Kinsmen of Another Kind

Gary Clayton Anderson

Kinsmen of
Another Kind

Dakota-White Relations

in the Upper Mississippi

Valley, 1650–1862

University of Nebraska Press

Lincoln and London

Publication of this book was aided by a grant
from the National Endowment for the Humanities.

Portions of Chapter 5 have previously been published in "American Agents vs. British Traders:
Prelude to the War of 1812 in the Far West," in
*The American West: Essays in Honor of W. Eu-
gene Hollon*, edited by Ronald Lora (Toledo: University of Toledo, 1980). Parts of Chapter 8 have
previously appeared in "The Removal of the
Mdewakanton Dakota in 1837: A Case for Jacksonian Paternalism," *South Dakota History* 10
(Fall 1980): 310–33.

The paper in this book meets the guidelines for
permanence and durability of the Committee on
Production Guidelines for Book Longevity of
the Council on Library Resources.

Library of Congress Cataloging in Publication Data

Anderson, Gary Clayton, 1948–
Kinsmen of another kind.

Bibliography: p.
Includes index.
1. Dakota Indians – History.   2. Dakota Indians –
Government relations.   3. Mississippi River Valley –
Race relations.   4. Indians of North America – Govern-
ment relations.   I. Title.
E99.D1A48   1984   977'.00497   83-23411
ISBN 0-8032-1018-3 (alk. paper)

Contents

Preface

This book focuses on interethnic relations in the upper Mississippi River valley. The land watered by this river was once the preserve of the eastern Sioux, or the Dakota people as they preferred to call themselves. The Dakotas, whose name was a native term meaning "allies" or "league," were feared by many of their neighbors when French fur traders first encountered them in the 1650s. Yet the French found them eager to make friends with whites and develop commercial ties. They extended the same spirit of friendship to the English and Americans who followed, and by the mid-nineteenth century the eastern Sioux people who remained in the upper Mississippi watershed—the Mdewakanton, Sisseton, Wahpeton, and Wahpekute tribes—were generally seen by white Americans as friends of the government and dependable allies. In many ways they had taken a far different path than had their more aggressive western Sioux relatives of the Missouri River, the Tetons, Yanktons, and Yanktonais. After they sold their lands in 1851 and moved onto reservations, however, elements of the Dakota bands in Minnesota rose up and killed nearly five hundred white Americans in August 1862. Although the conflict took a terrible toll, the insurgent elements among the eastern Sioux were ultimately defeated and driven west. The incident, known as the Sioux Uprising, closed yet another chapter in the often violent history of Indian-white relations on the American frontier.

Since the Sioux outbreak has been the subject of numerous books and articles, this narrative history does not reexamine the war in detail. Rather, it concentrates on the nature of ethnic contact along the upper Mississippi River before 1862, a period covering nearly two centuries. Three important themes emerge: early white explorers and traders became "enculturated" to Dakota social practices, adopting many of the customs that were essential for incorporation into the Dakota community; the economic context of ethnic relations changed from decade to decade as the Dakotas' belief in sharing of resources within the community conflicted with the demands of a European market economy; and, finally, the Dakota pattern of intratribal political authority weakened as Europeans, and later white Americans, began to participate in native consensus government. In other words, important ethnohistorical themes run conjointly with the chronological narrative. They focus on elements of a cultural "world view," be it European or native, that helps us understand the motives for early peaceful relations and their eventual disintegration by 1862.

A close look at the early years of evolving ethnic relations reveals that members of a strong, vibrant native culture eagerly sought relations with whites and virtually demanded that Europeans accept much of what the Indians perceived as appropriate behavior. French and later British and American fur traders lived and worked in what was really a Dakota world; early whites were not perceived as intruders. But once whites arrived in greater numbers it became the Indians' turn to ponder and ultimately absorb certain facets of Euroamerican culture, preserving the essentials of their life-style as much as possible throughout the process. Overall, both societies exhibited an inner strength that finally made assimilation difficult if not impossible, and this dichotomy proves important in understanding the breakdown of friendly relations.

If we consider specific aspects of the relationship, it seems clear that historians have been most inept at understanding how social ties evolve. The nature of Dakota kinship has been the subject of one or two anthropological treatises, but it is perhaps best outlined in a short book entitled *Speaking of Indians*, written by the Sioux scholar Ella Deloria. Kinship formed the social framework for the existence of the Sioux people and regulated their relations with outsiders. "By kinship all Dakota people were held together in a great relationship," Deloria points out. "Everyone who was born a Dakota belonged." But membership by blood was not the only means of access to Sioux society; by a secondary system, called "social kinship" or "fictive kinship," others entered the Dakota communal world. "Through this social kinship system," Deloria believed, "even real outsiders became relatives" and took a place in society.[1] Kinship systems, in other words, gave the Sioux a strong sense of identity that distinguished them from other people.

Such views of relatedness had enormous implications after Euroamericans began entering Sioux lands intent upon economic exploitation. White commercialists were products of a new, enlightened age that emphasized the inner-directed self and material gain. Nevertheless, early European fur traders were quick to see that adoption into native bands had enormous economic advantages, since Dakota kinsmen stood ready to assist their relatives by any means possible. Most traders accordingly married Sioux women and took Dakota names, at least while they remained in the west. Thereafter they were commonly addressed as "brother" or "father," a practice illustrative of the kinship incorporation that occurred well into the American period, when the common metaphor used to show the incorporation of the American president was the "Great Father." The father-son metaphor obviously denotes obligations not unlike those attending the relationship a Dakota son had with his father. Traders brought goods into Sioux lands, for example, and Indians gave them furs in exchange. But this obligation became a means to an economic end, and the rapacious exploitation of the fur trade and the later negotiation of land-surrendering treaties by the federal government were hung on the framework of a vulnerable and easily exploited native society.

Almost all whites who entered Minnesota after 1650 became, in the Sioux sense, kinsmen who were adopted into a band and given kin names in order to be viewed as friends or allies. But European kinsmen were expected to share and exchange resources so as to

make the community strong, an economic obligation commonly found
in communal societies. They in turn could expect assistance from
their Dakota relatives in time of need. Once a trader received a kin
name, he was formally considered a part of the Dakota *tiyospaye*, or
lodge group. This family relationship, based upon trust, reciprocal
sharing of resources, or blood ties, had special meaning to the Sioux,
since kinship relations dictated behavior patterns and the way other
people were treated.[2]

Nevertheless, there had always been outsiders who refused to
accept the responsibility that attended membership in Dakota society. To the Sioux people such interlopers, regardless of ethnic background, were enemies, unwilling to assist in the common struggle
for survival. This unique concept was clearly seen by an early missionary to the Sioux, Thomas S. Williamson, who wrote on 9 August
1849 that the Dakota people "have been accustomed to count all
men who are not Dakota, that is allies, as enemies."[3] Thus, to the
Sioux maintenance of kinship responsibilities was essential to peaceful
relations of any kind with traders as well as with the American bureaucrats and settlers who followed them.

Had the quantities of fur-bearing animals in Minnesota not eventually given out and had the throes of colonial competition and its
attendant aftermath of white settlement not brought this fur-trading
age to an end, perhaps the relationships forged by the early white
explorer-traders of the Sioux domain could have continued in a
peaceful vein for centuries to come. Unfortunately, traders made too
many demands upon Sioux resources, and entire populations of animals soon disappeared. Furthermore, ethnic relations entered a new
stage when American soldiers built Fort Snelling at the juncture of
the Mississippi and Minnesota rivers in 1819 and inaugurated an age
of Euroamerican settlement. The large numbers of whites who entered Minnesota in the four decades to follow subsequently weakened the kinship networks that had been formed among the various
ethnic groups in Minnesota before 1819. Only those white Americans who could benefit from social compliance, such as government
officials and traders, continued to reinforce bonds after the founding

of the fort. Moreover, mixed-bloods came to play crucial intermediary roles, using their ties in Dakota society but functioning more often than not within the imported market economy of whites. Simultaneously, economic maximization reached new levels, with the increasing white frontier population demanding that the Sioux people give up land and become dependent upon government annuities for survival. What had been a Sioux world just a few decades before quickly began to change; by the 1830s economic dependency created a neocolonial atmosphere from which the Sioux could never recover.

Attending the social and economic alterations brought to the Mississippi valley by Europeans were a host of new political problems. Consensus government, based upon the premise of majority consent, had been the hallmark of the Dakota political system. Working within band and tribal councils, native "speakers" played major roles by synthesizing issues and helping to form consensus. Early white traders were soon incorporated into this process, for kinship ties entailed taking part in the political mechanisms that governed the Sioux people. In the seventeenth and eighteenth centuries, more often than not the Sioux perceived traders as giving advice that was in the best interests of all concerned. But by the mid-nineteenth century, as government officials joined these discussions, it became increasingly difficult for the open Dakota political forum to function in the best interests of the Indians. By the 1850s, "speakers" were so closely tied to government officials or fur traders that they were no longer impartial, and mixed-blood intermediaries became yet another interest group that did not have the concerns of their full-blood kinsmen at heart. Without an effective political forum, factions became more difficult to control, especially when made up of young men.

Thus, over the two-hundred-year period from contact to the outbreak, ethnic interaction in Minnesota remained in a state of constant evolution, reaching a point by 1862 where a considerable number of Dakota people looked with nostalgia to the past, wondering out loud if life had not been better before the white man came. Yet others in the same villages had adopted farming, fostering a native polarization that threatened the very identity that had once been the strength of the eastern Sioux people. The factors that brought this condition about are what this book intends to explore. While at times one element of change—either social, economic, or political—may seem more important than another, all three were critical in determining the nature of ethnic relations in the upper Mississippi valley. Tragically, it is a relationship that was founded upon a strong bond of trust and friendship. Yet the relationship moved, ever so slowly, to one in which the bonds that had been so meaningful to the Sioux people as a whole became torn and tattered.

With the exception of the two introductory chapters on life-style, population, and migration, the book follows a chronological sequence, beginning with the fur trade era. By 1800, as chapters 3 and 4 illustrate, the English had constructed commercial networks in Sioux lands that owed their success to the acceptance of Indian social, economic, and political customs. Chapters 5–9 examine how ethnic relations withstood the transition from relations with traders to American occupation and the eventual negotiation of land-surrendering treaties. Despite the potential for violence, Americans assimilated Sioux customs and developed kinship networks much as the traders had done. Such tactics obviously go a long way in explaining the successful purchase of Sioux lands in 1837 and 1851. The treaties of Mendota and Traverse des Sioux, signed in Minnesota in 1851, resulted in the forced removal of the Dakota people to reservations in the western portion of the state.

Chapters 10 and 11 document the changes in ethnic relations during the reservation decade and show how these changes led to war in 1862. Central to understanding the reservation period is the realization that the Sioux people generally trusted whites and remained convinced that the "Great Father" would look after their needs. The willingness of a substantial portion of the eastern Sioux to give up their hunter-gatherer livelihood and become farmers is testimony of the growing belief on the reservations that change and the acceptance of white culture were inevitable. On the other hand, more

traditional Indians refused to acculturate, became critics of the treaties, and sought to protect their culture. It was this polarization,
brought about by significant social, economic, and political changes,
that eventually brought war to the reservations in 1862. The Epilogue looks at the results of this tragedy.

Before turning my attention to the early Sioux, I would like to
thank the many scholars and relatives who helped with the preparation of the manuscript. The list would certainly be incomplete
without mention of Herbert T. Hoover and Joseph Cash from the
University of South Dakota, who first introduced me to Indian scholarship and the Sioux. At the University of Toledo, Charles De-
Benedetti and Ronald Lora both showed a strong interest in my research. The Toledo years were most valuable, however, because they
offered me an opportunity to study under W. Eugene Hollon, who
directed my dissertation and tried ever so hard to teach me the ru-
diments of good writing. Few mentors have demonstrated greater
patience for students than Gene Hollon, and I am deeply thankful
for his interest in my career and for his continued friendship.

In the years of academic wandering that followed my acquisition
of a Ph.D. in 1978, I was fortunate to teach with numerous other
historians who either read parts of the manuscript or helped for-
mulate its content. The list includes Martin Lutter at Concordia College, Willard B. Gatewood at the University of Arkansas, and Paul
Kopperman at Oregon State University. In addition, I am much in-
debted for the financial and intellectual support that came from the
Center for the History of the American Indian at the Newberry Library, Chicago. While I was a fellow at the Center in 1980–81, such
fine scholars as Francis Jennings, Francis Paul Prucha, Jacqueline
Peterson, William Swagerty, and David R. Miller all listened patiently to what I had to say regarding the Sioux and offered criticism.
Other colleagues read the manuscript in its final form, including
Richard Haan from Hartwick College, Michael L. Tate at the Univer-
sity of Nebraska–Omaha, and Bruce Seely and Dale Knobel from Texas
A&M University.

Finally, despite all the assistance from my many academic friends, the book would not have been completed were it not for my parents (both the Andersons and the Larsens), and my brothers, who offered board and room while I worked month after month at the National Archives and the Minnesota Historical Society, and for my wife, Laura, and my daughter, Kari, who studied Sioux culture and linguistics and so patiently awaited my return from the research trips that seemed to drag on into eternity.

1

The Sioux and Their Ecosystem, 1650–1700

Thanks to Pierre Radisson, a traveler among the Sioux people in the 1650s, we can easily visualize the Sioux warriors. They carried bows and arrows, the arrow tips carved from the "stag's pointed horns." They dabbed their faces with several colors and tufted part of their hair, hanging turquoise stones from the lock. Men used bear grease liberally, no doubt to ward off the hordes of mosquitoes that infested the upper Mississippi valley, and most mixed a reddish earth with the fat to give their limbs and torsos a special tint. Warriors wore few encumbering clothes, merely tying a breechcloth over their nakedness in the summer. Tobacco pouches and ornaments such as crow skins dangled from their belts. All in all, these strapping specimens impressed Radisson to such an extent that he neglected to say much about Sioux women. The lapse illustrates the chauvinistic nature of Sioux society; most functions revolved around the excitement of the chase and the glories of war.[1]

The military prowess of these people impressed everyone who came in contact with them. Some early French explorers thought of them as the "Iroquois of the West," a meaningful comparison derived from years of fierce combat with this powerful eastern nation.[2] Other Frenchmen, like Antoine de la Mothe Cadillac, thought the Sioux surpassed the Iroquois "in bravery and courage." Their warriors, Cadillac cautioned, slept with one foot off the ground to be prepared for battle, with "daggers hanging from their wrists."[3] The explorer-trader Pierre Charles Le Sueur was another admirer. After visiting

their villages in 1700, he reported that Sioux fathers take "leurs en-
fans [sic] de l'âge de 9 ou 10" on raiding expeditions to teach them
the art of war before puberty.[4] But the French only echoed what
Algonquin neighbors had learned many years before. When asked to
describe the Sioux, they reverently exclaimed: "They are men."[5] At
French contact, the Sioux people were lords over a vast expanse of
territory extending from western Wisconsin into the eastern reaches
of what is today North and South Dakota. Even though the various
tribes lacked what might be described as a confederation, their warriors often acted together. When they did, the Sioux could field as
large an army as any native group in America.

Mobility went hand in hand with this aggressiveness. At French
contact, the western Sioux tribes—Yanktons, Yanktonais, and Tetons—roamed the prairie country between the Upper Mississippi
and Red River valleys. The French usually distinguished them from
their woodland brethren by referring to them as the "Sioux of the
West." With each passing decade the Yanktons, Yanktonais and Tetons moved farther west, and by the nineteenth century they had
settled in the upper Missouri watershed, an area rich in buffalo and
well worth the intertribal wars spawned by the migration. The
movement may have precipitated the decline of the Oćeti Śakowin,
"Seven Council Fires," an ancient league or alliance that according to
traditional accounts once united all Sioux tribes.[6]

The "Sioux of the East," or Dakota tribes—Mdewakantons, Wahpetons, Wahpekutes, and Sissetons—remained behind in the upper
Mississippi watershed.[7] Even so, they too were highly mobile. One
early observer, André Pénigaut, described them as being "toujours
errante," always wandering. They seldom stayed more than eight days
in one locality before striking camp.[8] This tendency to remain in
motion convinced at least one famous French traveler, Pierre de
Charlevoix, that the Sioux lacked a clearly defined occupational pattern. "A [Dakota] village which the year before was on the eastern
bank of the Mississippi," he wrote, "shall be this year on the western
bank, and that those who have lived for some time on the banks of
the river St. Peters [Minnesota] shall ... be at present in some meadow

a great distance from it."[9] His assessment contained more than a particle of truth; mobility did allow eastern Sioux groups to occasionally adopt the life-style of their western relatives and vice versa.

The upper Mississippi valley offered boundless advantages for mobile hunter-gatherers like the Dakotas. The rivers were natural avenues for travel, and freshwater lakes dotted the countryside, ideal locations for pitching the temporary deerskin lodges used by all the Sioux. The western half of their upper Mississippi domain was transitional prairie broken by clusters of hardwood and pine. In the south one could see sparsely covered hills from the west bank of the Mississippi River, while farther north the woodlands edged closer into the central portions of Minnesota. Some wooded oases on the prairies west of the Mississippi extended over rather large areas. Just east of the upper Minnesota River, the "Coteau de Grand Bois" formed a fifty-mile-long tree-covered strip meandering north and south. Straddling the lower Minnesota, another stretch of forest called the "French woods" ran from the heart of the Blue Earth country east to the Mississippi.[10]

Early travel accounts reveal that the Dakotas were an enterprising people who had developed a highly successful economy based upon this unique ecosystem. While men and boys hunted game, the primary subsistence source, eastern Sioux women tapped sugar maples, gathered berries, nuts, and roots, and, more important, harvested wild rice and perhaps some corn. Rice thrived in the northeastern woodlands, especially the marshes near Mille Lacs Lake, but it also existed in the Minnesota River valley, an area many of the western bands frequented. The various Sioux villagers probably ate either corn or rice according to availability. Although neither the Dakotas nor their western Sioux relatives were noted for their agricultural ability in 1650, corn was readily available through well-established trade networks with both the Missouri River and the Wisconsin tribes.[11] Because many of these resources were found in different areas of their domain, the Dakotas returned to specific localities at certain times of the year, thus producing a cycle that brought some order to an otherwise fluid existence.[12]

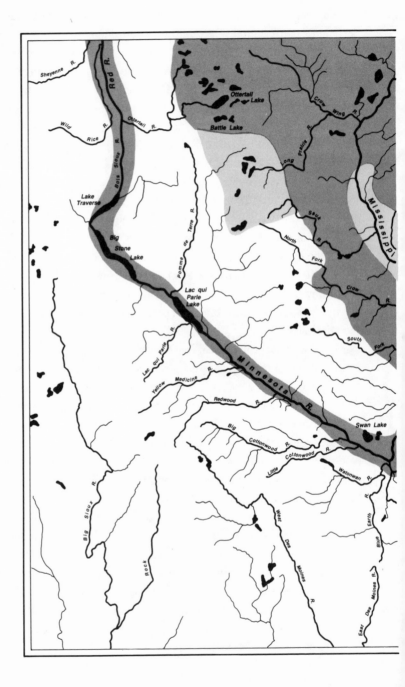

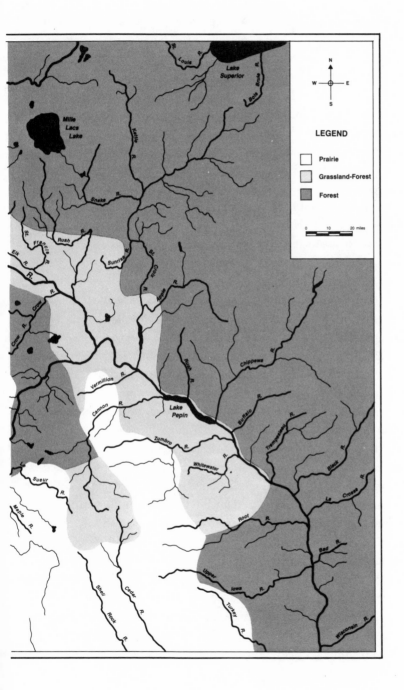

Lake
Superior

Mille
Lacs
Lake

St. Louis R.

Bois Brule R.

Kettle R.

Snake R.

St. Francis R.

Rush

Sunrise R.

St. Croix R.

Apple R.

Elk R.

Crow R.

Rum R.

Chippewa R.

Vermillion R.

Cannon R.

Lake
Pepin

Buffalo R.

Trempealeau R.

Zumbro R.

Whitewater R.

Black R.

Sueur R.

La Crosse R.

Maple R.

Root R.

Bad R.

Shell Rock R.

Cedar R.

Upper Iowa R.

Turkey R.

Wisconsin R.

The Dakotas, or eastern Sioux, retreated to the vast forests and tree-sheltered river valleys of northeastern Minnesota after harvesting wild rice in October. Virginia deer and elk offered a stable food supply throughout the winter, and they hunted them communally. The hunt was carefully orchestrated, with certain people assigned to paddle upriver and drive the animals out of the thickets while others stationed themselves back from the banks, ready for the kill. The hunters shared their meat with others in the village, reserving for themselves the skins and the distinction of success. Once the hunters were back in camp, the children loudly chanted the names of the providers until darkness fell. With the aid of snowshoes, the hunt continued all winter.[13]

In March or April the Dakotas returned to semipermanent villages to live off food stored the previous fall, supplemented by returning waterfowl and fresh fish. Lakes or large rivers were ideal locations, since they held stocks of fish and attracted game birds. Le Sueur saw Dakota warriors shoot waterfowl with bow and arrow *à la volée*, in flight, in 1700. Burial customs provided a second motive for establishing these semipermanent camps. The bones of those who died during the winter were preserved and carried back to the village for interment. Father Louis Hennepin was captured by "Issati," Mdewakanton Dakota warriors, who occupied encampments on the shores of Mille Lacs Lake in April 1680. One of the men carried with him the bones of a deceased relative that Hennepin had to "cover" with presents on the way to Mille Lacs.[14] Yet these villages never remained very permanent in the seventeenth and eighteenth centuries, since overhunting quickly depleted the game in the surrounding area. Hennepin found little game near the Mille Lacs village he visited. The people lived on a limited amount of wild rice, dried blueberries, and fish, from which the priest received an occasional meal.[15]

These Issati villagers, who camped haphazardly in several locales around the lake and on its islands, headed south toward the lower Mississippi River in July to hunt buffalo. This party of more than a thousand stopped briefly along the lower Rum River to make birch-bark canoes, then proceeded after organizing a "soldiers' lodge"—a committee of experienced warriors who knew how to overtake bison. The lodge fulfilled an important role by bringing order to the loosely structured woodland hunting camps. In the plains west of the Mississippi, the party discovered vast herds of grazing buffalo. One contingent killed 120 just west of Lake Pepin, a widening in the Mississippi River. The group once again headed toward Mille Lacs by late July, their small bark canoes loaded with huge quantities of smoked meat. After harvesting wild rice, which frequently was mixed with buffalo or bear tallow and stored with other preservable wild foods, the villagers began preparations for the fall woodland hunt, thus renewing the cycle.[16]

Travelers left sketchy accounts of the actual amount of resource wealth available to the Sioux, but most stressed the abundance of herd animals of all kinds both in the Mississippi valley and west of it. Nicholas Perrot, for example, traveled extensively in the Sioux domain during the 1690s and reported that it was a "happy land" on account of the large numbers of buffalo.[17] Le Sueur left a similar report; in one month his men killed more than seven hundred of the animals along the Blue Earth River. Modern scholars now believe that the bison herds alone averaged perhaps twenty-six animals per square mile. Such resources allowed large numbers of people to congregate in one locale. Radisson's report that more than seven thousand Sioux warriors came together in the camp he visited may be an exaggeration, but it illustrates the substantial size of some encampments and the corresponding resource base of these people.[18]

East of the Mississippi, early travelers frequently commented on the high density of game animals in the river valleys of western Wisconsin. The Chippewa River, for example, was initially called the "Bon Secour" by the French because of the number of "buffalo, stag, bears, and roedeer" found there.[19] Less is known of the regions above Mille Lacs Lake, but it has been suggested that the dense forests northwest of Lake Superior limited the populations of deer and elk, which normally prefer to browse in small openings in wooded areas. This may explain why Leech Lake and Sandy Lake constituted the northeastern frontier of Dakota hunting zones. Nevertheless, in 1680 Daniel Greysolon Duluth did discover nearly one hundred beaver dams along the St. Louis River, west of Lake Superior, impeding his way into Sioux country. Each had to be breached so his men could drag their canoes upriver.[20]

Abundance of this sort must have alleviated most fear of starvation. The only evidence of suffering is Hennepin's account of minor scarcity at Mille Lacs Lake. The area surrounding the lake, as well as much of the Rum River valley, was heavily traveled, frequently occupied, and consequently depleted of game. Yet even though Hennepin complained of tight rations, the men of the village were involved in a raiding expedition rather than hunting. Most likely, the period of relative want that the cleric observed in the spring of 1680 was the price paid for gathering to discuss the happenings of the winter and to seek glory and revenge in war.[21]

Sioux behavior was in part dictated by the abundant resources surrounding the people and by their fluid lifeway. An obvious outgrowth of prosperity was their delight in staging large feasts, a cultural manifestation observed by virtually every visitor to their country (even during the nineteenth century, when declining resources warranted conservation). These feasts often resembled the potlatch of the Pacific coast tribes, conducted to acquire status and demonstrate ability to provide beyond the needs of one's family. They could even be used to taunt relatives. A man prepared a huge meal for his kindred with the hope that they would be unable to consume all the food. Many ate until they vomited, while others gave in and paid a fine to their benefactor, a minor humiliation.[22]

Since the early Sioux were blessed with such a strong resource base, they had little need for a concept of conservation. Yet at the foundation of their religion and their hunting existence was a supernatural relation with the animal kingdom that guided the taking of game. Like many other North American tribes, the Sioux sought spiritual cleansing after killing animals for subsistence. "They bury the bones of the beaver and elk very carefully after eating the flesh," Jonathan Carver recorded in his 1766 journal, "thinking that the spirits of these animals have influence on the living ones and will inform them how they have been treated." Sioux hunters believed that if they failed to take such precautions, the game of the forests might abandon them.[23]

The Sioux also considered other animals to be invested with supernatural power. Crows, owls, and other birds, along with wolves, snakes, turtles, bears, and many others, are mentioned by early observers as creatures worthy of keen attention. Obviously, not all of these played important economic roles, and Sioux religion by and large transcended simple materialistic goals. The spirits of animals could cause sickness or good health, rain or sunshine, happiness or misery. The Sioux people remained convinced that animals possessed feelings and powers and that they could act for the betterment of the community or, just as likely, inflict spiteful revenge.[24]

The medium who helped interpret the spirit world was the shaman. These men and women, usually twenty or so in each village, were called *wicaśta wakan,* the supernatural people. Whites, even in the nineteenth century, found most of them difficult to understand and their secrets nearly impossible to penetrate. They set the moral tone for the village, giving it rules to follow in order to prevent disaster and be successful economically, and they cured the sick, most frequently by drawing harmful spirits from the body. Their use of magic often made them feared by the populace at large. Shamans were always watched more closely than other villagers.[25]

Shamans used taboos to help direct village life and thereby played an important role in creating a Sioux "world view." Recently scholars have even suggested that their interpretation of religion led to a "conservation ethic" that prevented overconsumption of game and that Europeans destroyed this process by curtailing the shamans' effectiveness.[26] Besides raising serious questions about the strength or survival ability of native religion, this thesis fails to address the nature of the hunter's relation to taboos. The Sioux hunter, for example, was superstitious in regard to his spiritual attachments to animals. He treated animals with respect to ensure his own future success. The type of institutional reverence necessary to create a "conservation ethic" was anathema to him, as missionaries quickly discovered. Moreover, as later travelers observed, animal-related taboos on hunting remained intact well into the nineteenth century. The evolution of a market economy, and the attendant slaughter of game, apparently did not affect Sioux beliefs regarding animals.[27]

This tendency to both exploit animals and pray to their spirits is a curious paradox. Animals provided food and shelter, but they were indiscriminately slaughtered. Even some early Europeans found this difficult to understand. Hennepin watched with astonishment in 1680 as the raiding party he accompanied stopped briefly to kill forty or fifty buffalo only for their tongues and a few other choice morsels. The hides and meat rotted on the ground. Le Sueur also gives the impression that the western Sioux declined to carry unneeded robes back to their camps, abandoning them on the prairies. When time permitted, however, they placed excess meat on scaffolds to protect it for later use.[28] Others in the west noted that early Dakota hunters constructed elaborate net enclosures for snaring moose and elk, taking whichever animal came into the trap. Perhaps the "philosophy" of Iron Shell best describes Sioux views toward resources: "Such things as cherries and even buffalo don't stay around long and the people must get them when they can."[29]

If necessity more than taboos governed resource acquisition, the Sioux had few cultural obstructions to prevent them from becoming active members of a market economy. Indeed, the only recognizable mechanism for conservation that did exist derived naturally from their cyclical lifeway. Game generally was left alone during reproductive periods and whenever it became scarce hunters traveled many miles for it; thus the villagers moved on, and this allowed regions to recover ecologically.

Geographic mobility also had much to do with the way Dakota society functioned. Whereas by the Renaissance Europeans had become conscious of landownership and more often than not endogamous, Dakota concepts of wealth were tied to game herds. Thus it was crucial to bring new blood into the society in the form of hunters. Taboos existed against marrying within one's own village, and the emphasis upon unique kinship bonds gave the village-oriented Dakota society a strong sense of tribal identity—of being Dakota.[30] So when Father Hennepin's Sioux captors asked how many wives he had, they scoffed at his answer that he "had promised the Master of life to live as they saw me"—in other words, alone.[31] Family, the elevation of young people to parenthood, village and tribal identity, and the creation of kinship networks all augmented the economic system that was peculiarly Dakota.

Consequently, within the extended family, which would easily include fifty people, and the village, which may have held upward of a thousand, family ties or kinship connections bonded uncles, brothers, and cousins in the common goal of survival. Hunting with primitive weapons clearly necessitated group action, and members of a family could always count on their relatives to assist them in acquiring food and protecting women and children. Sioux kinship ties were regularly reaffirmed by the exchange of presents, fostering a sharing of resources. It was exceedingly uncivilized to hoard food or fail to give presents to one's relatives. But entry into the family group remained relatively easy for outsiders provided they accepted the responsibilities attendant on admission. Captives often were incorporated into the extended families, taking the place of lost relatives. Euroamericans also found admission relatively easy. Whether the Sioux viewed such newcomers as "real" kinsmen, who could enjoy the same privileges as consanguineous relatives, or as "fictive" kinsmen, connected as a result of economic necessity, is impossible to determine. The only certainty is that the process of incorporation became so important that sacred rites existed to symbolize adoption. The ceremonies often included gestures used by a variety of native peoples around the world, such as smoking pipes, placing food into the mouth of a new relative, and crying over the individual's head.[32]

Political institutions evolved from the extended family units that made up villages and tribes. The council provided the formal means for political action, and at the village level it primarily discussed how resources should be gathered and what means were necessary to protect the society. By the historical period, the few records of tribal councils suggest that they were primarily interested in intertribal affairs. Councils were uniquely antifederal in that no decision could be made without strong consensus. Civil chiefs, who usually represented a village, always played important roles in council, gathering support for their views by oratory. The prestige of a chief rested almost exclusively on his ability to convince elders to accept his advice. Most civil chiefs ascended to the position by paternal descent, but unless he proved worthy to be a leader, a man was not listened to by the elders.[33]

Besides civil chiefs, the speakers, war leaders, and shamans played political roles, frequently analyzing issues in council and helping to shape opinion. Although mid-nineteenth century evidence suggests that speakers may have been elected, nowhere in the early historical material is this evident. War leaders, who were also religious men, had no civil power but were looked to for organizing hunts or when the village was threatened from outside. The war shaman depended upon the soldiers' lodge to effect order. This police force was charged with carrying out the will of the council and often disbanded when it had nothing to do. If, as occasionally happened, a member of the village was guilty of some infraction, the police might inflict a variety of punishments, including slashing his tent, breaking his bow, killing his favorite horse, or in extreme cases even corporal punishment.[34]

From what early evidence is available, it is obvious that consensus government did operate very effectively. When Father Hennepin and his two French companions first met a Sioux party in 1680, his captors angrily "wrenched our calumet [peace pipe] from our hands" and soon formed a council "to deliberate on what they were to do with us." While one or two powerful men in the group wanted to kill the Frenchmen, consensus dictated that they should live.[35] More than a century later, in 1817, the American Indian agent Benjamin O'Fallon found his Sioux hosts less accommodating. When O'Fallon pressed Wabasha's band to make peace with the United States after the War of 1812, the seventeen elders in council showed a divided front. Ten refused the offer and walked out of the council chambers. Despite the fact that Wabasha, a man of immense prestige among his people and with considerable oratorical skill, had decided to embrace O'Fallon's offer, the chief could not conclude a treaty without a consensus.[36]

At first glance it may seem that this depiction of the Sioux at white contact is rather idyllic. But that resources were abundant and that villages were stable and self-sufficient does not mean the Dakotas lived a life of ease. The constant movement essential for mere survival took a toll of tribal members of all ages, especially the very young and the very old. Moreover, hunting was never a safe occupation. During the winter, sudden snowstorms frequently claimed the lives of hunters who were far from camp. Above all, women had a burdensome existence, with little opportunity to accomplish much beyond preparing hides, making clothes, tending children, and preparing the camp for another move. Although statistics are unavailable, the rate of suicide was high among Sioux women.[37]

Nevertheless, the Sioux were a strong people in 1650. Although their society remained existence-oriented, political mechanisms met defensive needs and provided a firm basis for resource exploitation. In addition, abundant game gave them a strong sense of security and identity, and their migratory lifeway was well adapted to the diffused river network of the upper Mississippi valley. A slow decline set in thereafter, primarily owing to increased warfare and European-introduced disease. Yet the Dakotas were adaptable; they had already mastered one inclement environment. It remained to be seen to what extent their society would change in order to exist within the world that Europeans were introducing to America.

2

Population Decline in the Woodlands

Social scientists have traditionally been intrigued by the unique relationship the woodland tribes enjoyed with their environment. Only recently, however, have a few expressed confidence in the economic efficiency of a woodland hunting life. More often than not they perceive the relationship as an economic liability, since they assume that migratory peoples, compared with agricultural ones, have difficulty supporting themselves. To portray the early Dakota camps as efficient and stable, with a smooth rhythm as the villagers moved from one well-stocked game preserve to another, does indeed test one's faith in the early sources, especially when one examines the decimated condition of the eastern Sioux in 1850 after their ecosystem had been ravaged by the fur trade. By this late date, about 6,000 eastern Sioux remained in the entire Mississippi watershed, and they frequently suffered from want during the winter.[1]

The lack of interest in economic potential is further reflected in the failure of social scientists to assess demographic changes. While no evidence can clearly show that all Sioux bands were once woodland people, those that remained east of the Mississippi River at white contact were gradually declining in numbers. Any of three causes might be responsible for this restructuring. The Sioux were a warrior society, often embroiled in conflicts with neighbors. Warfare as a factor in population decline and forced migration must therefore be analyzed. Serious consideration must also be given to disease. The Sioux, like other North American tribes, had no immunity to European-introduced diseases such as smallpox, measles, and malaria.[2] All these afflictions took heavy tolls on native populations in the Mississippi valley. Finally, the Sioux were a fluid society, tied more securely to the movements of game than to the land. Voluntary migration has been used to explain the movement of the western Sioux onto the prairies. It seems unlikely that it would fail to affect the Dakotas.[3]

Nevertheless, it is essential to establish a base figure for Sioux populations in 1650 before attempting to assess the impact of warfare, disease, or migration. Social scientists have generally sought to establish estimates of early Sioux populations in view of the stark images of their suffering in the nineteenth century. Their figures have accordingly been small. On the basis of one French document, which could be interpreted much more liberally, a recent scholar concludes that the entire Sioux population, both eastern and western tribes, did not exceed 10,000 people in 1737. The author discards an estimate Le Sueur made in 1702, placing the number of Sioux at 4,000 families, even though the 1737 "census" is anonymous.[4] The transcription of Le Sueur's journal preserved by Claude Delisle demonstrates that stronger attention should be given to the explorer's figures. Although he saw only one western Sioux village—a Yankton camp—it numbered "plus de 150 cabanes [sic]," and Dakota informants told Le Sueur that the prairie Sioux all together equaled "plus de mille cabanes."[5] How many tepees actually existed beyond a thousand is anyone's guess, but since each held ten to fifteen people, the western tribes alone obviously surpassed 10,000 souls.

Even the dated research of anthropologist James Mooney places Sioux numbers at 25,000 in 1780, a figure gleaned from Zebulon Montgomery Pike's 1805 count.[6] Although recent scholarship has raised serious questions regarding Mooney's methods, his figure is a reasonable assessment for 1780. Unfortunately, other writers have erred by using Mooney's figures to represent Sioux populations in 1650.[7] Given that the North American tribes suffered constant attrition from European-introduced diseases, it would be strange indeed if Sioux populations either stayed the same or had been smaller than

25,000 at white contact. In fact, through analyzing the sources that have survived it becomes clear that significant demographic changes took place between Radisson's visit in the 1650s and that of Le Sueur a half-century later.

Early French observers certainly believed the Sioux numbered more than 25,000. In 1658, for example, Jesuits noted that the "Poulak," whom they identified as prairie Sioux, maintained 30 villages, while their woodland relatives, described as "Nadouechiouek and Mantouek," supported 40. If each of these numbered anywhere near the 150 lodges Le Sueur found in the Yankton camp, Sioux populations would have been enormous. Another Jesuit chronicler placed the total number of "Nadouesis," or Dakota settlements, at 30 a decade later, without mentioning the "Poulak." Perhaps these figures were poorly substantiated guesses, yet they do demonstrate the firm belief of early French explorers that the Sioux were one of the most populous nations on the continent. In addition, since the term "Poulak" is strikingly similar to the Cree name for the Sioux, "Poüelles," the Jesuits were likely receiving the bulk of their information from the Crees or closely related Algonquin neighbors.[8]

Admitting the validity of the Jesuit figures does pose problems, however, since it is impossible to determine the average size of a village. Only 1,100 souls were in the village Hennepin visited east of the Mississippi, whereas Radisson found 7,000 warriors alone in the plains camp he saw. In addition, Le Sueur made an extensive effort to list the Sioux villages in 1700 and came up with the specific names of twenty-three, fewer than recorded by the Jesuits.[9] The discrepancies might have resulted from the Jesuits' inability to distinguish between Siouan and Sioux peoples. Various Siouan linguistic groups including the Iowas, Omahas, Poncas, and Mandans lived on the periphery of Sioux lands and may have been counted as Sioux. Moreover, Jesuit figures may include the Assiniboins, who separated from the Sioux proper sometime after 1650.[10] On the other hand, dramatic changes may have occurred in the forty years before Le Sueur's expedition, and it is conceivable that his list is incomplete.

These factors amplify the difficulty of assessing the size of early Sioux populations.

Fortunately, some early sources provide numerical estimates. Médart Chouart de Grosseilliers gave the number of warriors among the "sedentary Nadwesseronons," or woodland Sioux, as 4,000 in 1658. Perrot set the number of Dakota warriors who used the canoe at between 7,000 and 8,000 before 1665. The Jesuits claimed in 1660 that Frenchmen, perhaps Radisson and Grosseilliers, had visited several villages that could send forth 5,000 men each.[11] Although this is probably an exaggeration, eastern woodland villages were obviously well peopled. Judging from Radisson's figure of 7,000 men for a single plains camp and the data supplied by Le Sueur forty years later, there must have been at the very least 8,000 Sioux warriors in 1658. Even Hennepin, who never visited the populous plains villages, indicated that the nation could raise "eight or nine thousand warriors" in 1680.[12] Although a figure of 8,000 men may seem excessive, so many early explorers could not all be wrong. Moreover, the figure seems reasonable, even conservative, when compared with the village numbers given by the Jesuits.

Since fur traders and missionaries failed to count women and children, calculating the total population requires some speculation. One would assume that the numbers of men and women remained fairly equal, yet men were often lost in intertribal wars and on hunts. This attrition may explain the high incidence of polygamy in Sioux camps and perhaps even the eagerness of the Dakota people to adopt male members into their kin networks. The polygamy protected widows and ensured most women of having at least one husband; a Jesuit in 1660 noted that some Sioux warriors maintained seven or eight wives, and another firsthand report by a French officer at Lake Pepin in 1727 places the number at ten for some men.[13] Although these figures certainly do not represent the norm, the French were quick to make the connection between the impact of war, the loss of men, and the existence of polygamy. In a memoir on the Sacs, Winnebagos, and Menominees, dated 1718, the author concluded that intertribal wars had so decimated these Wisconsin tribes that there were four women to every man.[14]

Among the Sioux the disparity probably never reached these levels, despite extensive polygamy. For example, the first population estimates accurate enough to permit some analysis of sex ratios come from Pike's 1805 count. He reported totals of 3,835 men and 7,030 women, for a ratio of 54 men to 100 women. There is some question whether war casualties were extensive in the seventeenth century, yet the Sioux had been fighting the Cree and Illinois tribes when Europeans arrived. In addition, even in the second quarter of the nineteenth century, when the presence of the American army limited intertribal struggles to small raids, Dakota sex ratios seldom rose above 75:100. It seems reasonable to assume that they were no higher in 1650. This would leave the total number of women in the society at about 11,000 at white contact and the total adult population at 19,000.[15]

Legitimate estimates for the number of children can also be formulated, since mortality patterns for native Americans do have some consistency. It is generally concluded that 50 percent or more of all children born in the early historical period died before the age of twelve. Therefore, while about half of every Indian camp consisted of children, often half of them did not reach adulthood. Infant mortality was especially high during the first few months after birth, and the chances of death usually did not decline until a child was weaned from mother's milk to the types of food consumed in a hunting society.[16]

Available statistics from the early nineteenth century support these conclusions. Pike recorded 11,800 Sioux children in a total population of 22,068. Two government vaccination reports for 1832 also provide significant information on the number of children and on child mortality. Of 1,562 Yankton Sioux immunized, 48 percent were listed as twelve or younger. Of these, 59 percent were six or under, and 41 percent fell within the age bracket seven through twelve. Children two and under suffered the most significant attrition. In a Mdewakanton band vaccinated in the same year, 62 percent were twelve and under. Although it is true that adults, especially men, were less likely to submit to vaccination, it still seems reasonable to assert that most Sioux camps in the nineteenth century were crowded with small children, with the numbers in each age group declining rapidly as these young people moved toward adulthood.[17]

Skeptics may point out that it is inconsistent to use nineteenth-century data to analyze populations from a century and a half earlier. But it is the size of the population, not the structure, that changes dramatically. The Sioux were still a hunting society in the early nineteenth century. All evidence considered, it seems likely that 50 percent of those living in 1650 were children. This would boost the total Sioux population in the Mississippi watershed to about 38,000 at white contact.

A figure this high should not surprise anyone familiar with the recent trends in New World demographic research. Mooney, like others who followed him, failed to comprehend the magnitude of the decline in native populations brought about by disease and warfare within a few years of European contact. New England Indians dwindled from about 90,000 people to 10,000 in the seventy-four years following 1600.[18] In comparison, the Sioux decline of from 38,000 in 1650 to 25,000 by 1780 is hardly excessive. Nonetheless, such a drop is important when one realizes that the Sioux most susceptible to European economic pressures and the wars and diseases that accompanied them were the Dakotas. The decline of the eastern groups and their migration into the Mississippi valley and beyond is a fascinating aspect of early Sioux history.

In the past the most compelling thesis for explaining Dakota movement into the west was one drawn from Chippewa oral history. Tribal accounts suggest that the Chippewas forced the Sioux to abandon the woodlands. Early French sources show, however, that the Dakotas maintained a general peace with the Chippewas until at least 1737. The movement of the Sioux into the west occurred for the most part well before that date, as is confirmed by French observers.[19] While Le Sueur was uncertain about the number of plains Sioux, he did place the woodland populations at about 900 men (300 lodges) in 1700, and a French estimate for 1736 noted that these numbers had dwindled significantly.[20] When we consider that seventeenth-century accounts mention from 4,000 to 8,000 woodland Sioux warriors, the real significance of the migration becomes apparent.

Although the Dakotas remained on friendly terms with the Chippewas well into the eighteenth century, the same was not true of their relations with other tribes. Fighting in the west intensified soon after the disastrous defeat and flight of the Huron Nation and their trading partners from the Iroquois in the late 1640s. Wisconsin and western Michigan quickly became an asylum for fleeing Sac, Fox, Potawatomi, Ottawa, Mascouten, Kickapoo, Miami, and Huron tribesmen.[21] The Sioux soon viewed these new residents of Wisconsin as a third threat to their security, along with the Crees and the Illinois. One large Huron village even settled on Pelée Island at the head of Lake Pepin and began raising corn. Initially accepted as friends, the Hurons ultimately quarreled with the Sioux and were driven back into Wisconsin. When Radisson and Grosseilliers arrived at Lac Court Oreilles a year or two later (1656?), the Hurons made every effort to appease their ferocious western neighbors. "Noboday durst offend them [the Sioux]," Radisson noted, "being that we were upon their land with their leave."[22]

The Hurons and their Ottawa allies supplied the Sioux with a few European-made trinkets, which stabilized the shaky détente found by the two French explorers, but a decade later they made another bid to oust the Dakotas from the woodlands. The expedition reportedly consisted of 1,000 warriors, but it was defeated with heavy losses.[23] Other Wisconsin Indians fared no better. Jesuits who visited the western shore of Lake Michigan in the 1660s found a constant state of warfare. The Dakotas had become so feared in eastern Wisconsin that the entire Green Bay area, an ideal location for settlement, was virtually deserted. The conflict also spread to Illinois. Near the southern extremities of Lake Michigan, Father Claude Allouez talked with a Miami chief who complained that both the "Nadouessious [Dakotas] and the Iroquois are eating us."[24]

Even though these wars unquestionably resulted in losses to the

Dakotas, Hennepin's historic trip up the Mississippi River in 1680 confirmed that the Sioux were securely implanted along the shores of Mille Lacs Lake. A second series of intertribal wars with the Sac, Fox, Miami, and Mascouten tribes, however, did erupt in the mid-1680s, and these had a more profound impact. During these campaigns, at least one Dakota village south of Lake Pepin was entirely overrun, leaving hundreds of casualties. The Sioux quickly rebounded and dealt the Miamis a devastating blow, but they continued to suffer losses well into the eighteenth century despite the trivial attempts of Cadillac, then commandant at Detroit, to end them. Ironically, many Chippewa warriors from Lake Superior fought alongside the Dakotas in these conflicts and continued to assist them into the second decade of the eighteenth century.[25]

While intertribal warfare may account for some population loss, recent scholarship has been more inclined to view European-introduced disease as responsible for major demographic changes among native peoples. Although evidence that specifically ties the Sioux to epidemics in the early period has yet to surface, disease did exist all around them. Perrot related that mysterious "maladies" had decimated the Winnebagos before the appearance of French traders in Wisconsin. In 1667 he witnessed firsthand the fear displayed by these same Indians at the report that the "pest [smallpox?] was at Montreal."[26] Daniel Greysolon Duluth also had a difficult time manipulating the eastern Sioux, Crees, and Chippewas after they had heard rumors that the "pestilence" was again among the French in the east. At about the same time severe epidemics spread to the Menominees in 1677 and the Mascoutens near Chicago in 1690, killing considerable numbers.[27]

Nevertheless, all these reports were for other tribes. Substantive evidence showing Sioux losses does not emerge until the eighteenth century. Smallpox struck the northern plains Indians in the late 1730s and again in the 1780s. Reports describing the first epidemic reached Montreal via traders working near Lake of the Woods. The Crees and Assiniboins suffered considerable losses. In 1781 the scourge returned to the plains. David Thompson reported that the disease "was caught by the Chipaways (the forest Indians), and the Sieux [*sic*] (of the plains) about the same time." The Sioux then spread it to many other tribes. Estimates of losses reached as high as three-fifths of the native population of the plains.[28]

But smallpox was not the only identifiable affliction that affected Sioux populations in the eighteenth century. Jonathan Carver visited the upper Mississippi River in 1766 and discovered that the Sioux quickly recognized the symptoms of "fever and ague (a disorder which the[y] greatly fear)." The Jesuits first reported such attacks (no doubt malaria) in northern Illinois in 1700, and Carver had seen intermittent fevers carry off nearly 100 Fox people on the Wisconsin River. This explains why Dakota leaders told Carver they did not want French traders from the lower Mississippi to enter their lands, since the Sioux realized that they, in contrast to their Lake Michigan rivals, always seemed to bring malaria with them.[29]

Assessing the impact of these various afflictions is obviously difficult. It does appear that Sioux populations were more seriously affected by disease in the eighteenth century than in the seventeenth. Theoretically, at least, epidemics do much to explain the general decline in Sioux populations from 38,000 at white contact to 25,000 in 1805, but they do not explain the dramatic movement of populations out of the woodlands. Looking more closely at the narratives that have survived, it becomes obvious that these changes were brought about by the only remaining alternative—voluntary migration.

Hennepin intimates that the vast majority of Sioux lived in the woodlands in 1680, but he visited few villages other than those of his Issati captors. Besides the latter, he mentioned the "Ouadebathon [Watpaton] River People," supposedly living in the "neighborhood" of Mille Lacs. Often confused with the Wahpetons (Leaf People), they were actually a distinct band of the Mdewakantons. Literally translated, the term means river (*watpa*) village (*ton*). The French trader Joseph Marin discovered that they had established semisedentary villages on the St. Croix River in 1753.[30] Hennepin's "Congaskethon" tribe is obviously a reference to the same people as Perrot's "Songaskitons" and Le Sueur's "Songasquitons." Frequently the subject of speculation, these villagers lived thirty or forty miles north of Mille Lacs, where Duluth visited them in 1679. Perhaps they were ancestors of the modern Sissetons, since Marin identifies them as the "Saisaiton" in 1753. Other than mention of the "Tinthonha," whom Hennepin calls "prairie-men," this is the extent of his information. In other words, Hennepin's account suggests that only Sisseton and Mdewakanton bands were living in the woodlands.[31]

Perrot followed Hennepin into the upper Mississippi valley, and his memoir offers a wealth of information on the western Indians in general. Nonetheless, one must turn to his famous and rather cavalier Lake Pepin proclamation of 1689 to find a brief account of the Sioux homeland. Besides claiming all of the upper Mississippi for France and noting that the Sioux were mere "proprietors," Perrot placed most of the Dakotas northeast of Lake Pepin, perhaps near Mille Lacs Lake. But he also mentioned that the "Mantantons," a Mdewakanton band, were then camped near the mouth of the Minnesota River.[32] Soon after trade began, the Mantantons settled near his post at Lake Pepin. The move undoubtedly represented a gradual southern migration induced by trade. Perrot also implied that another unnamed Sioux village had taken up a position on the lower St. Croix River. Nevertheless, the fighting that broke out in the later 1680s soon forced the Sioux to abandon Lake Pepin for the security of the swamps to the northeast.[33]

Le Sueur accompanied Perrot into the west and provided the first detailed analysis of Sioux occupation. He traded intermittently with the Dakotas for more than a decade, then departed for France in 1695. Once in Paris, he assisted the great cartographer Jean-Baptiste Louis Franquelin in drawing the first accurate map of the upper Mississippi watershed. Although the document indexes twenty-three Sioux villages, only twenty-two are included on the map. Of these, ten lie east of the Mississippi River while twelve are shown west of it.[34]

On the Franquelin map of 1697, most eastern Sioux villages clustered around Mille Lacs Lake. Unfortunately, the map is distorted so that actual distances are hard to determine. The "Ouadebathons," or Watpatons, were at this time north of the lake, rather than on the St. Croix River where Marin found them fifty years later. They had for neighbors the Sissetons, the "Ocatamentons," and the "Tangapssintons." The Issatis inhabited the south shore of Mille Lacs along with the "Ouaepetons" or Wahpetons, and the Mantantons. The new location of the latter band reflects their frequent movement. Three other groups of woodland Sioux occupied various positions on the eastern bank of the Mississippi River and probably spent considerable time chasing buffalo on the prairies.[35] Since Le Sueur knew substantially less about the western Sioux and the lands they occupied, the Franquelin map adds little to our knowledge of them. Suffice it to say that all twelve of their villages remained north of the Minnesota River and west of the Mississippi. The Wahpekute people, traditionally recognized as one of the four eastern Sioux tribes, were among them, as well as groups synonymous with the Yanktons and Tetons.[36]

Little would be gained by a careful delineation of the locations of these villages had Le Sueur not kept a journal when he returned to the upper Mississippi in 1700. In this later account he meticulously outlined the geographic locations of the various villages he had knowledge of, noting specific changes. A comparison of his journal with Franquelin's 1697 map shows a dramatic demographic transformation in the eastern Sioux lands since Le Sueur's departure in 1695. Four of the ten eastern villages had moved west of the Mississippi River. Included among them were the Wahpeton and "Tangapssinton" groups, both of which had been residents of Mille Lacs. The other two that migrated had previously occupied the eastern bank of the Mississippi River.[37]

Le Sueur also indicated that two other villages placed near Mille Lacs in 1697 had since changed names, even though they had remained in the woodlands. The Mantanton band of Mdewakantons were now described as the "village d'un grand lac qui se décharge dans un petit," rather than the "village de la Gross Roche." Since the Franquelin map clearly places the "Gross Roche" near the southwestern shore of Mille Lacs, the Mantantons apparently had abandoned the lake. A likely possibility for the "grand lac" that fits Le Sueur's new description is Lake Minnetonka, or the "great waters," a favorite Indian haunt west of present-day Minneapolis. The "Ocatamentons" also had moved, but whether they migrated away from the Mille Lacs lakeshore is impossible to determine.[38]

In sum, the concentration of Sioux in the east had dwindled significantly by 1700, and there is evidence that considerable fluidity existed even among those people who remained. Of the group later mentioned by French observers, only the Sissetons and three Mdewakanton bands—Mantantons, Watpatons, and Issatis—seemed to be consistently located in the woodlands. Of the three remaining eastern villages Le Sueur noted, one was identified as the "seekers of wild rice," undoubtedly a reference to their frequent migrations, another was placed north of Mille Lacs in 1697 but had moved three years later, and the third was so insignificant that Le Sueur failed to locate it initially on the Franquelin map.[39] More important, there is a distinct possibility that only Hennepin's Issati people maintained a semisedentary village at Mille Lacs by 1700. Perhaps this explains why the French cease referring to the lake as the center of woodland Sioux culture. Le Sueur, for example, noted that easternmost Dakotas lived above St. Anthony Falls (present-day Minneapolis) "dans une infinité de petits lacs et marais [marshes]."[40]

Voyageur traffic in the west diminished after the Le Sueur expedition returned to the Gulf of Mexico. Although French sources consistently mention the Sioux thereafter, little information on their locations surfaces until 1727, when a post was established at Lake Pepin. Pierre Boucher, Sieur de Boucherville, reached the lake with his small command in September. After the French had thrown up a stockade on the north shore, a woodland Dakota band of ninety-five tepees appeared and made camp. They stayed about a month, hunting and trading, then departed for their winter camp. Although the French mention contact with these people throughout the winter months, the Dakotas mysteriously disappeared in April. A French party sent to find them searched in vain for a week and returned after traveling more than a hundred leagues up the Mississippi River. Three months later the voyageurs learned that these woodland people had joined their western relatives on the plains to hunt buffalo and raid the Missouri River tribes. Since Hennepin's historic journey, the Dakota life cycle had altered to the point where they spent three months on the prairies rather than a few weeks.[41]

While the Dakotas now preferred to hunt buffalo each spring rather than go into a semipermanent camp as Hennepin's Issatis had done, in the fall they still maintained a village close to their rice crops. Boucherville noted, however, that when he sent envoys to this camp they were conducted "au Sault St. Antoine," or St. Anthony Falls. The cataract had apparently become the central rendezvous for the eastern Sioux. Whether all ninety-five tepees mentioned settled there is uncertain, but this assemblage undoubtedly represented the vast majority of the Sioux in the woodlands. Boucherville was careful to point out that they were still "toujours à la chasse" and moved every seven or eight days. Their frequent movement made it impossible for the French to study their language. Accordingly, the leaders of the expedition learned little more about the Dakotas, reporting back to eastern officials only that they were very numerous and that, along with their western relatives, they numbered ten villages.[42]

Voluntary migration has been suggested as a possible explanation for Sioux movement onto the plains. A recent scholar has even argued that the western Sioux crossed the Missouri and pursued an imperialist policy in order to acquire control of buffalo herds.[43] But the eastern Sioux have never been portrayed as buffalo hunters in the early period. Rather, they have been depicted as sedentary woodland hunters who showed little interest in the west until the Chippewas forced them beyond the Mississippi River sometime after 1737.[44] It is clear, however, that as early as 1700 the only woodland bands left in the east were Mdewakantons and possibly the Sissetons, and they were also depending on bison for a substantial portion of their food resources. Just when and why the Sissetons ultimately abandoned the regions north of Mille Lacs for the prairies is unclear. Strong pressure from the Crees, and after 1737 from the

Chippewas, may account for this occupational change. But the Mdewakantons were already in the Mississippi valley by the 1720s, where
they were found when Americans started coming up the river in the
nineteenth century.[45]

European commercial expansion undoubtedly provided a strong
incentive for migration out of the woodlands. From 1680 on, increasing numbers of traders frequented the Mississippi below Lake Pepin.
Many came from the Gulf rather than overland from Lake Superior.
Unfortunately, they left few details of their activities, but it is obvious
that the emergence of these men on the lower Mississippi made
occupancy of isolated, though protected, regions like Mille Lacs Lake
undesirable. It took Hennepin's party several days to wade through
the swampy country south of the lake in the spring of 1680. On the
other hand, villagers on the Mississippi could intercept French traders on the river below, harvest rice northeast of St. Anthony Falls,
and still reach western buffalo herds.

In addition, a decline in animal resources sometime after 1700
made occupation of the woodlands less desirable. Father Michel
Guignas, who accompanied Boucherville, noted after reconnoitering
the region around the Lake Pepin fort in 1728 that "those herds of
fallow-deer of all species, of which they tell such tales in Canada ...
are no longer in such numbers, and it is hard to kill any."[46] It does
not seem feasible that game could have declined so rapidly from
hunting. The French wanted beaver pelts, not deer or elk hides. Other
causes explain the change, however. An earlier French account noted
that a strange disease had struck the animal populations adjacent to
and south and west of Lake Superior in 1717 and again in 1718. "All
the elk were attacked by a sort of plague, and were found dead," the
informant explained. Indians who ate the infected animals also died.[47]

This plague, which struck at the heart of Dakota food resources,
when combined with the new trade avenues on the Mississippi and
the general migratory nature of the Dakota people, goes a long way
toward explaining the depopulation of the woodlands. Disease and
warfare played only minor roles in comparison. The shifts in population did much to reshape the demographic outline of the entire

upper Mississippi watershed. More important, they affected the balance of power in the region. Algonquin speakers from the east, unable to match the power of the Sioux before 1700, were slowly becoming an equalizing force. The Dakotas could no longer send forth the large armies seen by Perrot and Le Sueur after the Wahpetons and Wahpekutes moved far west of the Mississippi.

On the other hand, the Sioux remained fundamentally in control of their own destiny for many decades after 1700. Their reputation as brave and resourceful fighters and their willingness to give their lives in battle made adventurism by neighboring peoples a costly proposition. Thus the Dakotas never viewed the Algonquins as a threat to their existence, as previous historians have concluded. The older interpretations emphasizing forced migration have been based primarily on Chippewa bragging. Nevertheless, the Dakotas did realize that eastern neighbors held the key to consistent trade with Europeans, and they encouraged the French to breach the Algonquin barrier. Perrot and Le Sueur were the precursors of a new age that would greatly influence the social, economic, and political environment of the Dakota people.

3

Breaking the Algonquin Monopoly, 1670–1760

Dakota villagers probably saw firearms for the first time when the Hurons invaded their lands in the early 1650s. They logically assumed that an instrument that could make such noise had originated in the heavens. Thereafter, the Sioux called the gun *mazawakan*—sacred or mysterious iron. Hennepin found that by 1680 they readily understood the military advantages of modern weaponry. "Arrows only glance through the flesh they pierce," Dakota warriors told the cleric, "rarely breaking the bones of those whom they strike."[1] But the French musket was only the most conspicuous component of a whole new commercial world that included knives, hatchets, brass kettles, and trinkets. Not long after defeating the Huron and Algonquin allies in 1670, the eastern Sioux aggressively sought social and economic alliances in the east.

The Dakotas' incorporation of traders, their goods, and the advice they gave in council was not a radical departure from their past. The Sioux had been part of an extensive intertribal commercial network that stretched nearly from coast to coast. Archaeological and historical evidence, for example, shows that native commercial fairs were held annually along the James River of eastern South Dakota and at the Mandan villages on the Missouri centuries before Europeans arrived. Most of the tribal groups frequenting them remained socially, politically, and even economically distinct, so that carefully orchestrated rituals were needed to establish friendship for the purposes of trade. Since most native groups trusted only their own kinsmen and made war on anyone who did not hold a position within their society, rituals evolved that established temporary kinship bonds between villages and a system of reciprocal giving that initiated trade.[2]

The Sioux used the calumet or peace pipe ceremony as one way to "make relatives" or effect reciprocal giving. Teton variations of the ritual, as described by Black Elk, included a symbolic exchange of corn, robes, and tobacco as well as special songs and smoking the peace pipe. The event allowed outsiders to be temporarily incorporated into Dakota society, where they received kin names symbolic of being recognized as Dakotas. The exact nature of the kin relationship in the early historical period is impossible to determine. When villages came together to trade the bartering probably lasted only a short time, necessitating only temporary social ties. These "fictive" bonds served commercial purposes and obviously lacked the permanency that existed when an individual either was adopted or married into a band. Even so, the eastern Sioux appear not to have made a distinction between temporary ties and "affine," or more permanent, bonds with new relatives. The only rule that seemed to apply was that "fictive" and "affine" relationships worked as long as individuals reinforced them by exchanging gifts with newly made kin.[3]

European traders slowly came to understand the commercial implications of Dakota socioeconomic behavior. By a liberal use of presents and the creation of kinship ties, entire native descent groups could be obligated to hunt for their benefit and to turn their pelts over to their new relative, the trader. To ensure continued support over longer periods, Europeans frequently sought "country," or extralegal, marriages with Dakota women, making affine relatives of the women's descent groups. A trader usually selected the daughter of an important chief and stayed with her during the trade season. Occasionally these unions lasted for years, especially when the trader returned to the same band in the fall after marketing pelts in the east. On the other hand, Europeans who abandoned families were seldom disparaged by Dakota leaders. They needed males from outside the descent group to marry their women so as to prevent incest, a serious taboo, and Europeans had the added advantage of being able to offer their hunters manufactured goods, especially arms. In addition, since the descent group played a major role in rearing children, it was not necessary that the parents remain together. Parental separation occurred frequently in Sioux camps.[4]

Kinship and economic ties also allowed access to the Dakota political system. In seventeenth- and eighteenth-century America there were many pitfalls that fur traders had to avoid. Among them were pillaging by angry natives, the destruction of pelts through mishaps in storage or transportation, and, finally, the closing of hunting preserves owing to intertribal war. Once kinship bonds had been established, fur traders attained such an important status in Dakota camps that they were looked to for advice in council. Most important, this gave traders the chance to argue against intertribal war and even to negotiate peace treaties that would open debated lands. Of course such political influence was limited by the very paradox it created. With peace, tribes competed more readily for furs, and they soon fought over the resources the trader sought to make available for exploitation.

The degree of influence that early European traders attained in Dakota camps and the seriousness with which they took their kinship obligations depended upon a variety of circumstances. Some stayed in Sioux lands only a short time and used kinship as an expedient to economic profit. Others returned again and again, raising families and even educating mixed-blood children in the east. Those who became fixtures and returned each fall with manufactured goods generally found that their influence grew. Understandably, those traders who were less attentive to the responsibilities that kinship bonds engendered, such as assisting relatives and providing them with European-made items, lost status. As we shall see in the chapters that follow, at the height of the fur trade more than a dozen traders and their voyageur assistants worked each year in Sioux country. The number would dwindle by the late 1820s as the stock of fur-bearing animals declined. The economic degeneration of the fur trade also put strong pressure on long-standing kinship bonds.

Nonetheless, before such a mutually profitable relationship could be secured, either the Dakotas or the European traders had to breach the barrier thrown up by the eastern Algonquins. The Dakotas had generally been at odds with the Wisconsin tribes to the east as well as the Illinois and Crees in the south and north. These groups hoped to maintain a monopoly on firearms. Thus, in 1674 ten Dakota ambassadors appeared at Sault Ste. Marie, offering friendship to the small but important Saulteur, or Chippewa, bands that resided there.[5] The Sioux had not fought with the Saulteurs during the Huron wars three years before despite the profitable middleman trade the Saulteurs maintained with the Crees, archenemies of the Dakotas.

Initially successful, the council broke up when a Cree intruder stabbed a Sioux delegate to death. The incident provoked a desperate struggle in which the Dakotas killed most of the Chippewas in the council chambers before succumbing themselves. The Jesuits, who viewed this spectacle, were doubly distressed. Their small chapel that had been used for the council was destroyed, with the loss of much property, and the priests' hopes that peace would open the Sioux lands to Christianity were dashed. It took almost a decade before the Chippewas and Sioux put this disaster behind them, but the potential for reciprocal gain soon brought the two nations back together. In 1679 the Chippewas initiated negotiations and organized a diplomatic mission to the west.[6]

Just before their departure, a group of six or seven Frenchmen led by Daniel Greysolon Duluth visited Sault Ste. Marie. Engrossed with the possibility of reaching the Sioux country to trade, Duluth proposed to his Chippewa hosts that he accompany the party. The Chippewas heartily agreed, since they needed assistance in stopping the Sioux-Cree feuds, a major detriment to commercialism. During the summer, Duluth and his Chippewa companions negotiated a truce among the contending parties. Like many that followed him, Duluth failed in his efforts to stop Dakota-Cree conflicts. Only the Chippewas remained committed to the agreement. Indeed, they married their daughters off to Dakota warriors, establishing kinship links, and received permission to hunt and trade on Dakota lands.[7]

Duluth explored much of the upper Mississippi during his two-year stay in the Dakota domain. Being a military officer, he planted French flags in the Issati village at Mille Lacs as well as among the Sissetons and Watpatons (a Mdewakanton band) encamped north of the lake. Duluth remained unimpressed with the route to the Sioux via Lake Superior, and he returned by water in 1680, using the Wisconsin–Fox River passageway. This natural highway required only one short portage. Traders soon adopted it as the easiest route from the Great Lakes into the rich fur country of the upper Mississippi River.[8] Three years later Duluth was sending regular commercial caravans to the Sioux by this passage, and he had constructed a small fort somewhere on the headwaters of the St. Croix River. But war broke out with the Iroquois in 1684, and after his attention shifted to the eastern campaigns the bulk of the Sioux trade fell to Nicolas Perrot, a civilian who had been in the west since 1666.[9]

Perrot and several voyageurs arrived on the Mississippi with a large cargo of goods in the fall of 1685. In the spring he constructed Fort St. Antoine on Lake Pepin. Although Perrot spent little time at the post, it was occupied by at least a dozen Frenchmen until 1690. They armed many of the woodland Sioux for the first time and apparently carried goods north into Dakota villages.[10] Their efforts soon provoked disharmony, however, since the Wisconsin tribes felt betrayed by the French. Fighting had continued unabated between the Dakotas and their adversaries the Foxes, Mascoutens, and Miamis before Perrot's arrival; the only new dimension was the tendency of the Chippewas to join Sioux war parties. One such army, consisting of eight hundred men, had killed nearly sixty Fox warriors in a single engagement just before Perrot's arrival. Under such conditions it is no wonder that during the summer of 1686 a large number of Foxes, Mascoutens, and Kickapoos appeared at Lake Pepin, intent upon pillaging the small wooden stockade. Perrot saved his establishment by giving the war party presents and convincing them that he had forty well-armed men inside.[11]

After successfully handling the Wisconsin tribes, Perrot discovered that the Sioux showed signs of recusancy. They were peremptory and sullen and suspected the French of treachery. The Dakotas obviously could not understand how Perrot could establish ties with them and then exchange presents, the symbols of alliance, with their enemies. As Dakota warriors became increasingly haughty at Fort St. Antoine after 1686, demanding merchandise and pilfering small items, Perrot finally called for a council with their leaders. Rather than reaffirming any commitment to the Sioux, however, Perrot added some brandy to a cup of water, set it ablaze, then turned to the chiefs and threatened to do the same to their rivers and lakes should they continue to misbehave.[12]

Despite Perrot's claim that this chicanery worked, intertribal hostilities brought on by the trade increased, especially after rumors spread of the French defeat at Lachine in 1689. This massacre of several hundred people near Montreal by the Iroquois convinced many western tribes of the weakness of French arms. Fox warriors attempted to pillage Fort St. Antoine a second time and launched a raid on the Sioux for good measure. Both attempts failed, and the Dakotas prepared to retaliate.[13] Perrot frantically cajoled the four-hundred-member Dakota war party that had assembled, asking them to desist from fighting, but just as he seemed successful Fox and Mascouten warriors surprised a large Sioux village of eighty lodges (1,000 people) below the fort at Lake Pepin. Fifteen raiders died in the assault, but several hundred Sioux were killed. Perrot passed through the village shortly thereafter and reported that "nothing could be seen except melancholy remains."[14]

The attack upon the Sioux touched off a series of raids that made the lower Mississippi, Chippewa, and Fox–Wisconsin river valleys utterly unsafe for Frenchmen or Indians. Sioux villagers near Lake Pepin were supported in their quest for revenge by many other warriors who came down from the regions above the St. Croix River. Allied with a few Chippewas and Iowas, their forces on one occasion reached 1,200 men. The Sioux repeatedly struck the Mascoutens, and on one raid they completely devastated a Miami camp that was allied to that nation. The terrified Foxes soon sued for peace and returned all their Dakota prisoners, constructing palisades around their villages to withstand the anticipated Sioux onslaught.[15]

Although Perrot virtually abandoned trade during these troubled times, Pierre Charles Le Sueur maintained contact with the Dakota people by using Duluth's old route to their lands via Lake Superior. In 1695 he temporarily occupied a stockade on the Mississippi River and convinced a young Dakota warrior of the Mantanton band to join some Chippewa hunters he intended to conduct to Montreal. Governor Louis de Buade, Comte de Frontenac, greeted the party with an impressive honor guard of eight hundred smartly dressed soldiers and then led them to the council chamber.[16] A Chippewa spokesman first harangued the governor: "We come to ask a favour of you. . . . We are allies of the Sciou [Dakotas]. . . . Father, let us take revenge [on the Mascoutens and Foxes]." He was followed by a young Mantanton Dakota named Tiyoskate who made a tearful plea: "All the nations had a father who afforded them protection; all of them have iron. But he [Tiyoskate] was a bastard in quest of a father."[17] Tiyoskate's terminology symbolized the eagerness of the Sioux for European commerce. Yet his request went hand in hand with a proposal to create kinship bonds with the French nation. Frontenac recognized the importance of the requests and cavalierly granted Tiyoskate's wish for "iron," the equivalent of arms and goods. Unfortunately Le Sueur, who was ordered back to the Sioux country, left for France instead, intending to obtain a license to search for western mines. And poor Tiyoskate died after a month-long illness.[18]

The intertribal wars, along with the Iroquois troubles, devastated western commerce. Ironically, the decline failed to harm the European hat industry, based on the fur trade. Warehouses overseas had been overstocked for some time as a consequence of the prosperous 1680s. More important, commercial conditions allowed the Jesuits to gain the king's ear. The coureurs de bois, they complained, corrupted the Indians and should be ordered out of the west. Heeding this advice, Louis XIV ordered the evacuation of Wisconsin in 1696, only a decade after French commercialists had begun to harvest the vast wealth of the upper Mississippi valley.[19] Although the French lacked the western garrisons necessary to enforce this decree, only illegal European traders reached the upper Mississippi valley in the first decade of the eighteenth century.

Le Sueur remained the one exception. He received permission to enter the region by convincing French officials that he intended to explore for mines.[20] On his trip up the Mississippi, Le Sueur found the intertribal war still very much under way. Above the Illinois River, he learned of the defeat of the Piankashaws (relatives of the Mascoutens) at the hands of the Sioux and Iowas. The Illinois tribes in general had become so terrified of the Dakotas by this time that they disavowed any intention of avenging themselves on them and planned instead to raid the Missouri River Indians. Farther upstream Le Sueur met a party of Dakota warriors headed for the Illinois country, intent upon avenging three of their comrades who had been killed in the recent attack on the Piankashaws. He persuaded them to return with presents and promises of carrying goods to their people. Some Wisconsin tribes were retaliating for these blows, yet the two parties Le Sueur met on the Mississippi both had been unsuccessful, one having been forced to abandon its provisions and powder in the face of a Sioux counterattack.[21]

Despite the attacks and the trade embargo, most Mdewakanton warriors had firearms in 1700. A few coureurs de bois and the Chippewas apparently made up for the loss of the fort at Lake Pepin. Pénigault, a carpenter with Le Sueur's party, suggested that Pelée Island in Lake Pepin had become the rendezvous of French traders after the fort was abandoned. Cabins had been built on this treeless isle, along with large platforms for drying buffalo meat. Yet the war made wintering on the upper Mississippi dangerous. Perrot had obviously not convinced the Sioux that he had their interests at heart, and the Dakotas had grown accustomed to viewing Frenchmen on the river below Lake Pepin as enemies. The best a small party could expect was pillage. The only exception came when efforts were made to establish a proper social, and consequently commercial, climate.[22]

Le Sueur understood the relation between social alliances and trade. Nonetheless he selected a location for his mining venture far west of the Mississippi in the lower Blue Earth River valley. The Mantantons, with whom he had previously traded, immediately objected, telling Le Sueur that the site was on the lands of the western Sioux. They wanted him to return to their villages. Their leaders no doubt viewed his move as a threat to their successful middleman trade with the western Sioux, but, more important, his rejection of them was a social insult. Le Sueur countered by putting the Dakotas on the defensive. Two of his hunters had recently been robbed by the Issatis in consequence of his going west of the Mississippi. Thus he refused to council with any band of eastern Sioux, telling their representatives, "we shall no longer be good friends."[23]

A few days later the Mantanton chief "Ouacantapai," or Sacred Born, came and begged Le Sueur to listen to him. After the Frenchman finally agreed, Sacred Born began a long talk, frequently invoking the name of Tiyoskate, the unfortunate Dakota emissary who had died at Montreal after counciling with Le Sueur five years before, and weeping over Le Sueur's head. Next Sacred Born offered Le Sueur wild rice, placing three spoonfuls directly into his mouth. Finally the chief turned to the sixteen men and the handful of women and children who were at the council and explained that they were all relatives of Tiyoskate. At the mere mention of Tiyoskate's name the assemblage again broke into tears. All of this ritual was clearly designed to illustrate to Le Sueur that he too, by his relatedness with Tiyoskate, was in fact a kinsman of the Mantantons. The rice was a symbol of their willingness to share what they had with the French. Sacred Born concluded his presentation with the following: "Behold thy children, thy brethren, thy sisters, it is for thee to see whether thou wishest them to live or die. They will live if thou givest them powder and ball."[24]

The full nature of Le Sueur's kinship ties with Tiyoskate and the women and children present never surfaced in the discussion, yet the Dakotas obviously were pointing to a family bond. The response also helps explain why the Mantantons were so insistent on his re-

turning to their village; they undoubtedly assumed that he understood his obligations to help his people, all relatives of Tiyoskate. It
seemed only logical that when he passed up their village, as well as
that of their close relatives the Issatis, he should be punished and
reminded of those obligations. This in turn explains why two of Le
Sueur's men had their goods taken by men from the Issati camp.
Now aware of his error, Le Sueur responded to Sacred Born by an-
nouncing that he would hand out the required supplies. The Sioux
reciprocated by giving Le Sueur several hundred beaver robes.

After reaffirming his obligations, Le Sueur tried to lure the woodland bands to his fort on the Blue Earth River. He even urged them
to take up farming and thus supply his operation with corn. But
neither the Mdewakantons of Mille Lacs nor their Mantanton relatives ever stayed longer than a few days, and they had no intention
of abandoning the chase.[25] The Yanktons and Wahpekutes did move
south of the Minnesota River during the winter of 1700–1701, however, and settled near Le Sueur's stockade. They stayed in the area
until the fort was abandoned the following summer. The ore that Le
Sueur carried back to France proved worthless, making the continuation of the mining project unprofitable.[26]

The early experiences of Duluth, Perrot, and Le Sueur demonstrated that, although the Dakotas were eager for trade, commercialism was much more than an economic institution to these Indians.
A Dakota Indian did not have dealings with foreigners unless some
sense of trust was established through real or fictive kinship bonds.
Once these were created, it was impossible for the Sioux to understand how a trader could establish similar relations with others outside their tribal group. Abandonment required reprisals, in the form
of pilfering and threats, as Perrot discovered at his fort, or pillaging,
as Le Sueur found when his men bypassed the Mantanton and Issati
villages. Political influence also hinged on reinforcement of bonds.
Perrot had to resort to threats to assuage the Sioux in council in the
1690s, and Le Sueur found the Dakotas unwilling to leave his men
alone until he embraced past responsibilities.

After Le Sueur's garrison fled downriver to the Gulf of Mexico,

Queen Anne's War (1702–13) broke out in Europe. Although the conflict had only a minor effect on western affairs, it did help prolong the stagnation in the fur trade for at least a decade. During these years the Sioux stockpiled beaver pelts, sewing eight or nine together to make robes. When Le Sueur reached the Blue Earth River, a large number had already been preserved in this fashion, owing to the inactivity created by the decree of 1696.[27] Intertribal wars with the Wisconsin tribes also abated after 1702, as powder and lead became scarce. Antoine de la Mothe Cadillac, who commanded troops at Detroit, did what he could to prevent serious collisions by adopting a policy of "concentration," aimed at resettling many of the Wisconsin tribes near his fort. This partial evacuation of Wisconsin, coupled with the restrictions on trade, incidentally relieved many western intertribal pressures. Cadillac also issued a decree that levied a thousand-livre fine upon any Frenchman found illegally collecting beaver pelts.[28] Thus the Sioux were being isolated both from their enemies and from trade.

The French policy of evacuation eventually proved pernicious to colonial aims. Many native traders and hunters no longer felt obliged to sell their pelts at either Detroit or Montreal after 1700. They turned increasingly to the British, who offered higher prices. By the time delegates had signed the Peace of Utrecht thirteen years later, French policymakers suddenly realized they no longer could control the west commercially and inaugurated a plan of reoccupation. In the meantime the Foxes had reunited their people in Wisconsin and were enjoying a brisk trade, frequently with the British. Sometime before 1714 they even negotiated an alliance with the Dakotas. Accordingly, when French traders once again tried to reopen Sioux lands, Fox warriors pillaged their stores.[29]

Commercial animosity had grown to such levels by 1716 that a French army had to invade Wisconsin and extract a rapprochement from the Foxes. This only hardened their opposition, however, and three years later the Fox–Wisconsin River route was again under siege.[30] Realizing that the Foxes had a secure refuge in Dakota villages, the French attempted to lure the Sioux from this alliance by working through the Chippewas. In 1720 garrisons reoccupied Chequamegon Bay on the south shore of Lake Superior as well as Kaministiquia on the north shore. Both were stepping-stones to the Sioux, who were approached during the summer and pressured by the French to reject their Fox friends.[31]

As the plan matured, a woodland Dakota war party surprised the Chippewa Indians encamped at Kaministiquia and killed seventeen. Rumors circulated that the Foxes had poisoned the minds of their Dakota friends, apparently convincing them that the French and their Indian allies meant to betray them.[32] Increasing numbers of coureurs de bois from New Orleans also had reached the upper Mississippi by the 1720s. They competed with the brigades from Montreal and seemed to have had a hand in urging the Dakotas to break off negotiations with the French Canadians. Nonetheless, the Dakota raid on Kaministiquia only convinced the French in Montreal of the absolute necessity of building a fort in the Sioux domain. Without it the upper Mississippi might be lost to traders from New Orleans or, worse, to the English. By the 1720s Canadian policy revolved around neutralizing and eventually destroying the power of the Foxes.[33]

This presented quite a challenge. The Foxes, dedicated to protecting their trade monopoly, had organized a loose coalition around the Mascouten, Sac, and Kickapoo tribes in Wisconsin, as well as the Sioux. Rumors even placed the Otoes and Iowas in their camp.[34] By 1725 Sioux warriors had joined Fox raiders in the Illinois country, and the Fox had also disrupted French trade along the south shore of Lake Superior. The latter raids were primarily aimed at the Chippewas at Chequamegon Bay. This fighting understandably caused political difficulties for the woodland Sioux, yet they apparently remained on friendly terms with both the Chippewas and the Foxes.[35]

Finally, in an effort to break the Fox control of the western trade, several Montreal merchants received a three-year monopoly for the upper Mississippi in June 1727. It allowed them to bring nine canoes full of goods into the area the first year in exchange for supporting a small garrison. Passing through the Fox–Wisconsin River route, an accomplishment in itself, the trading brigade reached Lake Pepin in

September. Unfortunately, not long after the new post had been completed news arrived of yet another large French expedition against the Foxes, who were threatening to destroy the Lake Pepin fort and had already killed several French traders. Expecting an assault, commandant Pierre de Boucherville decided to abandon the Sioux post, leaving it in the hands of the several civilians who elected to stay behind. In final councils held with the Sioux at St. Anthony Falls, Sacred Born and his followers promised not to assist the Foxes in the upcoming struggle, an arrangement that demonstrated the strength of their new ties with the French.[36]

The Dakotas faithfully observed this pledge for the next two years, protecting the French from insult. In spring 1730 they even clashed with the Foxes, no doubt over the issue of the French presence. But the many years of Fox resistance to French colonial expansion were about to end. That fall, a combined force of more than 1,400 French and Indian allies invaded Wisconsin and laid siege to the Fox cantons. This movement, and a subsequent expedition in 1732, finally broke their grip on the Fox–Wisconsin River route.[37] The event had momentous implications for the Dakotas, who no longer remained isolated from consistent colonial exploitation.

After the Fox debacle, the French unfolded a major plan of westward expansion that soon took their explorers and traders well beyond the Mississippi River in search of the "western sea" as well as beaver. "Tranquillity," as the French governor Claude de la Boische de Beauharnois observed, made this dynamic thrust into the west possible. Opening intermediate posts at Rainy Lake in 1731 and Lake of the Woods in 1732, French traders under Pierre Gaultier de Varennes, Sieur de La Vérendrye quickly reached the prairies near the great bend of the upper Missouri River.[38] Meanwhile the monopoly on the Sioux trade was again farmed out, and the factors constructed a new, larger post near Lake Pepin. Early reports indicated that the Dakotas had "shown great satisfaction at receiving the French" and that sixty-two woodland tepees had arisen near the post, with more expected.[39] By the mid-1730s the French were at the height of their power in the west.

The opening of the upper Mississippi did more than attract traders. Some eighty lodges of Winnebagos followed the French into the region, intent upon using the Lake Pepin commercial center and the adjacent Sioux lands to advance their own economic well-being. In addition, the French brought in two missionaries with high hopes of converting the Sioux. The Winnebagos apparently were better received by the Sioux than were the missionaries. After several years of hard labor, the Jesuits admitted that they had converted only "a few old men and women ... beyond the age of sinning." Nevertheless, they boasted of accomplishing something. When sickness struck the Sioux children, a frequent occurrence with Europeans nearby, the missionaries baptized them "on the point of death."[40]

Within three years the eastern Sioux found themselves being transformed into a commercially responsive people. They turned to hunting smaller, more valuable animals for their hides and subsequently made huge profits for the traders. In 1735 alone the Sioux post, as well as the establishments near Lake of the Woods, shipped east nearly 100,000 prime skins, worth 178,000 livres.[41] Western tribes such as the Sioux and Crees had not been accustomed to traveling long distances to trade, and beaver populations in Sioux lands most likely had suffered little from earlier exploitation. Dakota resources probably compared favorably with those found at that time in Cree lands surrounding Lake of the Woods. Even though the Crees had carried a few pelts to the English and Chippewas for decades, early French traders noted in 1729 that they placed "little value" on beaver and used many of the skins to make winter coats that they discarded in the spring. Le Sueur had found the Dakotas doing virtually the same thing in 1700, and they no doubt had continued the practice until the French reappeared at Lake Pepin.[42]

Notwithstanding the profits that accumulated at Lake Pepin and the good treatment afforded the traders, the French remained dubious about the intentions of the Sioux. Governor Beauharnois and Intendant Gilles Hocquart both surmised that the Dakotas had little natural affinity for the French and tolerated their presence at Lake Pepin only because of the trade. Despite their caution, the French seemed oblivious to the impact their growing commercial system was having on intertribal relations.[43] The Sioux were asked to support French colonialism in the west while they watched La Vérendrye and his brigades push into the Lake of the Woods area, stocking post after post with arms and ammunition that went directly into Cree, Monsoni, and Assiniboin hands. The Sioux attack on the Chippewas at Kaministiquia may have been predicated on a similar concern, since the latter people were middlemen traders to the Crees. By 1733 these northern tribes had become well armed for the first time and began an aggressive campaign against the Sioux. La Vérendrye, unable to preserve the peace, managed only to extract promises that the war parties would confine their attacks to the prairie Sioux. But the Dakota bands east of the Mississippi now spent much of the summer hunting buffalo west of the river, and this made clashes between the two French allies inevitable.[44]

When the woodland Sioux retaliated, as they did in 1733, the only hope for the preservation of French presence lay in maintaining absolute neutrality. Unfortunately, La Vérendrye publicly sanctioned the recruitment of his eldest son, Jean-Baptiste, to join a Cree and Monsoni war party in May of the following year. The senior La Vérendrye contended in a letter to Governor Beauharnois that to deny the request would have left the French open to charges of cowardice. Although Jean-Baptiste left the party before it did any harm, the spectacle of La Vérendrye giving his son to a Cree war chief became public knowledge in the west a short time later, and the party the young man deserted raided the woodland Dakotas.[45]

La Vérendrye paid dearly for proving French valor. In June 1736 a mixed party of one hundred prairie and woodland Sioux and a few Chippewas from Chequamegon Bay captured several Frenchmen and Indians east of Lake of the Woods. Just as the Dakota warriors were preparing to burn the leader, René Bourassa, a Dakota slave woman attached to the voyageur mentioned that twenty-four Frenchmen headed by Jean-Baptiste La Vérendrye were on the river a short distance away. The Sioux released their captives and began to search for the other party. Finding the group on an island in Lake of the

Woods, the Dakota warriors first pretended to parlay and then turned on the French. All twenty-four members of the La Vérendrye party were killed.[46]

The Sioux massacre at Lake of the Woods was hardly an isolated incident. A month before, a Dakota party of fifty-four men had struck deep into the Illinois country, killing two French traders. Upon their return, they performed a scalp dance within sight of the Lake Pepin post.[47] Rumors also persisted that the Sioux had renewed their alliance with Fox survivors of the Wisconsin wars. By September 1736, relations between the French and the Sioux near the Lake Pepin post deteriorated further when a Dakota chief appeared sporting a silver earring taken from a victim of the La Vérendrye massacre. When the commandant asked where it came from, the chief laughed. The officer promptly "tore the seal away with the ear."[48] Finally, during the fall hunting season, a party of thirty-six woodland Sioux arrived near the French post and burned down the Winnebago stockade. Obviously the Dakotas were demonstrating to the French and Winnebagos that they considered these outsiders remiss in their kinship obligations. When the French commandant inquired of Sacred Born why his people continued to insult the French, the latter answered simply that it was done "with reflection and design."[49]

After the New Year, harassment reached new levels. The Dakotas soon gave notice that other Indian allies of the French would be forced off their lands. In March they killed four Chippewas from Chequamegon Bay just west of Lake Superior, and in May they raided the same tribe a second time. The Chippewas responded by enlisting the aid of the Winnebagos still camped near the French garrison at Lake Pepin. During the discussion between these two eastern tribes, several woodland Sioux arrived, which immediately provoked a skirmish. Thereafter the French recognized that their position on the upper Mississippi was no longer tenable, and the garrison burned the fort and disappeared downriver sometime during the summer of 1737. The Winnebagos and the Chippewas had abandoned the area a short time before, leaving the upper Mississippi solely in the hands of the eastern Sioux.[50]

At first glance the actions of the woodland Dakotas seem bewildering. Fur-trade colonialism usually implanted a dependency upon European arms that, once entrenched, few if any tribes could rebel against. The Sioux had asked, indeed begged, for French traders. Nevertheless Sacred Born, the venerable leader of the Mantantons that Le Sueur had dealt with, was at the head of the discontented faction. A large number of the woodland Sioux obviously found the interethnic community that emerged around the French garrison not to their liking.

Yet at least a portion of the Dakota population in the area had disagreed with Sacred Born and his followers. They informed the Lake Pepin commander that they were sorry for the actions of some of their young men. They wanted the French to stay.[51] Accordingly, the harassment campaign that followed was a good solution. It forced the French to depart even though a tribal consensus did not exist. The events demonstrated both the strengths and the weaknesses of Dakota politics; the tribe as a whole had to support a major policy decision for it to work, but when a consensus failed to materialize a faction could and often did act on its own.

Sacred Born's actions also illustrate the importance of maintaining a trade climate based upon reciprocity. To the Sioux, trade was a social as well as an economic function that could work only after the proper kinship and alliance pledges had been established. The French had violated their responsibilities by failing to provide for the welfare of their kinsmen. A look at the trade agreements assumed by French merchants bound for Lake Pepin in 1727 sheds some light on the situation. The contracts stipulated that the commercialists "shall not trade nor hunt in the direction of Point Chagouamigon [the point occupied by the Chippewas on Lake Superior] elsewhere than in the hunting grounds whither the Sioux go."[52] Since the post was leased at considerable expense, the hunting grounds contiguous to it became a capital investment that had to be quickly exploited. The restrictions were meant to prevent disruptive competition between the traders and the Indians at Lake Pepin and Chequamegon Bay.

But the traders failed to honor the divisions set down in Montreal. The Lake Pepin merchants encouraged the commercially active Winnebagos to live near them, probably out of distrust for the Sioux, and traded with the Chippewas whenever possible. The latter had been hunting intermittently on Dakota lands since the 1690s, and it must have been difficult to break this pattern. One wonders if the French even tried, since they paid for their concession by the year and cared little about which tribes harvested the pelts of the region.[53] The commercial agreements demonstrate that there was a need to regulate tribal access to various hunting zones in 1737. That the French and their Winnebago and Chippewa allies opted not to implement such restrictions undoubtedly led many eastern Dakotas to reevaluate their own relations with the expanding French commercial system.

The eastern Sioux life-style also differed from that of the woodland Chippewas and Winnebagos in one important way; the Dakotas had the option of hunting buffalo west of the Mississippi and continued to do so after the French built their post in 1727. Their diverse livelihood made it unnecessary for them to be so aggressive in the woodlands. Thus the French encouragement to the Chippewas and Winnebagos to use Sioux lands may have resulted from what traders perceived as Dakota inefficiency. Accordingly, the bulk of French merchandise went to Chippewa and Winnebago hunters, leaving for the Sioux only a few presents as symbols of the fictive kinship ties the French wanted to maintain.

On the other hand, it should not be assumed that the causes for war were solely economic. Trade was not a life-and-death issue for the eastern Sioux in the early eighteenth century, despite their eagerness for it. Game was plentiful, and the bow and arrow continued to be an effective means of taking animals. In addition, the Dakotas had few reasons to fear the Lake Superior Chippewas or the Winnebagos in 1736. Although they were clearly becoming a part of the European commercial process, the Sioux had yet to reach that state of dependency where they needed to extract maximum value from their resource base in order to survive. Unlike the Chippewas, Winnebagos, and French, the Dakotas still placed a strong emphasis upon social obligation and sharing when outsiders entered their lands, a process the others had apparently ignored in their combined quest for quick profit.

Nineteenth- and earlier twentieth-century historians viewed the period differently, pointing instead to the aggressiveness of the Chippewas and arguing that they initiated the war to drive the Dakotas from the woodlands. A recent scholar echoed this argument when he noted that the most important event for the eastern Sioux in the eighteenth century was "their expulsion by the Chippewa from their traditional homes around Mille Lacs Lake."[54] Emphasizing Chippewa imperialism perpetuates a myth; as we have seen, the vast majority of Dakota people had already moved into the Mississippi River valley before feuding broke out in 1737.

The legend of Dakota defeat persists because of the account of William Whipple Warren, a mixed-blood Chippewa who compiled his tribe's oral tradition in the 1840s and 1850s. Historians have deduced from Warren that sometime between 1737 and 1750 the Chippewas routed the woodland Dakotas in the three-day battle of "Kathio," a term mistakenly derived from the "Issati" village at Mille Lacs Lake.[55] Warren's informants indicated that five hundred Sioux lost their lives when the Chippewas crawled to the top of Dakota earthen lodges and dropped lighted charges down the smoke holes. The Sioux fought without firearms, they said, a key point that helped Warren explain the disastrous defeat.[56]

Written during the romantic age of William Hickling Prescott and Francis Parkman, the Warren account has been accepted for more than a hundred years. Yet it is not supported by French documents, has many inaccuracies, and runs counter to Sioux oral tradition. There is no doubt that some Dakota people had arms as early as 1690, and all accounts describe them as living in tepees rather than earthen lodges. It is also unlikely that such a major battle would have escaped the attention of traders at La Pointe, Green Bay, and Lake of the Woods, who often reported the most minor skirmishes after 1737.[57] When Dakota informants were queried in the 1850s (the same period when Warren gathered his information) they immediately dismissed claims of Chippewa conquest, pointing instead to the commercial advantages offered by the Mississippi valley as inducements for westward migration.[58] With such discrepancies in the oral accounts, it becomes essential that early French documents receive far closer scrutiny.

Although French observers failed to report major engagements in the woodlands in either the 1730s or the 1740s, they continued to follow events in the Mississippi valley after the evacuation of the Lake Pepin post. Contrary to Warren, these sources show that even though the number of woodland, or Mississippi River, Sioux had dwindled to a mere three hundred fighting men, most likely all of the Mdewakanton tribe, they still outnumbered the Chippewas inhabiting both La Pointe and the Keweenaw Peninsula.[59] Thus the easternmost Dakotas, augmented on occasion by close relatives living west of the Mississippi, had no difficulty protecting themselves. While they still considered the Mille Lacs country a part of their domain, it no longer had such strategic importance as the Mississippi, St. Croix, and Wisconsin rivers. The latter were still stocked with game and were tied to important transportation routes. French sources also suggest that while the new feuds that broke out in 1737 made woodland hunting dangerous, the fighting had little if any effect on migration.

Dismissing the myth of Sioux defeat at "Kathio," however, does not diminish the importance of events in the west after the French evacuation. During the 1740s, the French restored order and eventually established long-range kinship ties that became the foundation for consistent commercial exploitation. Initially they made little headway. Louis Denys, Sieur de La Ronde, the post commander at La Pointe, reported that in June 1738 the Sioux had killed thirty people, several of whom were members of the Chippewa village near his post. Nevertheless, within months the Dakotas expressed a willingness to reestablish bonds and trade. But when Chippewa delegates failed to keep a prearranged rendezvous to initiate the process, one hundred Sioux warriors fell on a Chippewa camp and killed several

men. Despite this setback, La Ronde seemed confident of his ability
to "restore peace." The Chippewas realized, he wrote, that unless the
feuding was brought to an end "they would Expose themselves to
die by hunger next winter." La Ronde unfortunately died before he
could effect a truce.[60]

Accordingly, French authorities appointed Paul Marin to restore
order in the west. Marin established himself at the Sac and Fox village on Rock River, but he soon made contact with the Dakotas and
convinced two of their leaders, Wabasha and "Sintez," to accompany
him to Montreal. Once in council with Governor Beauharnois, these
men asked for forgiveness for their "bad actions."[61] Beauharnois, assured by Marin of their sincerity, granted them their request for new
ties and soon contemplated restoring French trade posts on the
Mississippi River. Just as peace seemed imminent, however, Chippewa and Ottawa warriors ambushed two Dakota camps in quick
succession during the spring of 1741, killing seven in one and eleven
in the other. These losses, characteristic of the feuds that would
continue into the nineteenth century, were the most serious reported during the decade, and the Dakotas obviously perceived them
as examples of French treachery. Consequently, their warriors retaliated against a French trading brigade in Wisconsin, and eventually
their leaders sought out Marin for an explanation. "After the Father
of all nations [Beauharnois] had granted them their lives [peace]" at
Montreal, their chiefs said, they could not understand the actions of
the Chippewas and Ottawas.[62]

While Marin struggled to placate both the Chippewas and the
Sioux, tensions in the far west, building since the La Vérendrye massacre, erupted. In September 1741 two hundred Crees and Assiniboins surprised a prairie Sioux camp and killed at least seventy men
and uncounted women and children. La Vérendrye noted that the
captives taken by the Crees and Assiniboins "occupied in their march
more than four arpents [approximately seven hundred feet]." This
must have overjoyed the old voyageur, since it avenged the death of
his son and provided people to be shipped east for the small but
accessible Montreal slave market.[63] The debacle prompted old Sa-

cred Born to visit Marin in October. He obviously hoped to avert a similar disaster for his tribe, a real possibility should the Crees and Assiniboins join the Chippewas and Ottawas in an all-out war on the eastern Sioux. Marin told the Sioux leader he would have to take his concerns to Montreal, and he scheduled a peace conference for the following summer.[64]

The general council that convened at Montreal in July 1742 attracted nearly all the western tribes. Sacred Born and Leaf Shooter represented the Mdewakanton Sioux. During the meetings they bitterly complained that even though the French had "adopted" them, the Chippewas, Ottawas, and northern tribes continued to break the peace. Then, recounting the raid on their prairie Sioux brethren, an assault in which "160 of our men were killed," Sacred Born and Leaf Shooter said they had not yet acted to avenge their deaths only because Marin had "forbade our doing so." Yet the Dakota leaders were also conciliatory. Their people had broken the truce by killing both Frenchmen and their Indian allies. Thus they "begged for their lives." Finally, Sioux leaders asked that traders once again supply them and "give them sense" in dealing with their neighbors. Beauharnois responded warmly by saying that all past insults should be forgotten, whereupon he told the Sioux that they would once again become his "children" and eventually be granted a trader.[65]

The other tribes followed the Dakotas in accepting peace. Surprisingly, the treaty enjoyed some success, even though Beauharnois had no way of enforcing it. Scattered reports from the west thereafter divulge that the Chippewas and the eastern Sioux did reestablish kinship ties, and only a few references to small, isolated raids have survived. But in retrospect we see that a further decline in the fur trade did much to end feuding in the west. King George's War (1743–48) had brought a commercial blockade, and French officials found it exceedingly difficult to farm out the western posts. The lease system virtually fell into disuse.[66]

Even though the trade diminished, the Dakotas maintained ties with the French. When word of war reached Mackinac Island, a contingent of coureurs de bois deserted, heading west to live with the

Sioux. Although the commandant at Green Bay, Paul Louis Dazen-ard, Sieur Lusignan, visited the Sioux in 1746 and tried to coax his countrymen back, they refused. Lusignan, however, did convince four Dakota chiefs to visit Montreal on his return. While at the seat of government, they pleaded unsuccessfully for a post. By 1748 many western tribes had given up hunting for the French.[67]

The downward cycle reversed itself as soon as the war in Europe ended. By October 1749 Paul Marin had convinced the new gover-nor, Pierre-Jacques de Taffanel, Marquis de Jonquière, to reestablish a lease system. He volunteered to once again open the Mississippi valley to commerce. Marin believed that fortunes could be made in the region, since it held large numbers of beavers. The governor, in turn, received a partnership in the enterprise, which included plac-ing the La Pointe garrison under the command of the elder Marin's son Joseph and Green Bay under other associates.[68]

Paul Marin's trading venture in Sioux lands began in June 1750 and continued for nearly four years. With the aid of his son Joseph and perhaps a dozen other traders, Marin was able to send commer-cial brigades to nearly all the Sioux villages along the Mississippi River as well as to several on the Minnesota River. These posts cleared 150,000 francs annually, a strong indication of the wealth of Dakota hunting grounds.[69] Marin's success rested squarely upon his exten-sive understanding of Dakota culture; he fostered kinship ties with every important Dakota leader, gaining the trust of these people as no European had done since Le Sueur, and he kept outsiders like the Winnebagos and Chippewas at a distance.

Joseph Marin kept a journal of his trading endeavors with the Dakotas over the winter of 1753–54 that gives a clear picture of the way both he and his father operated.[70] Before leaving Green Bay in August 1753, Joseph ordered three canoes full of presents sent ahead for his Sioux friends. Once along the Mississippi, he counciled with many Dakota leaders, smoking the pipe and reaffirming kinship alli-ances. The presents, in turn, made the Dakotas obliged to listen to the words of "their father" Joseph Marin, a man who provided them with essential arms, powder, and balls. Once this sense of obligation had been reinforced, Joseph handed out "credits," as he called them, with the exhortation that the Sioux work hard at their winter hunts, securing the prime pelts necessary to cover this second outlay of goods. As with Le Sueur, there is no indication that Marin placed a specific value on the credits he handed out or on the few items he continued to distribute to hunters throughout the winter. Marin was able to use credit so cavalierly because he dealt with leaders of descent groups rather than with individual hunters. Establishing kinship ties with such men proved invaluable, since they assumed responsibility for collecting pelts from their young men.[71]

The exact nature of Joseph Marin's kinship ties with the Sioux is not evident from his journal. Europeans viewed "country" marriages with Sioux women as commercial arrangements and seldom recorded them. In a symbolic fashion, however, Marin's councils with Dakota chiefs demonstrated family relationships. Joseph often reassured Sioux leaders that they were "like my children."[72] And when a Mdewakanton came to report the murder of one of his fellow tribesmen, chiefs placed the dead man in Marin's hands. "He is your child, my father," the Dakota spokesman declared, "do with him as you will; see if you wish to go avenge his death or if you wish us to bury him and say no more." The use of the father-child metaphor was meant to show Marin that he had strong family responsibilities to the Sioux; yet it also illustrated that the eastern Sioux would carefully consider his advice, since children benefiting from the benevolence of their father were obligated to listen. The extent to which the Sioux intended to follow these kinship obligations is seen in their willingness to let Marin determine whether they would avenge the death of their relative.[73]

Beyond personal contact, the Marins also could use the close kinship bonds their men created to manipulate the Sioux. Several mentioned by Joseph Marin had probably been part of the group who deserted Mackinac in 1746 to live with the Dakota people. They wintered with individual bands in the 1750s and no doubt had consummated "country" marriages. The presence in Sioux camps of such voyageurs, a few of whom were bilingual, provided the first transitional links between European and native cultures. Their children would begin to function in such a capacity a generation later. Although attempting to assess the nature of their kinship ties with various Dakota bands is a futile effort, they probably acted as a diffusing network in spreading European influence throughout the Mississippi valley.[74]

The Marins used kinship ties as a means to ensure the gathering of pelts, but they also could be employed to stop intertribal wars and negotiate the division of hunting territory. Native hunters could not effectively exploit game preserves when they had to be on guard against intrusion by outsiders. For this reason Paul Marin initially sent his son to the Chippewa post at La Pointe so that a rapprochement could be established between the Sioux and the Chippewas. The elder Marin then negotiated a reasonable division of their hunting grounds that lasted until 1754. The agreement allowed the La Pointe Chippewas to hunt west to Sandy Lake. Joseph Marin apparently accompanied these people to this location sometime before his trip to the Mississippi. Farther south, the Chippewas worked on the headwaters of the St. Croix to its junction with the Snake River.[75] Whenever the Chippewas hunted beyond these borders, it was usually with Sioux kinsmen and after presents had been given to the Dakotas for the privilege. The younger Marin mentions that while he was at La Pointe the Chippewas had purchased the use of the Crow Wing River valley for the 1750–51 hunting season.[76]

The Dakotas, on the other hand, still dominated most of the Chippewa and St. Croix rivers, the regions directly south of Mille Lacs, and the upper Mississippi from below Lake Pepin to its headwaters, as well as a vast territory west of the river. Joseph Marin specifically mentions the existence of forty lodges (500–600 people?) of Watpaton Mdewakantons on the St. Croix River in 1753.[77] Other Mdewakantons apparently had semipermanent villages at the falls of St. Anthony and Lake Pepin. The Mantantons under Sacred Born and "Ouapati," perhaps a corruption for Wabasha, were still the dominant Mdewakanton people in this region. The "Meneouakatons"— Hennepin's Issatis—occasionally joined them, but they maintained a distinct band organization under their head chief, Iroquois. From the size of the Watpaton group, it seems likely that the three identified Mdewakanton bands totaled over one hundred lodges, or perhaps 300 men, in 1750. They still gathered wild rice south of Mille Lacs and returned to the Rum River during the spring to make canoes.[78]

The other three eastern Sioux, or Dakota, tribes remained west of the Mississippi in 1753. Although Marin had no contact with the Wahpetons and Wahpekutes, he did trade regularly with the Sissetons. Just when they migrated from their old homeland north of Mille Lacs is unclear. Marin implies that the Sissetons frequently camped with the Yanktons on the prairies southwest of the Crow Wing River, but both of these tribes were highly nomadic. The main Yankton camp, which Marin indicates held 160 lodges—perhaps 2,400 people—roamed clear to the Missouri River, while the Sissetons—80 lodges strong, perhaps 1,000 to 1,200 people—came to camp near Marin's stockade on the lower Mississippi during the winter of 1753–54. Both tribes were known to hunt in the woodlands south of Leech Lake during the winter, obviously to escape the harsh plains environment. Staying in this area any length of time, however, was contingent upon peace with the Crees.[79]

The Marins began to lose control of their upper Mississippi valley trading empire in the late fall of 1753 after their benefactor the Marquis de Jonquière left office. The first indications of trouble emerged after the new commandant at La Pointe, Louis-Joseph La Vérendrye, refused to support a 1752 peace proposal that Joseph Marin had initiated between the Crees and Dakotas. Shortly after the prairie Sioux raiders had taken two Cree captives, Marin convinced both sides to meet in the fall of 1753, exchange prisoners, and accept a truce. If the plan succeeded, Marin expected to station traders at the mouth of the Crow Wing River and on Leech Lake.[80] Unfortunately La Vérendrye convinced the Cree representatives to return to Lake of the Woods and evicted Marin's two traders from the upper Mississippi, intending to procure furs from the region for himself.[81]

After La Vérendrye forced Marin's traders to leave, he sent his

Chippewa hunters into the Crow Wing valley. Soon a Dakota hunter was killed, and Marin was faced with an intertribal war. He "covered" the death by giving presents to the family of the deceased, but the Dakotas made it clear the following spring that they would not allow the Chippewas to trespass on their land. "No one could be ignorant of the fact," a Sioux spokesman told Marin, "that from the mouth of the Wisconsin to Senue [Leech] Lake, these lands belong to us. At all points and on the little rivers we have had villages. . . . And today the Sauteux [Chippewas] want to take our lands and chase us away." Although many Sioux had been lost defending these lands, he said, neither the Chippewas nor Crees "ran us off that way."[82] The Dakota young men spoke of war, questioning the truce that "their father" Marin had requested them to embrace.

Joseph Marin promised Dakota leaders that he would carry their grievances to Montreal, and he encouraged several of their leaders to accompany him, but no record remains either of their arrival or of an official French response.[83] Furthermore, the French and Indian War broke out the following year, forcing both Marins to abandon their western posts. Their departure eventually led to the breakdown of an already shaky truce as traders from La Pointe increased pressure upon Chippewa hunters, pushing them farther west toward the headwaters of the Mississippi. The Dakotas, migrating south and west away from Mille Lacs Lake, still viewed this land as their own. The gradual changes in occupation patterns were hardly indicative of the superiority of one nation over the other; rather, they mirrored the evolving commercialism of the period, the Sioux becoming increasingly dependent upon traders in the south and the Lake Superior merchants acting as the catalyst to Chippewa migration west of Fond du Lac. With the possible exception of the Sissetons, the Dakotas were protesting the Chippewa presence in a region they had abandoned years before.

Students of the Indian have frequently pondered the revolutionary changes attending the introduction of European-made goods into native societies. Most agree that material changes took place, often of substantial proportions. This was certainly true of the Sioux, who in the 1680s turned quickly to using metal axes, knives, and kettles as well as firearms. Yet they were slow to incorporate capitalist ethics, insisting initially that trade be based on giving and need. When Sacred Born dealt with Le Sueur, he expected goods and gave furs in exchange, but the process was done without mention of price and fit into the framework of reinforcing kinship ties. The Sioux did not accumulate items and feel wealthier with a surplus. A concept of wealth existed only in that goods had a utilitarian value for the individual in his quest to preserve the group.

Identifying social and political changes that occur from the early fur trade has proved more nebulous. Stronger societies, such as the Sioux, seemed to have adjusted very well to the penetration of their lands by other trading Indians as well as by Euroamericans. This was true primarily because of the flexibility in their social and political systems. Yet European traders quickly realized that, while incorporation was a simple matter, age-old social and political rules existed that had to be obeyed. Traders could offer advice in council and use presents to gain political advantage, but a consensus of leaders and hunters in a particular village had to believe that a trader was in fact a sincere relative, committed to acting in their behalf. So it was that on many occasions as the Sioux came to council with the younger Marin they thanked him for coming with goods and presents, and gave special praise to Onontio, Marin's "father" in Montreal, who made such a relationship possible. They even made peace with tribes who had threatened them. In other words, political institutions were open to manipulation, if used properly, and this maneuvering went hand in hand with economic exploitation.

But fundamental to economic and political relations was the reinforcement of kinship bonds. Joseph Marin sent three boatloads of presents to the Sioux before he headed into their lands in 1753, even though he and his father had been trading with these people for several years. And he counciled with them often, rather than avoiding them as Le Sueur had done. To have neglected his Sioux relatives would have been an insult. Paul Marin had learned this after the French were expelled in 1737. He did not make the mistake of earlier traders, who had clear imperial designs that clashed with Sioux concepts of interethnic relations. Instead of encouraging the Chippewas and Winnebagos to follow him, he attempted to isolate each tribal group and work with them individually, giving each a prescribed hunting territory.

In essence, while the French did effect important changes in the west, they soon discovered that in order to successfully exploit Sioux lands it would be essential to become socially, politically, and economically enculturated into Dakota society. They had learned a lesson that would be invaluable to the relations that English and American explorers and colonizers were soon to establish with the Sioux.

4

Traders and the Evolution of Kinship Bonds, 1760–1800

During the French and Indian War (1754–63), the markets that usually stimulated the fur trade slowly evaporated. Posts at Green Bay and La Pointe remained open until the final defeat of General Louis Joseph de Montcalm, but the number of prime furs harvested by the western Indians declined as goods became unavailable. The English reopened western commerce in 1760, but they did little to reverse the downward trend. Stringent commercial restrictions prohibited bartering with natives beyond the confines of the military posts, most of which were east of Lake Michigan. Pontiac's uprising in 1763 also sent shock waves through the western trade system. Thus no one stepped forward to take up where the Marins had left off, and during the first few years of British rule only an occasional favorite of army commandants received permission to travel beyond Lake Michigan.[1]

Although the name Marin became less frequently spoken around Dakota campfires, the pause in imperial expansion was only temporary. But the Marins had taught the Sioux an important lesson; Europeans could become valuable social-political allies, assisting the Dakotas in the difficult quest for survival. This unique communal understanding—a conscious regard for the safety and welfare of one's relatives, sharing, and a strong sense of native identity and superiority—remained intact at the midpoint of the eighteenth century. Conversely, the Marins had demonstrated how susceptible the Sioux were to manipulation for economic gain.

Alexander Henry was one of the favorites of the British command who did receive permission to send traders into the upper Mississippi valley. He financed a commercial venture that apparently was placed under the control of one "Pennensha," a Frenchman living with the Sioux. Before departing Green Bay, this voyageur and his Dakota companions told a young British lieutenant named James Gorrell that the Sioux had little fear of the Chippewas. If the latter had any notions of hindering trade, Dakota warriors would "cut them off the face of the earth." Troubles between the two tribes, already evident in 1754 when Marin left, apparently had reached an impasse, yet the Indians with Penichon, as the name later appears, claimed that all other tribes were "slaves or dogs" of the Sioux.[2] Four years later, Henry himself journeyed west and discovered heightened hostilities between the Sioux and Chippewas. He wintered at La Pointe with the Chippewas, whom he found "almost naked" because they lacked traders. The Dakotas were contesting the region east of La Pointe, preventing the Chippewas from hunting, and in the spring of 1766 the Chippewas told Henry of an engagement in which four hundred of their men had challenged six hundred Sioux. These numbers were undoubtedly inflated, since the Chippewas could not have raised that many men south of Lake Superior. More important, the Chippewas had lost thirty-five warriors, an unusually high number considering that La Pointe, one of their larger villages, contained only forty lodges.[3]

Meanwhile another major expedition left Mackinac Island for the Sioux country in 1766. The explorer Jonathan Carver headed the party, which was under the tutelage of Major Robert Rogers, commandant at Mackinac. Rogers wanted Carver to discover the Northwest Passage. Instead, Carver spent six months among the Sioux, and from the journal of this experience he later published his famous *Travels through the Interior Parts of North America* (London, 1778).[4] The Dakotas impressed Carver; much of what he related about them is similar to the positive observations of his predecessors. "They pride themselves much in being good soldiers and brave warriours," he notes, "and truly they are much dreaded as such by all their neighbours."[5] This included the Chippewas, who according to Carver were now a constant enemy. The expanded warfare between the Dakotas and the Lake Superior Chippewas probably resulted from the removal of Joseph Marin in 1754. Once French traders at La Pointe were unchecked, they undoubtedly encouraged their Chippewa hunters to invade the Mississippi valley in search of game. This had been occurring as Joseph Marin was about to leave the Mississippi.

Nevertheless, Carver's journal indicates that the Sioux lived a better life than did their Chippewa counterparts, owing to the abundance of resources in their lands. "In short almost every necessary of life grows here [upper Mississippi] spontaneous," the English explorer exclaimed exuberantly. While the Chippewas were depicted as depressed by comparison, Carver thought the Sioux were "very merry sociable people, full of mirth and good humor. They spend whole nights in feasting and dancing." Maintaining this good life necessitated movement: the Dakotas seldom remained "more than a month in one place, in summer never so long as that." To facilitate such a life, they used tepees covered with elk or buffalo hides.[6]

Carver wintered twenty or thirty miles up the Minnesota River at the "Grand Encampment," supposedly a favorite Sioux haunt. During his six-month stay, he attempted to identify the major tribes. The list reflects his failure to learn the Dakota language, despite his claims to the contrary, and includes only one western tribe, the Tetons.[7] Yet three of the four eastern Sioux tribes are on the list. The Wahpetons frequented the "Grand Encampment" and hunted on the plains north of the Minnesota River. Carver included the Sissetons in a group described as the "River Bands." This suggests occasional occupation of the Mississippi valley. The others designated as river bands included the Mantantons and "Nehoggotowannah," both of whom roamed east of the Mississippi from Lake Pepin to the regions above the Falls of St. Anthony. A final entry on the list is the "Minewantonko," a reference to the Issati Mdewakantons.[8]

These tribes now had consistent contact with Europeans. Several unnamed traders who had been dealing with the Wahpetons waited to collect their "credits" at the "Grand Encampment." But most Sioux, especially the Mdewakantons, still repeatedly voiced concern over the small amounts of goods that reached their lands. Carver even found that some of the tribes "scearsly [had] any knowledge of spiriteous liquor," a clear sign of inactivity. Frenchmen from St. Louis had been filling the void created by British restrictions, but they lacked the inventories to satisfy the Sioux, and they carried "fever and ague" into Indian lands.[9] Consequently, when Carver returned east he carried with him welcome news of western commercial opportunity. The Sioux yearned to establish ties with the English, and their lands still offered immense fur resources. Pressured by commercial interest groups, the British government finally lifted restrictions in 1767.[10]

Once a liberal policy had been adopted, British officials turned to manipulating the western tribes as the French had done before them. Major Rogers, at Mackinac, initiated the process by calling the western tribes to a peace council in 1767. The delegates received substantial presents, and they promised to adopt the British as "their Father." The English Indian superintendent, Sir William Johnson, heard about the peace council secondhand and initially seemed pleased, especially with the reported comments of the Sioux, who unlike the Chippewas had stayed neutral during Pontiac's Uprising. "A peace has been lately patched up between the *Chipeweighs* and the *Sioux,*" Johnson wrote to superiors in London, "who are the only Nation capable of checking the insolence of the former." The Sioux had even offered to march "5,000 men against the western confederacy [Pontiac's sympathizers]." The next year, however, Johnson's enthusiasm waned. Intertribal fighting broke out again, and he learned that traders rather than British arms would benefit from the peace efforts.[11]

The failure of the 1767 accord did little to hinder British commercial expansion. Some forty-three new licensees listed Wisconsin as their destination that year, and another seventeen gave the Mississippi River.[12] While French freebooters robbed a few Englishmen along the Wisconsin River in 1769 and 1770, the number of Mackinac canoes in the west increased every year thereafter. General Thomas Gage considered a proposal to build a military post at the mouth of

the Wisconsin River to protect Englishmen, but by 1773 British traders had become so dominant in Wisconsin that they incorporated
many of their French rivals.[13]

The New Englander Peter Pond was one such free trader, and
from Pond's narrative we learn much more regarding the effect of
early consistent trade upon Dakota institutions. Pond fitted out twelve
large canoes at Mackinac, hired voyageurs, and set out for the Mississippi in late summer 1773. His journal, written in a quaint, pho-
netic style, gives an excellent account of commercial escalation in
the west. The trip by the Fox–Wisconsin River route went smoothly.
The only incident of note occurred at a Fox village. An epidemic
much like the one Carver had witnessed just seven years before had
swept through the town, carrying off "Grate Numbers of Inhabetans."
Nevertheless, upon arriving at Prairie du Chien Pond discovered "a
Larg Number of French & Indians Makeing out thare arangement for
the Insewing winter." Many Frenchmen had arrived via keelboat from
New Orleans, carrying wines, cheese, ham, and other items. Other
British traders also had reached this increasingly important rendezvous. Rather than proceeding beyond it, however, many handed out
"credits" to the Indians and mixed-bloods and settled down to await
their return in the spring.[14] Issuing goods in the form of credit each
fall had obviously become standard practice in commercial circles,
but it seems unlikely that most Indians fully understood the implications of the concept.

After resting several days, Pond embarked on the Mississippi, intent upon working in the Sioux heartland. This was a gamble, considering Pond's limited knowledge of the region. Being understandably cautious, his party "wen[t] on Sloley to Leat the Nottawasease
[Sioux] Git Into the Plain." Pond had heard that the Dakota now "tru-
beld" traders for goods and robbed those who were unknown and
unable to protect themselves. Luckily he faced no such demands,
since he lacked the kinship ties necessary to guarantee the safety of
his commercial brigade. While the Dakotas hunted on the prairies,
Pond reached the Minnesota River and constructed a wintering
shelter. Sioux hunters arrived in December with many beaver, otter,

fox, and wolf pelts. Pond did his "bisnes to advantage," no doubt owing in part to the voyageurs who had accompanied him. Nevertheless, a Frenchman nearby gathered many more skins. After they became friends, Pond inquired about the secret of his success. The trader replied that the Yankees had not caught onto the "rite Eidea." The Frenchman always left a few small brass rings, medals, and awls unattended for the Indians to pilfer. This "thievery," along with the use of some credit, constituted the give and take of gift exchange that went on regularly among kin.[15] Pond failed to understand its significance, since such a strategem doubtless ran counter to his Yankee upbringing.

Once he was back at Mackinac, Pond's venture proved an unqualified success despite his lack of trading acumen. He paid for his goods, taken on credit from a merchant, and had nearly enough pelts left over to purchase next year's outfit. But as he prepared to return, merchants from Lake Superior arrived "with the Disagreabel News that the Nawasease [Dakotas] & Ochpowase [Chippewas] had Bin Killing Each other." The flare-up had occurred during the spring, the traditional time for young warriors to mount raids. Pond and his colleagues discussed the problem with the post commander, Captain Arent Schuyler de Peyster, who suggested that another peace conference be held. Pond volunteered to take the invitations to the Dakotas, and to make the offer attractive the merchants jointly purchased "Six Belts of Wampum," or presents, for their leaders.[16]

The Yankee trader arrived at his wintering grounds without incident and quickly sent couriers "into the planes" to alert the Sioux about the impending council. In the spring of 1775 several of their chiefs joined him and proceeded east. A confrontation took place at the mouth of the Minnesota River, however, that Pond could hardly understand. Several Chippewa traders who had wintered near the headwaters of the Mississippi suddenly appeared with their Algonquin delegates. "I was much surprised to Sea them [the Chippewas] so Ventersum among the People I had with me," Pond recorded, "for the Bad [blood] was Scairs cald the Wound was yet fresh." The convivial relations even survived the trip, and the Sioux and Chippewas readily accepted the terms set forth by the merchants. The agreement stated that the Sioux "Should Not Cross the Missacipey to the East Side, to Hunt on thare Nighbers Ground.... The Chipewase Likewise Promis On thare Part Strickley to Obsareve the Same Reagulations ... [and] will not cross the River."[17]

Chippewa traders obviously had dominated the negotiations, looking out solely for the benefit of their hunters. They must have felt pleased to think they had acquired the rich beaver country east of the Mississippi so cheaply. Pond had spent the winter with the Sissetons and Wahpetons and seems to have been unaware of the existence of the Mdewakantons.[18] There is no evidence that they attended the Mackinac peace council, which, along with the difficulties of language, may explain the Dakotas' acquiescence to the agreement.

The Mdewakantons had no intention of obeying any division agreed to at Mackinac. Most of them still hunted the eastern tributaries of the Mississippi. Charles Gautier de Verville, on a recruiting tour for the British government in 1778, visited the Mdewakantons "on the upper part" of the St. Croix River, where they were entrenched along with their French traders. A few Winnebagos had joined them on this occasion, establishing fictive or temporary kin ties, and their hunters seemed quite unafraid of the Chippewas. Indeed, Verville noted that the latter were not "so strong as they [the Sioux] in winter quarters" and had tried to make up for the deficiency by giving the Dakotas some poisoned oil. The trick made many ill but did not alter the military imbalance.[19]

Verville also observed that since Pond's visit the Wahpetons had moved closer to the mouth of the Minnesota River, where they met their traders. Considering the positions of both the Mdewakantons and Wahpetons, it appears that the increased trading activities of the 1770s had induced the eastern Sioux to gradually return to woodland areas where beavers and other prize fur animals were more abundant. They were much farther east than where Carver located them. Yet Marin had placed the Watpaton Mdewakantons on the upper St. Croix River in 1753. The Sioux had apparently hunted this river continuously ever since the days of first white contact.[20]

After the American Revolution broke out, Gautier and others attached to the British cause courted the Dakota chiefs, especially the influential and pro-English Wabasha. Considered a man of "very singular and uncommon abilities," Wabasha received a commission as a "general" in the British army, probably during a 1778 visit to Montreal, and was said to be able to raise two hundred warriors "with ease."[21] Captain De Peyster at Mackinac had been partially responsible for Wabasha's support, providing him with presents on many occasions. "King Wabasha," as De Peyster styled him, reciprocated by giving the captain a beautiful wampum belt at the outset of the war. Not only did Wabasha bring his tribe over to the British, but several officers at Mackinac also thought he was responsible for holding the allegiance of the Sacs and Foxes.[22]

The Dakota role in the American Revolution was limited mostly to protecting Prairie du Chien. The only exception came during the summer of 1780, when Wabasha's warriors led the charge on the Spanish garrison at St. Louis. On this day the Sioux and Chippewas fought side by side as they had occasionally done in the past, and the assault failed, according to one observer, only because the Sacs and Foxes refused to follow Wabasha's men. The British officers in charge had the highest praise for the warriors under Wabasha, and one young lieutenant went so far as to say that they did "nothing inferior to regular troops." Each morning they religiously cared for their powder and arms, and they could be depended upon to abstain from brandy and wine, seldom the case with their European counterparts. Obviously the Dakotas under Wabasha viewed certain British leaders as allies and kinsmen, and they saw it as their moral duty to fight for them.[23]

Wabasha's donning a British uniform came at a time when significant commercial changes were unfolding in the western Great Lakes trade. Despite the loss of the Atlantic coast colonies, the English were able to control and expand their western trade for several decades after the Revolutionary War. The organization of the North West Company in 1779 marked the beginning of the new commercial era. This firm turned to the regions northwest of Lake Superior for pelts after fighting along the Ohio valley disrupted hunting during the Revolution. A rival to the North West Company, ostentatiously named the "General Company of Lake Superior and the South," or the Mackinac Company, appeared in 1785. It concentrated wholly on the Sioux trade.[24]

The founders of these companies realized that too many traders had entered the lands west of Lake Michigan just after the Revolutionary War. They sought to incorporate the most successful men into brigades that would monopolize particular regions and tribes. This stratagem worked well with the Chippewas, and it quickly led to the dependency of these people upon a small group of Euroamericans who were exploitative by nature and unconcerned about the impact of the trade upon Chippewa resources and culture. English corporations also tried to promote monopoly in Sioux lands. But too many traders, declining European prices, and too little organization hindered company efforts toward maximization. The Mackinac Company broke up in 1788, and attempts to create even small partnerships experienced only limited success in the period before the outbreak of the War of 1812.[25]

Increased competition on the upper Mississippi prompted British traders to disperse to more remote hunting grounds as traditional locales like Lake Pepin and the lower Minnesota River were abandoned. When Charles Patterson, agent for the Mackinac Company, organized the Sioux Outfit in 1785, he selected no fewer than six wintering stations. Patterson himself built a stockade well up the Minnesota River among the Sissetons and Wahpetons. Murdock Cameron and Joseph Renville (not to be confused with his son, an important métis Sioux trader of the same name) took brigades beyond Patterson to the Tetons and Yanktons on the plains. The company had two posts on the Chippewa River, still a prime fur-producing zone. A Frenchman named La Batte managed one on a tributary, and Alexander La Framboise and Jean Baptiste Perrault took charge of the other. Finally, James Aird and Joseph Rocque constructed a third post among the "tribe of la Feuille," or Wabasha's people, somewhere north of the Minnesota River. Other men joined this core of Sioux traders after 1785. Among the newcomers who appear regularly in the records were Robert Dickson, Jean Baptiste Faribault, Louis Provençalle, Joseph Rolette, Jacques Porlier, Etienne Campion, Archibald John Campbell, and the young métis Joseph Renville.[26]

With so many men in Sioux lands, it became impossible for any one group to dominate the trade as the Marins had done in the 1750s. Thus more and more English traders sought a means to limit the negative effect of competition. Strong kinship attachments and influence with the Dakota political system seemed to offer the best solution, and Englishmen and their French companions quickly sought out unions with the most comely female members of the most important Dakota descent groups. These bonds served to prevent outsiders from pirating furs from the villages the traders were attached to. They provided the foundation for a sociopolitical network of people and outposts that survived into the mid-nineteenth century.

Joseph Renville was typical. He purchased a woman from Red Wing's Mdewakanton village in 1779. The union produced a son, who eighteen years later became a trader and married a Mdewakanton of the Little Crow band.[27] Joseph Ainsé, a British Indian Department official who traded with the Sioux for only two years, was also quick to purchase a Mdewakanton woman. His daughter by this consort later married Jean Baptiste Faribault, forging kinship ties with the Sioux for her ambitious husband. Faribault later attempted to gain title to an island in the Mississippi, supposedly given to his wife by her people.[28] Perhaps the most celebrated of intermarriages was that of the well-born Robert Dickson to "Toto-win," a sister of the Sisseton chief Red Thunder. After Dickson took on Renville's son as a clerk in 1797, his family influence included two of the four eastern Sioux tribes—the Mdewakantons and Sissetons. Two other key Sioux traders took wives among Renville's people. James Aird, who began trading permanently with the Sioux in 1779, married no less an individual than the daughter of the first chief Wabasha. And Thomas G. Anderson, who came into the Sioux land after the turn of the century, later took a daughter of this union as his first wife.[29] Finally, the only American on the upper Mississippi, Archibald John Campbell, married into the Mdewakanton tribe sometime before 1790. By his wife's death in 1801 Campbell had at least five children, one of whom went on to become noted as the government interpreter for the Sioux.[30] In sum, these examples serve only to show that, regardless of position or ethnic background, traders in Sioux lands subscribed to the "custom of the country" and purchased wives. Their Dakota kinship ties provided a family linkage, welding Indians and Europeans into a unique social and commercial network.

While these unions may have stemmed from romantic or physical attachment, the commercial overtones were overwhelming. Kinship bonds were essential if a trader was to consistently succeed in obtaining pelts from the Sioux. By 1800 traders gave "credits" in the form of goods each fall and relied upon these items to be "covered" with furs in the spring. Bartering with affine relatives gave traders an added edge against outsiders, especially if they happened to be influential in the village soldiers' lodge. This institution could be used to protect a trader's goods, collect pelts in the spring, and prevent competitors from breaching an established kinship commercial network and stealing returns.[31]

The value of kinship ties obviously depended upon the importance of the family with whom a trader established affine relations. Dickson, who wed a chief's sister, had extensive influence with his wife's people. Joseph Rolette, a Frenchman who ventured into Sioux country in 1800, purchased the hand of Wabasha's niece. Thereafter he received assistance from the chief whenever his clerks faced competition or hunters from the band were reluctant to hand over pelts. Even Ainsé found occasion to use his new connections among the Mdewakantons. In the spring of 1787 he came in contact with a stubborn hunter who refused to turn over skins as payment for credits. The Englishman turned to the subchief Red Wing, an important warrior of the tribe from which he had taken a wife. Red Wing called on the "warrior Indians," or soldiers, who broke into the lodge where the skins were stored and turned them over to Ainsé.[32]

Nonetheless, on occasion traders found that even kinship bonds did not prevent the loss of goods or afford protection. Some men purposely went into Indian lands late in the fall to avoid giving credits. They would then trade for furs spoken for by others. Rum became an important tool in this nefarious business, since latecomers often lacked close ties with any tribe. Unfortunately, alcohol use soon forced more respectable traders to stoop to the same practice, initiating a problem that grew worse in the nineteenth century.

The experiences of Jean Baptiste Perrault illustrate how traders unconnected with the Sioux worked. While encamped along a tributary of the Wisconsin River in 1788, Perrault used rum to barter for pelts with some of Wabasha's hunters, even though he knew other traders had already purchased them with credits. He then opened communication with the Chippewas from Lac Court Oreilles in western Wisconsin. As luck would have it, six Chippewa hunters showed up at his post just before the arrival of twenty-eight Mdewakanton Sioux under a rising young chief named Little Crow. "I leave you to imagine our dismay," Perrault wrote in his narrative, for he feared a collision would take place that would threaten his trade. Even though the two adversaries danced the calumet and made peace, a few Sioux killed two Chippewas from ambush as they left the stockade. Perrault decided to stay on even after the murders and nearly perished at the hands of an avenging band of Chippewas. He had no one to rely on for protection except a handful of Menominee hunters who had joined him at Green Bay.[33] Although events are unclear, it is not likely that Little Crow was unaware that an attack on the Chippewas would place Perrault's post in jeopardy.

But even when traders had firm ties, problems could develop. Archibald John Campbell traded in the upper Minnesota valley near Little Rapids in 1794, apparently with the Wahpetons. A young voyageur in his employ, Coteaux, had married a Dakota woman of the band nearby, but he soon found her to have "moeurs [morals] irréprochables." The bride's father took umbrage at this criticism and finally killed his son-in-law. This created a problem for Campbell, who felt obligated to demand satisfaction. The irate father, on the other hand, threatened Campbell and nearly killed him. Only the appearance of Jean Baptiste Faribault and several men stopped the execution.[34]

The treatment the Sioux afforded Campbell was unusual; more often than not when villagers became discontented with traders they simply withheld furs, causing loss of credits issued in the fall. Yet even when the best of conditions existed traders often failed to collect a few skins each year, as hunters were killed or deserted to other Europeans. In addition, intertribal warfare could make it impossible for hunters to gather the skins necessary to pay their debts. A combination of these difficulties apparently beset Joseph Renville in 1787, when he failed to collect one thousand beaver pelts the Dakotas owed him. The Sioux and Chippewas had been fighting that fall, and Joseph Ainsé had called many of them to council at a time when they should have been hunting. Renville also claimed that Ainsé had illegally used government presents to lure pelts from his Indians. Even though Renville admitted he had never experienced such losses before, his troubles seem to show that, while kinship ties were essential, they did not ensure success.[35] Accordingly, traders gradually increased their exchange rates, tried to instill a capitalist ethic among Sioux hunters, and worked to convince the Dakotas to honor these obligations.

When intertribal war became a serious commercial problem, as it did for Renville, the English, like their French predecessors, tried diplomacy. A petition written by Montreal merchants in 1787 declared that, although the upper Mississippi was abundantly stocked with game, the traders "do not procure from it one fourth part of the furs which it is capable of producing annually," owing to the fighting. The memorialists wanted the government to distribute presents to the western nations and call on them to embrace peace. The merchants felt the government should stress that all traders were "children of the same father" with equal rights to work in the western trade and that the Indians should stop fighting over the pelts necessary to pay them.[36]

The British Indian Department sent Ainsé to the Sioux in the fall of 1786 to bring them east to council. He reached the Minnesota River in early winter, where he discovered "a large number of Sioux of all the different villages ... [preparing] to go to war against Sauteux [Chippewas]." Meanwhile another Dakota war party returned from a raid on the Chippewas with sixteen scalps and three prisoners. "The arrival of this party caused a little interruption to the peace which I proposed," Ainsé concluded, as the women "tore the still bloody & ragged scalps from [the] hands of the warriors" and sought to obtain control of the prisoners. Ainsé succeeded in negotiating a delay in the departure of the raiders, and the next day he used presents to secure both the prisoners and a pledge of peace.[37]

After visiting several other Sioux villages and also the Chippewa camps well east of the Mississippi, Ainsé brought representatives from all these tribes together at a spot ten leagues up the Minnesota River, probably near the "Grand Encampment" Carver noted many years before. After eight days of negotiations and feasts, the leaders agreed to a truce and followed Ainsé east to sign treaties.[38] At Prairie du Chien, in a festival atmosphere, more solemn pledges were made. On this occasion Perrault witnessed an event that easily may have rivaled in symbolism and grandeur the movements of a British column of troops. After the Dakotas had formed into one line, the Chippewas and Menominees made another and the Sacs and Foxes gathered in a third. Then, according to Perrault, "these three lines formed three triangles ... [and] an orator from Each of the Confederates, with Each one their attendant, placed themselves in the center of the three triangles, each holding in his hand the pipe of peace." Chants followed, and the lighted pipes were exchanged. All smoked the sacred pipes except one young Sioux warrior, who, upon being rebuked by one of his chiefs, acceded to the "fictive" bonds pushed by the English.[39]

No doubt weary from celebration, the leaders of the tribes proceeded to Mackinac Island and on 10 July 1787 signed articles of peace written by Montreal merchants. This agreement, sealed by a "Belt of Peace," the links of which the Indians promised to preserve "from Rust as long as the Rivers flow &. the Rocks endure," contained four basic articles. The first pledged support of the British "father," and the fourth contained a clause designed to encourage the tribes to resist the advice of "bad birds," no doubt referring to the Spanish at St. Louis. But articles two and three dealt specifically with the fur trade. They cajoled the delegates to deal honestly with traders and pay their credits. Article three also included a clause whereby the Indians agreed to hand over any tribesmen guilty of robbing or killing a trader.[40]

The Dakotas were well represented at the 1787 Mackinac peace council. Red Wing spoke for the Mdewakantons. Delegates for the Sissetons, Wahpetons, and Wahpekutes also attended. Even the Yanktons and Tetons sent men to hear what the British had to say. Just how well they all understood the treaty is difficult to determine. Surely Wabasha's son, already a noted war chief who had declined the invitation to come east, wanted no part of it. He led his Mdewakantons against the intruding Chippewas while the negotiation was still in progress.[41] The Sioux leaders in attendance probably viewed the agreement as a reaffirmation of their strong bonds with the traders, who by extension were tied to the British government. The English "fathers" reinforced this bond with a large number of presents, including three hundred blankets, fifty guns, chief's coats, and a host of lesser items. As in the past, the acceptance and use of the father-child metaphor was not an imputation of inferior status but rather a symbol of the Dakota conception of gift-giving. Dakota fathers always willingly shared whatever they possessed with their children.[42]

Young Wabasha's rejection of the peace process made it practically impossible for much good to come out of the negotiation. Obviously a consensus had existed among the Sioux delegates at Mackinac but not back on the Mississippi. In addition, traders were clearly as responsible for the wars as were the Indians, even though they seemed unwilling to assume any blame. They increased economic pressure on the tribes and their resources during the 1790s and continued to build wintering stations in or near the zones they contested. Consequently the Sioux and Chippewas were fighting so fiercely over the region between Prairie du Chien and St. Anthony Falls that Dickson reported in 1793 that it was "virtually unfrequented by Indians."[43] Similar conditions existed between Lake Superior and the Red River. But, unlike the Sioux, the Chippewas were already suffering from a lack of resources and were forced to tread ever deeper onto Dakota preserves. The encroachment virtually ensured fighting.[44]

Sioux warriors did surprise the Chippewas from Sandy Lake in 1797, killing forty-five, a terrible defeat considering the small population of most of their villages. William Whipple Warren obtained an oral history account of this engagement that suggests the attack nearly destroyed the Sandy Lake band.[45] Nevertheless, the Chippewas continued to enter the debated zones for game. Some even ventured out onto the prairies southwest of Leech Lake and into the tributaries of the Red River. The Sissetons and Wahpetons contested these areas with the Chippewas, and they were especially dangerous for the Chippewas, since the mounted Sioux occasionally maneuvered themselves upwind of their enemies and set the tall prairie grass on fire. The bleak material conditions of the Chippewas necessitated boldness, as David Thompson noted in his journal of 1798. Nearly every Chippewa he saw was "very poor from the animals being almost wholly destroyed" west of Lake Superior. He did not see "a single duck" in their canoes, since they could not afford ammunition. Yet the men of Sandy Lake, despite their defeat the year before, were once again headed for the "war grounds" to hunt.[46] Rather than being successful imperialists, the Chippewas generally moved onto lands in northeastern Minnesota after suffering severely at the hands of the Sioux or after the Sioux had abandoned the area.

In 1800 the eastern Sioux were still wealthy in comparison with their Chippewa neighbors. Abundant resources such as buffalo allowed them to live in substantial villages rather than small family hunting units. Ainsé visited four in the Minnesota River valley in

1786–87. Most of the people were probably on their winter hunts when Ainsé arrived. Nevertheless, he recorded demographic data that gave populations of 204 and 230 men for the first two encampments encountered near the mouth, and 260 warriors for the third, farther upriver.[47] Reports of early traders suggest even larger populations at times. For a period of years, the Mdewakantons supposedly united into a huge village of four hundred lodges on the lower Minnesota. Traditions say that the second Wabasha helped form this camp, called "Tetankatane." Correctly spelled Titankatanni, meaning great old village, the encampment was later considered the spiritual home of the nineteenth-century Mdewakantons.[48] Although Ainsé obviously did not see four hundred lodges in one camp during his visit, the first village on his list probably was the Mdewakanton center. It seems plausible that the other two were Wahpeton and Sisseton villages, since Ainsé did identify the fourth as the Wahpekute camp. It held 200 men, which brought the total number of Mdewakanton, Wahpeton, Wahpekute, and Sisseton warriors to about 900, supporting a population of perhaps 4,200 people.[49]

These figures were far less impressive than those of earlier decades. It is fair to assume that the Dakotas suffered from the dreadful smallpox epidemic that killed many Algonquins and Assiniboins north of them in 1782–83.[50] Yet the Dakotas still fielded a military force equal in all regards to that of the Chippewas and Crees. They had established permanent commercial contact with the east, securing the latest munitions, and they still controlled the strategic areas along the Mississippi River that allowed access to valuable resource zones, sheltered campsites, and traders.

Yet above all the Dakotas had established rewarding and workable relations with Europeans, from whom they benefited in at least two important ways. Traders now regularly carried into Dakota lands goods that enhanced native life. There is no evidence that the Sioux saw the use of metal pots, combs, needles, and knives or other weapons as cultural degeneration. They readily embraced the new material world offered by Europeans, even though they increasingly found that their new Euroamerican relatives were inclined to place specific values upon such items rather than sharing them in the traditional norm of simple exchange. Second, traders became full-fledged members of the Dakota bands, taking wives and fathering children. In the Sioux world view, this obligated them to assist in-laws materially and to help sustain the village. No wonder Dakota leaders agreed to European treaties. They were viewed as nothing more than attempts by white kinsmen to better the conditions of the Sioux people.

Nevertheless, the framework for Indian-white contact along the upper Mississippi in 1800 had many rough edges. While whites often realized they had assumed certain social responsibilities in Dakota villages, they were clearly not as committed to the relationship as their Sioux counterparts. In European social circles, taking a wife did not bind a husband to support her extended family. While traders may have taken wives with the intention of supporting the children of the unions, it seems unlikely that they ever morally obligated themselves to their spouses' other relatives. Yet they used such relatedness to advantage in the fur trade. In addition, a few Europeans used kinship bonds only as long as they served an economic end, then abandoned wife, children, and relatives for another geographic area of trade. And yet others never took wives at all, purchasing women casually and relying on fictive bonds and presents to acquire pelts.

In a political sense also the two differing world views seemed at times to clash. While traders certainly used their relatedness to influence Dakota consensus government, the attempt to mold such a forum into a binding contract was foreign to the Sioux. Yet they signed three such contracts, or treaties, in the later eighteenth century. From what little evidence has survived of these negotiations, it seems reasonable to assume that the Dakotas viewed the discussions as positive. They had on many occasions negotiated peace with the Chippewas, exchanged women, and hunted together for a season or two. But war had never been a constant state that could be brought to a permanent close by a contractual agreement. Feuds with other tribes occurred not only because of competition for game, but from more complex motives such as the need to avenge the loss of relatives and the desire to acquire glory. The Dakota commitment to European treaties, then, existed as long as the consensus regarding peace survived. As soon as a minority within a particular village felt it was time to strike an enemy, the peace fell apart.

While the British would not have great success in building inter-tribal peace in the west, they did experience some political gains. By and large, the Dakotas did come away from the various negotiations at Mackinac convinced that the English were their kinsmen and allies. Dakota warriors willingly fought for England during the Revolution and stood ready to answer any call in the future. Of course such support was tied to the commercial and social relations that had been consummated by traders in the west, a condition the British government readily recognized. In the final analysis, despite the ceremonies, the negotiations of treaties, the handing out of medals bearing the insignia of the British king, and the distribution of military coats, Dakota-white relations in 1800 relied almost exclusively upon the web of individual bonds of a political, social, and economic nature that cemented friendship between the Sioux and their Euroamerican kinsmen.

5

Conflicting Loyalties, 1805–20

While British traders were nurturing family bonds with the Dakotas
and expanding their commercial network, a political upheaval took
place far to the east. Most western tribes had little understanding of
the antagonisms or issues surrounding the American Revolution. Yet
in the final settlement of the dispute, negotiated in Paris in 1783, an
important change occurred that affected the lives of the Dakotas and
their neighbors. A new boundary separating Canada and the United
States placed the portions of the Sioux domain lying east of the Mississippi squarely within the perceived limits of the new republic.
The American "long knives," as they were called, purchased French
claims to Dakota territory west of the Mississippi exactly two decades later. By 1805 the United States was ready to press its claims to
the vast upper Mississippi watershed.

The British decision to give up the upper Mississippi had been
made in London rather than in Canada; Sioux traders were initially
incensed. During the 1790s they openly conspired with the Canadian lieutenant governor George Simcoe to reverse the Paris accords
and bring transportation avenues into Sioux lands under British
control. The one major advantage they had was their trade network,
whereby a commercial umbilical cord joined the Dakota people to
Montreal rather than New York. Conversely, Simcoe recognized the
importance of the Sioux in any struggle for the west. He had heard
that they were "the bravest warriors in America" and that they could
raise six thousand men. Simcoe recommended that England build a

fort at the mouth of the Wisconsin River in order to continue supplying the Sioux with English arms.[1]

The Dakotas were oblivious to the diplomatic and political maneuvering in the east until 1797, when the United States moved troops into the old fort on Mackinac Island. That occupation inaugurated a fierce struggle to control the western hinterland.[2] As the United States and England finally squared off to decide who would rule the upper Mississippi, the Sioux remained adamantly tied to their British traders, who, more than ever before, had a hand in the destiny of these Indians. But since relations with the Sioux evolved from individual contact rather than loyalty to any one flag, and since western tribesmen had become increasingly dependent on European-made arms by the late eighteenth century, whichever nation could best offer the social, economic, and political advantages that these Indians had gained from whites in the past would ultimately win their loyalty.

The British had the advantage of experience. Yet after the United States purchased Louisiana from France in 1803 the young republic seemed to be in a commanding position. A handful of British traders, including Robert Dickson and Rexford Crawford, sought a rapprochement with United States officials two years later and accompanied two large eastern Sioux delegations to St. Louis in May 1805 to meet General James Wilkinson, the ranking United States officer in the west.[3] The party included some thirty "handsome able-bodied men" from the upper Mississippi and Des Moines rivers. The Dakota delegates conducted the interview "in admirable order and with . . . decency and decorum," according to the chronicler of the event. In their lengthy addresses, Dakota spokesmen indicated that the traders had encouraged them to visit their "new father." They admitted they had been "fools" in the past and had given up their "old father [England]." Yet behind this diplomatic jargon was an ulterior motive. Dakota warriors had killed a drunken Frenchman in self-defense some time before and wanted a pardon from the Americans. Dickson and Crawford had no doubt warned the Sioux that the American garrison at Mackinac might cut off trade. Thus the Dakotas presented themselves as "children," who in the Sioux world view could not be denied a request to their father. Wilkinson graciously granted the men who had committed the offense "their lives," and the Dakota delegates departed well pleased with their visit. Wilkinson likewise spoke glowingly thereafter of the Sioux and of the success of this first crucial council.[4]

While the Dakota delegates had a specific reason for visiting St. Louis, so did their British kinsmen. Dickson, Crawford, and a third colleague, James Aird, promptly followed up the negotiations in May with applications for American citizenship. Wilkinson refused the peace overture, however, and even issued a proclamation in August prohibiting British trade west of the Mississippi River. Jay's Treaty of 1795 had granted Canadians commercial access to American soil, but Wilkinson smugly argued that Louisiana, and thus the Minnesota River, had not been part of the republic when Jay negotiated the agreement.[5] The general surmised that force would be necessary to implement the decree, so he selected Lieutenant Zebulon Montgomery Pike and nearly two dozen men to reconnoiter the upper Mississippi and purchase land for forts both at Prairie du Chien and at the mouth of the Minnesota River. Troops could then be detailed to close off other trade routes via Lake Superior. Reaching Prairie du Chien on 4 September 1805, Pike acquired the assistance of Sioux traders James Fraser, Pierre Rousseau, and Joseph Renville. They accompanied him, on and off, throughout his journey and provided a wealth of information on the Dakota people.[6]

Once above Prairie du Chien, Pike soon made contact with the Mdewakanton people, who had undergone considerable change over the two decades since Ainsé's visit. The old Mdewakanton village of Titankatanni on the Minnesota River had broken up, scattering people in several directions. The dispersal, caused by declining game herds, had dissolved the old band affiliations noted by early chroniclers; the Mantanton, Watpaton, and Issati divisions had disappeared, and five new bands had evolved. Wabasha, son of the earlier chief of that name, seemed to be the dominant Mdewakanton leader. His villagers (a remnant of the Mantanton people) now called themselves the Kiyuksa band. They periodically migrated between the mouth of the

Upper Iowa River and Lake Pepin. Pike found young Wabasha cordial, but many of the chief's warriors had been drinking when the lieutenant arrived and fired their muskets into the water, seeing how close they could come to Pike's boats. Above Lake Pepin, a second Mdewakanton village under the war chief Red Wing had sprung up near the mouth of the Cannon River. These people called themselves the Hemnican band, which referred to their geographic position near a large hill often called the "barn." The last village along the Mississippi held the Kaposia band under Little Crow II. Traditionally known for their nonsedentary ways, the Little Crow people had constructed eleven bark-covered lodges just above the mouth of the St. Croix River. The change in housing suggested a growing dependence upon corn, but when Pike arrived the Kaposia band was hunting on the St. Croix River, and the lieutenant left word for them to join him with the other Mdewakantons at the mouth of the Minnesota River.[7]

Once at the Minnesota River, Pike met two other important band leaders, one of whom signed the treaty he negotiated with the eastern Sioux. "Le Fils de Penichon," the métis son of a French trader by that name, had risen to a position of leadership over the remnant of the Titankatanni village, still situated on the Minnesota about nine miles from its mouth.[8] The second key leader Pike met that day was identified as "Le Demi Douzen," or Six. Better known as Shakopee, he led the remnant of the Issatis who had earlier followed Iroquois. The band's village, thirty miles up the Minnesota, frequently hunted buffalo and went by the name Tintatonwe, the prairie villagers.[9]

Pike learned less about the other three eastern Sioux tribes, but he did obtain population statistics and information on their trade and location. If we compare these with the data compiled by Lewis and Clark in 1805–6, a sketch of these groups emerges. The Wahpekutes still roamed the country south of the Minnesota River and frequently camped in the Blue Earth River valley. Pike counted their strength as 80 warriors, while Lewis and Clark estimated the total at 150. Many Mississippi River traders disliked the Wahpekutes because they had a reputation for pillaging boats from Mackinac and often traded with men from St. Louis. Pike came away thinking they were "vagabones"; Lewis and Clark, on the other hand, judged the Wahpekutes to be industrious and had heard that they treated their traders "tolerably well."[10]

The Wahpetons and Sissetons roamed the central and upper Minnesota River valley. They left the river in April, hunted on the plains until August, and in winter sought relief from the cold in the smaller Crow and Sauk river valleys. Pike placed the Wahpeton population at 180 warriors, while Lewis and Clark estimated 200. However, Pike's figures for the Sissetons were 360, nearly double the number reported by Lewis and Clark.[11] It seems that Pike's figures were more reliable, since he received information from traders who were consistently among these tribes.

The reports of both the Pike and the Lewis and Clark expeditions contained a wealth of information on trade. The latter men had heard that the Wahpetons were now exploiting their hunting grounds to the fullest extent. Accordingly, competition for pelts frequently brought clashes with the Chippewas, who had invaded the Crow River valley. Pike discussed the conflict with the son of the Wahpeton chief Red Eagle, who informed him that Robert Dickson had encouraged the Sioux to push farther north that fall, since Dickson believed Pike would temporarily negotiate a truce. As for the Sissetons, they too were heavily involved in trade with Europeans. Yet Lewis and Clark contended that their lands north and east of Big Stone Lake still contained untapped resources. They also had become adept at using their favorable geographic position to carry on an extensive middleman trade with tribes on the Missouri. People from several tribes regularly met along the James River in May to exchange goods for hides. Even a few Wahpetons, Wahpekutes, and Mdewakantons joined the Sissetons in these commercial fairs.[12]

Taken as a whole, eastern Sioux populations and life-style had changed little since the visits of Pond and Ainsé. Adding the 300 warriors in the Mdewakanton camps, their villages still held about 900 men in 1805, or 4,000 to 5,000 people. Although travelers could now more often see a corn or bean field on the periphery of their encampments, the Dakota people continued to rely heavily on hunting for subsistence. Nonetheless, changing economic conditions had broken up the larger villages seen by earlier travelers, and this had affected tribal unity. Wabasha's people, for example, had separated from the Mdewakantons proper. Although we know less about the other three Dakota tribes, the Sissetons also had a splinter group living along the banks of the Blue Earth River, and the Wahpetons would undergo a similar division a short time after Pike's visit.[13]

Perhaps the fragmentation partially explains why Pike chose to treat only with Little Crow and Penichon during his brief negotiation on 23 September. They represented villages with the best claims to the approximately 100,000 acres that he purchased for a fort at the mouth of the Minnesota River. Past historians have viewed this negotiation as high-handed, primarily because Pike failed to obtain the signatures of other leaders and deferred to Congress the amount to be paid for the land.[14] The latter omission does bring into question the fairness of the document. Pike later claimed he had obtained the land "for a song." The only tangible benefits the Sioux received at the time included $250 in presents, most of which went to Little Crow and Penichon as gifts.[15]

Ironically, the Dakotas probably thought they were getting a bargain. In a letter to Wilkinson, written after the negotiation, Pike noted that the Sioux "had bound me up to many assurances that the post shall be established." Pike also admitted he had pledged the government to help the Dakotas in their war with the Chippewas, should the latter refuse overtures of peace.[16] Mdewakanton leaders had obviously viewed Pike and the Americans as future allies and kinsmen, and the proposed fort offered a sure means of supply, comparable to the direct connection the Chippewas enjoyed with Sault Ste. Marie and Mackinac Island. Finally, Pike guaranteed the Sioux that a government factory or trading house would be established at the new American fort. "The Indians," he exclaimed to the Dakotas in council, might then procure "all their things at a cheaper and better rate."[17]

While the Dakotas applauded the Americans' intention to build a military-commercial establishment on the upper Mississippi, they greeted Pike's efforts to secure peace between themselves and the

Chippewas with less enthusiasm. Most leaders realistically observed that it would be difficult to restrain young warriors. They also questioned the sincerity of the Chippewas. The hunting grounds of western Wisconsin and northeastern Minnesota had been contested by these tribes for more than sixty years. Temporary armistices had been negotiated by the combatants as well as by Europeans, but the love of fighting, the need to avenge death, and the growing importance of dwindling game herds all made obtaining a consensus for peace nearly impossible. It seemed that the negotiators wanted peace, but they were unwilling to abandon the debated zones, the crucial sacrifice necessary to stop the fighting. This also held true for the traders. Nevertheless, Pike assured Dakota chiefs that he would bring Chippewa representatives down from the northern Minnesota woodlands to negotiate.[18]

While proceeding up the Mississippi, Pike encountered many Chippewa leaders and also visited the two main North West Company trading posts on Sandy Lake and Leech Lake. He found the Chippewas to be "neither ... so brave nor generous as the Sioux" and concluded that many were "cowards." His comparison was derived from his observations of the overuse of alcohol by the Chippewas and the better material conditions among the Sioux. In addition, the Chippewas refused to attend the peace council that Pike attempted to organize. He could only convince them to send pipes, hardly a clear demonstration of a desire to end the hostilities.[19]

While coming down the river, Pike was flushed with the success of his expedition. In final councils with the Sioux at the mouth of the Minnesota River, both Little Crow and Red Wing pledged themselves for peace, and about forty Dakota leaders from the Mdewakanton, Sisseton, and Wahpeton tribes smoked the Chippewa pipes. The British government, Pike noted, had "requested, commanded, and made presents" to the Indians, but "all this [was done] at a distance." Pike felt that he had succeeded because he had gone among the tribes delivering lectures that "commanded them, in the name of their great father," to end the intertribal struggles.[20] Wilkinson also voiced approval. At Pike's urging, a large body of Dakota men with four principal chiefs descended the river in May 1806 and counciled with the general at St. Louis. "The great power and I can add the apparent dispositions of the Sioux, give them strong claims to our attentions and courtesy," Wilkinson later concluded in a letter to Henry Dearborn.[21] Although he was clearly exaggerating his accomplishments, Pike had established a footing for American expansion into the upper Mississippi.

Shortly after his return to St. Louis, Lieutenant Pike was sent on a more dangerous expedition to Mexico. General Wilkinson also departed St. Louis abruptly after becoming involved in the Aaron Burr conspiracy. Thus at a crucial time the task of expanding Pike's modest beginnings in diplomacy fell to others. In 1806 the War Department did appoint Nicholas Boilvin subagent to the Sacs. He eventually set up headquarters at Prairie du Chien and opened council with the Sioux. Another veteran of thirty years' trade with the Dakotas, Pierre Dorion, was commissioned to represent the United States along the Des Moines and Missouri rivers.[22]

The new agents soon discovered a growing aversion among British traders to Wilkinson's proclamation. Englishmen asserted that Spain had never stopped their parties from crossing into Louisiana and that the Jay Treaty granted them the right to traverse United States territory regardless of when it became a part of the republic. Several defied the proclamation and visited the Sioux on the upper Mississippi River in the fall of 1806.[23] Meanwhile, Robert Dickson and backers from several important Montreal trade houses formed a new company to exploit the Sioux trade. The American commanding officer at Mackinac Island, Captain Josiah Dunham, complained that this would surely bring "misery, oppression, & wretchedness to the aborigines, and a total exclusion of every American [from the trade]."[24] But before the new monopoly had a chance to flourish news arrived in the west of a clash between the American cruiser *Chesapeake* and HMS *Leopard*. The incident prompted President Jefferson to embargo all commerce in fall 1807, regardless of the provisions of the Jay Treaty. This led to the confiscation at Niagara of several British boats loaded with goods destined for St. Joseph's Island (a British island near Sault Ste. Marie) and the Mississippi trade. Dickson gave up all plans of wintering in the west, abandoning the Sioux.[25]

The embargo and the subsequent withdrawal of the British from the west presented a golden opportunity for American commercial expansion. The United States constructed a new fort and trading post at the mouth of the Des Moines River in the spring of 1808. It served the Sacs and Foxes as well as the Wahpekute Sioux. John Johnston, the factor, soon petitioned his superiors for more goods. He expected to fill the vacuum left after his British counterparts failed to show up among more northern Dakota tribes in the coming fall.[26] Another factory, under J. B. Varnum, took shape at Mackinac Island, designed to control the Wisconsin trade. In addition, Archibald John Campbell received a commission as a new agent to the Mississippi River Sioux. Campbell had refused to join the new Mackinac Company and was portrayed by both Captain Dunham and Governor Meriwether Lewis as having substantial influence with the Wahpeton and Mdewakanton Sioux.[27]

As the British receded from the northwest, American officials found the western tribes more pliable. The Dakotas, in particular, voiced strong approval of their "American father" in councils held at Prairie du Chien in 1809. Their only complaint dealt with Pike's failure to replace the British medals he had collected with ones showing the likeness of the American president.[28] The Wisconsin tribes followed suit. Only the Rock River Sacs seemed implacable. But Boilvin believed they would be overawed if the Dakotas remained in the American camp, since the Dakotas held the "balance of power" in the upper Mississippi watershed. The Sioux were "powerfully influential from the River Saint Pierre [Minnesota River], to this place [Prairie du Chien]," he wrote to the secretary of war, "and all traders calculate on doing but little without the *favor* and *approbation* of the Sioux."[29]

Unfortunately, the continued support of the Sioux depended upon the reinforcement of these friendly ties with trade, and the United States was unable to fully exploit the new economic opportunities north of Prairie du Chien. Traders from the states preferred to tap the Missouri River rather than the upper Mississippi, and Johnston's plan to send goods to the Mdewakantons was thwarted after the military refused him an escort for the journey. The one man who did concentrate on the Sioux trade, subagent Campbell, died in a duel with a British trader shortly after he received his commission.[30]

American officers also found it impossible to control British access to the Dakota domain and to compete with the quality of their goods. Of the few natives who left their wintering grounds to venture to Lake Michigan, most went to the British at St. Joseph's Island, where they received items that best suited their needs. The American steel traps, factor Varnum noted, were "so miserably made" that they would never sell. Simultaneously, British traders illegally entered American territory, disregarding Wilkinson's proclamation. Dickson led a large party past the Mackinac garrison at night in 1810 and wintered on the upper Mississippi River without molestation.[31]

Boilvin informed his superiors of the harm men like Dickson were doing. The Indians "loudly complain," he wrote the secretary of war in August 1810, "saying that the Government of the United States gives them but little for their support." The British, he added, at least kept them from starving, despite American endeavors to close western rivers to their brigades. Yet many natives also told Boilvin that they feared the Americans and British would one day fight, making supplies nearly impossible to obtain. Boilvin appeased the discontented Indians by handing out presents. He soon discovered, however, that the new Indian superintendent, William Clark, would not or could not reimburse him for these added expenses.[32]

By spring 1811 Boilvin knew he had lost the prestige Pike had initially gained among the upper Mississippi tribes. "I am too weak by myself to impress them [the Indians]," he wrote to Washington officials. Boilvin implored his superiors to establish a garrison and factory at Prairie du Chien. This was likely to hold the loyalty of the Sioux, who now complained vociferously that their "American father" failed to "take sufficient care of them." Their pelts, according to Dakota spokesmen, had suddenly become worthless, and they would soon "want everything" and "die in wretchedness." Accordingly, a handful of illegal British traders regained their former positions in Dakota camps almost by default. They reportedly told the Mdewakantons that if it were not for their "Old English Father," they would not have "a single blanket to cover themselves with."[33]

William Henry Harrison's attempt to dislodge the Shawnee Prophet and his followers from their town on Tippecanoe River forced many northwestern Indians to choose sides. Many living east of Lake Michigan had a strong attachment to the British, developed through years of watching the aggressive Americans. Indians in the upper Mississippi valley, on the other hand, had found the Americans untrustworthy for other reasons. The Americans had pledged their support to the Sioux on several occasions and had failed to reinforce these bonds. Dickson had again evaded the American garrison at Mackinac Island in 1811 and carried stores to the Sioux. Upon his return in 1812, the extent of the decline in American influence became evident, as many Mdewakanton Sioux spoke out strongly for the English.[34] Wabasha told Dickson that the Dakota people lived by their English traders, "who have always assisted us, and never more so than this year, at the risk of their lives." Then Wabasha spoke of the Americans; their words were "not the songs of truth." Red Wing was less conciliatory: "We abandon forever any connection with the Liars [Americans] who have uniformly deceived us," he proclaimed.[35] The British had quickly overcome their earlier failure to reinforce kinship ties with presents and goods.

The European war that spread to America in 1812 had a debilitating effect on Indian tribes contiguous to the frontier. In the upper Mississippi valley the suffering actually began several years before the hostilities. The embargo of 1807 and subsequent efforts by Americans to limit the access of British traders to potential allies had caused extreme shortages of munitions, clothing, and metal implements. Dickson, appointed British Indian agent at the outset of fighting, described the conditions of many western tribesmen in 1812 as "truly deplorable."[36] He used the discontented and near-naked hunters to form an army in Wisconsin during the summer. These warriors, along with British volunteers, quickly forced the surrender of Mackinac Island in July. A few months later, agent Boilvin fled Prairie du Chien.[37]

Kinship ties to individual British traders ordained what path the Sioux would take in the war. Nevertheless, the Mdewakantons also needed European armaments for hunting. Social ties went hand in hand with economic necessity. Red Wing told Dickson that he could only "rejoice" at being asked to once again join the British, who had "conferred so many benefits on our nation."[38] Menominee, Winnebago, and Chippewa warriors also replied favorably to Dickson's invitation. The majority of Sacs and Foxes, however, lived closer to the Americans and opted for neutrality.[39] Nevertheless, with many of the Indians in Wisconsin behind their cause, little prevented the British from marching on St. Louis. Fortunately for the United States, eastern campaigns distracted Dickson and his partisans.

Most British allies remained near Green Bay and Mackinac throughout the winter of 1812–13, eating provisions and taxing the resources of the English commissary. Only the Mdewakantons, now under Wabasha, stayed in the west for their winter hunts. In February 1813 they received orders to muster at Prairie du Chien; ninety-seven Sioux warriors joined in the campaigns near Detroit the following summer.[40] They fought at Fort Meigs on the Maumee River and later at Fort Stephenson near Lake Erie. The failure of the English to storm these strategic points discouraged the Dakota participants, and the distasteful tendency of other native allies to roast American captives convinced many to leave. By September most had reached Mackinac, where they complained to the British commander that they had received few goods for their service. The Dakota desertion came at a crucial stage, since their warriors had already reached their villages when the contest for the western lakes was decided on the Thames River in October.[41]

British Indian allies showed increasing frustration as the war entered its second year. The poor showing at Fort Meigs had not been entirely responsible; superintendent Clark noted in December 1812 that a majority of the eastern Sioux had preferred neutrality, and this was also true of other western Indians. Clark even felt that those west of the Mississippi might be approached by United States agents, and he immediately sent spies among them. His efforts did have some effect, since the vast majority of the Sioux never did join the British, and a few like the Wahpekute leaders Little Dish and French Crow were everywhere known as "rather American inclined." They had strong ties with the old French trader Dorion, who was in the American camp.[42]

Dickson had worried about the influence of the American agents. He had spent nearly £2,000 on gifts for the Sioux during the first six months of the war to counter their efforts. The Mdewakantons received the bulk of this aid, leaving most Dakota warriors west of the Mississippi untouched by Dickson's gift-giving.[43] This may explain why a delegation of "interior," or prairie, Sioux approached the Mdewakantons in April 1813, bidding them join an expedition against the Sacs and Foxes. The foray would have broken up the British league by inaugurating an intertribal feud.[44] Although the Mdewakantons declined, the incident demonstrates the growing effectiveness of American intrigue. Years later, Clark admitted that his strategy during the war had been to counter the British by encouraging the tribes west of the Mississippi to go to war against those east of it.[45]

Meanwhile, even Mdewakanton support of the British war effort faltered. Dickson was unable to get supplies into the west in the fall of 1813, and Red Wing defied him in October by attacking a Chippewa camp. Dickson was furious, charging that the "Sioux have behaved like villains." Just why Red Wing attempted to break up the British Indian alliance is impossible to determine, but both the Red Wing and the Little Crow villages were closely related to Archibald John Campbell, the former American agent, who had had five children by his Dakota wife, all living with the Sioux.[46] Red Wing soon sent wampum belts to the Missouri River Sioux who had contact with Americans, suggesting that they join him in a visit to see Clark at St. Louis. Although Red Wing failed to make the trip, the noted Mdewakanton warrior Tamaha did go and later acted as an agent for the United States.[47] Even the dedicated Wabasha wavered. He had received several American flags and medals before the conflict, and when it seemed as though the British would be unable to supply his people with arms, powder, and lead he brought them out to show his tribesmen his influence with the "long knives."[48]

Dickson finally arrived on the upper Mississippi with five canoes loaded with supplies in February 1814, six months after the Sioux complaints at Mackinac. Wabasha gratefully received the goods and asked Dickson to forgive Red Wing. But the supplies were too few and too late to please most of the dissatisfied elements, and the Sioux had no sense of loyalty to any nation-state. When an army under Clark appeared before Prairie du Chien in June, the Indians of the area, including three Sioux bands, offered no resistance. Even the retaking of the Prairie du Chien fort by the British in July did little to rekindle spirit in their cause. Wabasha's band stood by the British, but it took no part in the fighting. Wabasha followed closely the advice of his relative, Joseph Rolette, a trader who halfheartedly embraced the British. But Rolette seemed to sense by 1814 that the Americans would eventually regain the upper Mississippi, and his Mdewakanton kinsmen spent most of their time after the surrender protecting the defeated American garrison from the Winnebagos, who seemed intent on slaughtering the defenseless troops.[49]

Disaffection of surrounding tribes completely precluded a British offensive from Prairie du Chien. The only purpose for maintaining the garrison over the winter of 1814–15 was to retain the neutrality of the Indians. Wabasha continued to support the British outwardly, but the commanding officer knew the chief regularly received emissaries from the Yanktons and Wahpekutes, tribes sympathetic to the United States.[50] Yet Wabasha, the key to holding the region, had to be placated; he continued to receive supplies from the garrison, often at the expense of other Indians and perhaps even the British troops, who were starving by winter. The difficulty forced Rolette, the beef contractor, to turn to the Wahpekutes, whom he thought might sell buffalo to the troops. Instead, a lone member of the tribe murdered Rolette's two messengers, forcing a showdown. The Wahpekute chief

French Crow avoided fighting by surrendering his nephew to a firing squad.[51] The execution only compounded the troubles of the beleaguered British garrison.

Elsewhere in the Sioux domain British prestige also suffered because of their agents' inability to meet the needs of native hunters. Traders, headed by James Aird, did enter winter quarters along the Minnesota River in the fall of 1814, and they reestablished commercial ties with the Sissetons and Wahpetons. But Aird was able to give fifty lodges of Sioux only ten double-handfuls of powder. By March this band had not been heard from, and reports of mass starvation circulated everywhere. The Sioux were "dying with hunger from want of ammunition," according to one observer, and some traders themselves nearly perished.[52]

Consequently, traders and Indians alike rejoiced when the war ended in April 1815; the only uncertainty that clouded the celebration was just what the peace would bring. Some Mdewakantons understandably feared American occupation, even though they had offered less than enthusiastic support for England. On the other hand, Clark felt that the only visible evidence of British influence by the armistice remained on the upper Mississippi near Lake Pepin, where Wabasha, Little Crow, and most of their followers were being told that the war had been carried on for their welfare, and that if the Americans ever occupied Prairie du Chien, the Sioux would lose their land forever.[53]

Great Britain had evacuated Wisconsin and Mackinac Island by summer. In leaving, the British handed out small rewards such as a cannon to Wabasha's band, and their agents attempted to explain the peace in council. British officers told tribal delegations that their soldiers were no longer necessary to defend Indian lands. The commanding officer at Mackinac, Lieutenant Colonel Robert McDouall, assumed that provision had been made in the London accords for the preservation of Indian sovereignty. He encouraged the western tribes to stand their ground against the United States and strongly hinted that England would help them do so.[54] Washington officials, however, had no intention of allowing Britain to create a neutral zone in the northwest. As the Union Jack came down in the west, the War Department planned the construction of forts at Green Bay, at Prairie du Chien, and near the Falls of St. Anthony on the upper Mississippi River.[55]

Before the military occupation of the upper Mississippi, Americans negotiated four treaties with the Sioux on 19 July 1815, just north of St. Louis. The councils attracted few of their principal leaders, many of whom were discouraged from attending by British traders. Among the eastern Sioux delegates, the only truly influential men were Red Wing for the "Sioux of the Lakes" and Running Walker for the Wahpetons, suggesting again the influence that Americans had gained in the villages of these men. The agreements forgave past injuries, established perpetual peace, and provided a pledge of allegiance to the United States.[56]

As the discussions near St. Louis got under way, Colonel McDouall inaugurated plans of his own to offset them. He retained hopes of building an Indian confederacy in the west, using the Mdewakanton Sioux as a bulwark. By September the colonel had sent Thomas Anderson and several other traders to the Dakota tribes, exhorting them to resist the Americans. According to agent Boilvin, who had recently returned to Prairie du Chien, these men had poisoned the minds of many Indians regarding American intentions. Boilvin felt that the presence of British partisans on the upper Mississippi would certainly forestall the American occupation of Prairie du Chien.[57] Clark also perceived the seriousness of the threat to American plans. He quickly sent several men to the Sioux to trade and distribute presents. The agents selected for this job included such old hands as Pierre Chouteau and Manuel Lisa, as well as Clark's young nephew, Benjamin O'Fallon.[58]

Events along the upper Mississippi reached a climax during the summer of 1816, when American troops began building forts at Prairie du Chien and Green Bay. Surprisingly, none of the disaffected natives resisted. Several hundred of them under Wabasha and Little Crow, however, did visit the British at Drummond Island in June. Colonel McDouall, now under orders to preserve peace, had to concede to the Indian delegates that they must accept American rule. Wabasha immediately pressed his old ally for an explanation, claiming that "an omission appears to have been made at the treaty made between the Big Knives [Americans] and English." Wabasha had been under the impression that the British would help them resist American occupation. Little Crow astutely observed that "the good work you had begun for your Indian Children was entirely laid aside, when you buried the hatchet."[59] He later told Colonel McDouall privately that he thought the new American forts would cause his nation's "final extinction," since they would surely stop British traders as they had done before the war. The colonel generously handed out presents at the council's close, noting to his superiors that the Americans would no doubt view his kindness as an attempt "to renew the war."[60]

While the discussion went on at Drummond Island, American commissioners made one last bid to treat with the eastern Sioux near St. Louis. These negotiations did have a secondary purpose: the pledges of peace included an omnibus clause reaffirming all previous agreements, such as Pike's 1805 pact. More than forty Dakotas "touched a pen" to the 1816 accord. Nearly one-fourth were principal men. The list included French Crow and Tasaugye, chiefs of the Wahpekutes, Bad Hail and Penichon from the Minnesota River Mdewakantons, and Red Wing, Iron Cloud, and Marching Wind from the friendly Red Wing band. Even White Dog, second chief in Wabasha's village, accepted the treaty.[61] Many eastern Sioux obviously were convinced that Great Britain had abandoned them, breaking longstanding kinship bonds.

Wabasha's and Little Crow's bands came face to face with this new political reality when they descended the Wisconsin River on their way home from Drummond Island. Near Prairie du Chien, the new American commanding officer, Brevet Brigadier General Thomas A. Smith, hailed their party of ninety followers. The general noted in a letter to Clark that their sail-draped canoes "hoisted no flags & gave no salute," showing a break with the British. Yet Smith demanded that they camp below the town, even after Wabasha expressed a wish to join his tribesmen who had just returned from St. Louis. They had pitched tents above Prairie du Chien on a spot traditionally reserved for the Dakotas. General Smith retorted that he allowed only the Dakotas who had made peace at St. Louis to camp above the town and launched a gunboat to enforce the decree. Wabasha's followers "were not well pleased at this reception," Smith wrote, but they set up camp and prepared to hold a council the next day. Meanwhile their leaders asked to visit their relatives north of town. Smith consented, and a long discussion ensued in a tepee surrounded by American flags. A consensus seems to have been reached the next morning when Wabasha and Little Crow solemnly gave up their British flags and medals and pledged "the protection of their American father." The admonished Indians then reapproached Prairie du Chien by river with American flags flying from the bows of their canoes.[62]

After the Dakotas landed, a celebration took place, with toasts of grog to the "American father." General Smith ordered the regiment's "Rifle Band of Musick" to play while all the Dakotas cheered the president in unison, denounced the British king, and shook "the flag staff" of Old Glory. According to Smith, Wabasha led his men in this pageantry, "shaking the flags with much zeal." But not all the Dakotas were in a festive mood. General Smith learned that Red Wing's band had been unable to obtain ammunition and clothing for some time. Red Wing complained that since the traders had deserted them they "had to cloath themselves with grass & eat the earth." The Sioux had surely learned that regardless of the kinship ties they had established with traders, they were now vulnerable to the economic system and to the foreign competition over it. Nonetheless, Smith gave Red Wing's view short notice in his report and came away from the councils convinced that Wabasha, a man of "dignity and superior understanding," was won over to the American cause. To some degree he was correct. The ceremonies described by Smith illustrate a willingness on the part of many Dakotas to create fictive kinship ties with the Americans.[63]

Yet Smith failed to see how important trade had become to the establishment of friendly relations with the Sioux. Clark lacked his optimism, especially since British traders had filtered back into Dakota lands immediately after hostilities ceased. Indeed, rumors circulated that Robert Dickson intended to draw off many eastern Sioux warriors to the Red River and use the newly formed Lord Selkirk's colony near present-day Winnipeg as a staging area to supply them. Dickson had begun to construct a stockade between Big Stone Lake and Lake Traverse, convincing Clark to appeal to the War Department for funds to counter his influence. Before an answer arrived, Clark enlisted O'Fallon to serve as an agent to the eastern Sioux and to spy on Dickson.[64]

O'Fallon wintered on the Chippewa River in 1816–17 with a small group of Red Wing's hunters who had already expressed their friendship for the United States. Yet his initial report to Clark emphasized the continued influence of the British over most eastern Sioux. In May 1816 the president had granted bonded foreigners the right to trade temporarily on American lands until others could supply the Indians. They were obtaining licenses at Mackinac Island for a mere fifty dollars, and O'Fallon thought they were taking advantage of this privilege. The British traders "left no means untried in endeavouring to make the minds of the Indians corrupt," he reported to Clark. They tampered with "the little influence the Americans had acquired," and they even monopolized boatmen and interpreters at Prairie du Chien, so that Americans would be unable to hire experienced help. In these circumstances, O'Fallon was not surprised when the rank and file of Wabasha's village received him coolly.[65]

The next year, O'Fallon and a handful of other Americans made some inroads into Mdewakanton Sioux camps. The expedition of Stephen H. Long, launched in July, may have played a role in this change, even though his small force of ten men passed quickly through eastern Sioux lands and deferred to O'Fallon negotiations with Dakota leaders. Long had been ordered to select sites for military forts along the upper Mississippi, survey the Indian villages below St. Anthony Falls, and show the American flag.[66] Not long after Long's return to Prairie du Chien, Shakopee and Wabasha showed strong friendship toward the Americans. "Bad Birds [British] have attempted to whisper in my ears," Shakopee told O'Fallon by fall. "They told me to turn my back upon the smooth face chief [O'Fallon]." But Shakopee claimed that he had rejected their advice forever. He wanted O'Fallon to visit him the next year with presents and to "drag from amongst them the dogs [British traders]" that were corrupting his young men. Wabasha also spoke of the "lies" the British had used to "shut our ears against truth." In both instances O'Fallon smoked with these leaders, securing fictive bonds, and promised them American traders to provide for their needs. Throughout the winter, O'Fallon's prestige rose as various Sioux leaders came to see him at Prairie du Chien. One, in a sweeping metaphor, denounced the British: "the red coats [British] appear no longer gay. The greedy but *timid* wolf . . . sought the thicket for a hiding place."[67]

O'Fallon returned to the upper Mississippi in the spring of 1818 accompanied by a force of fifty United States infantrymen. This party, by far the largest to date of any foreign nationality to invade Sioux lands, made a striking impression upon the Indians. The troops manned two "fortified" keelboats and stopped at every Mdewakanton village along the Mississippi. The party then entered the Minnesota River and ascended it to Shakopee's camp, thirty miles from the mouth. To add prestige, the Americans announced their presence at every encampment with a salute from each of the swivel cannons mounted on the bows of the vessels.[68]

The show of force brought many Sioux men over to the American side, yet some still felt disposed to refuse O'Fallon's overtures. The lack of consensus seemed evident at Wabasha's village, where the chief embraced O'Fallon but others in the camp were obdurate. When O'Fallon sat down to council with the seventeen elders of the band, ten of them refused to shake hands and promptly left the chambers. O'Fallon's inquiries into the cause garnered this response from Wabasha: "a few . . . had not yet become reconciled to the Big Knives— [and] view them with indifference." The Americans had still to keep the promises made by Pike more than a decade before. Even so,

Wabasha promised to drive the discontented men from his band if such conduct continued. Of course the chief had no such power and could only gain face by mildly berating O'Fallon for the actions of some Americans. He voiced displeasure with the conduct of a handful of loggers, apparently from the Prairie du Chien fort, who had invaded his domain that summer and taken lumber.[69]

Little Crow seemed nearly as indifferent to the United States as did the men at Wabasha's camp. O'Fallon found him absent from his village on the trip upriver in 1818 as well as when the expedition returned to Prairie du Chien. O'Fallon soon learned that Little Crow had joined Dickson and Renville on the upper Minnesota River and that forty of his men were acting as guards for the British traders. Renville had served as Dickson's clerk before the war, and through marriage and his own kinship background he had close relatives in Little Crow's band. This situation seemed ominous, but Little Crow had also selected a narrow spot along the Mississippi, just above the St. Croix River, and constructed fortified blockhouses that commanded the passage. He had said that no Americans would be allowed to pass.[70]

How much of the scheme can be attributed to Dickson is anyone's guess, but O'Fallon promptly arrested the English trader, whom he encountered by chance along the upper Mississippi. In March 1817 the president had revoked the right of foreigners to trade on American soil, thus putting Dickson in violation of American law.[71] On his way downriver O'Fallon stopped to lecture Little Crow's followers. "Sioux, from this day you must date your change," he angrily asserted, "or this river's surface will be covered with our boats, & the land with troops who will chase you as you do the deer." The band was represented in council by Grand Partisan, a witness to Pike's treaty thirteen years before. He rose, trembling somewhat at this threat, and responded by explaining that he had last conferred with Pike, who promised that the "red coats" would be excluded from Sioux land. But they had returned and Pike had lied. Notwithstanding, Grand Partisan then noted O'Fallon's "triumphant flag waving over our land" and the troops with him "glistening before us." He, at least, promised to take up with Little Crow the issues O'Fallon had raised.[72]

The other Mdewakanton bands that O'Fallon visited were markedly different in their attitudes toward Americans. Red Wing and White Dog had been friendly since the war's end, and Penichon and Black Dog, band chiefs from the lower Minnesota River, had either sent representatives to the 1816 peace treaty or attended in person. Even Shakopee's people, far removed from any American presence at Prairie du Chien, listened attentively to the agent's words. Described by O'Fallon as "one hundred & thirty six desperados," Shakopee's band had been expecting an attack from the Chippewas when the Americans arrived. Shakopee adroitly asked O'Fallon in council if he would not allow them to counter the anticipated raid, and when the agent advised them to "raise not the tomahawk but in good cause," Shakopee's warriors sprang to their feet, discarded their blankets, and prepared for war.[73]

Shortly after O'Fallon returned to St. Louis in 1818 he received news of his appointment as Indian agent for the Missouri River.[74] But as he prepared to leave he could reflect upon considerable success, for the majority of eastern Sioux villagers now seemed amenable to American occupation. In every discussion with the Dakotas, O'Fallon had made it clear that the reestablishment of trade at pre-1805 levels rested upon acceptance of American rule. And, like Pike, O'Fallon had argued that a military post would be an essential factor in maintaining permanent commerce. Even before Secretary of War John C. Calhoun ordered the construction of a military post near the confluence of the Minnesota and Mississippi rivers in the spring of 1819, most eastern Sioux had accepted such an occupation as judicious. In addition, O'Fallon stressed the willingness of the American "father" to assume the responsibility of caring for his people, the Sioux, of helping to end intertribal war, and of preventing starvation. The Americans, he promised, would become benevolent providers to an even greater extent than the French or English before them. Those Sioux Indians who had doubts had at least grown accustomed to the American presence by the end of O'Fallon's tenure as agent.[75]

Nevertheless, Washington officials still remained cautious and ordered the Sac and Fox agent, Thomas Forsyth, to accompany the new garrison upriver that summer and distribute $2,000 worth of presents to the Mdewakanton people. This amount had been penciled into Pike's accord by the Senate at ratification in 1808. Colonel Henry Leavenworth had been assigned the task of building the new fort, and Forsyth joined his command of ninety-eight regulars and twenty boatmen at Prairie du Chien, where they proceeded upriver with a flotilla of fourteen small boats, two larger keelboats, and a barge.[76] This fleet stopped at the various Mdewakanton villages to allow Forsyth to council with the Sioux. At Wabasha's camp he outlined Leavenworth's construction plan, telling the leaders in council that a fort at the mouth of the Minnesota River would serve three purposes: it would provide protection from other Indians such as the Chippewas, offer a blacksmith shop to repair the weapons and tools of native warriors, and contain a trade center. Forsyth also urged the Sioux to recognize the neutrality of the Mississippi River, which was necessary for free trade.[77]

Forsyth probably used the same arguments at each camp thereafter, emphasizing the positive economic assets of the new army garrison and the Americans' willingness to create friendly bonds rather than any restriction the garrison might place on Sioux sovereignty. All the Dakota leaders seemed convinced of the validity of this argument, even Little Crow, whom Forsyth now described as a "steady, generous, and independent Indian." Little Crow now acknowledged the Pike treaty and the right of troops to occupy the mouth of the Minnesota River. He had even given up his efforts to prevent American traders from going upriver. He now viewed the future garrison as an asset, telling Forsyth that finally the Sioux would have "their father near them." Of the other Dakota leaders who came to receive presents and whiskey from the Indian agent, only Shakopee expressed discontent with the Americans.[78] His objections, however, stemmed from the small number of presents he received, not from a disenchantment with the new garrison that took shape that fall. Considering the general candor of the Sioux in council, this is strong testimony to the success of earlier American diplomacy.

By November the post had received 120 reinforcements, and a stockade had been constructed on the south bank of the Minnesota River. But the work progressed slowly and came at a considerable cost in soldiers, who by the winter months suffered from the cold and from scurvy. Since Leavenworth finally decided that the location of the post contributed to the sickness, he moved the garrison into tents north of the river in May 1820. By fall Colonel Josiah Snelling arrived at this new camp and replaced Leavenworth. He selected the final location for the fort along the cliffs overlooking the Minnesota and Mississippi rivers and completed construction. The new post was deservedly named Fort Snelling a few years later.[79]

A permanent Indian agent joined the new military community in 1820 and became the spokesman for government policy. Lawrence Taliaferro, a Virginian, took the job after resigning from the army. Taliaferro served the Sioux at the new St. Peter's Agency near Fort Snelling for nearly twenty years and played an important role in fashioning early government policy. The new agent's character was not without flaws, but he was an honorable man and asserted upon retiring that he was leaving the Indian service "as poor as when I first entered."[80] Perhaps Taliaferro's most telling fault was his vanity. His extensive journals are filled with pretentious comments on the importance of his role in the Indian service.

The establishment of Fort Snelling and the employment of a permanent Sioux agent in 1819 marked the beginning of the end of British intrigue among the Dakota people and simultaneously opened a new era in Dakota relations with whites, once based solely upon the reciprocal interaction of individual traders and Dakota bands. The fort and a permanent agent introduced the added dimension of more extensive interethnic interaction, with the garrison, ranging in size from several dozen men on active duty to several hundred, providing the key element in this change. The short stay of the soldiers and their eagerness to acquire Indian women posed some problems for the Sioux, who found it difficult to create meaningful kinship ties with such a fluid community. But if Sioux leaders ever thought seriously about forcing the garrison to leave—and there is no evidence that they did—the military capability of their new neighbors made expulsion difficult if not impossible.

Although one might assume that the garrison would eventually cause a breakdown in reciprocal relations, and though government officers at times expressed fears that trouble might erupt, Indians and American soldiers did learn to coexist on the upper Mississippi River. They did so primarily because Sioux society possessed the ability to adapt to the military community. Dakota men and women living near the fort established, on a limited scale, both fictive and affine relations with members of the garrison, just as they had done with the traders who preceded them. On the other hand, the early Americans, both traders and government personnel, assimilated to various degrees key aspects of the Dakota world view.

While Fort Snelling became the hub of a unique multiethnic society, it also played an economic and political role. The garrison held supplies of food and goods that Dakota people could barter for, it housed a blacksmith who fixed weapons and tools, and it provided protection and support for the flood of traders who entered Dakota lands each year by 1820. In addition, it offered a neutral ground for council, where Sioux, Chippewa, Winnebago, Menominee, and American diplomats gathered to work out problems. Naturally, on every occasion where Americans were involved, they tried to encourage the adoption of policies favorable to the United States.

Yet the use of the garrison as a coercive force in these negotiations was not very effective with the Sioux. Traders and the Indian agent, when working together, had far more success. Both used presents and the manipulation of the kin networks they created among Sioux leaders to maintain the American presence. Consequently it seems unlikely that the Dakotas viewed the invasion of their country negatively. In 1820 they had merely exchanged a small strip of land, on which the fort sat, for a permanent "father." The British government, which had failed to provide them with necessities, had been replaced by the American government. Fort Snelling may have symbolized American occupation to whites, but, as Little Crow noted, to the Indians it illustrated the concern the Americans had for their increasingly dependent native children. Neither the British nor the French had ever sent their young men so far west, and the presence of American soldiers merely confirmed what Pike had so long ago promised; to many Dakota people, the American invasion offered the pledge of easy access to goods, abundant presents to reinforce kinship ties, and the friendship and assistance of those responsible for such benevolence.

6

Intertwining Loyalties

During the decade that followed the founding of Fort Snelling, the Dakotas came to grips with the American presence, and government officials encouraged their accommodation by using the same kinship and gift-giving institutions that earlier traders had employed. Continuity rather than change dominated early intercultural exchanges near the fort. But behind these cordial scenes many subtle social, political, and economic pressures were at work. American "civilization," with its attendant acculturative mechanism, was slowly becoming entrenched. Concurrently, trader manipulation reached its utmost level. Although the eastern Sioux remained militarily strong throughout the 1820s, they were being beset by seemingly insignificant changes that would soon form the basis for an all-out assault on their culture.

Pressures that produced the most change in the 1820s were political and economic, the end products of increased commercialism and the expanding role of the federal government. Traders had become essential to Sioux survival, and the Dakotas' growing dependence on them made it possible for Euroamerican kinsmen to strip the land of animal resources. The assault on the upper Mississippi River ecosystem, although destructive of the native economy, paradoxically had become essential to the existence of the Dakota hunters. It financed large purchases of kettles, combs, and jewelry for their women and bought fancy shirts, metal implements, arms, and whiskey for themselves. The Sioux seemed powerless to stop the ecological rape of their lands, and it soon forced them to make adjustments. The Mdewakantons, for example, found it necessary by the 1820s to hunt farther west each year, turning to such nontraditional resources as muskrats for pelts and food.

Government pressures stemmed from the need to support extraterritorial privileges for white citizens in Dakota lands and the desire to stop intertribal warfare. These policy concerns prompted officials to preserve Dakota leadership groups so that they might maintain stability and a sense of responsibility within their bands. Simultaneously, it led to intervention in the Sioux process of consensus decision making, the political mechanism based on council discussion that led to policies acceptable to all concerned. The army allowed the Indian agent, Lawrence Taliaferro, to handle interethnic relations. Yet the garrison was generally represented in major councils by the commanding officer, who became in the Indian sense a chief soldier or policeman. In the early years at the fort, the commanding officer spent most of his time trying to stop intertribal war by arresting Indians who raided other tribes.

In acting as a policeman, the commanding officer at Fort Snelling had a difficult time effecting meaningful kinship ties with Dakota leaders. This was also true of the garrison, which had limited social contact with the Sioux. Yet a few officers and men did use presents to make friends and took Dakota women as wives or concubines. Since many soldiers remained only a short time at the fort, however, the Indian agent was far more able to develop a kinship network in Dakota villages. Through gift-giving, creation of kinship ties, and the employment of mixed-blood assistants, who also had strong bonds with the Sioux, Taliaferro became far and away the most influential government employee on the upper Mississippi. The use of such traditional cultural mechanisms by the agent caused many Sioux to believe the government had a genuine concern for their welfare. By the late 1820s Taliaferro had formed a small but effective sociopolitical faction in the Dakota community, most notably among the bands near the fort, that had striking similarities to those formed by traders decades before.

Friendly bonds between Indians and government officials evolved despite significant expansion in the fur trade that threatened the economic existence of the easternmost Dakota bands. During the 1820s traders rushed to monopolize and maximize the Sioux trade. John Jacob Astor formed the American Fur Company in 1817 to take advantage of the void left when Canadians departed. Astor thought he could quickly grab a monopoly of the commerce along the upper Mississippi, and he sent his business manager, Ramsay Crooks, west to coordinate these efforts. It took Crooks ten years to accomplish the task, since several other entrepreneurs had the same thoughts as Astor. Indeed, Crooks was unable to find anyone to carry goods to the Sioux until the fall of 1818, when he brought James Lockwood into the company fold.[1]

Lockwood and his four or five clerks faced stiff competition from a horde of other expectant capitalists. Dickson continued to work from his post on Lake Traverse until 1822, when he and his partners, Kenneth Mackenzie, William Laidlaw, and Daniel Lamont, formed the Columbia Fur Company.[2] Bostwick and Stone, a third major mercantile group, had beaten Crooks into the field and temporarily procured the services of Joseph Rolette. In addition, even the government factory at Prairie du Chien put traders on the upper Mississippi, financing several who worked out of Fort Snelling. When other small independents were added, the eastern Sioux had more traders than they really required.[3]

Nonetheless, the American Fur Company outlasted the others because of its leadership, financial reserves, and sophistication. It combined a unique mixture of Jacksonian entrepreneurship with the idiosyncrasies of traditional social trade patterns. In many ways the company was one of the first vertically integrated firms in America. It worked to control fur resources and transportation systems in the west as well as markets in New York and abroad. It also cultivated politicians in Washington, maintaining lobbyists who prevented the passage of restrictive laws and urged the repeal of measures that stood in the way of the company's expansion.[4] Yet it adapted well to the conditions in the west, Crooks recognizing that he would

have to deal with traders who understood the customs and person-
alities of the various tribes the company wished to conduct business
with. In the case of the Sioux, he turned to men who had established
kinship ties before the War of 1812.

This excluded Lockwood, who had only recently reached the west.
Crooks replaced him in 1822 with the more dynamic Joseph Rolette.
Hazen Mooers was recruited next. He had married into the Sisseton
tribe and took charge of the Lake Traverse post. Alexis Bailly, Rolette's assistant, controlled the brigades sent among the Mdewakantons. The company's success soon attracted other veterans, including Jean Baptiste Faribault, Joseph La Framboise, and Louis
Provençalle. Faribault had relatives among the Red Wing Mdewakantons and also traded with the Wahpekutes. La Framboise had married the daughter of a Sisseton chief living in the vicinity of Swan
Lake; Provençalle had established similar ties with the Wahpetons
near Traverse des Sioux, raising a large mixed-blood family.[5] Thus
Crooks had expanded the company's trade and its social connections to include all four eastern Sioux tribes by the mid-1820s.

But the early consolidation fell far short of monopoly. Competition provided the Indians a prosperity reminiscent of the 1780s and
1790s, with traders generously giving out credits and presents to
keep hunters from deserting to others with their furs and to pacify
native relatives. Although the number of presents was probably not
as substantial as in past years, these practices were anathema to
Astor and Crooks, who realized how seriously they cut into profits.
Crooks wrote Rolette in 1827 to complain about Mooers, who was
"extremely extravagant" in his dealing with his Sisseton in-laws, giving the women "many goods for making clothes, etc."[6] But Rolette
took no action against his Lake Traverse partner, since he realized
the importance of such exchanges. Accordingly, the Dakotas viewed
traders as crucial friends and allies. Their major fear in the 1820s
was that another war might disrupt the commercial system and leave
them without goods.[7]

The steady competition produced dramatic ecological changes,
as staple animals declined in number. Major Stephen H. Long, whose

second expedition toured the northwest in 1823, took special note of the lack of game along the river valleys. A noticeable decline had occurred since 1817, as herd animals disappeared "very rapidly" from Sioux country. The hunters with Long's party took only two or three dozen game birds between Prairie du Chien and Fort Snelling and saw no deer or buffalo at all.[8] Even less game existed between Fort Snelling and Big Stone Lake, where Long and his cohorts took only two birds. As provisions gave out, guide Joseph Renville feared that the Americans would starve. Indians encountered along the way indicated that those Sioux living near the lake "were reduced almost to a state of starvation by the delayed visit of the buffalo."[9] Fortunately, upon reaching the lake the party found that these reports had been exaggerated. Meat could be procured from large herds north of Lake Traverse.[10] Nonetheless, the Long account illustrates that game in the heartland of the Sioux domain had been seriously depleted by 1823.

Despite the utter exhaustion of game along the main river courses, large numbers of animals existed in the debated zones lying between the Sioux and the Chippewas. Long's expedition found that the contested land extended over much of central Minnesota. In the Red River valley alone, a huge chunk of land lying between Ottertail and Turtle rivers was fought over.[11] Moreover, the 1820 Lewis Cass expedition that explored the upper Mississippi reported that much of the river above St. Anthony Falls was disputed. This included the Crow Wing, Sauk, and Rum river valleys. But the land south of the Minnesota, especially the headwaters of the Des Moines, also had become a contested zone. Here the Sacs and Foxes sought to dislodge Dakota hunters.[12]

Ecological decline forced the Sioux to turn increasingly to agriculture. Although the Sissetons and Wahpetons reportedly had cornfields in the 1770s, planting seems to have increased among the Mdewakantons after 1812, even though production was not substantial.[13] While he was a member of Cass's expedition, Charles Christopher Trowbridge visited Little Crow's camp at harvest time in 1820. He reported that, although corn had become "almost their only food" during the summer, the band quickly consumed the crop. Upon being asked to a feast, Trowbridge agreed hesitantly, since Little Crow's people proposed to eat the corn before it had ripened. In a large bark house the Indians had prepared "four or five fires over each of which hung a large drop kettle filled with corn." After appropriate songs and dances, each member of the band "filled his wooden bowl, holding probably two gallons and commenced eating." The scenes that followed "ceased to be interesting," according to Trowbridge, since he had never witnessed such gluttony, and he quickly departed. He came away thinking that the Mdewakantons had reached a point of near-starvation because their men were "too indolent to hunt."[14]

Actually, Trowbridge passed very quickly through the countryside and failed to understand the cyclical aspect of Sioux food gathering. Long found the Mdewakantons hunting in the summer, and the band had probably just returned from a summer hunt to tend their crop when Trowbridge arrived. The Dakota men no doubt realized that daily searches for game in the immediate vicinity of their camp were useless. Moreover, the feast Trowbridge attended was likely a "feast of the new crop," a ritual that inaugurated the harvest season. At a feast of this sort participants received a gift if they finished their corn first, thus explaining the gluttony observed by the Americans. The situation was similar for other villages along the Mississippi and Minnesota rivers. They all had planted corn by the 1820s, and an occasional patch could even be found in clearings several miles from the Sioux camps. Shakopee's people reportedly had undertaken the largest agricultural effort among the Mdewakantons, while the Sissetons had substantial fields on several islands in both Big Stone Lake and Lake Traverse. Some sources say Hazen Mooers introduced such cultivation among the Sissetons, though they had obviously planted off and on for some time before his arrival.[15]

Perhaps the best gauge for the state of the Dakota economy is found in the returns of the American Fur Company. Data for the 1820s have survived only for the years 1820 and 1827, and these two lists of pelts indicate that populations of prime fur-bearing animals clearly had declined. In 1820 the company's three Sioux brigades under Lockwood took 760 beaver pelts. Seven years later Rolette, with more men and goods, brought in only 321. Even though competitors perhaps did as well, these figures hardly compare with those reported on an 1805 return: the Sioux alone collected an estimated 8,000 beaver skins in that year. The taking of deer and elk also declined. Rolette's men, who concentrated their efforts in the woodlands, gathered 6,000 of these skins in 1827, whereas 15,000 had been taken from the Dakotas twenty-two years before.[16]

In addition to the figures above, the invoices for the 1820s include much larger numbers of less valuable skins. Rolette's men took an unbelievable 68,000 muskrats, or "rats," in 1827, worth twenty cents apiece to the Sioux hunter. Buffalo hides also averaged between 500 and 1,000, probably the most that eastern markets could digest. They sold for three dollars a robe, but the tanning done by Indian women was time-consuming. While many more packs of furs were being shipped east during the 1820s, they were worth less than the large numbers of beaver and otter skins that had come from Dakota lands two decades earlier. Rolette's returns brought $25,000, and it seems unlikely that his competition, which had dwindled by 1827, did any better.[17] The estimated value of the 1805 return was $75,000. Such comparisons illustrate that the Sioux hunter still had much to offer traders, but they also indicate that taking large numbers of muskrats had become necessary to offset lost income. "Rats" now constituted an incredible 85 percent of the pelts taken by Rolette's men in 1827.[18]

The shift to exploiting muskrats prompted changes in food-gathering cycles, especially among the Mdewakantons. Small parties of their men frequently went west in the 1820s to hunt rats on the prairies. The animals congregated in stagnant sloughs and could be easily killed with spears by individuals rather than by communal parties. The growing muskrat bonanza led to fluctuations in Mdewakanton occupation patterns. Black Dog's people near Fort Snelling broke up into several small hunting parties for better rat hunting. Long met the chief and a few of his relatives on the upper Minnesota River in 1823. Penichon's camp also declined; Taliaferro told the chief that when his village contained only his relatives, the government could no longer recognize him as a Dakota chief.[19] Only Wabasha's people seemed to adjust successfully. They seasonally vacated their village sites on the Mississippi for new hunting camps on the headwaters of the Upper Iowa River, where they had access to both buffalo and muskrats.[20]

For those Mdewakantons who remained in established villages, mere survival became difficult. The handful living close to the fort occasionally relied on the generosity of the garrison or the agent. Travelers frequently mentioned their destitution. Others who were more enterprising collected wood or made items to barter with soldiers. The Chippewas often functioned as a third partner in this commerce, frequently exchanging bark canoes for necessities.[21] But despite the apparent difficulties many Mississippi River Mdewakantons still returned to the Chippewa and St. Croix rivers to hunt deer. In addition, the Sissetons, the Wahpetons, and Shakopee's Mdewakantons continued to exploit the Sauk and Crow rivers.[22] Unfortunately, reports arriving at St. Peter's Agency by 1827 mention their failures in winter quarters as frequently as their successes.

Although alterations in the Dakota ecosystem partially explain the subtle changes in occupational and food gathering patterns, numerous other forces contributed to culture change in the 1820s. Permanent trade posts were established after the War of 1812 rather than temporary wintering stations.[23] This alteration in the commercial process gave traders a better opportunity to bypass chiefs and manipulate large numbers of hunters. The year-round occupation of Sioux lands also increased external pressures on hunters, who now more frequently looked to the trader than the chiefs for advice individually or in council. Minor changes in the credit system led to an even more pronounced breakdown of communal economics. Traders now kept lists of hunters and the exact amount of goods each had received in the fall. The use of individual accounts made it more difficult for chiefs or soldiers' lodges to control the annual take in pelts or the distribution of presents.[24] Finally, traders now acted as brokers, often telling hunters which pelts would fare best in the

marketplace. Even though Indians often refused to follow the traders' directions, the fur trade was well along the way to becoming
less of a reciprocal exchange and more of an economic function.

Such growing dependence on traders had political implications;
councils and chiefs were becoming more susceptible to their mach-
inations. Unfortunately, these changes were occurring at a time when
a generation of important Dakota leaders was passing. This was especially true among the Mdewakantons: Shakopee died in 1827, Red
Wing two years later, Penichon in 1833, and Little Crow and Wabasha
in 1835 and 1836, respectively.[25] All were past the prime of life when
the first indications of economic instability hit. Others stepped forward to lead, but they lacked the prestige of their predecessors and
found it difficult to attain a following in a society increasingly manipulated by whites.

For the most part, factionalism had always been a part of Sioux
politics, but the pressure on leadership, especially among the Mdewakantons, was new. Their chiefs noted the changed political atmosphere in council with Taliaferro by the end of the decade. Although
they did not blame whites directly, several leaders realized by this
time that the traders' use of alcohol was partially responsible for
their troubles. In the past chiefs had controlled access to liquor,
keeping it away from young men. As the role of traders expanded,
however, they began bypassing village leadership groups and distributing liquor directly to young hunters. Traders now gave the most
successful young men a keg each spring, an entirely new practice
that reinforced the hunters' economic obligations to the trader rather
than their accustomed roles in the band. The minor Mdewakanton
chief Black Dog told Taliaferro that men who received the reward no
longer listened to their leaders. It "ruins the hunters generally," he
noted, and frequently "causes difficulty" in the village.[26]

Although the decline of political leadership was more complex
than this, Taliaferro agreed that alcohol had been debilitating. Unfortunately, Congress had left too many loopholes in the Indian Intercourse Acts, a series of laws designed to regulate Indian trade and
prevent the influx of spirits. Men working for the various commercial

companies were allowed to carry into Dakota lands nearly two gallons of whiskey per month for each boatman in their employ.[27] A law passed in May 1822 also gave government officials the right to search vessels and seize liquor destined for the Indians, but it was obviously impossible to distinguish between legal and illegal alcohol. In addition, large quantities of spirits could be shipped into military reservations like Fort Snelling and into civilian pockets like Prairie du Chien. Understandably, officials felt confused about the regulations and preferred to avoid the legal action that often occurred when agents and military officers attempted to enforce poorly constructed laws.[28]

American Fur Company agent Joseph Rolette and his assistant Alexis Bailly soon "monopolized" the whiskey trade with the Sioux, as one government official put it.[29] Bailly's boats seldom if ever were searched, and he further avoided inspection by obtaining licenses from friendly agents, such as Nicholas Boilvin at Prairie du Chien or George Boyd at Green Bay. Colonel Snelling and Taliaferro both deplored this nefarious trade, but it was not until the fall of 1825 that they were able to convince the War Department to issue a blanket directive excluding spirits "altogether" from the Indian country. On the strength of this order, Snelling made a spot check of Bailly's boats in July 1826. The trader had taken the usual precautions of having Boilvin give written "permission" for him to carry alcohol upriver. But Snelling, supposedly supported by the War Department, seized the sixty-four gallons on board. Bailly sued both Snelling and Taliaferro, who had issued his own proclamation against the introduction of spirits three months before, and it soon became evident that a departmental directive did not constitute law on the frontier. Rather than face penalties in court, Snelling returned the cargo, extracting a minor concession from Bailly: thereafter, Rolette's assistant agreed to leave an invoice of his goods when he passed Fort Snelling.[30]

Traders like Rolette never publicly admitted using liquor in the trade, but they did so because it offered such an effective tool in manipulating the Sioux and because it provided an edge over competitors. Mackenzie, a company opponent, used liquor regularly at

Lake Traverse even though neither he nor his men fell afoul of Taliaferro or Snelling.[31] But the most consistent use of spirits in the trade
came along the Sioux-Chippewa border. The American Fur Company even petitioned the government for the right to use alcohol
legally to compete with the English. Fully fifty Wahpetons and Sissetons crossed over to Crow Island in the Mississippi in 1825 and
bartered for liquor with men from Astor's firm. They gave up all their
prime pelts in the process. The next year Philander Prescott, a trader
working for Mackenzie, reported to Taliaferro that his trade had been
"nearly ruined" by whiskey peddlers from Lake Superior.[32]

Most of the spirits that reached Dakota bands south of the Minnesota River came directly from Prairie du Chien. Many times the
Indians themselves simply went to town and bought kegs. Taliaferro's journal contains numerous accounts of what happened
thereafter; a drunken frolic usually took place in which villagers were
often killed, and the band affected had to split up to avoid further
bloodletting by vengeful kinsmen. A typical encounter of this sort
occurred in 1826 when the sons of Little Crow nearly cut off the arm
of a young hunter after receiving several kegs of whiskey from Rolette.[33] Perhaps the most celebrated case happened at Wabasha's village four years earlier, when Rolette sent his father-in-law liquor to
induce him to run out a Green Bay competitor. The chief's men, in a
state of drunkeness, went beyond the orders and burned the intruder's newly constructed post to the ground. Taliaferro used the incident to attract attention in Washington to the problem of alcohol
availability.[34]

Most American Fur Company officials viewed efforts to control
liquor use as misguided philanthropy by men who failed to understand the frontier environment. Spirits had already been in the trade
for several decades, and the Indians wanted them. Furthermore, Taliaferro used liquor in councils with the Dakotas, creating a double
standard that the Indians found confusing.[35] Actually, what Taliaferro and Snelling grew to dislike in the 1820s was not necessarily
the use of whiskey, although it proved degenerative for much of Sioux
society, but the power it engendered for the company and the dis-

order it often provoked. Taliaferro soon concluded that the American Fur Company was run by men of "mean principles and low origins."[36] Prescott, who later entered government service and knew all the Sioux traders working for the company, tended to agree. Of three with whom he had business contacts, two cheated him and the third attempted to seduce his Indian wife.[37] In truth, ethical merchants simply did not survive among the Sioux by the 1820s.

Taliaferro did attempt to limit the growing influence of the company in 1824. Implementing a new law that gave the agent the authority to select trading locations, Taliaferro told the company it could occupy posts only at Lake Traverse, at Patterson Rapids, at Traverse des Sioux, near Fort Snelling, and at the mouth of the Chippewa River. Company officials complained loudly, and Crook's assistant Robert Stuart concluded that Taliaferro had been "grossly imposed upon" by Mackenzie.[38] Under political pressure from the company, the secretary of war directed William Clark to give the matter his "immediate attention," suggesting that sites selected should "subserve the convenience of the Indians and the traders."[39] Faced with opposition, Taliaferro slowly increased the number of posts to thirteen by 1826, more sites than the company needed. And two years later Rolette had become so bold in disregarding the location law that he simply informed Taliaferro where his traders were going and asked that the sites receive official sanction.[40]

Ironically, while traders inadvertently caused sociopolitical change, local government officials bolstered more traditional leadership groups, hoping to use them to control the Sioux rank and file. Taliaferro, especially, worked as a stabilizing force, dealing with and supporting the status quo. He maintained a system of protocol in his councils, being certain not to give individual Dakota leaders more or less attention than their rank deserved. Positions in the hierarchy were symbolized by three different medals. Tribal chiefs received the largest, while band chiefs and village headmen were given correspondingly smaller medals. Although it has been asserted that Taliaferro tried to "make chiefs" during the 1820s, it was more that he advised band leaders to select a responsible man to represent them. He understood that leadership depended solely upon a man's ability to give good advice.[41]

Nonetheless, Taliaferro did meddle in Dakota politics by allying with Mdewakanton leaders close to the fort in what became a unique and worthwhile sociopolitical relationship based upon extensive gift-giving and the kinship attachments that he, and the men who worked for him, maintained. His interpreters Duncan and Scott Campbell had strong Mdewakanton ties, and along with traders such as Mooers and Prescott they lent the agent considerable support.[42] In addition, Taliaferro had magnified his influence immeasurably by forming a "country" union with the daughter of the war chief Maḣpiyawicaṡta or Cloud Man, of Black Dog's village. The union was soon blessed with a child, christened Mary.[43] All these relationships made possible the creation of a unique kinship "network system" that was structured along traditional Dakota cultural lines and provided the agent with a strong base of support for his policies. The network generally proved invaluable when Taliaferro dealt with Black Dog's and Little Crow's camps, but its influence dissipated when Taliaferro counseled the more western bands that visited him infrequently.[44]

Yet kinship ties only provided access into Dakota society; Taliaferro reinforced these bonds continually by issuing presents and giving good counsel. A pattern soon developed whereby at least twice a year Dakota leaders came to hear his advice. On each visit an established ritual occurred in which the men would shake hands, present and smoke peace pipes, and, at the conclusion of the discussion, receive an outlay of presents, sometimes equaling forty dollars per chief. The Dakotas accordingly gave Taliaferro a place in their social scheme, calling him Maza Baksa, "Iron Cutter," referring to his role in distributing metal implements.[45]

When a particularly important issue had to be resolved, the councils at the agency attracted the headmen of several tribes. Leaders struggled to find a consensus acceptable to all and often incorporated Taliaferro into the political decision making. Although the agent frequently did not get his way, as was the case with any other chief present, he was able to present his views in the forum and be assured that they would be considered.

With whiskey, ecological change, and the political manipulation of outsiders common by 1827, it may seem contradictory to suggest that most Dakota people still maintained cultural continuity with the past. But the Sissetons, Wahpetons, and Wahpekutes benefited from their isolation, living most of the year on buffalo, which made them less susceptible to changing economic conditions. They also employed the communal hunt and a soldiers' lodge and simply had little contact with the fort. Members of the Long party might be accused of adhering to the "noble savage" myth when they described Sisseton and Wahpeton leaders in 1823. They were stately and dignified, several supposedly over six feet tall. Most seemed young and dashing, a stark contrast to the Mdewakanton Red Wing, who when speaking for his band begged Long that "some of his 'Great Father's milk' [whiskey] might be given them to gladden their hearts."[46]

The members of the Long party took only a cursory glance at the Indians they visited. Had they probed deeper into evolving Indian-white relations in the region, they would have discovered that the Sissetons and Wahpetons were also far more independent of government action. The fort had to some extent intimidated the Mdewakanton bands living near its walls, but the failure of the government to spread its influence much beyond the vicinity of Fort Snelling is convincing evidence of the restricted scope of overall Dakota decline.

The limitations on military influence became evident in September 1820, when army officials learned that the Blue Earth River Sissetons had killed two of Manuel Lisa's traders on the Missouri River. Colonel Snelling dispatched a messenger to invite their chiefs to the agency for a council, where he promptly charged the leaders with the murders. The chiefs did not deny the affair and *"reluctantly"* agreed to leave two hostages at Fort Snelling until the perpetrators gave themselves up. But not long after the two warriors had been incarcerated, they made it known to their guards that they needed to step outside the gate "for a necessary occasion." Once beyond the confines of the still incomplete walls, the two men made their escape.[47]

All Snelling could now do was caution against dealing with the Sissetons and send word advising them to live up to their initial agreement. He soon found, however, that his lack of ties with these people hindered diplomatic progress. Snelling then turned to Colin Campbell, son of Archibald John Campbell, who agreed to approach the Sissetons again. Surprisingly, the warriors from the guilty village returned to the fort, and their war chief turned over one of the murderers and prepared to take the blame for the second, his own son, upon himself. In a ceremony symbolic of submission to American authority, both men surrendered to Colonel Snelling. An Indian carrying a British flag led the procession, followed by the murderer and his chief, "their arms pinioned, and large splinters of wood thrust through them above the elbows." Colonel Snelling, who recorded the scene, thought this demonstration was meant to show his men that Sissetons did not fear pain, death, or the Americans. The murderer "wore a large British medal" around his neck but carried skins in his hands as an offering. Both men sang their death songs, and the Sissetons that followed behind joined in the chorus.[48]

Colonel Snelling ordered the British flag burned, and as the murderer gave up his medal a blacksmith stepped forward and "ironed" him. When the chief also offered his wrists the colonel graciously refused, saying that he would simply remain a hostage. The guilty man was soon sent to St. Louis for trial, but the secretary of war, touched by the old chief's demonstration of love for his son, ordered his release. Most military officials agreed that the surrender itself and the punishment of one man provided sufficient restitution.[49] Of course the government at the time failed to realize that the submission represented the influence of Colin Campbell and his kinship ties rather than respect for the American military. It also seems clear from the exchange that the Sissetons came to the fort hoping to establish fictive ties with Snelling. It must have shocked them when he seemed to accept the offer and then took their young man away. Allies would not act in such a fashion.

Snelling's actions failed to make a lasting impression on the western Dakotas. Throughout the summer of 1821 most of their leaders simply avoided the Americans at Fort Snelling, and those who did show up to council with Taliaferro often demonstrated a decided preference for the British. Some Mdewakantons did not help matters. Shakopee sent alarming messages up the Minnesota River, emphasizing the unfriendly nature of the soldiers and the agent. He seemed intent upon keeping the Sissetons isolated, or perhaps he was still disgruntled over the small number of presents he had received from Forsyth in 1819.[50] British officials in Canada also felt disposed to meddle in affairs south of the border. After 1819 the Northwest Company supplied the métis Joseph Renville, who had a post in the vicinity of Lake Traverse. He reportedly flew the British flag at his establishment and supposedly had threatened to use whiskey to incite the Indians against the Americans should they interfere in his trade. But after the consolidation of the Hudson's Bay Company and the North West Company in 1821, Canadian authorities gradually withdrew their support, forcing Renville to turn to Mackenzie for goods.[51]

With such intrigue in the west, it is no wonder the western Sioux distrusted Americans and occasionally caused them difficulty. In 1822 a relative of the man sent in chains to St. Louis avenged the insult by attacking a mixed-blood trader along the Minnesota River, and two more American traders were killed on the Missouri by the Sioux a few years later. Yet the most serious crisis developed during the summer of 1823, during Colonel Henry Leavenworth's expedition up the Missouri River. Leavenworth intended to reduce the Arikaras after they had attacked an American trading brigade, but his plan failed and a few Sisseton Sioux began joining the Arikaras in what military officials suspected would be war on the United States. Complicating matters even more, two white deserters from Fort Snelling and two métis were killed below Lake Pepin in July 1824. Although Colonel Snelling received permission from the War Department to train a twelve-man dragoon or mounted force to capture individuals who threatened or took the lives of whites, he was unprepared for a full-scale war.[52]

As these events unfolded, the army reevaluated its role in Sioux country. Considering that fewer than one hundred men were often on active duty at Fort Snelling, it was decided that the colonel would pursue a "defensive" posture, dispersing hostile parties in the immediate vicinity of the fort and protecting boat traffic on the Mississippi.[53] The decision undercut Snelling's ability to protect whites, and the murder of the traders and the men below the fort went unpunished. Thus, white travelers crossing Sioux lands west of Fort Snelling did so at their own risk.

Although many western Dakotas defied the army's efforts to create an arbitrary rule, the Mdewakantons close to the fort remained friendly throughout the early 1820s, primarily because of Taliaferro's kinship ties with the Sioux. These bonds gave him far more influence than Snelling could possibly achieve. They even provided a means for limiting the destructive intertribal warfare that had been disrupting the Sioux-Chippewa border country for nearly a century. The government felt morally obliged to stop the contests. It would be virtually impossible to instill "civilization" in the Indian camps if the raiding continued. Moreover, Secretary of War Calhoun realized that if his cherished removal policy were to be implemented and the Indians east of the Mississippi concentrated west of the river, the intertribal squabbles would have to cease. Woodland tribes would rebel rather than be placed between warring plains enemies. Thus Taliaferro assumed he had a mandate to end the feuding.[54] Unlike the army that acted like a policeman, however, he presented himself to the nearby Mdewakantons as a fatherly adviser who saw peace as the way to a happier life.

The first opportunity to contain the outbursts of violence came in July 1820 when Governor Lewis Cass appeared at St. Peter's Agency with 150 Chippewa chiefs and braves ready to treat with the Sioux. Taliaferro quickly cast his support behind the council, informing Colonel Leavenworth, who was still in command at Fort Snelling, that he would conduct the parlays on his own with Cass. Dakota and Chippewa delegations met on 31 July and concluded a peace. Trowbridge, who recorded the events, noted that both sides proclaimed that the agreement should be as "lasting as the sun." Since only segments of both nations were present, however, Trowbridge remained skeptical about the lasting effect of the accord.[55]

The agreement of 1820 was one in a long line of discussions between the Sioux and Chippewas that thereafter occurred annually at the agency. These treaties never ended the violence, yet they did have an important effect on the intertribal relations for the Mdewakantons, limiting their feuds with the Chippewas to an occasional attack on an isolated hunting party. In 1821, for example, several discussions took place during the summer. One went on for five days and attracted 450 Chippewas and 395 Sioux. Another major treaty was negotiated in 1823 with similar numbers of delegates present.[56] During the latter council, which had a carnival atmosphere, the Dakotas formed a line 150 yards long and approached the Chippewas with flags flying, "singing the peace song." The Chippewas then advanced chanting the "brave's song" and gently pressed hips with their Dakota counterparts. With this pageantry out of the way, everyone shook hands, smoked pipes to create fictive bonds, and pledged to remain at peace.[57]

During these affairs the Campbell brothers acted as interpreters, translating the Chippewa into English and Dakota, and vice-versa. Taliaferro acted as compromiser, reaffirming the agreements each year with large numbers of presents. The Dakota band chiefs Little Crow, Penichon, Black Dog, and "Kocomoko" frequently spoke during these discussions, expressing their strong desire for peace. "We about here [the fort], wish to be good children," Penichon pointed out at one juncture. Kocomoko reiterated these views, saying that he felt "every man of sense in the Sioux Nation" ought to accept Taliaferro's advice and end the war. Black Dog also had few reservations about the value of Taliaferro's counsel. "We have been a long time at war," he noted, "but since our Father [Taliaferro] came into our Nation, our young men have sense, and our wives and children rest quiet."[58] These were not empty words. Taliaferro's kinship network gave him legitimate influence with these people individually as well as within their political system. He also had convinced them that they could better exploit the debated zones by remaining at peace with the Chippewas.

The agent's counsel meant less to the western Dakotas, no doubt because they lived beyond the effective range of Taliaferro's kinship network and received fewer presents than those Indians living near the fort. But it is also unlikely that verbal and economic coercion would have done much good. The troubles in the west were mainly with the Sacs and Foxes who lived in the lower Des Moines River valley. Because of their increasing destitution, they needed to wrest from the western Dakota tribes game preserves on the upper portion of the river. In 1822 alone, nearly one hundred casualties occurred in engagements fought over the valley. The fighting had become so intense that the War Department had even asked Congress for authority to use troops in stopping it. But Congress would not approve the bill, and the army had to settle for the same defensive strategy on the Des Moines as it had used on the Minnesota River.[59]

Without effective military help the burden of ending the feuds continued to fall upon the Indian agents. After the early failures, Taliaferro decided in 1823 to take the Sioux leaders to Washington for consultations with the secretary of war. The agent hoped that touring the capital and other American cities would overawe them. It took time to organize the trip, and the delegation did not depart until the summer of 1824. Unfortunately, few western Dakotas joined the group, and Taliaferro's good intentions also suffered when the Sacs and Foxes killed the Wahpekute chief Cloud, one of the delegates. He had left the riverboat carrying the delegation to return home and met his fate near Charles Bay, Missouri. Nonetheless, not all of Taliaferro's plans went astray; while in Washington he convinced Calhoun to call for another, much larger conclave to be held the next summer at Prairie du Chien.[60]

Governor Cass and the superintendent of Indian affairs, William

Clark, opened the Prairie du Chien council in August. They spoke to delegates from many different tribes including the Dakotas, Sacs and Foxes, Chippewas, Menominees, and Winnebagos. More than three hundred Sioux representatives alone made the trip. Clark set an unusual tone by loudly declaring that the government wanted no Indian land. Rather, its representatives had come to create a lasting peace. After arguing that the western Indians were responsible for their own suffering, Clark proposed to put an end to the feuds by drawing tribal boundaries.[61] The lines would define hunting territories and supposedly end the causes for most disputes.

The various delegates quickly gave their consent and outlined their domains. Chippewa spokesmen claimed virtually all the land east of the Mississippi River. In the west they argued for a boundary that commenced at Crow River and included the Sauk River watershed. Little Crow and Shakopee angrily protested. The former argued that his band controlled lands up to the St. Croix and Chippewa Falls, regions fifty miles east of the Mississippi. Shakopee, on the other hand, considered both the Sauk and Crow Wing rivers north of the Mississippi to be his hunting ground. Similar conflicts erupted with the Sacs and Foxes, who claimed a boundary extending from the Upper Iowa River, above Prairie du Chien, to a point on the Sioux River, fifty miles above present-day Sioux City, Iowa. The Wahpekute chief Tasaugye objected, forcefully asserting that his people had always hunted down the Des Moines to the Raccoon Fork. From these descriptions, Clark obviously realized that the contested zone in the north encompassed a stretch of land fifty to eighty miles wide running through western Wisconsin and central Minnesota. In the south, the debated zones practically equaled the northern half of the state of Iowa.[62]

Clark and Cass encouraged compromise during the second week of the council. They assumed that tribal spokesmen had exaggerated claims to allow for bargaining. But good maps of the region were nonexistent, and government negotiators had little idea of how to recognize a legitimate claim. Regardless, any compromise agreed to by leaders while being boarded and cajoled by whites would hardly be acceptable to the rank and file of any of the tribes at home.[63] Nonetheless, lines were ultimately drawn to separate the contending tribes. The Chippewa-Sioux boundary split the difference between each of the claims, but the unknown geography of the Des Moines watershed made it difficult to create a fair line in the south. The boundary that was finally agreed to supposedly ran through the "second fork" of the Des Moines River to the mouth of the Sioux River on the Missouri. The Wahpekutes, however, had always considered the "second fork" to be the Raccoon River, whereas Clark later contended that it was actually a smaller stream well above the Raccoon. When the Wahpekutes realized the mistake and protested, Clark refused to accept their version despite Taliaferro's agreement with it. Surveyors recognized Clark's error in the 1830s and diplomatically referred to his river as the "second or upper fork" so as not to confuse it with the real one.[64]

In the final days of the meetings, government officials liberally handed out rations and alcohol to demonstrate their good faith and generosity. But the celebrations soon soured when several of the delegates came down with "intermittent" fevers. Prairie du Chien lay in a marsh that was prone to visitations of malaria. As the sick Sioux and Chippewa delegates left for home, fur traders were entrusted to assist them. Several of the most debilitated were unfortunately abandoned for dead along the Mississippi. The Sisseton leaders decided that the government had plotted against them. Taliaferro hurried to counter such rumors with more whiskey and presents. Such an inauspicious beginning to the peace policy, however, did not surprise some white observers. Although Taliaferro and Clark seemed confident of success, Governor Cass remained skeptical. He privately told James Lockwood that the Indians would go to war as soon as "they were ready."[65]

The hostilities Cass had predicted began in the fall of 1826 when French Crow, a Wahpekute chief living with Wabasha's people, led a war party against the Chippewas that killed and scalped one lone hunter. Taliaferro quickly sent word of the attack to Clark, but he failed to receive instructions. The government had made a treaty, but it had not created the machinery necessary to punish violators. Meanwhile the agent counciled with the Sioux, telling them he would "shut his door forever" against French Crow. "My heart beats strong for the welfare and happiness of every soul of your Nation," he declared.[66]

While most Mdewakanton chiefs agreed with him, many young warriors did not. They had yet to prove their valor in war so as to gain recognition in their bands. The opportunity to demonstrate their courage came on 27 May 1827 when a group of Chippewas arrived at St. Peter's Agency to discuss the newly announced transfer of their land to the control of Henry Schoolcraft's Michigan Superintendency. As usual the Chippewas traded brown sugar and bark canoes with the Sioux during the discussions and invited their customers to a feast that evening. Shortly after 9 P.M., several Mdewakanton and Wahpeton warriors left the Chippewa encampment that had been set up for the night just below the walls of Fort Snelling. After walking no more than thirty paces, they wheeled and fired into the tents, killing two Chippewas and severely wounding others. The incident enraged Taliaferro and Colonel Snelling, since it had occurred directly under the American flag. It was a challenge to their authority and to the peace process.[67]

The agent had the wounded rushed to the council house, where a Chippewa warrior, Strong Earth, supposedly made an impassioned plea for justice. Colonel Snelling recorded the speech in his diary: "Father, *look at your floor*," the chief began, "it is stained with the blood of my people, shed under your walls. . . . If you are a great & powerful people why do you not protect us? If not, of what use are all these soldiers?"[68] Snelling promptly sent the speech off to General Henry Atkinson, noting, perhaps with some satisfaction, that the "transaction" that had taken place was a good example of the "efficacy" of Indian treaties, negotiated at huge expense to the American people. But the colonel also seemed distraught over his own inability to handle the Indians. The army might as well have "Men of *Straw* with wooden *guns* and *swords*" at Fort Snelling, he moaned, rather than an immobile infantry regiment with orders to remain in a defensive posture.[69]

The crisis quickly turned to a showdown the next morning when a large group of Dakota warriors appeared in front of the garrison showing little or no remorse over the incident. Snelling sent out two well-armed companies that secured nearly a dozen captives. Although Taliaferro guaranteed them their safety if they came peaceably, the colonel, still furious, gave the captives three days to turn over the guilty parties or face the gallows. Cooler heads prevailed, and four men were handed over who supposedly had participated in the attack. Two came from Shakopee's band, and the others were Wahpetons from the Little Rapids of the Minnesota River. Snelling gave these men to the Chippewas, who graciously allowed them the opportunity to run for their lives. All four were cut down and scalped in front of the garrison.[70]

Taliaferro expected war with the Sioux to result from these actions. Yet he grudgingly sustained Snelling. Clark and General Atkinson also gave the colonel a strong commendation for his decisive actions.[71] Snelling's response seemed ill-timed a month later, when news arrived that the Winnebagos had risen against white miners in what was later called Red Bird's Outbreak. Government supply boats were attacked on the Mississippi, and one nearly fell into the hands of the Indians. Rumors circulated almost immediately implicating the Sioux in the war. Thus when Colonel Snelling prepared to reopen the river, he drew up plans to burn Wabasha's village to the ground should he encounter any resistance. He also wrote Taliaferro that the agent should anticipate the evacuation of Fort Snelling. The Colonel expected *"Indian War & Nothing Short."*[72]

Strong sympathy for the Winnebagos existed at Wabasha's camp. Notwithstanding, Snelling did not come to blows with these warriors. The Winnebagos had been abused by whites for some time, and the attack on the boats was reportedly triggered when several Indian women were kidnapped by soldiers. But at no time did Wabasha's followers show any unified desire to assist their Siouan neighbors. Wabasha moved to the Red Cedar River in an obvious endeavor to stay clear of the problem, and four Dakota men from his faction appeared at St. Peter's Agency to declare their neutrality. Only a handful of Dakota men seemed implicated, several of whom had intermarried with the Winnebagos and regularly allowed their kinsmen to hunt on lands claimed by Wabasha's band. They quickly sent pleas for assistance to Dakota relatives near Fort Snelling and on the Minnesota River.[73]

Among Dakota warriors above Wabasha's village, Snelling's actions still rankled when requests for assistance arrived. Those who supported hostilities generally came from Shakopee's village, the home of two of the men executed in May, and from among the Wahpetons and Sissetons. Several of their war chiefs considered accepting the war belts that came from the Winnebagos. But Taliaferro received daily reports from Mdewakantons close by about the actions of the agitated factions, and his network continued to function throughout the crisis. The agent learned, for example, that the uncle of one of the men shot at Fort Snelling, a member of Shakopee's band, had held a feast in which he swore to kill "our Father [Taliaferro] . . . and Campbell."[74] Under the Dakota kinship system, he was duty bound either to protect his brother's son or to avenge his death. Fortunately, the Winnebagos came to terms with the United States late in the summer, and the popularity of resistance waned.

Sioux timidity is explained in part by their hunters' strong dependence on commercialism. Both hostile and friendly elements realized that a war would sever contact with traders. The son of old Red Wing spoke for the friendly group, insisting in council with Taliaferro that he must "keep open the *Road* for their traders."[75] But even Wabasha's war chief, Lark, a man closely related to the Winnebagos, eventually pleaded that the traders not be removed from his village. In finishing his speech he noted that the plains Sioux could "jump on their horses & with their bows & arrows . . . kill what they want."[76] His people were no longer so fortunate and needed guns and ammunition to kill small game so as to survive.

Taliaferro, on the other hand, pointed to his moderating role in the crisis. Although government officials probably viewed his claim as boasting, his kinship bonds clearly played a decisive role in forestalling violence. He had given presents on a much larger scale during the crisis, especially to the relatives of the men executed at the fort. This reinforcement of kinship obligations made it difficult for hostile elements to forge a consensus. In a final report to Washington, written in October, Taliaferro emphasized the "great want of unanimity" in Sioux camps as a primary reason war leaders failed to organize resistance.[77] While the agent had no illusions about the seriousness of the events of 1827, realizing full well that a clash had been narrowly averted, he did believe that his influence with the eastern Sioux had been crucial in preventing trouble.

The events of 1827 illustrate the increase of social and economic pressures that American occupation and consistent trade brought upon the Sioux. Yet the Dakota people had adapted well to the new conditions, primarily because of their historical reliance upon mobile food gathering and their social flexibility. They had socially incorporated white traders, allowing them to become members of Dakota society, and government officials for the most part used trader connections and presents to effect similar relations. The only exceptions to this were certain military figures, and even they tried to remain on friendly terms with the Indians, though at times they did not know how to reinforce kinship bonds. Fortunately, when reciprocity seemed on the verge of collapse, as in 1827, Taliaferro used his kinship network to defuse the troubles.

More important, as the 1820s went by, relations between Indians and whites on the upper Mississippi became more stable. Peace councils like the one in 1825 provided an opportunity for most Dakota leaders to meet and discuss problems with whites. To be sure, there were misunderstandings, even when professionals like William Clark were in charge, but by and large each passing year provided the Indians an opportunity to create those individual ties that were at the core of peaceful Dakota contact with outsiders. Consequently, a transformation took place in which soldiers who sat by

Taliaferro's side during council discussions gradually benefited from his kinship network. When Sioux Indians later met these men alone on the Mississippi, the two groups smoked, ate together, and parted friends, despite the fact that they had had little previous contact. This was much different from Father Hennepin's confrontation with the Sioux a century and a half before.

The occupation of Fort Snelling, on the other hand, occurred at a time of accelerated social and economic change. For the most part the alterations were self-induced, with Sioux hunters going out of their way to obtain whiskey and to work within the maximization scheme begun by traders. Yet even though the hunting of large numbers of muskrats illustrates ecological decline, the Dakotas saw their traders as more essential to their survival than ever before. The pressures of the 1820s were nonacculturative, for they placed little strain on the evolving friendship of Dakota and white leaders despite the troubles of 1827. The minority of warriors who wished to punish the whites during the Red Bird Outbreak had an obligation to avenge the men who were handed over to the Chippewas. Their quarrel was not with American occupation, but with the whites who had been personally responsible for the deaths of their kinsmen.

For their part, Taliaferro and Clark were concerned about the dwindling game, the growing use of alcohol, and the intertribal feuds. Both had selfish reasons, since problems of this sort made their job of controlling the Sioux more difficult. But Taliaferro also hoped to steer the Dakotas clear of the degradation that the more eastern tribes had already suffered. He knew that as Mdewakanton bands hunted farther west each fall and summer the time was fast approaching when massive changes would be necessary to prevent starvation and possibly extinction. Clark, too, was worried about the Sioux. He realized that even though the Dakota hunter continued to think of himself as a free spirit, ecological changes would soon force him into an awkward and dangerous era in his history. "This period," he wrote in 1826, "is that in which he ceases to be a hunter, from the extinction of game, and before he gets the means of living, from the produce of flocks and agriculture."[78]

The eastern Sioux were rapidly approaching this watershed. Despite the weakness of the American garrison and the seemingly unobstructed sovereignty of the Sioux people, government plans would soon be inaugurated to transform the sacred weapons of the Dakota hunter into the tools of the husbandman. It would be difficult indeed to convince warriors to incorporate such a foreign program, since nothing in their past relations with white men had prepared them for it. Euroamericans had previously reinforced Indian culture rather than trying to change it. The success of this transformation would rest to a large measure on the smooth implementation of government programs that preserved as many as possible of the traditional mechanisms of native interethnic relations.

7

The Origins of Government Paternalism, 1827–36

The confrontation at Fort Snelling in 1827 presaged a new era of tensions between whites and Indians on the upper Mississippi. Mounting economic difficulties underlay the trouble, as animal resources continued to decline, forcing intense competition among Indians for game. By the mid-1830s, only buffalo and muskrats remained in numbers worth commercial exploitation, and most of these were in the west. The struggle at the fort also symbolized the expanding role of the federal government, which was on the verge of implementing a new policy regarding Indian-white relations. Often called after its foremost proponent, President Andrew Jackson, the policy had two major tenets: the peaceful settlement of the west by Euroamericans and either the acculturation or the forced removal of tribes that delayed white expansion. Dakota social and political institutions faced inevitable pressures as a result of this settlement and the policy attending it. The eastern Sioux were soon to be swept into a period of complex negotiations with government officials that inaugurated a new phase of intercultural relations.

Despite the premise of cultural disruption and land alienation that characterized Jackson's Indian policy, in its inception it was politically essential and relatively humane. Jacksonians borrowed heavily from Thomas Jefferson, who placed Indians on an equal plane with white Americans and attributed obvious dissimilarities to environmental influences. Jeffersonian paternalists felt that the "noble savage" could be transformed from savagery to civilization, which in practical terms meant turning a hunter into a farmer. Yet cultural prejudices among most westerners denied the Indian acceptance into the American mainstream, and in practice acculturation became secondary to dispossession, or removal beyond the Mississippi. For many tribes this meant giving up woodland homes for the foreign environs of the plains.[1]

Most Dakota villages were beyond the artificial border established by proponents of removal. Yet the Mdewakantons did hold some land east of the Mississippi, and it would not be long before the policy affected Sioux claims to what is today northern Iowa. Although the Dakota people initially had little to fear from Jackson's programs, they increasingly felt the influence of removal policy as federal officials urged the Sioux to halt intertribal warfare, sell "excess" lands, and take up farming. In addition, Washington bureaucrats were often joined in these endeavors by local officials and fur traders, who manipulated Dakota kinship connections and used annuities and presents to promote their own self-interest as well as removal policies.

Paternalistic concern for the Sioux began in the late 1820s when officials in Washington realized that neither acculturation nor removal could occur without the suppression of intertribal warfare. Indeed, the immediate goal of removing the Sacs, Foxes, Winnebagos, and Menominees west of the Mississippi depended upon providing a peaceful atmosphere in Iowa; besides, most officials agreed that tribal feuds were degenerative and should be prevented for moral reasons.[2] Agent Taliaferro had tried, with mixed results, to halt the fighting. He had learned that though presents, kinship bonds, and good counsel were enough to influence bands living near Fort Snelling, these tactics failed with more distant villages. Thus government policymakers pressed for stronger measures to end tribal feuding along the Mississippi and to the west.

As the War Department pondered alternatives, intertribal strife over debated zones intensified, stimulated in part by a monumental change then under way in the commercial trading system. In 1827 John Jacob Astor and Ramsay Crooks came to terms with the small group of competitors who remained in the Mississippi watershed.

Bernard Pratt and Pierre Chouteau reached an agreement with them first over the division of the upper Missouri region, including the territory lying west of Lake Traverse. Kenneth Mackenzie of the Columbia Fur Company gave in shortly thereafter, leaving Astor and Crooks masters of the entire Dakota trade. By fall, eastern Sioux hunters faced a monopoly that brought an immediate drop in the value of their pelts, a decline in presents, and an increase in the price of goods.[3]

This commercial concentration quickly altered the trading process. The new monopoly made it almost impossible for Indians to take credits from one merchant and sell their pelts to another. Rolette even constructed contractual agreements that defined the villages and specific hunters assigned to each of his brigades; conducting business with an Indian belonging to someone else could result in a $200 fine.[4] The commercial process actually went beyond maximization by the 1830s; try as they might, most Sioux men could no longer consistently feed their families from the chase.

Along with declining game, there were substantial changes in the cost of goods. Taliaferro indicated that some markups in 1828 rose from 100 to 200 percent: "30 muskrats equal to $7.25 was paid for 1 tin kettle holding 2½ gallons—first cost $2.25 at Bailly trading H[ouse]," he recorded. A musket worth about $6 now sold for 110 rats, or about $18.[5] The inflation made it increasingly difficult for hunters to pay their credits each spring. A credit list for 1828, for example, illustrates that, of sixteen men who received goods in the fall, none were able to pay their full debts in the spring. The repayment rate for the group averaged only 58 percent of the debt each hunter owed.[6] The failure to pay credits prompted traders to be more niggardly in the fall with the least successful men.

Dakota hunters first complained to Taliaferro about the new policy in November 1827. According to the agent, many objections came from "very respectable persons" who realized that without company competition they faced exploitation. In January of the new year, Wahpeton hunters from the Sauk River traveled overland to tell Taliaferro that Louis Provençalle no longer provided for their needs and even refused to give powder to some men. The Wahpekute chief Tasaugye appeared in April and dejectedly asserted that his trader "could not supply more than one-half [of his band's men] & the rest starved." Not surprisingly, resistance to the selective crediting of hunters erupted; angry warriors killed Provençalle's clerk in March 1829 over the credit issue.[7]

Faced with a declining economy, many Dakotas either returned to a more subsistence-oriented lifeway or pushed deeper into debated zones, clashing with the Sacs and Foxes and the Chippewas over pelts.[8] By 1829 Wanmdisapa, Tasaugye's nephew, spoke bluntly to Taliaferro of the dilemma his people faced. "Traders we want," he began, "but it appears to me that to get skins they wish to push us into the Jaws of our enemies." Wanmdisapa's wife was decapitated by a large Sac and Fox raiding party in April 1829, and the raids and counterraids that followed throughout the summer caused several dozen casualties. After the death of his wife, Wanmdisapa requested that the agent force the Sacs and Foxes to surrender the murderers as the army had done with his people in 1827 at Fort Snelling. An embarrassed Taliaferro could not explain how it was that the Americans lived so close to the Sacs and Foxes along the lower reaches of the Des Moines River and yet could not stop their war parties.[9]

Whereas the Wahpekutes expressed disenchantment with government officers for failing to enforce the treaty agreements of 1825, some Mdewakanton leaders felt the treaties worked to their disadvantage. The need to defend hunting grounds lay at the root of their aversion. "We made peace to please you," Little Crow told the agent in June 1829, "but if we are badly off we must blame you for causing us to give up so much of our lands to our enemies." Black Dog likewise expressed resentment over the tendency of the Chippewas to take advantage of the peace process. "If we had been left as we were," he concluded, "we could have hunted our game & disposed of our enemies whenever they came our way."[10]

As officials sought diplomatic solutions to the feuds, most agreed that they resulted from the government's failure to adequately survey the 1825 treaty boundaries. Joseph Street, the Winnebago agent, adhered to this basic view, although in a detailed letter to Washington he added that the government ought to create buffer zones between the contending tribes and eventually place eastern Indians, such as the Winnebagos, on them.[11] Secretary of War John Eaton apparently liked this plan, especially as it applied to the Sioux and the Sacs and Foxes. In the fall of 1829 his office authorized Clark to organize another council to be held at Prairie du Chien to implement such a policy. This time, however, Washington officials made it clear that Colonel Willoughby Morgan at Fort Crawford (Prairie du Chien) would handle the negotiations. The last-minute change from Indian Bureau personnel to a military officer reflected the growing belief in Washington that army participation would be necessary to pacify the tribes.[12]

Clark seemed pleased with the proposed role of the military, since he wrote Taliaferro that "the government is determined to interfere in the [intertribal] wars."[13] The commitment came none too soon. A month before the tribes met, a large party of Sioux and Menominees surprised a Fox delegation ten miles below Prairie du Chien and killed ten of their ambassadors. The incident understandably stirred up the Sacs and Foxes, whom Clark felt were none too ready to end the fighting; they seemed to be winning the upper Des Moines River from the Sioux, and they desperately needed these hunting grounds. Complicating the issues, white miners had crossed the Mississippi and settled on Fox lands near present-day Dubuque. Thus the Sacs and Foxes were nearly as angry with the whites as they were with the Sioux.[14]

The military soothed these feelings by driving off the white miners and having troops escort the delegates to the council grounds. Nonetheless, when the council convened in July many leaders were missing from every tribe. The Wahpekutes, for example, had no recognized chiefs on the grounds, yet the government anticipated purchasing lands from them for the proposed "neutral" ground. The western Chippewas and the Sissetons, contenders for the Ottertail Lake country of central Minnesota, also avoided the discussions. Even more discouraging, once the council got under way the speeches degenerated into a barrage of recriminations, each side blaming the other. Colonel Morgan remained undeterred, concluding that "the government has come to the resolution of enforcing peace between the Indians ... not only from consideration of humanity, but with the view of favouring the policy of emigration." He threatened the Indian leaders with military action, telling them that he would "march an army" into their country and chastise those who refused to accept the peace.[15]

In essence, the army pledged to end intertribal hostilities at the Prairie du Chien treaty of 1830. The assembled tribes, in turn, agreed that violators of the general peace would be punished by the government.[16] Finally, American officials purchased a tract of land extending twenty miles on each side of the Sac-Fox-Sioux boundary line of 1825 to serve as a neutral zone separating these contending peoples. The Wahpekute French Crow, who had for some years lived with Wabasha's Mdewakanton band, represented his tribe in the negotiations for the land. In exchange for the zone, the eastern Sioux received a yearly annuity of $2,000.[17]

As tidy as the treaty seemed, it was hopelessly flawed. Besides securing a land purchase from representatives not empowered to sell, the War Department soon realized that enforcing the peace would be difficult and expensive. The first violation occurred as the council broke up when Medicine Bottle, a warrior from Little Crow's band, led a party up the St. Croix River and killed five Chippewa hunters. Although Medicine Bottle and his followers were temporarily imprisoned at Fort Crawford, the cost of holding them soon brought their release.[18] The next series of raids erupted in the west, where Taliaferro and Clark had tried to negotiate compliance with the peace process. By autumn Colonel Morgan had received so many reports of violations that he deemed it militarily impossible to apprehend those responsible. Even more disheartening, by the summer of 1831 disgruntled Sac and Fox warriors carried intertribal disputes to the gates of military establishments, surprising a Menominee camp within earshot of Prairie du Chien and brutally murdering twenty-four people. Although some warriors were arrested, they too were soon freed like their Sioux counterparts. No laws existed for trying Indians charged with intertribal warfare, a final oversight in the 1830 negotiation.[19]

Many officials realized that resource depletion figured heavily in the warfare. An army patrol sent into the upper Des Moines watershed in the fall of 1831 reported that the Wahpekutes relied almost entirely on game. They had to hunt in the debated zones or else face starvation; accordingly, they suffered substantial losses in defending these lands.[20] Similar conditions applied northwest of St. Peter's Agency as the Wahpetons and Sissetons engaged in a life-and-death struggle with the Chippewas to control the headwaters of the Sauk and Crow river valleys. Members of Renville's soldiers' lodge ransacked Benjamin Baker's Chippewa post on Crow Wing Island in February 1833 in an obvious attempt to discourage Chippewa competitors. The incident provoked a series of letters between Washington officials and local traders regarding Renville's influence with the Wahpetons near his post. Renville's brother-in-law had headed the raid and his brother Victor was killed by Chippewa warriors as the party returned home, providing a stimulus for further retaliation.[21]

Now aware of the inability of the military to deal effectively with such trouble, the commissioner of Indian affairs ordered Taliaferro to demand that Renville surrender the marauders. When Renville hedged, Taliaferro suggested that the government either recall all traders or send in a military force. Army officials chose the latter course and ordered Lieutenant Colonel Zachary Taylor at Fort Crawford (Prairie du Chien) to "separate the Sioux and Chippewa" and arrest Renville. Taylor objected, writing General Atkinson that his limited force of "one hundred and fifty men, marching between two hostile tribes of Indians, consisting of several thousand warriors, would have rather the effect of producing a contemptible opinion of our power." A fortuitous outbreak of cholera incapacitated his regiment and allowed the future president to throw the problem back into Taliaferro's lap. The agent finally managed to convince the disgruntled Wahpetons to meet with the Chippewas at the headwaters of the Crow River and conclude a brief peace.[22]

By 1834 nothing seemed to indicate that the first necessary element of the Jackson policy—the peace process—was working. Nevertheless, Indian Bureau personnel continued to give lip service to the 1830 treaty in the west. The Sioux-Sac-Fox boundary was finally surveyed in 1833, and the Chippewa line was completed to Ottertail Lake two years later. Neither of these efforts produced much change, despite a decline of fighting in the south brought about primarily because of Sac and Fox losses suffered during the Black Hawk War of 1832. Indeed, the peace process seemed to take a decided step backward when the War Department asked a large Sioux contingent to join them against the Sacs and Foxes and the Dakota warriors surprised and massacred nearly one hundred Sac and Fox people above Prairie du Chien. The Chippewa line also was disputed by both sides, and angry hunters moved the survey stakes as quickly as they were set.[23]

While Taliaferro and military officials struggled to enforce the peace, the efforts became more difficult every year and often led to confrontations similar to that of 1827. One incident occurred in 1835 when the agent sent friendly Indians to Shakopee's village to arrest several men who had killed three Chippewas. The warriors at the village were inebriated and celebrating the scalp dance when the agent's envoys arrived. Unable to effect an arrest, Taliaferro requested an army patrol. Before the troops arrived, Shakopee's people cut their corn and fled up the Minnesota River to Lac qui Parle. Ultimately, the agent had to call on trader Joseph Renville to bring in the troublemakers.[24] Taliaferro's alternative was to take hostages and exchange them for the men sought by the military, a measure that now created tensions between officials and Indians previously friendly to the government.

Although well intentioned, the peace initiatives of 1830–35 had little chance of success in light of the crumbling fur trade economy. With the 1827 merger, the commercial system based upon reciprocal exchange had been replaced by a corporate monopoly that cared little about the hunter or his family. The most immediate change was the increasing tendency of traders to resort to fraud or alcohol to increase profits. Although declining company competition made using liquor unnecessary, it provided a cheap alternative to more durable goods.

Whiskey naturally compounded problems for Taliaferro and the Sioux, encouraging intertribal fighting and a general disregard for government policy. The agent fumed over the loopholes in the federal laws designed to stop its importation. In August 1830 he finally issued an independent proclamation prohibiting the use of all spirits within his agency. Clark sympathized with the idea, as did the commissioner of Indian affairs, but neither felt the proclamation had any legality.[25] The uproar the agent created did convince the army to once again encourage military officers to search trade canoes. Prodded by superiors, Captain W. J. Jouett at Fort Snelling stopped two caravans of trade goods in August 1832 under the commands of Louis Provençalle and Hazen Mooers. The searches netted eleven and six kegs of whiskey, respectively. In all, Jouett surmised that he had taken the equivalent of five hundred gallons, once the contents of the barrels were diluted with water.[26] Ironically, a month earlier Congress finally had passed a new intercourse law that in effect made Taliaferro's proclamation the law of the land. Thereafter, traders wisely bypassed the fort and instead shipped liquor via the Des Moines River. However, the easiest way to avoid the law was to invite Dakota hunters down to Prairie du Chien each year to receive a liquid "present."

After officials clamped down on the use of liquor, the American Fur Company introduced more stringent retrenchment policies. Gifts at the start of the hunting season now went only to the heads of influential families who could help in the collection of furs. In this fashion kinship responsibilities were maintained with a portion of the Dakota population at minimum cost. Even the amount and type of credits given these people were curtailed; Rolette, for example, decided to give out only powder and tools needed for hunting and often refused even these necessities.[27] Obviously Sioux hunters, who had become accustomed to receiving new outfits of tools and arms each fall, found it difficult to adjust to the change. Traders next turned to repossessing goods that had not been fully paid for with spring returns. Repossession had occurred on a minor scale during the 1820s, but it escalated under the company monopoly, since traders no longer had to be concerned about hunters' abandoning them for other traders. Taliaferro recognized that credited goods came to the Sioux hunters at three times their original price. Yet he counseled the Indians to pay their debts and even allowed his interpreters to help collect items in spring 1832. By June Dakota leaders complained vociferously of the practice; Little Crow stated that "it would be better at once to knock us in the head—than to starve us to death." Without guns, knives, or hatchets, his men had no way of procuring food until these items were reissued for the fall hunts.[28]

Taliaferro handed out a few fishhooks and lines to alleviate suffering in 1832, even though he realized that fish had never been a mainstay of the Sioux diet. But the problem reappeared the following spring, forcing Taliaferro to resort to another proclamation. He informed traders that if they suffered assault at the hands of Indians while in the process of taking back goods, the government would not protect them. Reaction came quickly: Joseph R. Brown, a clerk working for Bailly, was stabbed at Red Wing's village; Jean Baptiste Faribault suffered a similar wound near Little Rapids; Wahpekutes looted Bailly's supply wagons near the Des Moines River; finally Faribault, Provençalle, and a few others found that warriors were killing their livestock, the Dakotas in one instance shooting eight hogs and two cows.[29] Clearly, Sioux actions attested to their belief that some traders were no longer living up to kinship obligations. Bailly blamed Taliaferro for the unrest, telling Major John Bliss that the agent's proclamation had put traders "out of protection" and endangered their lives. Taliaferro disagreed, noting that only a handful had suffered losses, mainly those men who persisted in repossessing goods. He gleefully confided in his journal that the Dakotas "did not like these people" anymore. He considered their loss of influence to be his gain.[30]

In defense of the traders, they did have large expenses, and those who worked with Indians in the field made little money. Philander Prescott, for example, noted that even when Indians arrived to pay their debts they expected to be fed for two or three days. Traders generally gave away a thousand meals over the season besides the usual presents and credits. And Indians had a unique view regarding the debts they contracted. "Time does diminish, in their view, the obligation to pay a debt," Prescott noted, "because they say the white people can get goods by merely going after them, or writing for them." In addition, when a trader received new supplies the Indians could not understand why he needed to be paid for the old ones. The Dakotas saw material items as mere conveniences that one should not so much possess as share.[31]

In 1832 most problems over credits were still confined to the Mdewakantons and, to a lesser extent, the Wahpekutes. Joseph Renville at Lac qui Parle, by all accounts, continued to enjoy the strong support of the Sissetons and Wahpetons. His livestock roamed the prairies near his establishment unmolested, and he could generally count on the Indians living nearby to protect him and his family from the Chippewas. Renville's success was derived mostly from the large soldiers' lodge he controlled, manned by relatives with whom he had formed a strong kinship attachment. He still rewarded the loyalty of these warriors with presents and access to credit. Hazen Mooers likewise refused to change, freely giving credit at his Lake Traverse post.[32]

Nevertheless, Renville and Mooers were becoming anachronisms. They identified too closely with native culture, continuing gift-giving even after it had become impractical. The company's pressures on these men to adopt retrenchment increased markedly after Alexis Bailly was replaced as head of the Sioux Outfit. He had finally been caught carting liquor into his posts in 1834, and Taliaferro thereafter refused to grant him a license. The fur company was by this time looking for new blood and sent a young Detroit entrepreneur, Henry Hastings Sibley, to replace Bailly. Whereas Renville and Mooers preferred native life-style Sibley yearned for the city and white civilization. More important, he sought to transform the fur trade into a completely modern business.[33]

Sibley had even less concern for the welfare of the Indian than his predecessor. He viewed the trade as a business rather than as a paternal relationship and he did whatever was necessary to maximize profits. Under him, credits generally were limited to powder, lead, and shot. A handful of Shakopee's men were not even this fortunate, complaining to Taliaferro shortly after Sibley took charge that they could get *"nothing"* from their traders, "not even a flint much less traps & ammunition."[34] The old hunters were most frequently discriminated against. It now took a robust man to chase down increasingly scarce game, and traders simply cut off all goods to older men regardless of their past records. Smoky Day, an old hunter from Traverse des Sioux, considered this unfair since he had killed 3,700 muskrats the year before. "Mr. Bailly used to feel something for us old *fellows*," he disdainfully wrote to Sibley through a translator, "you are a young man and want nothing but Young men."[35]

After curtailing the use of credits in the east, Sibley turned to the upper Minnesota River. In fall 1835 he sent Brown to assist Mooers at Lake Traverse. Actually Brown acted as a spy, reporting in detail how Mooers ran his department. When Mooers's creditors paid only part of their large debt in the spring, Brown wrote Sibley that it resulted from "bad management."[36] Old Mooers was removed from the post he had held for nearly twenty years and replaced by Brown. This prompted a visit to St. Peter's Agency by the Sisseton, Wahpeton, and Yankton hunters who had worked for Mooers. They opposed the firing of their old friend and kinsman and argued that Brown did not care for their welfare. He had prevented them from freely entering his private chambers in the Lake Traverse stockade, and he had held back credits. Consequently, some Dakota Indians took goods from Missouri River traders that fall and avoided Brown.[37]

Disdain for Brown may also have arisen from what George W. Featherstonhaugh, who visited Lake Traverse in 1836, described as Brown's reputation as a "gay deceiver amongst the Indian fair." It seems that Brown had adopted the indecorous practice of taking young Dakota girls as wives and then leaving them. He had already abandoned several women near Fort Snelling and was showering a fourteen-year-old with gifts when Featherstonhaugh arrived. Traders near Lake Michigan had begun the practice in the eighteenth century; exploiting pubescent females lessened the chances of catching disease. While sexual manipulation of Dakota women by whites had yet to become a problem in most eastern Sioux villages, native leaders knew about men like Brown. Unfortunately, their dependency on manufactured goods now precluded their putting a stop to it.[38]

The decline in resources had reached a crisis stage by the mid-1830s. Without the small advances of powder and ball, eastern Dakota hunters realized, their families would starve. The Mdewakantons and Wahpekutes were the hardest hit; an 1834 return shows that between those two peoples only 118 beavers were taken. Deer had likewise dwindled for the more eastern Dakota people to fewer than 600 skins yearly, and Taliaferro reported that hunters returning from the debated zones on the St. Croix River had not killed any in 1836. The number of muskrats taken also peaked in the 1830s, at the same time that prices offered for them fell. They were worth nearly twenty cents early in the decade but slowly fell in value to ten cents by 1840. As animals declined and prices fell, indebtedness rose for the few successful Mdewakantons who could still get credits. Ninety-nine hunters on an 1831 Mdewakanton list owed Bailly 169 muskrats apiece on average at the close of the hunting season. By mid-decade, average indebtedness had risen to more than 400 rats per Indian.[39]

Conditions were better west of Lake Traverse where buffalo were still plentiful, but even there resources seemed to be declining. Brown reported to Sibley in 1836 that his post at the lake would collect eighty packs of bison robes, forty of rats, and two of prime furs. While buffalo seemed numerous, Brown and others realized that many Indians as well as the Red River métis now competed for them. Frequently, this resulted in the animals' being driven far north of Devil's Lake or to the Missouri River, often at the time when they were needed to prevent starvation.[40] The Sissetons and Wahpetons had accordingly become more protective of their hunting zones by 1836, refusing to let even the Mdewakantons use them. After being informed of these restrictions, Sibley made a trip to Traverse des Sioux to mediate, since he had credits among the Mdewakantons, who now depended entirely on western hunting grounds. He had to threaten the upper Sioux with the withdrawal of all company men to convince them to leave the Mdewakantons alone.[41].

The serious economic problems caused a handful of Mdewakanton men to seek alternatives to hunting. Several, including Little Crow and Black Dog, had asked the agent to help them become better farmers before 1830. Taliaferro had responded by acquiring one or two plows for their use.[42] But in 1829 Taliaferro's father-in-law, Cloud Man, approached the agent and requested plows, harnesses, and seed. Cloud Man had traveled west the previous fall and had been caught in a blizzard on his return in the spring. He now felt it was necessary to give up the hunt for farming. Taliaferro helped him select a location for an agricultural village near Lake Calhoun, west of Fort Snelling. The agent named the experiment Eatonville, for the new secretary of war John Eaton. Taliaferro then convinced Philander Prescott, who had been thrown out of work by the merger of the American and Columbia fur companies, to take up residence at Eatonville and instruct the Sioux in farming. Prescott moved his Dakota family, headed by his Mdewakanton father-in-law Keiyah, to the lakeshore and began breaking land in 1830.[43]

This farming community represented the first serious effort to assimilate the Mdewakantons, and it attained some degree of success. The population increased from eight in 1830 to well over one hundred at mid-decade. Crops of all kinds were soon in production, including squash, potatoes, cabbage, pumpkins, and corn. By 1835 the Lake Calhoun people harvested nearly one thousand bushels of corn. Yet most of the surplus food was still not preserved for use in the winter. Taliaferro found that much of it was given to relatives who lived outside the community, showing that traditional values based upon shared resources continued to thrive at Eatonville. The village also lacked root houses for storage, making the production of large surpluses impractical. The only markets for excess produce were the traders and the soldiers at the garrison. Finally, the Indians at Lake Calhoun left periodically to hunt like their Dakota neighbors, abandoning their bark cabins for several months at a time.[44]

Eatonville residents were not agricultural entrepreneurs. If anything, they represented a Dakota subculture. The founders, Cloud Man and Keiyah, had strong kinship alliances with whites, relations that actually subverted their former tribal roles as warriors. Three of Cloud Man's daughters took white husbands and raised mixed-blood families, making his extended family more an appendage of white than of Dakota society. Keiyah also had become a pawn of the Americans around Fort Snelling after his daughter married Prescott. In addition, vaccination records kept by Taliaferro show an inordinate number of women and children in the village, further suggesting the total dependency of the occupants on whites. Many of these women and children were attached to officers or enlisted men at the fort, from whom they received rations.[45]

Taliaferro recognized the vulnerable nature of his little community. He subsidized its members with supplies and tools, frequently purchased out of his own pocket. He also steered as much as possible of the annuity money from the 1830 treaty into Eatonville. Much of the effort is explained by Taliaferro's realization that a successful agricultural experiment would be a symbol to the Dakotas of the benefits of white culture. Taliaferro's resources were limited, however, and he realized that the project would need financial support from the government. Accordingly, he launched a campaign to convince Washington officials that a small investment would bring substantial progress toward "civilization" among the eastern Sioux.[46]

Simultaneously, the agent worked to convince the Sioux that, though a few traders might abandon them, the government would never do so. The $2,000 annuity became a lure to gather native support, since most of the money partially replaced items lost through declining trader support. Taliaferro used the fund to purchase goods that he divided three ways: shares went to Tasaugye's Wahpekutes, Wabasha's Mdewakantons, and the Indians living in the vicinity of the agency. In addition, at Taliaferro's insistence, the treaty set aside

$700 to be used exclusively for agricultural tools. Taliaferro spent this money on plows, livestock, and hoes, most of it going to his friends at Eatonville. Giving plows and oxen to the Dakota men who could best use them constituted an obvious reward for their agricultural progress and reinforced kinship connections.[47]

The example set by the 1830 annuities made many Mdewakanton leaders realize that the government could relieve the economic pressures brought on by declining animal resources. The small allotments of supplies also projected concern on the part of government officials. Even the blacksmith, provided under the treaty, became an immense asset to the Sioux. Wabasha briefly boycotted the annuity distribution when he discovered that the smithy would be established at St. Peter's Agency rather than near his village. The shop produced rat spears, hoes, and metal traps, relieving the Indians of the necessity of purchasing these expensive items from traders. The blacksmith also mended broken guns and kettles. The annuities handed out by the mid-1830s did not end suffering, but they did illustrate to those Indians who received them that the government felt genuine concern for their welfare. They also convinced Sissetons and Wahpetons, who were excluded from the distribution, that treaties offered certain advantages.[48]

No one symbolized this concern more than Taliaferro. He frequently visited the fort to purchase meat and flour for destitute Indians, often using his private funds. He convinced the fort surgeon to help fight epidemics, vaccinating most of the Indians within easy reach of the agency. This did not halt occasional visitations of smallpox, cholera, or malaria, but the eastern Sioux came to trust the agent more deeply than ever before owing to his efforts. His advice became especially valued after an 1836 smallpox epidemic carried off old Wabasha and more than one hundred of his people while villages near the fort suffered only minor losses.[49]

Taliaferro realized that if the eastern Sioux were to survive they needed a stable economy, and he also saw that such a development would lead to intertribal peace. Thus the agent concluded during the spring of 1836 that it was now time for an energetic government to get behind a coordinated acculturation program. He suggested that the Sioux sell more of their land so that the revenue could support the necessary agricultural revolution. He honestly felt that a land sale was essential if the Mdewakantons, who had declined to fewer than 1,400, were to survive as a tribe.[50] Taliaferro knew he would have to convince the Indians of the beneficial nature of his program, yet he had been courting the Dakotas for years with presents, convincing them that the "Great Father" was concerned for their welfare. Not surprisingly, then, when the famous chief Wakinyantanka, or Little Crow III, nearly perished from a snowstorm while hunting in the fall of 1835 and came to Taliaferro begging for a "plough and a yoke of oxen and a man to assist in opening a farm," all the elements of a major cultural transformation seemed to be at hand.[51] Taliaferro felt safe in putting his plan in front of Washington officials.

He opened his campaign to effect a treaty in May 1836, writing to Clark of the Mdewakantons' extreme need for farm tools and instruction. Only a small number of Indians, he asserted, had settled at Eatonville, and it was time to expand upon their modest success. The agent suggested that the Mdewakantons would be willing to give up their lands east of the Mississippi River for the small sum of $192,000, paid in annual installments of $12,000 over sixteen years. Taliaferro had not consulted the Indians about this figure; he had already learned through experience that a larger annuity would only attract white adventurers and whiskey peddlers. The sum proposed, however, would provide the means for agricultural development.[52]

In closing his proposal, Taliaferro cast his treaty in the same light as others being negotiated during the period of Indian removal. "I beg leave to assure the President," he wrote in his letter to Clark, "that my influence is such that I can and will answer his [Jackson's] views in defiance of the combined efforts of any set of men in this country."[53] The remarks were undoubtedly aimed at the traders, since the agent suspected they would meddle in the civilization program. But it made good political sense to sell the negotiation as part of the national removal policy.

Caught off guard, Superintendent Clark wrote Commissioner Elbert Herring that he knew nothing of a desire by the government to purchase more Sioux land.[54] But Taliaferro's proposal did complement well the Indian policies of the age. The Dakotas roamed east of the Mississippi River but had hunted out these lands and were in need of annuities. The agent's support for a removal treaty hardly indicated disregard for the Indians. If anything, it demonstrated compassion. Taliaferro also knew that a treaty for lands east of the Mississippi would only slightly inconvenience his charges, since only one of their villages remained in the region.

At first Washington bureaucrats informed Clark that there were no funds for the negotiations. But in August Wisconsin Territory was organized, and much of the Dakota domain was included within its administrative limits. Territorial Governor Henry Dodge became superintendent of Indian affairs for the region, and Taliaferro's agency was transferred to his control. Dodge immediately urged the removal of Indians from the lower extremities of the territory. This included the Winnebagos, with whom he negotiated in the fall.[55] Bolstered by Dodge's sympathy, Taliaferro reintroduced his treaty idea, this time sending it directly to the president. By the end of the year all the machinery had been put in motion to ensure a treaty. Even the traders, hopeful of acquiring payment for past Indian debts out of the proposed compact, had begun to discuss how they might best control the proceedings.[56]

The movement toward another major treaty negotiation illustrates how rapidly the government became involved in Dakota tribal affairs. From mere concern over intertribal wars, policy initiatives had expanded to include economic support and rehabilitation programs. Although ulterior motives existed, for the most part these efforts were paternalistic. Most western officials felt that a humane Indian policy was in the best interests of the United States as well as of the Indians. In addition, the Dakotas living farthest east seemed willing to accept guidance from Washington. They considered government representatives like Taliaferro and Campbell to be kinsmen, and the $2,000 in annuities handed out each year reaffirmed this reciprocal relationship. Although a portion of their people disagreed with efforts to enact a peace policy, others thought peace with their neighbors was preferable to war. All Dakota leaders seemed convinced that the government was trying to help them, especially those who had suffered from the wars.

Mdewakanton leaders were doubtless blind to the changes that dependence on annuities would bring, but they trusted Taliaferro and recognized the serious degeneration that had occurred among their people. "It seems that everything is changed for the worse," an entreating subchief noted in council with the agent in the fall of 1836. "The land is bad [referring to smallpox] ... and your advice is this day asked for my people."[57] Even the Sissetons and Wahpetons made it clear in conversations with Taliaferro that much had changed in a few years. Their leaders noted that they "were not like the Sioux [Mdewakantons] nearest the fort." These relatives were now unable to take care of themselves.[58] The easternmost villagers had become, in the terms of one traveler, a "sad, squalid-looking" group of people who were ready to accept help from their Great Father.[59]

Considering the past relations that Dakota leaders had had with whites, they had few if any reasons to be worried about negotiating with Washington officials. Their cultural concept of negotiation was based upon a political process in which all parties discussed issues until a good solution had been reached. Discussions were leisurely and could go on for days. The Dakotas anticipated that the council in Washington would be such a forum and that the result would benefit them. Despite the increased role of military officers, government agents, and traders in this consensus process, there is no reason to believe Dakota leaders felt they had lost control of their political destiny. They had problems to discuss with their benefactor, and he had always been sympathetic to their needs.

The record of white Americans in regard to economic assistance was also unblemished. In fact they had become the source of most essentials necessary for Sioux survival. It is true that some traders had fallen into disfavor because they failed to reinforce kinship ties, but traders by and large still provided most of the manufactured goods the Sioux used, and the Indians realized that the game they offered in payment had diminished markedly. More important, Dakotas assessed relationships individually and generally did not think in terms of "them" and "us." All traders gave some presents and credits, even if only a bit of tobacco. Individual Indians who were refused simply took it as a personal insult and acted accordingly. Thus traders as a group were never condemned, and in the mid-1830s the Sioux were still quick to affirm that they "lived by their traders."

Such a unique perception of politics and economic relations was made possible in part by the kinship system that linked the Sioux to their white relatives. Dakota leaders, especially among the Mdewakantons, still had strong affine and fictive kinship bonds with both traders and government personnel. It was inconceivable in the Sioux cultural milieu that people who were related and who had time and again demonstrated a concern for the well-being of their relatives should be considered undependable and viewed with suspicion. Indeed, Dakota leaders had no reason to doubt the intentions of men such as Taliaferro, Bailly, Faribault, or even Sibley. Relatedness was considered an asset, and the Sioux intended to take advantage of it in the upcoming negotiations, for they had been told many times over, and had come to believe, that their father in Washington wished to take care of his red children. In the Dakota world, a father never denied the request of a child.

Dispirited, hungry, and aware that game was fast disappearing from their land, the Mdewakantons were eager to travel to Washington. This optimism did not seem to change when Taliaferro asked them if they desired to sell a portion of their land for a much larger annuity. Thus the eastern Sioux faced their first great dilemma in the spring of 1837. They would be asked to dispose of their birthright to forestall tribal disintegration and starvation.

8

Culture Change and the Assault on Land Tenure

After New Year 1837, rumors of a treaty spread rapidly up the Mississippi River. Congress had taken up the issue in January, sending out
requests to the War Department for information on the land to be
purchased. But a new president, Martin Van Buren, and a new commissioner of Indian affairs, Carey Harris, were just entering office
and the new administration was unable to commit itself to negotiations until summer. It did so reluctantly even then, since a serious
depression had hit the country in June, plunging the federal government into debt, and frontier settlers had yet to pressure the Sioux
for their land.[1] By fall, Dakota leaders were faced with the reality of
selling a section of their Minnesota landholdings. Little did they know
this decision would greatly affect their entire hold on the Mississippi watershed and accelerate the process of culture change.

Dakota leaders undoubtedly considered their experiences with
whites in discussing the proposed treaty. They had certainly come
to trust Taliaferro and his sage advice. Fortunately for the government, other Dakota mixed-bloods also spoke in favor of negotiation.
In the earlier 1830 accord they had received a large tract of land
(forty-seven by fifteen miles) lying astride Lake Pepin.[2] Another treaty
meant an even greater reward. In addition, traders threw their support behind a treaty, realizing that it offered commercial advantages
as well as a chance to recoup lost Indian credits. Thus white kinsmen who had lived with the Dakota people for many decades had
something to gain from negotiation.

Other national and local reformers joined government officials and traders in supporting treaty negotiation. Both elements hoped to introduce acculturation programs. Protestant missionaries had visited the upper Mississippi as early as 1829, and six years later they had established the first substantial stations. To them treaties meant funds for farming programs and schools, institutions that would help convince the natives to adopt Christianity. Although they differed with traders, mixed-bloods, and even government agents on how the proposed treaty should be written and implemented, reformers remained relatively silent on such technicalities in 1837. They simply added their voices to the already substantial consensus.[3]

During the winter of 1836–37, Governor Henry Dodge of Wisconsin joined the treaty advocates. After a tour of upper Wisconsin, he made several emphatic reports on Indian affairs to his superiors in which he stated that the country belonging to both the Sioux and the Chippewas "abounds in pine, is barren of game and unfit for cultivation."[4] Timber remained its only resource. Dodge also noted the desperate condition of the Indians. Fur traders were seizing upon their misfortune by extorting extralegal contracts to exploit the timber. Henry Sibley, Hercules L. Dousman, Lyman M. Warren, and William A. Aitkin had forced a contract for timber-cutting rights on the Chippewas in March 1837. Chippewa leaders consistently turned down the offer until "the wine arrived."[5] Other entrepreneurs had more grandiose plans that even included using the government mill site at St. Anthony Falls. There was talk of building a timber empire on the upper Mississippi.[6] No wonder Dodge's reports stressed the need to purchase timber resources. The lands were being illegally stripped of trees with the Indians obtaining no pecuniary benefits.

Meanwhile news arrived in Washington of a bloody encounter between Tasaugye's Wahpekutes and the Sacs and Foxes. The latter had also struck the Winnebagos east of the Mississippi River, disrupting the emigration of this tribe to Iowa. Governor Dodge immediately notified the War Department, expressing fears of an impending Indian war. Commissioner Harris suggested to the acting secretary of war that either three mounted companies be dispatched to Wisconsin or the tribes be brought to Washington to settle their differences. Clearly concerned, the War Department authorized the latter course. Almost as an afterthought, Harris added in his instructions to Dodge that negotiations for Sioux lands could take place while the Sioux were in the east.[7]

While officials awaited the arrival of the eastern Sioux in Washington, Governor Dodge and General W. R. Smith received commissions to treat with the Chippewas for their timber lands. Taliaferro witnessed the negotiations that took place at his agency. The commissioners quitted Chippewa claims in July for $700,000. Unfortunately, the treaty was marred by the demands of traders for special payoffs as well as by claims that the Chippewas received too little for their land.[8] Taliaferro feared that traders might also attempt to meddle with the Mdewakanton negotiations, a concern that seemed justified after American Fur Company agents gained access to his confidential 1836 treaty proposal. They quickly noted Taliaferro's failure to include substantial sums for the payment of Indian debts, and they questioned the agent's relatively small recommendation for annunities. "It is of great importance to us," Sibley concluded in a letter to Ramsay Crooks, "that Major T [Taliaferro] be not appointed a commissioner [for the Sioux treaty] inasmuch as he is known to be inimical to the Am. Fur Co."[9] Sibley asked Crooks to lobby against Taliaferro's appointment as a treaty commissioner.

It is not clear what role if any Crooks played, but in his final instructions to Dodge, Commissioner Harris suggested that all Indian agents stay at their agencies, where they could perform "the most useful service."[10] The directive provoked a strong indictment of the company from Taliaferro, who charged that American Fur exceeded "in strength and influence the great 'bank of the United States,'" an institution that was then seen by Jacksonians as the epitome of evil. The company was a "giant" that had usurped control of Indian policy from the government, exploited pine lands in Wisconsin, and "enslav[ed] the poor Indian, body and mind, to their dictatorial will."[11] Dodge rejected Harris's suggestion and ordered Taliaferro to form the treaty delegation and lead it to Washington.

This support did little to end trader harassment. Dousman soon informed the Mdewakantons that their agent wished them to receive only one-tenth what their lands were worth. Simultaneously, Dousman confided to Crooks that the Indians were "willing to sell their country" and that the traders should concentrate on having a large fund for debts included in the final accord.[12] By early September Dousman wrote Sibley that the company could document debts of at least $50,000, then added that, if it were left to Washington officials, "we can prove claims to much more." He closed by counseling Sibley, who was headed for Washington, to "leave no *stone unturned* to get something handsome for us."[13]

Despite delays caused by another Sac and Fox attack in July, Taliaferro left the agency on 18 August with the twenty-one-member Dakota delegation. Taliaferro had recruited mixed-blood assistants, "suitably rewarded," to aid the exodus. This group included interpreters Scott Campbell, Augustin Rocque, and Peter Quinn and traders Duncan Campbell and Alexander Faribault. Only Faribault worked for the fur company at the time.[14] Mixed-bloods played a key role in the negotiation of the treaty that followed. They had considerable influence with full-blood relatives and were wooed by both government officials and traders.

The Dakota delgation sat down with Secretary of War Joel Poinsett and Commissioner Harris on 21 September at Dr. James Lurie's Presbyterian church in Washington. People who did not work for the government were barred from the council chamber, including Sibley, Oliver Faribault, Benjamin Baker, and Francis LaBathe. After passing the calumet to reaffirm friendly bonds, Poinsett came directly to the point: "Your Father desires to place the great river [Mississippi] between you and the whites." Poinsett wanted the delegation to arrive at a price for their Wisconsin pine lands. Although Big Thunder, or Little Crow III, who had assumed control of his father's band sometime before, promised to answer, the next day, 22 September, the delegates said they had not contemplated selling so much land. Poinsett countered by offering one million dollars for the region east of the river. The delegates asked for more time to discuss the proposal.[15] Clearly the council was not following the pattern the Sioux had expected. The Americans seemed unwilling to participate in the give and take necessary to form a consensus.

When the council resumed the next day the Mdewakanton leaders pleaded their case. "I see all your people are well dressed—we are obliged to wear skins," Little Crow complained. "When the amount [one million dollars] is divided among our people, it will not be much for each." He and the other members of the delegation thought their land was worth at least $1,600,000. Dakota leaders had apparently listened to Dousman. Finally a few delegates, especially Grey Iron from Black Dog's village, suggested that the Wisconsin land was better hunting territory than the prairies west of the Mississippi River. This attempt to stall the proceedings fooled no one, since all the lands east of Lake Traverse were terribly depleted of game.[16]

Poinsett refused to budge. "What your father has offered for the land," he asserted, "is the real value—it is sufficient to buy a great many comforts." In addition, if the president had considered the true value of the land, the secretary argued, "he would not have offered more than one half that amount." Poinsett remained unenthusiastic about bargaining for a region that was considered to be of marginal use, especially after the national economic downturn. The Indians could take the offer or leave it.[17]

At this point, Okapota, a subchief from Penichon's village, rose to respond to Secretary Poinsett. "What you have said is all very true . . . your agent [Taliaferro] knows the country." The delegates, he continued, "did not come to Washington to go home empty." Others followed as nearly every leader had the opportunity to express his views on the proposed cession. Although many Indian leaders thought they should get more money for their land and some no doubt were confused by how rapidly issues were being discussed, none voiced serious reservations about the need to sell. The Mdewakantons feared above all else returning without a treaty. Their people were expecting a solution to their economic troubles as well as additional annuities, and over the weekend the delegation gave in to Poinsett's price.[18]

On Monday, 25 September, the secretary of war presented the leaders with an outline of how the money would be divided. The hand of Taliaferro was evident in the development of the document, which differed only slightly from the final draft of the treaty.[19] In general terms, the treaty provided the tribe with $25,000 in food, farm tools, and goods annually for twenty years. Another yearly annuity of $15,000 would accrue from a permanent trust fund of $300,000 and would be paid forever. The few changes that did occur between the initial draft and the final treaty were in the amounts set aside to pay off traders and mixed-bloods. Funds for the former were increased from $70,000 to $90,000, and the subsidy to be given the latter rose from $100,000 to $110,000. Poinsett opposed these changes because they reduced other funds, yet he gave in to tribal leaders.[20]

With details worked out, the chiefs and braves addressed government officials for the last time on 29 September. Many seemed nostalgic, well aware of the significance of the paper they were about to sign. Iron Cloud, chief of Red Wing's village, noted that he had not had a good night's sleep for some time. "I hope it [the treaty] will satisfy our people," he worried out loud. "I feel very uneasy about giving up these lands as you would not give us our price." Perhaps the thoughts of Iron Walker, the only Wahpeton attending, best exemplified those of other leaders: "They [delegates] feel sore about parting with their country, it would bring a great price if you could cut it up and bring it here." Shortly thereafter all twenty-one delegates signed the treaty, some more reluctantly than others, but all aware of the need to bring something home.[21]

Several parties did object to the treaty. On the day of the signing, Sibley wrote Ramsay Crooks that the whole document was "but one series of iniquity and wrong."[22] He found a minor clause that gave Scott Campbell a $450 annuity for twenty years particularly loathsome. The grant also included title to a section of land then partially occupied by Sibley's trading establishment. Taliaferro had obviously made some concessions to hold sway over the delegation. This clause was later taken out by the Senate. Even so, Sibley concluded at the time: "This is the boasted paternal regard for the poor Indian. 'O

Shame where is thy blush!'" Traders had been so completely excluded from the negotiation by the "paternalists" that Sibley did not
even see the final draft of the treaty until it was being signed.[23]

After the seven days of negotiation, efforts to settle the conflict
between the Sioux and the Sacs and Foxes seemed anticlimactic.
Indeed, the government devoted only the afternoon of 5 October to
the issue, perhaps because of the near-row that ensued when the
representatives of the tribes met for the first time. After taunting each
other the tribal leaders finally sat down to talk. The Dakota Cloud
Man began by suggesting that Poinsett "take sticks and bore the ears"
of the Sacs and Foxes so they would listen to overtures for peace.
Keokuk, the Sac chief, then declared that it would be necessary to
bore Mdewakanton ears "with iron."[24] A reporter for *Niles' Register*
questioned the prudence of putting the two groups in the same room.
Sibley thought that Poinsett had failed to use a "firm tone" and that
as soon as the Indians got home the wars would resume.[25]

When the Mdewakantons reached St. Peter's Agency, they found
general approval for their actions. Three of the delegates passed word
back to Taliaferro, then taking a two-month furlow, that they wanted
him to be sure "not to undo any part of the treaty."[26] By late fall 1837
the Mdewakantons seemed utterly convinced that the treaty would
solve their material ills. Many even refused to go on winter hunts
and preferred instead to await the annuity shipments. Furious over
this turn of events, Dousman wrote Sibley in December that the
Mdewakantons "say it is not necessary to work for the traders any
more as they will now have plenty to live on independent of the
traders' goods." The Mdewakantons, claiming that their debts had
been paid by the treaty, also refused to honor commitments made
for credits.[27] Unfortunately, by January 1838 bands in the vicinity of
the agency had to beg food from Fort Snelling. Starvation seemed
imminent unless the treaty was quickly ratified.[28]

The Senate Committee on Indian Affairs sent several other treaties to the floor but initially passed over the Mdewakanton agreement. In March the senators sought advice from Secretary Poinsett,
questioning whether the purchase was necessary. Poinsett defen-

sively answered that Congress had sanctioned the negotiation upon the recommendations of Taliaferro and Dodge, "men well acquainted with the interests of the government in that portion of the country." Poinsett then proceeded to defend the treaty in the Jacksonian rhetoric of the day. He noted that the natives were starving and that "liberal treaty stipulations would give them more advantageous and permanent benefits as well as removing them from the corrupting influence of whites." Poinsett also believed the treaty would bring stability to the upper Mississippi, diminish intertribal wars, and be a positive way of projecting American influence into the region. Finally, he appealed to the nationalism of the senators, emphasizing that this removal treaty would flesh out the natural borders of the republic.[29] Still the Senate balked, unwilling to approve a major expenditure during times of economic uncertainty.

Meanwhile spring brought worsening conditions in the west. A handful of traders informed the Sioux that they had sold their land too cheaply. Whites were also settling east of the Mississippi, building houses and planting crops. "These things seem hasty on their part," Little Crow told Taliaferro; "they might at least wait until the news of our treaty is fully known."[30] At the same time, small groups of Winnebagos continued to cross the river, headed for new lands in Iowa. The invasions increased tensions around Fort Snelling and worried Major John Plympton, the commanding officer. He had fewer than fifty men on duty and could not police the area. To appease the Sioux, he wisely handed out rations to hungry warriors.[31]

By late June Taliaferro became concerned over the delay. Attacks on livestock had reached unprecedented levels despite the ration distribution. Traders held back credits and refused to take muskrats owing to depressed markets. Little Crow warned the agent to expect violence. "A man may starve one & two days & even three," he said, "but on the 4th, he becomes desperate & kills the first thing that crosses his path."[32] Taliaferro finally wrote Commissioner Harris a despairing letter. "What mortal man could do, has been done ... to keep my *miserable* and *starving people* quiet until we hear from you— if the treaty has not been passed over by the *Senate* all will be well."[33]

Fortunately the accord received congressional approval on 15 June, and news of its passage reached the Sioux agency a month later. Within days, starving Indians found traders willing to advance goods on credit, with the promised annuities as collateral. Moreover, corn crops were now edible, albeit underripe. By September the agent had developed budgets for each aspect of the annuities, earmarking funds for agricultural equipment, goods, and food. Meanwhile the Indians eagerly awaited the steamboats that carried their annuities.[34]

When the items arrived in October, however, both Taliaferro and Sioux leaders were disappointed. St. Louis suppliers had been unable to properly fill the $10,000 order for guns, blankets, and kettles, and some articles sent in their stead were worthless to the Indians, purchased at "scandalous" prices. *"Fine Cloth*—& casinets [castanets]—shawls—handkerchiefs [etc.] ... do not suit our people," a Dakota leader told the agent. Another problem arose over the $15,000 payment derived from the $300,000 trust. The Indians could not understand why they had to wait until 1839 for the interest to mature. They expected the money immediately. Taliaferro convinced the disgruntled leaders to wait a year for the cash and to accept the goods offered.[35]

Four days later the food annuities arrived. Over $5,000 worth of flour, corn, pork, and salt was divided into seven shares, based upon the various populations of Mdewakanton villages. Shakopee's camp received the largest allotment, 328 barrels in all. Grey Iron from Black Dog's camp claimed the smallest portion, totaling 158 barrels. The food annuities did much to subsidize the meager economy of the Mdewakantons, and they made up for the scarcity of guns and blankets.[36]

The government worked to improve its record in distributing the Mdewakanton annuities in the years that followed. But the combination of undependable congressional appropriations and slow water transport frequently caused delays and even brought Taliaferro's resignation in 1839. He had promised to distribute annuities on 1 June 1839, but when the appointed day came they were still in St.

Louis. When the goods arrived in August the quality of most had been significantly improved, but the 114 guns sent were far fewer than the 350 requested.

After Taliaferro had submitted his resignation, his father-in-law Cloud Man tried to talk him into staying. But the agent had confided in his journal in 1836 that he would leave after a treaty had been implemented, and the War Department had already named a successor, precluding his return. Taliaferro departed the agency for good in November 1839, after twenty years of service.[37]

Amos Bruce, Taliaferro's replacement, received better cooperation from Washington. His first distribution, on 1 June 1840, included 300 Northwest guns, a weapon for nearly every warrior in the tribe, several hundred blankets, and a host of lesser items such as knives, kettles, scissors, and looking glasses. Dakota leaders were "much pleased" with the improvements, and thereafter few complaints surfaced over either the quantity or the quality of goods or food.[38] Yet the Indians complained to Bruce about the cash annuity. Treaty writers had specifically reserved $5,000 of this $15,000 to be spent by the president on Dakota education. When the Indians failed to receive the entire amount, traders began encouraging them to demand this "education fund." Dousman thought that if the Indians emphasized their destitution in council with the agent he could use their speeches as leverage with the Indian Bureau. When Bruce reported the conspiracy, Washington officials were even more determined to preserve the fund for schools. This did not sit well with Dakota leaders, who continued to bring up the issue thereafter.[39]

Nevertheless, these minor complaints did not detract from the overall success of the annuity system, which obviously saved the Mdewakantons from utter destruction. One can only speculate on what might have happened without it; certainly many tribal members would have joined other Sioux bands on the Missouri River. But with annuities, the Mdewakanton villages prospered. From a population of about 1,400 in 1836, their numbers grew to 1,668 in 1839. One hundred more people were added by 1841, and two years later the population had expanded to nearly 2,000. The increases continued until midcentury, when the seven Mdewakanton villages contained 2,250 Indians, an incredible 60 percent increase over fourteen years.[40] The expansion can be attributed to two sources. Annuity rolls show that the percentage of children rose dramatically, from 33 percent of the population in 1844 to 45 percent in 1849. It seems that a more consistent food supply and the consumption of bread cut down on infant mortality. Second, external additions occurred as band members living with the Wahpetons and Sissetons on the upper Mississippi River came home. Frequently they brought along relatives from the upper tribes who were attracted by the annuities.[41] The fluid nature of Dakota band membership allowed for the immediate incorporation of these distant relatives.

As Taliaferro organized the annuity distribution, government commissioners W. L. D. Ewing and S. J. Pease arrived to pay the mixed-bloods their $110,000. The agent did not begrudge them the money, since he believed that if "anything of a beneficial tendency" were to be accomplished with the Sioux, the support of these bicultural people would be necessary.[42] Unfortunately factions had evolved within their ranks, and those that aligned with the agent, including Scott Campbell and Philander Prescott, soon found themselves pitted against the Faribaults, Alexis Bailly, and Samuel Stambaugh, the sutler at Fort Snelling. The commissioners sided with Stambaugh and adopted a list of 143 mixed-bloods (10 percent of the Mdewakanton tribe), drawn up in five categories by Faribault according to degree of blood. The first class received $1,500, with amounts declining to $400. Taliaferro's half-Dakota daughter was placed in a lower bracket, probably to spite the agent for his meddling.[43]

During the treaty negotiation, some discussion had also been given to the possible allotment of the "half-breed" reserve, the portion of land given to the mixed-bloods in 1830. Again Campbell, Prescott, and their backers supported a proposal that limited a distribution of the lands to literally one-half Sioux people. Stambaugh and Bailly, on the other hand, developed a less rigid scheme that would include anyone who was at least a quarter Dakota. The debate was carried back to Minnesota after the Indian commissioner refused to push for the allotment. Without hope of a solution, the issue was left for another time, though petitioners continued to bombard the Indian Bureau with appeals for the distribution of the land.[44]

After the mixed-bloods were paid off, traders approached the commissioner's table at St. Peter's Agency. A fund of $90,000 had been included in the accord to quit their debts, money that Sibley and others quickly decided to accept despite their initial dislike for the treaty. The American Fur Company received most of the fund, since many individual traders now owed them debts. In a sense the company made a windfall profit on the treaty, for most of the "credits" they claimed were unpaid by the Indians were covered by the high prices charged.[45]

The payment made to traders and mixed-bloods set precedents for future negotiations. Thereafter these groups came to expect pay-offs when the government proposed to treat with the eastern Sioux. Traders began planning for the next land sale almost as soon as the ink had dried on the 1837 accord. Many mixed-bloods likewise found employment as government farmers and blacksmiths, thereby becoming more strongly attached to Jacksonian removal policies. In spite of becoming a politically distinct group, the mixed-blood community remained as dependent upon traders and government assistance as their full-blood relatives.

The only people who did not benefit from the treaty were the western tribes—the Sissetons, Wahpetons, and Wahpekutes. Once the Mdewakanton annuities had been distributed, they came to the agency seeking a share for themselves. Taliaferro tried to explain that they would have to sell land to acquire government assistance. This did little to appease them, since they felt that the Mdewakantons should share their good fortune. The upper or western Dakotas had allowed eastern bands to hunt on their lands for many years. They now faced economic problems of their own, and at least some of their leaders asked the agent if they too might sell land to the government.[46]

The declining price of muskrats had much to do with this plea. By spring 1838 Joseph Rolette had heard that prime rats could not be sold in New York even for a dime, which forced many traders to stop taking them. Such an event had never happened before, and Sisseton leaders came to Taliaferro complaining loudly that their traders seemed disposed "to desert us in our extremity."[47] Then in April news arrived of the murder of an American fur trader on the James River. He had been working at Lake Traverse under Joseph R. Brown, who was himself shot and wounded. Sibley ordered the evacuation of the Lake Traverse post after the assault, and since it served smaller establishments on the James and Sheyenne rivers the company virtually closed down its operations west of Lac qui Parle. At the western posts still operating—Lac qui Parle, Traverse des Sioux, and Little Rapids—the Indians were sullen and refused to hunt for the more valuable but nearly extinct prime fur animals.[48]

On top of these misfortunes, smallpox struck again in the summer of 1837. The initial reports put the most serious Sioux losses at Devil's Lake, where the Yanktons and Yanktonais had large villages. But the infection quickly spread east to the Minnesota River valley. Over the next two years, losses mounted among the Dakota bands. Unfortunately, trader reports failed to mention specific numbers. It does seem certain, however, that the Minnesota River Sioux suffered much less than Indians along the Missouri River. Renville had made piecemeal attempts to vaccinate the upper Sioux before 1835, and missionary Thomas S. Williamson, as well as explorer Joseph Nicollet, promptly obtained vaccine from the authorities at Fort Snelling to carry on the effort.[49]

Nonetheless, when agent Taliaferro made his final report to the Indian office regarding Sioux affairs in September 1839, he quickly pointed to the degeneration that had occurred in the west. With the exception of sporadic buffalo herds and muskrats, most game animals had disappeared from Sisseton, Wahpeton, and Wahpekute lands. The Indians raised some corn, but hardly enough to last through the fall, and they had surprisingly few horses. The Sissetons numbered 1,500 people, but the Wahpetons now numbered only 750 and the Wahpekutes merely 325. The smallpox had sapped their strength. Taliaferro recommended the negotiation of another treaty for part of their lands, a step that was not unpopular to the suffering western Dakotas.[50]

The War Department ignored Taliaferro. Yet conditions elsewhere convinced the government to treat with the upper tribes after all. Some 36,000 Indians still wandered throughout the area that is today Wisconsin, Iowa, Illinois, Michigan, and New York. Indian Bureau officials decided to purchase approximately five million acres from the Sioux and move the eastern tribes there. They believed that Minnesota would be an ideal location for another "Indian country" similar in design to Oklahoma. Thus in May 1841 Governor James Doty of Wisconsin ascended the Mississippi to negotiate with western Dakota leaders. While en route, he wrote to Dousman, requesting assistance from the traders. Since Sibley's men were obviously being courted, they decided to extend their assistance to Doty.[51]

Fearing delay, the governor purchased canoes at Prairie du Chien rather than waiting for a steamboat. With the help of traders, who spread the word among the upper bands, he convened a council on 29 July 1841 at Traverse des Sioux. In a matter of six days the governor reached an agreement, purchasing from the Sissetons, Wahpetons, and Wahpekutes some thirty million acres, which included all their holdings in Minnesota. Stephen Return Riggs, a missionary who was present at the signing, noted that the governor had acted so quickly that many important Sisseton leaders were absent, including such major chiefs as Sleepy Eyes and Burning Earth. On 11 August Doty reached a similar agreement with the Mdewakantons for the purchase of their land claims west of the Mississippi River. To acquire sufficient signatures the governor spent over $12,000 for food and presents and used another $1,000 for what amounted to bribes.[52]

The treaties included a large annuity. One million dollars was to be invested for the Sissetons, the interest, amounting to $50,000, being handed out each year in cash. The treaty also set up specific reservations for each tribe, the largest consisting of 200,000 acres. The Sissetons, Wahpetons, and Mdewakantons were to be settled north of the Minnesota River and the Wahpekutes south of it. Most of the remaining land between the Iowa border and the Minnesota River would be reserved for migrating tribes and not open to white settlement. Finally, the accords promised that gristmills, sawmills, and schools would be constructed on the reservations and that each Indian would receive a yoke of oxen, one cow, five sheep, two swine, a house, a spinning wheel, and a loom. After the individual had plowed his land for two years he would be eligible for United States citizenship. Doty aptly termed the treaties a "radical" departure from the past.[53]

While little information has surfaced on the pressures exerted on the Indians to obtain approval, they must have been considerable. Mixed-bloods and traders played key roles in molding native sentiment. Accordingly, the treaties included a $300,000 fund to cover traders' claims against the Sioux.[54] Before the negotiations, Doty also promised mixed-bloods that the government would purchase their reservation at a substantial price and put them in charge of the new reservations. He kept both bargains, buying mixed-blood lands for $200,000 and recommending that such men as Jean Baptiste Faribault, Joseph La Framboise, and Joseph Renville, Sr., be employed as new agents for the reservations. Another ploy used to garner support was the inclusion in the treaties of a regulated trading system. The treaties allowed individuals to be given commercial monopolies on the new reserves and to sell goods at fixed prices. Alexander and Oliver Faribault, Philander Prescott, Alexander Graham, Joseph Renville, Jr., Hazen Mooers, and Louis Provençalle, among others, were to be commissioned traders. Sibley received support for the job as superintendent of Indian affairs that Doty envisioned would put the entire scheme in motion.[55]

Doty justified these unusual arrangements to the secretary of war by arguing that the mixed-bloods and related traders provided the "connecting link between the savage & civilised man, & ought to be employed by government as its agents, interpreters, & teachers." The governor felt that most were well educated and ought to be given an opportunity to "establish a character for themselves—to obtain a place in civilised life." Implying that mixed-bloods were educated

yet not anchored in "civilised life" apparently presented no contradiction to the governor.[56]

Despite the belief held by Doty and his cohorts that the Dakota
treaties would solve the northwestern "Indian problem," the Senate
tabled both documents in September 1841. Opposition surfaced for
several reasons: the bureau had not authorized such an extensive
purchase, and senators, especially Thomas Hart Benton, were un-
sure of the wisdom of creating another Indian territory like Oklahoma. Sibley and other traders used their contacts in Washington to
lobby extensively for adoption. Even missionaries pushed for passage.[57] But by the spring of 1842 ratification looked doubtful. At this
point Sibley began working with bureau officials to modify the original documents, cutting out some of the annuity provisions. Even
this failed to placate a hostile Congress, and Doty's "radical" acculturation program was defeated on the Senate floor by a vote of two
to twenty-six on 29 August.[58]

Although treaty advocates lamented that rejection would cause
massive starvation for the western Dakotas and delay their eventual
incorporation into the American mainstream, they must have realized that Taliaferro's efforts to create farm communities among the
Mdewakantons had had little success by 1841. Thoughts of quickly
turning the more nomadic upper bands into quiet agriculturalists
raising sheep and swine were incredibly naive. Taliaferro, writing
from Pennsylvania, said as much himself in a letter to the Indian
Bureau. He also attacked the accords for their embarrassing generosity to traders.[59]

Taliaferro's "civilization" plan unquestionably had far fewer pitfalls than Doty's, yet the Mdewakantons avoided the opportunity to
become farmers. One reason for its failure was Taliaferro's, and later
Bruce's, inability to find competent instructors to run the project.
Those that Taliaferro tried to recruit seemed "ill disposed ... to be
Indian slaves." In their place he hired four missionaries, an Irishman,
and two mixed-bloods. To assist them in maintaining equipment, he
expanded the corps of blacksmiths to six, most of whom were Ca-

nadian by birth. Taliaferro believed that missionaries or men raised in the fur trade would make poor instructors.[60] Unfortunately, his predictions were accurate.

Mdewakanton leaders had their own views about the farming system. They naturally wanted to use the system as a means to assist relatives and applied pressures to ensure the selection of farmers culturally acceptable to them. Shakopee, for example, finally convinced Taliaferro to hire the mixed-blood Oliver Faribault, the son of Shakopee's trader. Young Wabasha, who became a chief after his father died in 1836, likewise persuaded agent Bruce to employ James Reed, a relative, in 1842. But the most interesting case of Dakota nepotism developed at Little Crow's village, where the band boycotted and destroyed the primitive school begun by the missionary/farmer Thomas Pope, so as to obtain the farming job for young Alexander Faribault, a relative of Little Crow. Even though Pope resigned, Taliaferro decided that Faribault was too inexperienced for the job and hired someone else.[61]

When Dakota leaders and their people failed to get their way or felt that farmers needed to be put in their place, they killed the work oxen necessary to keep the agricultural projects functioning. Little Crow's village had been issued nine cows in the spring of 1839, and only six were alive by July when Pope resigned. Wabasha's people likewise slaughtered livestock, forcing the removal of their farmer in 1841 so that Reed could be employed. On occasion, the Dakotas had good reason for demanding change. Reed's predecessor, the missionary J. D. Stevens, had taken the government-issued oxen east of the Mississippi and opened land for himself. But most Dakota men had no intention of becoming husbandmen. The treaty supplemented their income as hunter-gatherers and allowed them to continue the chase as their forefathers had done for centuries. Therefore by 1849 about fifty acres of land was plowed each year per village, all by whites.[62]

Taliaferro left the agency before the utter failure of his agricultural program became obvious. He had believed that, once given a chance to farm, the Mdewakantons would change. This had not happened by the 1840s, primarily because the Sioux did not want to become farmers and because of a major contradiction inherent in the government's acculturation plan—Indians who were being fed had no reason to adopt agriculture as a means to feed themselves. Missionaries quickly noted the illogic of the situation, also arguing that annuities postponed the evolution of the work ethic and individualism. "The time they [the Sioux] employed in hunting before they were furnished with these things [annuities] they now spend in feasting, dancing, etc.," one disgruntled station worker wrote in 1840.[63] At a time when government programs were floundering, missionaries sought to force a spiritual transformation upon the Sioux that would convince them of the superior benefits of Euroamerican civilization.

Mission workers had had little to do with negotiating the 1837 accord, but they soon developed a keen interest in Dakota acculturation and the implementation of the treaty. Permanent stations had been built in Sioux lands two years before, and the number of missionaries grew rapidly. The largest contingent had ties with the Boston-based organization the American Board of Commissioners for Foreign Missions (ABCFM). Thomas S. Williamson, J. D. Stevens, and Alexander Huggins established the first Dakota missions at Lac qui Parle and Lake Harriet in 1835. The Pond brothers, Samuel and Gideon, soon joined the staff of these stations, as did Stephen Return Riggs. Other missionaries followed, including several Methodists, two Swiss Protestants, and a Catholic, but their stations survived only a few years. By the late 1840s the ABCFM dominated the field, with seven missions in operation at various times throughout the decade.[64]

ABCFM missionaries initially believed that they could make Christians of Indians before inculcating a sense of Euroamerican civilization. Consequently they felt that Sioux religion posed the major obstacle to their success. The Dakotas had a polytheistic world view that helped regulate their hunter-gatherer subsistence cycle and defined individual Dakotas' relation to the world around them. Central to their religion was a spiritualism derived from visions that guaranteed the preservation of the individual as well as the group. As many as twenty "shamans" per village interpreted dreams, cured the sick, and worked to bring about successful hunts. Attending their efforts were institutional rituals such as dances, feasts, fraternal organizations like the soldiers' lodge, and "medicine" societies.[65]

Mission workers clearly underestimated the strength of Dakota religion and initially failed to understand how it integrated Dakota culture. They saw rituals as mere "superstitions" rather than as true spiritual experiences. Workers assumed that when they learned the Dakota language they could effectively offer the Sioux a superior Christian alternative to this "devil" worship.[66] But after the Ponds at Lake Harriet had studied the language for four years, they still found it difficult to "preach Christ Crucified." The inability to translate the cultural nuances of Christianity destroyed early optimism. The consistent rejection also prompted a closer look at Dakota religious institutions, so that Williamson confessed they were more entrenched in the culture than he had first realized.[67]

Still, Williamson's mission did achieve some minor success during the latter 1830s, primarily owing to the patronage of Joseph Renville, the bicultural trader of the American Fur Company, who had eight children. Taliaferro had convinced him to help Williamson and Huggins get established near his stockade by pointing out the educational and cultural advantages that missionaries would offer his family. In addition, four of Renville's cross-cousins, Wamdiokiya, Paul Mazekutemani, Cloud Man (not the Mdewakanton of the same name), Abel Itewawinihan, and his brother-in-law Tacanhpitaninya also lived with families close to his trade center. These men acted as leaders of the twenty- or thirty-member soldiers' lodge that Renville controlled. Williamson soon found that the lodge and Renville's kinship ties gave him access to the more important families at Lac qui Parle. Throughout the winter of 1835–36, Williamson used the lodge as a school and a church.[68]

Missionaries found a more receptive attitude toward Christianity at Lac qui Parle because Renville acted as a culture broker. He joined the church in 1836, with his wife and several children. The first full-bloods, six women—also closely tied to Renville—took communion a year later. Yet Dakota men, even those directly related to Renville, were more cautious. Riggs later noted that while they frequently listened patiently to the arguments of the station workers, by 1840 most "were still eminently Dakotas in their social feelings and family relations."[69] They had agreed to name their lodge Wowapi Wakan Okondakitchie, which meant "friends of the holy book [Bible]," but the name was only a new label for what clearly remained a Dakota institution.[70]

Renville's cousin Wamdiokiya exemplified the extent of the cultural change among the Lac qui Parle soldiers. He had made the best progress toward learning how to read and write in Dakota, and Williamson encouraged him to serve as an itinerant teacher among the Sissetons and Wahpetons at Lake Traverse by 1839. However, the murder of one of Wamdiokiya's wives in the spring brought a sudden halt to Williamson's plans. Wamdiokiya's thoughts immediately turned to revenge, and he organized a war party to strike the Chippewas. The missionaries tried to stop him, saying they would pray for his failure. Station worker Amos Huggins even refused to grind corn for the expedition. Wamdiokiya retaliated for this breach of Dakota etiquette by killing several cattle; he could not understand how men who were connected with his lodge could refuse him assistance. His party left for the Chippewa country without the corn, and the raid proved unsuccessful. Wamdiokiya, who was also a shaman, concluded that his learning to read and write had forever sapped his *wakan*, or power, as a "seer" of war; he never went into battle again.[71]

Over the next two years a significant number of Dakota people accepted Christianity. Most of them were women. Riggs suggested that members of the "fairer sex" more readily converted because they held such a low position in Dakota society. Sioux men cared little about their women's religious affiliation. Men, moreover, were forced to make more profound cultural changes when they became Christians, such as giving up war, the hunt, sacred societies, and feasts. Thus, when Simon Anawangmani took the vows in 1841 he faced constant ostracism, even from women and children. His sacrifice hardly matched that of Tacanhpitaninya, the second Dakota man to apply for admittance a few months later. Tacanhpitaninya had two wives, and the missionaries unsuccessfully demanded that one be "put aside." Thus, to acquire church membership, Indians had to adopt Euroamerican standards of behavior, even though they might continue to function in their own culture. By 1842, thirty-nine native women and three men had reached this level of acceptance. Over the next six years several more men joined, most of whom were Renville's relatives.[72]

The year 1842, however, was the high point. Many church members moved away thereafter and lost contact with the missionaries. A prolonged drought seemed responsible for the migration. The religious decline also coincided with a deterioration in Renville's economic status. He had fallen further and further into debt to the fur company and by 1843 was no longer able to reinforce kinship ties. His soldiers' lodge broke up, and harassment of Christians rose markedly.[73] Finally, opposition to Christianity grew among traditional Dakota shamans, who increasingly saw missionaries as a threat to their own congregations. There had been a "honeymoon" period of sorts in the later 1830s when shamans had listened to the teachings of the missionaries and found little harm in them. After the mission churches demonstrated some success, however, Indian religious leaders became more cognizant of the narrow philosophical nature of Christianity, and they came out strongly against it.

A few of the old Lac qui Parle members joined new congregations at the Mississippi River villages of Little Crow and Cloud Man. However, the stagnation in the native church convinced missionaries to work toward more dramatic cultural changes. By the late 1840s they concluded that the entire Dakota population must adopt Euroamerican behavior if universal conversion were to occur. The chase and its perceived lack of industriousness, the use of common property, and improper socioeconomic sexual roles, the missionaries convinced themselves, prevented real progress toward Christianity.[74] So long as most Sioux Indians continued to be hunters, missionaries knew the conversion process would never expand beyond a handful of the faithful.

This assessment led to more interest in educational systems and ultimately to a greater concern with federal acculturation programs and financing. In a sense, mission schools enjoyed more success than churches. The school at Lac qui Parle, for which attendance records exist for the years 1839 and 1844–46, had no fewer than 236 students annually. Many attended infrequently, but a substantial minority learned to read and write in Dakota, and a few, mostly mixed-bloods, studied English and mathematics.[75] Government officials expressed amazement at the students' rapid progress. Many learned to write intelligible letters in the Dakota language in six months. The ABCFM missionaries, with the help of Renville, successfully translated and had printed a host of materials for use in the Dakota schools, mostly books of the Bible, primers, and hymnals.[76] In all, more than four hundred Sioux and mixed-bloods had received some basic education by midcentury.

Nevertheless, as it had in response to the other missionary efforts in the 1840s, resistance also erupted to the school program. Some Dakota men, such as Wamdiokiya, saw learning as a magical experience. Others came to believe that the written word "could not lie." The mysticism of learning posed threats for native shamans, whose powers could seldom match the "talking" paper of the missionaries. Some men also apparently disliked the notion of their sons' becoming more learned than themselves in these strange customs. Thus Dakota men from soldiers' lodges began preventing children from attending classes. Violators had their blankets cut up.[77]

Attempts by traditionalists to disrupt schools reinforced the missionaries' beliefs regarding culture change. It also convinced them to look favorably upon government assistance. Schools at Lake Pepin, Wabasha's village, and Lake Harriet had each received $500 grants from the Mdewakanton education fund in 1839, but the rest of this fund, which increased annually by $5,000, was drawing interest in a St. Louis bank. By 1845 certain mission workers felt the money should be used for boarding schools, and several workers ultimately received the sanction of the Indian commissioner to take ten or fifteen Dakota children into their homes. For its part, the government agreed to contribute $50 a year to the upkeep of each scholar.[78] Although

Riggs suspected the concept would distract the workers from their general purpose of evangelism, the change underscored a growing trend: if missionaries could not immediately persuade the Sioux to act like white people, they had to insulate as many as possible from the "evils" of Dakota culture.[79]

Missionaries likewise became more aware of the positive role the federal government could play in creating the right climate for culture change. The proliferation of whiskey, for example, was seen by both missionaries and federal officials as a degenerative influence that had to be stopped. Alcohol became easily available in large quantities after white settlers took up lands east of the Mississippi River. Intemperance constituted a major problem for Samuel and Gideon Pond at Lake Calhoun, and it quickly spread west to Lac qui Parle and beyond. The Minnesota River Sioux realized they could reap huge profits by trading spirits for horses to the Yanktons on the James River. In 1844 enterprising Dakota merchants carried in at least twenty barrels. Little Crow IV, or Taoyateduta, gained a reputation as a very successful whiskey dealer. Martin McLeod, who had reopened the Lake Traverse post for Sibley, reported that the sales were hurting his trade.[80]

Government officials were no more effective in stopping the liquor trade in the 1840s than they had been earlier. Military officers sent petitions to Washington asking for stronger laws against sale of alcohol by whites and even sent out patrols to various places, including the mixed-blood reservation, to shut down dealers who were violating the law. Bruce cooperated with these efforts and even Sibley lent a hand, taking a job as justice of the peace in order to apprehend violators of the intercourse law. Strangely, the most progress was made when missionaries, agents, and traders alike begin obtaining temperance pledges from notorious Dakota drinkers. By 1844 Sibley had more than forty names on his pledge, some Indians agreeing to abstain for as long as a year.[81]

Missionaries also strongly supported efforts to end the long intertribal wars. The consequences the fighting had for the mission program struck home in July 1839 when four Chippewa men separated from two friendly parties and killed a Dakota at Lake Calhoun. Mde-wakanton leaders saw this act as especially treacherous, since the Chippewas had recently smoked with them at Fort Snelling. Warriors from several villages formed two armies, pursued the Chippewa delegations, and surprised them on the Rum and St. Croix rivers. A slaughter ensued in which more than one hundred Chippewas and at least twenty Sioux lost their lives; the war that followed broke up Eatonville and the Lake Harriet mission.[82]

The Chippewas soon retaliated, setting the stage for another series of general raids. Captain Electus Backus, commanding at Fort Snelling, lacked a strong force to preserve order, and once again the government turned to negotiation. On 4 August 1843, Dakota and Chippewa representatives signed still another peace treaty, but this one included an unusual clause: thereafter, Sioux and Chippewa bands that were attacked would be allowed to collect compensation from the forthcoming annuities of the aggressors. The injury clause did not affect the Sissetons, Wahpetons, or Wahpekutes, but it had an important impact on the Mdewakantons.[83] The next year when four Wahpetons living with Shakopee's band killed a Chippewa, Bruce acted on the new formula. He told Shakopee that his annuities would be withheld until he turned over the murderers. The chief promptly sent out nineteen of his men to seize them. Shakopee then sought out the Chippewa chief Hole-in-the-Day and settled the affair with presents. This solution markedly contrasted with the way Shakopee's villagers had responded to a similar request for violators of the peace in 1835.[84]

Unfortunately, the government abused the new rule. After a Sisseton war party killed a white cattle drover in the fall of 1844, Bruce refused to hand out the Mdewakanton annuities under the pretext that his actions would keep their warriors peacefully waiting on the Mississippi River. A military force was sent to Lake Traverse and captured several men responsible for the attack, thereby defusing a tense situation. In 1847 Bruce extended the leverage provided by annuities when a few Mdewakantons joined a Wahpeton war party that killed nine Winnebagos on the neutral ground of northern Iowa. He held back government assistance for six months until it became obvious that the Mdewakantons had little to do with the troubles.[85]

This use of annuities as a way to limit intertribal fighting underscores the failure of the government's acculturation program. Such support was theoretically supposed to tide these people over until they became successful farmers. Actually, the eastern Sioux underwent few noticeable cultural modifications as a result of the 1837 treaty, living much as they had before the establishment of Fort Snelling. Annuities had led to rejuvenation of the Mdewakantons in the east rather than their cultural demise. And the fact that such a renovation came at a cost of increasing economic dependency seemed to have caused little alarm in the 1840s.

Ironically, although government annuities symbolized economic depression, they also reinforced the reciprocal bonds that had become the fiber of peaceful relations between Indians and whites. Officials who handed out thousands of dollars worth of goods each year clearly were perceived by the Sioux as allies and friends. In addition, hunters soon discovered that traders once again extended credit, knowing they would be able to collect unpaid debts out of treaty payments. Traders' books were now kept in dollars rather than muskrat pelts, reflecting the growing importance of purchasing items with money.[86] Finally, village chiefs took charge of the distribution of government-supplied goods and food and had some say in the allotment of government jobs, thus increasing their political prestige. Even though annuities had made the eastern Dakotas highly dependent upon the federal government, they seemed to enhance both the social and economic ties that had traditionally bound the various ethnic groups together in the Mississippi River valley.

On the other hand, the negotiations of 1837 and 1841, and the intertribal peace treaty of 1843, illustrate that significant political degeneration continued in eastern Dakota camps. Traditionally, councils had been forums where issues were considered and leaders worked to establish common ground. But while annuities made the Sioux economically dependent and reinforced kinship ties, they also bound native leaders to listen carefully to government officials, much as those chiefs had done when traders spoke in their councils. The influence gained by white officials came from a sense of obligation inherent in Dakota culture. When a Dakota Indian wished to present an argument to other men in his village he called a feast, feeding those men he wished to lobby and thus obligating them to listen carefully to his point of view. If the men were close relatives, which was often the case, they could seldom deny a request. In substance, by the later 1830s government officials, traders, and even mixed-bloods applied these techniques, using annuities and presents as a means of creating obligations. And since such obligations bound individuals, it became exceedingly difficult for Dakota leaders to act independent of these outside influences. Consensus became more difficult to obtain, and when leaders did arrive at major decisions, such as in 1837, they frequently represented the will of whites more so than Indians.

An increase in interest groups—government as well as economic—also produced a cultural factionalism that had not previously been evident in Dakota villages. This factionalism took on kinship parameters, with groups forming around key relatives who showed decisive leadership. The Eatonville community, under Taliaferro's patronage, offers the best example. Western Dakotas came to see it as a subculture that was completely dependent upon the agent and garrison, and it offered an economic alternative to traditional hunting and gathering. Eatonville was soon followed by the various "Christian" fellowships and schools that sprang up at the ABCFM missions. Other small groups of Indians tried to follow the examples set by government and missionary farmers and educators. They were occasionally joined by a few mixed-bloods who had been displaced by the decline in the fur trade. That such groups threatened traditional Dakota culture is demonstrated by the opposition they engendered. Factions that ever so slightly abandoned key elements of Dakota culture had less common ground with traditional groups.

Nonetheless, most Sioux seemed unconcerned with the alterations that were occurring around them by midcentury. Even the Mdewakantons made a rather smooth transition from venison and wild rice to pork and flour. The lesson of relatively painless adaptability made an impression upon the less experienced western Dakota tribes. They saw only that annuities had refurbished their eastern relatives and that the treaty of 1837 was an example of the great generosity of their father in Washington. But the Mdewakantons were no less grateful and remained convinced that white Americans were their friends and kinsmen. They had no reason to believe that the Great Father was any less benevolent than he had always professed to be.

9

The Treaties of 1851

The eastern Sioux enjoyed a respite from government acculturation pressures after the defeat of the Doty treaty in 1842. But the economic problems that had stirred Dakota interest in another land cession simply grew worse, particularly in the west where natives could not depend upon annuity subsidies. Traders seized upon the difficulty, planning strategy for a new negotiation not long after the Senate rejected Doty's effort. They slyly reminded Indian debtors that a land sale would provide funds to erase indebtedness and bring an abundance of goods. Dakota leaders unquestionably pondered long the pros and cons of such a novel idea as they suffered through the seemingly endless northwestern winters.

Discussions of the growing number of whites who had settled on the east bank of the Mississippi River no doubt crept into these forums. Although government authorities had once viewed the river as a natural boundary separating Indian and white, this attitude changed after Congress created Minnesota Territory in 1849. A year later census records showed that more than five thousand whites had already taken up residence in the territory even though only a narrow strip of land between the Mississippi and St. Croix rivers was open to settlement. The territorial organization soon attracted a newspaper and politicians, and intense speculation arose regarding the future opening of land west of the Mississippi.[1]

Missionaries and promoters in Minnesota had sought to justify a land sale well before the first territorial governor, Alexander Ramsey, reached the new capital at St. Paul. They had argued that a cession would benefit both the country and the Indians by opening new lands to settlement and promoting "civilization" among the natives.[2] Missionary letters and memorials showed a strong concern with institutional civilization, considered crucial to their endeavors by the late 1840s. Riggs now believed that no Indian tribe in America could "long hold arable land in common" and thought the tribal tenure of the Sioux people should be replaced by individual ownership of small, agriculturally manageable plots.[3] ABCFM workers finally concluded that the ultimate goal of mass conversion could come only on the heels of a dramatic social, political, and economic reorientation. By 1850 they had composed an "Outline of a Plan for Civilizing the Dakotas," in which the evils of large villages, tribal government, and the community system were carefully elucidated. The plan called for a future treaty to include manual-labor schools so that Dakota children could be separated from their parents, the encouragement of the nuclear family, and the development of a body of "civilized" law. "Disintegrate them [the Sioux] as far as possible," Riggs wrote. "Encourage them to be thrifty farmers rather than poor villagers."[4]

Most of what the missionaries proposed made good sense to government bureaucrats. Like the station workers, they recognized that Taliaferro's earlier "civilization" plans had accomplished little. Robert G. Murphy, who was Sioux subagent briefly in 1848–49, as well as his successor Nathaniel McLean had even tried unsuccessfully to dismiss the farmers. McLean, Governor Ramsey, who was also Indian superintendent, Commissioner Orlando Brown, and his successor Luke Lea felt by midcentury that more control over the Dakota people would be necessary to teach them the arts of husbandry and save them from destruction. These men accepted the need for a major policy change, frequently described as "confinement." They wanted the four eastern Sioux tribes placed on one small reservation so agricultural and educational programs could be consolidated.[5] As Agent McLean noted: "The agency, manual-labor school, missionaries, a large farm, surrounded by Indian populations, upon whom the influence might operate would ... produce a salutary effect upon the habits of these sons of the forest."[6]

The proclaimed humanitarian concerns of federal authorities and missionaries complemented the political necessity of wresting the regions west of the Mississippi from the Indians. Governor Ramsey fully understood that his political future in the territory depended upon opening the trans-Mississippi region to settlement. This convinced Ramsey, a Whig, to work with the Democrat Henry Sibley, who had been elected territorial delegate. Both men used their influence in Washington to persuade the secretary of interior to open new treaty negotiations. He finally complied in late summer 1849, selecting Indian Superintendent Ramsey and John Chambers, formerly a territorial official in Iowa, to act as commissioners. In the instructions sent out to both men, Commissioner Brown suggested that Doty's aborted treaty should serve as a guide and that approximately two and one-half cents an acre would be an appropriate price for the twenty million odd acres between the Minnesota River and the Iowa border.[7]

Ramsey and Chambers were new to the business of making treaties. Both men arrived in St. Paul well after most Indians had left for winter quarters. But neither their inexperience nor the lateness of the season were as severe an obstacle to their efforts as Sibley's opposition. He had learned that Chambers had no intention of honoring trader claims against the Sioux, and when Ramsey asked him to help in assembling tribal representatives, Sibley made a halfhearted effort. Moreover, the commissioner soon found numerous rumors in circulation, including stories that prophesied a military occupation of the Dakota domain. In desperation, Ramsey sent an urgent letter to Riggs at Lac qui Parle, asking him to help bring down the Sissetons and Wahpetons. But the damage had been done, and the upper Indians procrastinated too long to effect a treaty in 1849.[8]

When the commissioners finally sat down with a handful of Mdewakanton leaders in October, the chiefs promptly submitted a list of grievances, drawn up, not surprisingly, in Sibley's hand. They insisted that the $50,000 "education fund" be distributed, that the agent appoint more of their mixed-blood relatives as farmers, that the soldiers at Fort Snelling compensate them for firewood, and that the government honor promises made by earlier agency employees for the delivery of some horses.[9] In Ramsey's mind these demands seemed trivial, but he decided against pressing the chiefs. Manifestly impressed with Sibley's influence with the Sioux, Ramsey and Chambers quietly closed the council.

Ramsey apparently approached Sibley over the winter regarding treaty matters. The full particulars of these meetings have not surfaced, although Sibley did illustrate his position in a letter dated 15 September, just before the ill-fated council. The Minnesota delegate informed Ramsey that his endeavor to treat would fail as long as the Indians were prevented from paying their outstanding debts. Sibley indifferently advised the governor to go ahead with his intended councils, and he closed his letter by suggesting that whenever Ramsey decided to purchase the Dakota domain he should first rid the commission of the unyielding Chambers. By December Ramsey had substantially adopted Sibley's views, even to the point where he endorsed a plan to quadruple the price offered the Sioux from two and one-half cents an acre to ten cents, producing additional revenue to pay the traders.[10]

Although Sibley had his way with government officials, he recognized that some Dakota leaders might be reluctant to sell. A few opponents could be found in every Dakota band, especially among the Mdewakantons, who already had annuities and would be called on to give up all their land. Yet Sibley understood the Dakotas' generosity and their strong proclivity to reciprocity. By 1850 he instructed traders working under him to be liberal with credits and to reinforce kinship ties with all four eastern Sioux tribes. As luck would have it, Sibley's own father-in-law, Bad Hail, had risen to the position of speaker for the Mdewakantons.[11] Other leaders in this tribe who were sympathetic to the traders included Wakute, or Shooter, Good Roads, and Shakopee, the last being described as the "part parcel of Oliver Faribault." On the other hand, Sibley's men considered the young Little Crow, who had succeeded his father as chief in 1846, and Wabasha to be undependable, even though both were closely related to various mixed-bloods who worked for the company. More important, no one knew what the rank and file in Mdewakanton villages would do about a treaty negotiation. Overall, the traders working under Sibley felt that their kinship networks would garner strong support from the Sissetons and Wahpetons and that at least half of the Mdewakanton leaders would accept their advice.[12]

Despite the lack of consensus in Dakota camps, economic dependency proved a valuable ally in dealing with recalcitrant leaders. Mdewakanton villagers had become so accustomed to eating flour, pork, and beef that many refused to tend their cornfields. Prescott, who had lived with the tribe since 1820, noted the dietary change, even suggesting that hungry Mdewakanton children would spit out boiled corn and cry for bread.[13] Such cries had increased by the later 1840s, however, since populations had grown appreciably, prompting a per capita decline in government food distribution. The newly acquired tastes made the tribe more susceptible to traders who sold large quantities of food on credit and took payment from the cash annuities.[14]

While the lower bands were thought to be favorably inclined toward a cession, the Sissetons, Wahpetons, and Wahpekutes clearly wanted a treaty. They had spoken favorably about a treaty since the late 1830s, largely because little had changed in the interim to alter their views; in fact, economic conditions in the west had taken a further downturn. Martin McLeod, Sibley's trader on the Minnesota, had reported some starvation among the western tribes nearly every year during the 1840s. The news for March 1846 was typical: "there is but one cry of starvation here resounding from the lakes to the hills." Even when a few buffalo could be found east of the James River, the Sissetons and Wahpetons were ill prepared to kill them, for starvation had forced them to eat their horses, dogs, and even the skins covering their tepees.[15] The loss of equipment, especially horses, prevented extended hunting campaigns.

The growing difficulty in the west made it especially easy for Sibley and McLeod to ingratiate themselves with various Sioux bands. As the negotiations grew closer, they reinforced old, often neglected kinship bonds and promoted a friendly political environment by judicious use of credits and presents. Ironically, McLeod had chastised his two clerks, Joseph and Gabriel Renville, for using the "old system of crediting" over the 1848–49 trading season. But now earlier retrenchment policies were jettisoned in preparation for the treaty. In their eagerness to court tribal leaders among the upper Sioux, traders encouraged Indian visits to the Mendota warehouses, placing a burden on company stores.[16] Fred Sibley, Henry's brother, thought the Sioux were taking advantage of the situation and angrily wrote to his brother, "I wish the infernal Indians would stay in their country."[17] Sibley and Ramsey also did their best to alleviate starvation, convincing the Bureau of Indian Affairs to provide small sums for Sioux relief in 1850. Nonetheless, the upper Indians now suffered constantly. McLeod believed they realized hunting would not support their families. The Sissetons and Wahpetons were ready to sell "a large portion of their country," he felt, "if liberally dealt with."[18]

Nevertheless, McLeod still worried about possible tampering with the Indians by outsiders unsympathetic to the traders' debt claims. Henry M. Rice, a local politician whom Sibley had vigorously opposed both politically and commercially, harbored serious thoughts of intervening in the treaty process, though he had never traded with the Sioux. Sibley apparently used various commercial considerations to convince him to leave the negotiations alone in 1851, but most traders put little faith in Rice's promise.[19] Rice bided his time, waiting for an opportunity to make some gain from the land sale.

After Rice the missionaries seemed the likeliest threat, especially in terms of tampering with the upper Sioux. They had influence with several important leaders including Walking Spirit, the hereditary chief at Lac qui Parle, his war chief the Sisseton Cloud Man, and Red Iron, the subchief of Sleepy Eyes's people. All three men had learned to read and write Dakota, though only Walking Spirit was sympathetic to Christianity. Walking Spirit had told Riggs that the one shortcoming preventing him from joining the church was that he had had ten wives, which made him "a great sinner," as well as that, of the two who remained, the one he wished to "send away" did not want to go.[20] What worried the traders was that Walking Spirit and other principal men who had missionary training were expected to weigh the terms of a treaty more "objectively" than those Dakotas concerned only with the annuities offered. The missionary-trained members of the Sisseton and Wahpeton delegation finally included the three chiefs named above, as well as Henok Mahpiyah-dinape, Paul Mazakutemani, Peter Big Fire, and Simon Awanwang-mani. The latter men, generally the sons of important Sisseton-Wah-peton men, had adopted farming and had no ties with traders. Yet Sibley ultimately reached an understanding with the missionaries whereby the clerics promised to use their influence to support those treaty clauses providing for debts in exchange for articles promoting acculturation.[21]

The last political faction, the mixed-blood relatives of the eastern Sioux, could generally be counted on to stand by the traders. Most were directly related to the leading men in the trade or their under-lings, and Sibley made a substantial effort to use these kin bonds. By 1851 the company employed a large number of them, including the Renville and Faribault brothers, the sons of two of Minnesota's earli-est permanent fur dealers. In addition, Fred Sibley noted in a letter to the Missouri commercialist Pierre Chouteau that many mixed-bloods had recently been extended credit by his brother when they had failed to get support elsewhere. The elder Sibley anticipated collecting these debts from the treaty funds and of course intended to use indebtedness to hold mixed-blood supporters.[22]

Sibley also pushed for the sale of the "half-breed" tract, a ploy that ingratiated him with the Minnesota mixed-bloods. Although Ramsey had negotiated an agreement with the mixed-bloods in 1849 whereby they were to receive $200,000 for their Lake Pepin lands, the docu-ment never made it to the Senate floor for a vote: most senators considered the price exorbitant.[23] Yet company officials could assure the mixed-bloods that their lands would certainly be purchased when the government extinguished Sioux title to the regions west of the

Mississippi, giving mixed-bloods added incentive to encourage their full-blood relatives to sell.

Everyone in Minnesota was primed for a treaty by the fall of 1850. Sibley even boasted to Chouteau that the Indians would sign whenever "we tell them to do so" and that he intended to "dictate" the result.[24] All that remained was for Congress to appropriate money and for the executive branch to decide upon a second commissioner to accompany Superintendent Ramsey. The governor thought he had the perfect candidate in Hugh Tyler, a close political ally who had once asked Ramsey to secure for him the position of Sioux agent. Sibley concurred in the nomination, knowing that Tyler would complement Ramsey's views. But the Minnesota clique ran into stiff opposition from the Ewing brothers of Ohio as well as from Rice, who generally opposed Sibley. When it looked as though Sibley and Ramsey would lose, Congress passed an appropriations bill that required commissioners to be government employees. The job then fell on the new Indian commissioner, Luke Lea. Sibley had courted Lea for some time and felt much relieved at hearing that the Ewing candidate would be ineligible.[25] It looked as though the Mendota trader would dictate the Sioux treaty after all.

As the commissioners traveled west to St. Paul they worked out a few minor details. Tyler, who had been selected to serve as supply agent, went ahead to obtain provisions to support the Indians during the negotiations. Horses had been issued to the Mdewakantons the year before to satisfy one of their basic complaints; Ramsey and Lea also made preparations to distribute the "education fund" to satisfy another. Since the secretary of war had purposely left treaty instructions vague, the negotiators made a crucial decision to treat first with the Sissetons and Wahpetons. McLeod had been advising this course for several months, since he felt sure the upper Sioux would sell their lands. A cession in the west would also force the Mdewakantons to sell, since they could hardly expect to hold land in the center of a territory that was rapidly being settled. Thus, once in St. Paul, the commissioners and an entourage of newspaper reporters, assistants, and traders headed west to Traverse des Sioux on the steamboat *Excelsior*. Ramsey and Lea were ready to meet the upper bands by 1 July.[26]

Spring rains had drenched the upper Minnesota valley, making travel difficult, and five days after arriving the commissioners found only one thousand Indians present. The upper Sisseton chiefs still remained at far-off buffalo lands. McLeod headed for Lake Traverse to hurry them along. Meanwhile, various other groups straggled in, including a few Mdewakantons, who feasted on the government stores of beef and flour and played the ancient game of lacrosse. With the exception of the impatient commissioners, everyone seemed in a festive mood. Finally, after nearly two weeks, tardy Sisseton leaders showed up, and the council opened on 18 July. Ramsey addressed the Sioux leaders first, voicing the concern of the "Great Father" for the starving condition of their people. They had plenty of land, he said, but it was of no use to them since it produced so little food. Ramsey proposed to swap land for annuities.[27]

On the following day the commissioners expected an answer. Instead, Sioux leaders sat quietly on the ground under a large awning of boughs and said nothing. No one felt prepared to speak for both tribes, and the Indians had no intention of hurrying such important discussions. Finally Orphan, the Lake Traverse Sisseton chief, answered for his people. He had learned that some white man—apparently McLeod—had told his soldiers to return home, and he felt obligated to include them in the discussions to ensure consensus. Ramsey berated the chiefs for stalling, arguing that only the chiefs needed to sign the treaty. At this Sleepy Eyes lamented the absence of his Lake Traverse relatives and left the council chamber. A cry of joy swept through the crowd of Dakota young men standing nearby. They had planned a lacrosse match at the end of the discussions and were eager to begin. The commissioners viewed the demonstration in a different light, suspecting that it signaled the end of negotiations. They abruptly cut off rations and prepared to leave. Only the timely intervention of the traders saved the treaty. They smoothed over the disagreement and brought the delegates and commissioners back together on 21 July.[28]

The council now went more smoothly, with Extended Tail Feathers, a respected Lac qui Parle subchief, apparently speaking for both tribes. He had been an ally of the traders and asked to be excused for not expressing sooner his wish "to give you our country if we are satisfied with your offer." The commissioners presented a set of terms that were intensely debated that evening and much of the next day. Some leaders thought that the million and a half dollars offered was insufficient, while others complained about the amount of land to be sold. A few chiefs also had a difficult time grasping the implications of changing ownership, despite the efforts of Riggs, the traders, and the many educated Indians to explain the proposition. Finally, on 23 July leaders had agreed to the terms and professed willingness to sign the document. The missionaries had translated the treaty into the Dakota language, and it had been thoroughly studied by the educated men. Walking Spirit and Orphan, as traditional head chiefs of the tribes, stepped forward to sign. Thirty-three other headmen followed.[29]

In all, the two tribes relinquished title to their lands lying between the native boundaries set down in 1825—roughly from central Minnesota to northern Iowa. The western limit of the cession fell on a line running from the Red River south to the Sioux River. The eastern boundary, abutting Mdewakanton lands, remained undefined. A reservation had been selected along the upper waters of the Minnesota, including ten miles of land on either side of the river from Yellow Medicine Creek to Lake Traverse. For its part, the government agreed to keep $1,360,000 in the Treasury for the upper Sioux for fifty years, paying them 5 percent interest annually, or $68,000. Actually the money was never put in the Treasury, and Congress had to appropriate the interest each year. Of this amount $40,000 was to be handed out in cash, a large sum that the missionaries felt would promote fiscal responsibility. Handouts of food had been the nemesis of past civilization programs, and the mission workers wanted a large proportion of the money distributed even if it benefited the traders. Of the remainder, the government pledged to spend only $10,000 on food and $18,000 for education and farming.[30]

Finally, the first section of article four delineated a special sum of
$305,000, often called "hand money," to be spent during the first year
to open farms, support the Indians until the first year's interest came
due, and allow "the chiefs" in open council to "settle their affairs."
Traders had planned from the start to earmark most of this money
to satisfy their claims against the Sioux. Immediately after the treaty
was signed they had enlisted the help of certain missionaries and
mixed-bloods to convince the delegates to sign a second document
called a "traders' paper," which pledged $210,000 of the fund to them
and $40,000 to the mixed-bloods. The disposition of the hand money
had been discussed in at least one soldiers' lodge a day or so before
the treaty signing, but most of the upper Sioux leaders thought they
had initialed a second copy of the treaty rather than an obligation to
the traders. As the last signature was inscribed on this two-page
document, a stormy controversy erupted.[31]

Objective observers who had no interest in the traders' paper often
disagreed over its validity. Riggs, for example, had been at the meeting when interpreters supposedly told Dakota leaders of their obligations to pay debts under the treaty. He thought the amount and
the distribution plan were justified. Agent McLean, on the other hand,
noted that no schedules stating who would receive what had been
attached to the paper when the chiefs signed it. McLean doubted
that the Indians understood what it purported to do, and he re-
sented Ramsey's efforts to convince him to witness and verify the
document. Two subchiefs, Running Walker and Cloud Man, who had
close fictive kinship relations with the missionaries had told the agent
they would sign another paper in his presence, but McLean wanted
a formal council, something traders preferred not to risk. A day after
the paper had been signed, several chiefs did draw up a list of 160
mixed-blood relatives who would benefit from the hand money; the
traders attached a schedule for their funds immediately thereafter.[32]

After succeeding with the Sissetons and Wahpetons, the commissioners headed down the Minnesota River to Mendota, where they
opened council with the Mdewakantons and Wahpekutes on 29 July.
Lea confidently proposed extinguishing title to their Minnesota lands

for $800,000 and distributed a treaty paper that probably had been drawn up on the riverboat. Wabasha unabashedly responded, "According to what our Great Father ... said [in 1837], we have some funds laying back in his hands." The chief was referring to the education fund that the Sioux had asked for during negotiations in 1849. Lea assured Wabasha that it would be paid as soon as the Mdewakanton chiefs signed the treaty. But the next day Wabasha returned Lea's proposal without comment; silence fell in the council chamber. The commissioners wisely decided to give the chiefs more time and adjourned the meeting. On 31 July Little Crow finally rose after another long, awkward silence and said, "We will talk of nothing else but money [the education fund] if it is until next spring." Lea then professed to be injured by their suspicions about his integrity, but the ploy did no good. Nothing could be accomplished until the issue of the education fund had been resolved. Rations were cut off, the council was discontinued, and the commissioners turned to the traders and mixed-bloods for help.[33]

Over the next few days several private discussions took place. Apparently Mdewakanton leaders agreed to negotiate earnestly in exchange for $30,000 from the education fund. By 5 August a written treaty had been translated into Dakota by Gideon Pond. Assuming that differences no longer existed, the commissioners then called a formal council and presented the pen to Little Crow. He still refused to sign, as did Wabasha. Instead, the chiefs brought up the issue of the reservation boundary, pressing Lea to move the line south, farther down the Minnesota River. Some leaders also spoke against the funds set aside for civilization programs, pointing out that farmers and schools had never benefited their people in the past. Lea, tired of the whole affair by now, responded with veiled threats of force. Ultimately Wabasha broke the standoff by turning to the warriors, seated behind the delegation, and remarked: "You have said, young men, that the chief who gets up first to sign the treaty you will kill." Medicine Bottle, who spoke for the soldiers, responded that his followers had no more objections because the price paid for the land had been increased nearly twofold from Lea's original estimate, and the reservation had been moved farther south. Medicine Bottle then pointed to Little Crow and encouraged him to sign. Symbolically, the young chief, who had spent some time in mission school at Lac qui Parle and who had only five years before succeeded his father as chief, wrote out his name, Taoyateduta. Other leaders thereafter added their marks, building the list of names to sixty-three.[34]

In exchange for their lands west of the Mississippi, the Mdewa-kantons and Wahpekutes were to receive a twenty-mile-wide reservation on the Minnesota River, stretching from Little Rock to the Yellow Medicine River, and other economic aid and material benefits worth $1,410,000. The accords earmarked $30,000 for mills and schools and another $220,000 to finance removal and pay debts. Once again the treaty specifically noted that this latter fund should be distributed by the chiefs "in open council." Sibley had convinced the Wahpekutes to sign a traders' paper granting $90,000 of this fund to cover their trade debts, but the Mdewakanton chiefs had refused his overtures. Initially Sibley seemed unconcerned over this turn of events. Most Mdewakanton chiefs had assured him that they would honor their obligations to traders.[35]

The government promised to place the remaining $1,160,000 into a trust fund for fifty years, from which 5 percent interest ($58,000) was to be paid annually to finance food distribution, civilization projects, and a $30,000 cash annuity. The resources still due the Mdewakantons under the 1837 treaty were also to be converted to a cash annuity, though the funds were to be shared with the Wahpekutes. The final stipulation of the agreement called for the sale of the "half-breed" tract at a price of $150,000. Here, the commissioners took the precaution of allowing Congress to strike out the article without affecting the remainder of the Mendota treaty.[36]

A general euphoria swept Minnesota at the conclusion of negotiations. The Mdewakantons spent the $30,000 from the education fund within a month of its distribution, thereby lubricating the local economy. The missionaries expressed general approval of the accords, Riggs writing in the New York *Independent* on 16 October that the treaties would surely "make men" of the Sioux. If the treaties failed to "make civilized and Christian men and women of them," he prophesied, "they must perish."[37] Ramsey too thought the treaties would provide for the "concentration" and eventual "civilization" of the Dakota people. "They will be surrounded by a *cordon* of auspicious influences to render labor respectable, to enlighten their ignorance, to conquor [*sic*] their prejudices," he wrote Lea in November.[38] All attention now focused on the Senate, where confirmation hearings were expected in early 1852.

Before the congressional review got under way, trouble broke out. Hundreds of settlers flocked onto Sioux lands in the fall and took up claims. Lieutenant Colonel Francis Lee at Fort Snelling had neither the troops nor the inclination to prevent the invasion. Land speculators in St. Paul held meetings and pledged to fight eviction. Ironically, the Sioux benefited from the white presence, because many settlers felt disposed to feed hungry Indians during the winter, since they themselves were illegal occupants. Yet when the number of settlers increased in the spring and the treaties had still not been ratified, tensions began to build.[39] Sibley understood the possible repercussions of the usurpation of Sioux lands, but it soon became clear that he, like other officials, intended to do nothing about it. "Let the people go on to the purchased country in the thousands if they will," he wrote Ramsey.[40] The invasion provided him with an excellent bargaining tool to use against reluctant southern senators.

Dakota discontent also erupted when many of their leaders learned the particulars of the traders' paper, the document that detailed debt payments to traders. The Sissetons Cloud Man and Walking Spirit, though initially supportive of the debt payments, now told McLeod they were "dissatisfied with their proportion of the distribution [of hand money]." Most likely Cloud Man was unaware of the amounts involved when he agreed to re-sign the document in front of agent McLean.[41] In November 1851 disgruntled factions found an ally in Madison Sweetser, a shrewd politician who had come west purposely to benefit from the treaty. Sweetser had married into the Ewing family, had a brother in Congress, and apparently intended to work with Rice. He brought a large supply of goods to Traverse des

Sioux to use in making friends and built a trading house. In the meantime, Rice watched affairs at St. Paul and did what he could to prevent the Mdewakantons from signing any obligation with Sibley or his traders.[42]

Sweetser soon found allies in agent McLeod and various Indian leaders. McLeod spoke to him of the "great wrong and injustice" done the Sioux by the treaty. This led Sweetser to gleefully boast to George Ewing that he would have "no difficulty in getting his [the agent's] signature to any paper which the Indians will sign." Sweetser also borrowed one of Rice's mixed-blood employees to act as interpreter and clerk at his new post. With the blessing of the agent and the assistance of a few mixed-bloods, Sweetser then sent out invitations for Dakota leaders to meet at his store. Twenty-one responded, and on 6 December they signed a document that denounced the traders' paper and gave Sweetser power of attorney to act for them. The signatures included a large number of men who had missionary training, such as Red Iron, Paul Mazakutemani, Cloud Man, and Simon Anawangmani, as well as more traditional leaders including Sleepy Eyes and Running Walker.[43]

After meeting with Sweetser, the delegation descended upon St. Paul to see government officials. In discussions with McLean, the agent agreed to forward their complaints to Washington. McLean reported that the discontented faction did not oppose the sale of the land—only the method and proposed distribution of their hand money. The traders' paper, the agent concluded, had been secured through "deceit and fraud," and at least one Dakota group wanted officials to know they expected it to be nullified. Next McLeod escorted the group over to Ramsey's residence, where they more or less demanded to know what the governor proposed to do. Ramsey read the treaty aloud, declared that the language was specific, and stated that the money had to be paid "to the chiefs and braves of the tribe, in such manner as they in open council should determine."[44] The governor gave his word that the Indians would be allowed to pay as much of their trade debt as they wanted.

The actions of this group and Sweetser's meddling soon stirred

Sibley's faction to action. They realized the effect adverse propaganda could have on the Senate. In the west, McLeod began working to counter Sweetser in December 1851, doing his best to keep Indian leaders away from Traverse des Sioux where Sweetser had his store and trying to line up support for a "paper" that would revoke the one Sweetser had obtained.[45] Sibley also labored to effect some understanding with the Ewings in Washington and encouraged his partner, Hercules Dousman, to work on Rice. By spring neither McLeod nor Sibley had made much headway. The harsh weather and the dispersal of the bands hampered McLeod's effort, and when a group of upper Dakotas finally did visit Mendota in March 1852, Fred Sibley reported that they were "much divided among themselves" over the debt issue. A month later when McLeod presented leaders with his document, Orphan, Walking Spirit, Extended Tail Feathers, Running Walker, Red Iron, and Sleepy Eyes, most of the important upper Sioux leaders, refused to sign it. Sibley had no better luck, since both the Ewings and Rice professed to be unconnected with Sweetser.[46]

By the time McLeod's paper reached Sibley in Washington, it was of little use. Surprisingly, the Senate showed little interest in the traders' paper controversy, preferring to lay Sweetser's power of attorney aside after minor debate. What did concern that august body was the location of future Dakota reservations—senators wanted them moved west of the territory or eliminated—and the clause in the Mendota treaty calling for the purchase of the Dakota mixed-blood tract. When the Senate finally ratified the treaties in June, it eliminated the clauses pertaining to reservations and to the mixed-blood tract. Few people who joined in the celebration that erupted in the streets of St. Paul on 17 June with news of the treaty's passage, noted that the "Great Father" had deprived the eastern Sioux of their only remaining lands in Minnesota; most observers thought Sioux acquiescence to the Senate "amendments" would be a mere formality.[47]

The optimism seemed unwarranted when Indian leaders who understood the significance of the changes immediately balked. Wabasha scornfully remarked in July: "There is one thing more which our great father can do, that is, gather us all together on the prairie and surround us with soldiers and shoot us down."[48] What is most surprising is that Dakota intransigence held even after food became scarce and Ramsey refused to hand out annuities. Conditions among the Sissetons and Wahpetons especially had deteriorated. Few of their bands had even planted corn during the summer in which the treaty was negotiated, and over the following winter starvation became common. Worse, McLeod noted in May 1852 that the buffalo had "failed totally on the usual ranges." One Sisseton band had devoured two hundred horses, and rumors persisted that another band of perhaps two hundred lodges had nearly perished.[49] Hunger became an ally for Ramsey and the traders; Fred Sibley even noted that the upper bands "looked to their [future] annuities as their only hope of salvation."[50]

Nonetheless Henry Sibley left nothing to chance in Washington. He convinced Commissioner Lea that the amendments could be confirmed by the Indians without the benefit of a "formal council." Sibley hoped to obtain their acceptance before Congress adjourned, after which appropriating the funds necessary to pay traders would be impossible. He realized that if the issue dragged on his opponents would create additional obstacles.[51] By midsummer this seemed to be the case, as the Minnesota delegate learned of the missionaries' discontent. Their plans had focused on a policy of concentration that would expedite civilization and Christianization programs, and without a reservation the Dakotas were likely to scatter in many directions. Thus Samuel Pond, Williamson, and Riggs began speaking out against the amendments. They were joined by the opportunist Madison Sweetser, who had ferried several thousand dollars worth of supplies up the Minnesota River by August and stood ready to thwart the Ramsey-Sibley clique. Thus, when Ramsey approached the Sissetons and Wahpetons at midmonth he found them unwilling to consider his proposition.[52]

Ramsey immediately sought a compromise, suggesting to Lea that whites would not want the original reservation lands for at least two decades. He also wondered if the president could not be convinced to reserve this land for the Sioux, since the amendments did allow the president the prerogative of selecting a reservation for the Dakota people "at his discretion." Sibley embraced the idea, reassuring the missionaries that the Sioux could move onto the lands marked out for them in the original treaties. The clique then recruited Henry Rice at a fee of $10,000 to sell the amendments, a move designed to neutralize Sweetser. Rice finally convinced the Mdewakantons and Wahpekutes to re-sign the amended Mendota treaty on 4 September 1852. Prescott, who interpreted for him, remarked that the chiefs had been fed "like gluttons" for days to get their consent. Ramsey allowed Rice to pay for the feasts with funds set aside for removal and subsistence.[53]

By this time, however, the old lands of the Mdewakantons had already been overrun, and there was little hope of regaining them. The signed amendment also gave the governor authority to draw money from the federal treasury to fulfill article four of the treaty, the part dealing specifically with hand money. After several weeks of negotiations—most in private—on 8 September the upper Sioux also signed the amendments. Red Iron, Walking Spirit, Sleepy Eyes, and a few other leaders boycotted the discussions, but a majority of leaders gave their approval to the Senate changes. Ramsey took both documents to Washington, where he convinced the president to grant the Sioux right of occupancy for five years on their earlier assigned reservation. He then picked up gold and bank drafts totaling nearly $600,000 and headed back to Minnesota.[54]

Meanwhile Sibley returned to St. Paul to oversee the crucial distribution of the money. He confidently wrote Dousman on 16 September that Ramsey seemed "well-disposed & willing to do what is right."[55] His optimism grew after he received a note from Tyler informing him that the money would be "properly disbursed" and that there would be no need for "blackmail." Tyler also advised Sibley to keep working on the Mdewakantons, since they had yet to sign a traders' paper. By early November when Ramsey returned with the cash, however, only the Wahpekutes were willing to accept their trader obligation without challenge. They initialed receipts for $90,000 set aside in their treaty, and the governor gave the money to Sibley, who first deducted 10 percent for acting as "attorney" for the claimants, then distributed the fund, most of which went to himself and Alexander Faribault.[56]

The Mdewakantons proved far less obliging, though by no means united in their opposition. They refused Sibley's final overtures to procure a traders' paper, and in a formal council held on 8 November their chiefs demanded that Ramsey pay the funds reserved for debts—later arbitrarily established by the governor at $90,000—into their hands as the treaty clearly stated. But Ramsey declined, stating simply that he thought it was "proper" for them to allow him to pay their debts. The governor then threatened to take the funds back to Washington and withhold the annuities, whereupon Wabasha replied that he might just as well do so.[57] As the council broke up, interested traders noticed that several Mdewakanton leaders disapproved of Wabasha's uncompromising attitude. Good Roads spoke up in favor of signing the receipt, as did Bad Hail, lately a spokesman for the Mdewakantons as well as Sibley's father-in-law. Bad Hail had a son in the Fort Snelling stockade, charged with raiding the Chippewas, and Ramsey had clearly implied that the youth would be released if the Indian leaders signed receipts for the money.[58]

Resistance unraveled the next evening as Ramsey made a few minor concessions and Sibley promised more gifts. The governor agreed to turn over $20,000 cash to the chiefs so they might pay their mixed-blood relatives as they wished, a tactic that instantly encouraged mixed-bloods to throw their support behind Ramsey and Sibley. Wabasha later testified that mixed-bloods Jack Frazer, Joseph Rock (or Rocque), and several others had coerced him to sign, saying that if he refused the other chiefs would do so and he would be left out of the payment. Frazer was Wabasha's first cousin, and Rock was also closely related to him. Alexander Faribault also put kinship pressure on his relatives Little Crow and Shakopee, specifically addressing the former as "brother" and promising him $3,000 in cash if the chiefs signed the receipt. "Brothers" in Dakota society had a strong responsibility to help each other, and Faribault was symbolically giving Little

Crow an ultimatum. In addition, Sibley used open bribery, telling Mdewakanton leaders that he would give them "seventy horses and double-barrelled guns and pistols" after the document had been signed.[59] On the night of the ninth these pressure tactics succeeded. At Franklin Steele's house, Wabasha and Shooter initialed the receipt. In turn, each received a bag of gold worth $2,857.14, one-seventh of the money reserved for mixed-bloods. Frazer took the money and apparently kept most of it himself; the other band chiefs signed the following day. Hugh Tyler took the $70,000 that had been set aside to pay debts, deducted 15 percent for his services, and handed the rest out to the traders.[60] In the end, individual kinship ties had been the determining factor in acquiring the needed signatures.

In mid-November Ramsey traveled to Traverse des Sioux to obtain a similar receipt from the Sissetons and Wahpetons. Although he previously had promised these people he would turn the fund for subsistence and debt of $275,000 over to their leaders, he now refused to do so. Red Iron, a farmer and a friend of the missionaries, led the resistance against signing the necessary receipt, supported in part by a soldiers' lodge. Red Iron used the lodge to keep other chiefs from attending a council with Ramsey, a tribal prerogative he enjoyed because Traverse des Sioux fell within his band's territory. However, Ramsey tricked Red Iron into appearing before him on 22 November and, backed by a company of troops, had the chief arrested. In the heat of the discussion that followed Ramsey arbitrarily dispossessed Red Iron of his chieftainship.[61]

This usurpation of traditional authority provoked Red Iron's soldiers and forced Ramsey to employ a new strategem. During the early days of December he convinced traders and mixed-bloods to bring in one or two chiefs at a time, and he handed out annuities to anyone who would sign the receipt. Even so, Ramsey found only eleven men willing to place their marks on the receipt, four of whom might be considered subchiefs. To make that document appear as though the Indians had signed it in a formal council on the same day, Ramsey added the date 29 November.[62]

Meanwhile, several upper Dakota chiefs and headmen formed a

protest movement. Henok Maḣpiyahdinape played a principal role, as did Cloud Man, Running Walker, Lorenzo Lawrence, and Peter Big Fire. Red Iron was allowed to join them after Ramsey had secured his receipt. Although most of these men had strong attachments to the missionaries, they now acted very much on their own, even though they used Sweetser's trading house as a place for meetings. On 2 and 3 December the group formulated and signed two documents dealing specifically with the hand money. The first called for the formation of a committee composed of Sweetser, Williamson, and McLean to examine traders' debts and determine just compensation. The second, written in Dakota by Henok Maḣpiyahdinape, proposed to distribute the Sisseton and Wahpeton money as follows: $100,000 to the Indians, $70,000 to the traders, $60,000 to the mixed-bloods, and $45,000 to be reserved for subsistence and removal. Maḣpiyahdinape termed the document a "national protest," but he used the first person singular to plead for his people: "Father, my money, which I ask you to give me, you will now deliver all to me and I will do as I like with it." Ramsey was presented with both papers as he prepared to return to St. Paul.[63] Once back at his house, the governor ignored the protest and turned $250,000 of the Sisseton-Wahpeton money over to Tyler, who subsequently deducted 12 percent to 15 percent and gave the funds to traders and mixed-bloods, the former getting nearly all of the money.[64]

Of the $370,000 that fell into the hands of traders and mixed-bloods in November and December 1852, the exact distribution remains unknown. Tyler took more than $50,000 for simply distributing the money, but it would be ludicrous to assume that Ramsey, who gave him the job, received no share. Dousman later declared that a large part had been used to bribe senators in Washington. Other rumors charged that $40,000 had been placed in a bank in Pennsylvania, the home state of both Ramsey and Tyler.[65] Fur company employees also did very well by the treaty. A receipt in the Sibley Papers shows that the company alone took in $105,618.54, which was divided into four nearly equal shares of $26,404.63. Sibley, Dousman, McLeod, and Ramsay Crooks were the beneficiaries, but Sibley and others close to him also had private debts that were collected from mixed-bloods and other traders. This appears to have created some hard feelings, since most of the mixed-bloods felt their share remained small compared with those of fur company officials. Even a few of Sibley's closer partners opposed the 12 percent to 15 percent surcharge imposed by Tyler and Sibley, but Ramsey's threat to distribute the money among the Indians silenced these protests.[66]

Shortly after the hand money distribution, several newspapers reported that gross improprieties had taken place. To silence any allegations of a coverup, Sibley called for a Senate investigation in January 1853. Ramsey and Sibley both acquitted themselves well in the preliminary hearings, pointing to the supposedly huge debts the Indians owed and claiming that the natives were incapable of handling the large sums necessary to pay them.[67] While Congress geared up to look more deeply into the issue, Willis A. Gorman replaced Ramsey as governor and Indian superintendent. By June, the president ordered Gorman and John M. Young to take testimony in Minnesota relative to Ramsey's actions. Throughout the several hundred pages of questions and answers they recorded runs strong evidence of fraud and conspiracy.[68]

Although the Senate ultimately cleared Ramsey, Gorman pressed on with the attacks into the fall, mostly for political reasons. Sibley finally concluded that Gorman should be stopped, or "the devil will have to pay." Joseph R. Brown succeeded in ending the new governor's curiosity by pledging to throw the support of his newspaper, the *Minnesota Pioneer*, over to Gorman.[69] By spring 1854 territorial and federal officials put the Ramsey investigation behind them, and the former governor went on to a long and illustrious career in Minnesota politics. But the final act of the sordid affair was yet to be played out; in May Ramsey asked Sibley and representatives of the fur company for $5,000, since he had fulfilled "implied promises" in the past and had sustained expenses defending himself in Washington.[70] Although the noted Minnesota historian William Watts Folwell recorded in his private papers that Ramsey was "too smart to leave

tracks," at least this one document has survived, showing circumstantial evidence of bribery. Ramsey noted in his diary on 8 May that
the traders had agreed to pay, but "to guard against improper infer-
ence will not do it now."[71]

Historians have viewed the 1851 treaties at Mendota and Traverse
des Sioux as a "monstrous conspiracy."[72] After deducting the money
that went to traders and mixed-blood relatives, the Dakotas received
about seven cents an acre for their Minnesota lands. Yet by concen-
trating on the hand money issue, historians have overlooked what
the negotiation shows about Indian-white relations. Through kinship ties and material support, the federal government had built a
strong pattern of friendship with the Dakota people before 1851. One
can only marvel at the unusual degree of trust most Sioux leaders
had in their white and mixed-blood relatives. A vast majority of Indians obviously believed a land sale would benefit them. The success of the 1837 treaty and the declining living standard of many
Sioux people were strong incentives for accepting the government's
argument. It is also probably true that most Dakotas never dreamed
that federal negotiators would ask for all of their lands; the Great
Father had never been greedy in the past. Yet when it became obvious that the government wanted a radical relocation, not even then
did a large number of leaders unify sufficiently to resist the accords.
The small factions that did assemble were easily outmaneuvered by
traders, mixed-bloods, and Washington bureaucrats.

Despite certain difficulties with generalizations, those among the
Dakotas who spoke out most strongly against the amendments and
the illegal distribution of the hand money were men who had some
education and had little need for annuities. Many exemplified the
discontinuity that was slowly evolving in Sioux society and were already being identified as "nonblanket" Indians. Undoubtedly they
saw the traders' paper as a gross fraud and wanted very much to
maintain the reservation clause. It would be a mistake, however, to
assume that they spoke for the missionaries or that they were Chris-

tians. They organized the protest against Ramsey's actions for their own reasons.

The nonblanket faction also had little desire to reinforce kinship ties with traders. Most obtained a livelihood by farming or through trading with smaller St. Paul merchants. Red Iron, for example, was a farmer who noted at the Ramsey investigation that he had no trader and therefore should not have to pay the whites anything. "I had one once [called] Mr. Provençalle," he said, "but he is dead, and I have not said that I would pay him anything."[73] Other missionary-trained Indians who also did some farming took the same attitude. Even so, Red Iron was far from abandoning his traditional culture; he turned to a soldiers' lodge to fight Ramsey, and men in his village were willing to follow him. It would also be a mistake to assume that only nonblanket Indians opposed either the treaties as originally negotiated or the amended versions. Men who were not dependent upon traders often acted in the best interests of their people. Wabasha and Sleepy Eyes clearly fell into this category. Both had strong doubts about the treaties from the start, but they received little support from fellow chiefs.

That men who lived by hunting and annuities would agree to the treaties, even as amended, should not be surprising. Trader support had been essential to their survival for many years, and the treaties promised the continuation of a hunter-gatherer economy, even though they contained "civilization" programs. More traditional Indians also placed strong reliance on their kinship connections with whites and mixed-bloods, who in turn used these kinship networks to influence the negotiation. For these social and economic reasons more traditional Sioux, especially among the Sissetons and Wahpetons, seemed less concerned about either the reservation issue or the hand money controversy. For example, Orphan, the Sisseton chief from Lake Traverse, gave no indication of being discontented about his treaty while giving testimony to the Gorman commission in 1853. "The Great Father had sent them [Ramsey and Lea] there to get a small portion of our land," he said, and his people had agreed.[74]

In addition, for some leaders the treaties were a dilemma. Many Mdewakanton chiefs had maintained kinship ties with traders and government officials for years. They wanted no part of the changes that had occurred at Lac qui Parle, and they prevented schools and farming from taking hold in their villages. They also preferred to stay on the Mississippi River even though they could no longer follow traditional paths without annuities and often had to beg food from nearby whites. But when traders, mixed-bloods, and government officials pressured them, they felt obligated to listen. Many of these men were perceived as kinsmen who had aided their families for years. In the final analysis many felt they had no choice but to accept the inevitable, and they later justified their actions by pointing to the economic depression they faced. "We were forced to sign for fear of starvation," Shooter noted in 1853.[75]

Finally, no political alternatives to the negotiation existed. With the exception of a few minor disagreements over money and terms, the Sioux seemed to be at a loss when it came to countering the offers of the commissioners. When leaders like Sleepy Eyes, Little Crow, and Wabasha questioned the treaty, their arguments were almost apologetic, obviously reflecting their fear of offending white kinsmen. And when a diplomatic breakdown seemed possible, other more pliable leaders spoke out in favor of government alternatives. No consensus ever had a chance to form, and traders and mixed-bloods were left to work individually on chief after chief, filling them with fears of what might happen if they did not accept the generous offer the Great Father had tendered.

In sum, various Dakota factions had different opinions regarding the 1851 treaties both before and after they were negotiated and ratified by Congress. Social, political, and economic factors inherent in the evolution of interethnic relations led to this complex situation. The degree of influence that can be attributed to any one factor varied from tribe to tribe and even from village to village, which makes emphasizing one above the others difficult if not impossible. Suffice it to say that, after the treaties were in force, what had once been a

Dakota world was on the verge of collapse. Only a handful of Sioux seemed to fully understand this in 1852. The others would slowly learn the meaning of the negotiations as the policy of "confinement" was implemented and as white pioneers poured onto the land that had once been the Dakota domain.

10

The Failures of Early Reservation Development, 1853–57

Unknown to most Dakotas, the treaties of 1851 were tools of reform rather than examples of reciprocity. Government officials expected to consolidate the Indians on the lands assigned to them, thus preventing clashes with whites, and to introduce a "civilization" program. Yet few if any bureaucrats knew in 1851 what such a plan entailed. Only the missionaries, who had been with the Sioux for a decade and a half, had a precise idea of what constituted acculturation: the station workers hoped to "individualize" the natives and promote single-family homesteads. Civilization, in other words, was seen as a preliminary to Christianity. Certainly had the Dakotas perceived the intentions of either group—government officials or missionaries—it would have been more difficult to obtain their signatures in 1851. It remained to be seen how long it would take the Sioux to learn the true nature of the 1851 accords.

Several complications prevented the unveiling of the government's acculturation scheme in the early 1850s. Paramount among them was maladministration on the reservations. Officials argued incessantly over procedures and in the process wasted both time and money. Allotment, for example, or the development of individual farms, did not receive strong government attention until after 1858. Meanwhile, minimal pressure from white settlers allowed the Dakotas continued access to ceded lands throughout the decade. River valleys and forested oases in the prairie country were slowly being put to the plow, with whites reaching the southeastern border of the reservations in 1854, yet the "Big Woods" north of the Minnesota and several picturesque valleys south of the river still offered sanctuaries for small hunting parties up to the time Minnesota became a state in 1858. Finally, troubles with the Yanktons in 1855 and a clash between isolated settlers and nonannuity Wahpekutes near Spirit Lake, Iowa, two years later kept the reservations in a state of uneasiness and further hindered development. These factors granted a reprieve to Dakota traditionalists, who could draw annuities in the 1850s and still continue to roam the countryside as hunters rather than adopting an agricultural life.

Removal and reservation development fell under the overall supervision of the new territorial governor and Indian superintendent Willis A. Gorman, who assumed office in May 1853. Gorman faced a multitude of problems. Settlers called for the concentration of the Indians on the reservations, yet nothing of a substantial nature had been done by former governor Ramsey to prepare for their reception. Four government farmers working under Philander Prescott had begun breaking land on the reservations and a contract had been let to a private firm to open six hundred acres more, but warehouses and provisions to feed Indians had been neither built nor planned. In May Gorman found that the Sioux would not relocate unless they could be assured of receiving rations upon arriving in the west. The superintendent agreed to let them plant on their old lands at least until the reservations were ready to accommodate them.[1]

A month later this compromise proved unworkable. Whites invaded Red Wing's old village and burned the bark lodges. Further contests soon erupted over the cleared and plowed fields at Shakopee's and Wabasha's villages. Rather than resist, the Indians appealed to the governor for help. Gorman responded by issuing annuities in exchange for the Indians' moving west. Throughout the summer and fall small parties, often described as "naked and destitute," advanced up the Minnesota valley. By November Gorman could report that only a handful of Dakota people lingered in the immediate vicinity of the Mississippi.[2]

Just as they had feared, most Dakota immigrants found little succor awaiting them in the west. Ramsey had spent most of the funds that the treaties specifically set aside for removal to finance the feasts necessary to obtain Indian consent to the Senate amendments. Furthermore, at the suggestion of both missionaries and traders, direct annuity support came mostly in the form of cash rather than food. Many Indians were able to purchase food from traders, but funds were insufficient to provide sustenance through the winter. While Dakota hunters stalked ducks, tended a few rows of corn, and generally placed their welfare in the hands of their "Great Father," the officials in charge of the reservations slowly came to realize that agency farms were the only clear means by which the easternmost Dakota bands would be able to feed themselves.[3]

Gorman turned the responsibility for agricultural improvement over to Robert G. Murphy, the agent who replaced McLean in the summer of 1853. Murphy surveyed the reservations in July and selected a site eight miles below the junction of the Redwood and Minnesota rivers for the lower Sioux agency, to serve the Mdewakantons and Wahpekutes. A few weeks later he submitted an ambitious and costly development plan to Gorman, calling for the construction of buildings, the purchase of sixty three yokes of oxen, and the employment of farming superintendents, schoolmasters, housekeepers, and forty white laborers. Murphy intended to build a gigantic model farm, spending $23,100 the first year.[4] In his enthusiasm, he neglected certain important details such as organizing the transportation system that would be essential for moving supplies to the agencies.

Gorman remained skeptical, as did the new Indian commissioner, George Manypenny. Both men noted that the Indians did not yet hold clear title to the reservations and seemed reluctant to settle on them, despite the president's assurance of their right to temporary occupancy. Manypenny sympathized with their hesitancy, pointing out to Gorman that it would be unwise to invest heavily in farming when the land might have to be relinquished. In addition, he was becoming suspicious of Murphy's competence. The agent's first-quarter returns showed a proclivity to be loose with money, a tendency that disturbed the frugal commissioner.[5]

Events soon convinced Manypenny that other Minnesota Superintendency employees, including Gorman, also deserved watching. The commissioner's concerns stemmed from a Sioux flour contract that Ramsey had negotiated before leaving office. The former governor had advertised for bids in early 1853, receiving five offers ranging from $4.64 to $6.90 a barrel. Ramsey then sat by as the contractors conspired among themselves. Ultimately the man offering to sell flour at $6.90 was the only bidder left and received the contract, which cost $3,000 more than the lowest bid. Since Ramsey had departed, the commissioner called on Gorman to investigate the fraud. The new superintendent, while critical of Ramsey, recommended that the government honor the contract and even praised the honesty of the contractors, who, it seems, had political clout in the territory.[6]

While Manypenny pondered this advice, the missionaries Riggs and Williamson sent their own emissary, Seliah B. Treat, to Washington to see him. The American Board workers were concerned over the lack of progress on the reservations and had given Treat some disturbing information about Gorman. Treat told the commissioner that the superintendent had purchased a young Sisseton girl and cohabited with her during the annuity distribution in the fall of 1853.[7] Undoubtedly convinced that both the agent and the superintendent were either immoral or dishonest, Manypenny sought ways to get rid of them both and prevent the squandering of Sioux money. There was some discussion of removing Gorman, or so the president told Treat, but when this failed to materialize Manypenny clamped down on funds and ordered Gorman to keep a strict accounting of every penny spent on the reservations. His campaign to prevent fraud resulted in his refusing to release the large sums of money already appropriated by Congress for reservation development.[8]

Manypenny's new austerity views doomed Murphy's farm program. The agent received permission to employ one superintendent and a few hands, but the purchase of substantial numbers of draft animals and the construction of buildings other than storehouses was temporarily refused. Although the number of agency personnel grew steadily thereafter, Manypenny did his best to keep a tight rein on spending by encouraging contracts for specific tasks; thus Murphy had to justify and order in advance any supplies or equipment necessary to run the Sioux farms.[9] Unforeseen expenses would have cropped up for the most farsighted agent, which Murphy was not. Bordering on incompetent, he never overcame the restrictions Manypenny placed on him.

Nonetheless several hundred acres, most of it near Redwood Agency, were broken in 1854. Yet most of this new cropland lay fallow throughout the summer, since Murphy had failed to order seed.[10] The agent also tried to open lands for the Sissetons and Wahpetons near a new agency designated for them at the mouth of the Yellow Medicine River. Here Andrew Robertson, who had married Robert Dickson's mixed-blood daughter, directed farming. Unfortunately the fields selected for the experiment were extremely rocky. The plows broke after completing just twelve acres and had to be sent back to Redwood for repair. Riggs, who watched with deep interest, also noted that all the workmen whom Murphy had provided with spoiled pork and sour flour came down with severe dysentery.[11] Despite the setbacks, Gorman reported to Manypenny in the fall that the farming had been prosecuted with "more than common vigor and success."[12]

These problems might have been resolved had Murphy been at his post, but he was not disposed to stay at Redwood Agency because there was no house for his family.[13] Lieutenant Colonel Francis Lee, then in charge of constructing Fort Ridgely in the southeastern corner of the reservation, scornfully reported to superiors that during his first full year of service Murphy had spent only three brief periods near the agency. By July 1854 Colonel Lee feared that the agent's negligence would prevent the Indians from receiving their food annuities. He had learned that most of the provisions stored at Redwood had been allowed to spoil, and Murphy had yet to have the rations and supplies scheduled for distribution in August shipped from St. Paul. "I fear they will remain in St. Paul indefinitely," the colonel reported, "perhaps till they, too, are all spoiled."[14]

Two flatboats reached the agency in October, allowing the agent to formally call for a distribution and hand out funds, but they carried only a small portion of the rations necessary to feed the Indians and brought no goods at all. Army officials received reports of actual starvation at the agencies. The desperate agent turned to distributing the spoiled meat and flour.[15] One army officer reported that when the barrel staves were removed the flour "stood alone and was as hard as a similar lump of dried mortar." The pork, also, had become "so offensive," as one chief reported to the officer, "that he tired of carrying it and threw it away after leaving the agency."[16] By November Murphy attempted to head off starvation by moving new supplies of food overland from Henderson, Minnesota, fifty miles east of the lower agency. When an early snow descended upon the plains, however, all hope of relief failed. By that time the several thousand Sissetons and Wahpetons had received a mere twelve barrels of flour and several beef cows that Murphy had herded north from his farm in Illinois to sell at fifteen cents a pound.[17]

Indian leaders were quick to note that the fine promises made at the 1851 treaties had not materialized by 1854. The officers in charge of Fort Ridgely heard numerous complaints through the fall, and fears of an "outbreak" filled their reports. Military men were apprehensive, largely because most Dakota Indians refused to stay on the reservation where they could be watched. Many Sioux left immediately after the annuity distribution in 1853, and their numbers grew the next year when it became obvious that Murphy could not feed them. These people established camps in the Big Woods and along the Cannon and Blue Earth rivers. As ducks and geese returned in the spring they congregated in larger villages near the Minnesota River, stretching from the town of Shakopee upriver to the agency. Most of these people now believed they could show up at the agency in the summer and fall, draw rations and funds, and spend the rest of the year off the reservation.[18]

This freedom, however, did not erase the growing Sioux anger over the treaties. Moreover, the continued reliance on hunting, especially in the Big Woods, often led to war with the Chippewas. The clashes during the 1850s seemed at times to be a way of venting anger brought on by the failures on the reservations and by the growing intrusion of white farmers on old hunting grounds. Dakota warriors commonly raided the Chippewas for scalps that they tauntingly paraded on poles through the streets of Minnesota River towns. Shakopee's people were in the forefront, defiantly holding scalp dances during autumn 1853 and 1854. "They have been afraid to show their hostility to the whites," Samuel Pond concluded while at the town of Shakopee in the fall of 1854, "but they have made us as much trouble as they dared to by attacking the Chippewa."[19] In a sense, a psychological duel was being fought.

The Chippewas soon retaliated, attacking Little Crow and a mixed-blood companion within earshot of Fort Ridgely in June 1854. Little Crow escaped with a slight wound, but his friend was killed. The army captured seven of the Chippewa offenders and incarcerated them at the fort. The next day, as workmen continued to erect barracks, 150 to 200 armed Dakota warriors dashed into the compound, overpowering the guard. Soldiers scrambled for rifles and miraculously saved the Chippewa prisoners from the mob. The Sioux finally agreed to withdraw, but they remained in an ugly mood for some time thereafter, angry at the troops as well as at agency workers.[20]

The intertribal violence and the reservation supply problems seemed to engender stronger remonstrations from generally friendly Indians. The normally amicable Red Iron, for example, demanded that plowing be done for his people in 1854, and so did chiefs located at Lake Traverse and Big Stone Lake.[21] Hunting Indians, on the other hand, repeatedly showed up at the agency hungry and begging for food. When it was not forthcoming, they raided the government fields, and in July 1855 a small number of them broke into the Redwood warehouse. Some supplies had been reserved for white laborers, and Dakota men could not understand why workers should

eat while their children starved. When possible, Murphy or his sub-
ordinates handed out a few rations, extracting pledges that bound
the Indians to stay on the reservations in exchange for food. Most
warriors broke the agreements as soon as their women had planted
in the spring or harvested in the fall.[22]

While the agent and superintendent reluctantly accepted the desertion of the reservation each fall, this was not true of the missionaries, who had their own views on acculturation. At the very least,
confinement was a necessary aid in dismantling the communal life-
style of the Dakota people. Obviously this had not occurred, and by
now the missionaries knew better than to expect rapid change. Accordingly, they began constructing their own acculturation programs as the Senate debated the treaties in 1851–52, hoping to attract treaty funds for education and development but aware that
funds for boarding schools and new stations would probably have
to come from private sources.[23]

Williamson and Riggs led the proselytizing efforts on the new reservations, while old colleagues, including Samuel and Gideon Pond,
opted to stay in the east. Williamson had already begun work on the
new station of Pajutazee, near the Yellow Medicine River, or upper
Sioux, Agency, when the Senate gave final approval to the treaties.
Two Indian villages quickly sprang up nearby, one under the Christian sympathizer Running Walker, the old Lac qui Parle Wahpeton
chief who had recognized the value of farming some time before.
Williamson estimated that the number of husbandmen in this village
alone had grown to nearly twenty by the fall of 1852. Other villagers
showed at least a nominal interest in farming, especially at Riggs's
Lac qui Parle mission, the other American Board station that survived the transition to the reservation.[24]

The Presbyterian mission workers had one advantage over their
government counterparts; they had won over a small core of Dakota
men who had already embraced farming. Although most were not
professed Christians, they had known the missionaries for nearly
two decades and had established fictive kinship ties with them. Most
were related to Joseph Renville and came from Lac qui Parle. Riggs

and Williamson believed these men would set an example for others. By 1853 Riggs had launched a newspaper campaign to convince bureau officials that the "concentration" plan that had seemed so promising would succeed only if strong emphasis was placed upon alloting lands to individual farmers. The "model farm" emphasized "common" or band fields and discouraged individualization.[25]

After fire destroyed his Lac qui Parle mission station in the spring of 1854, Riggs saw an opportunity to once again take the lead in showing government officials how acculturation should be effected. He gathered fifteen Dakota families whom he believed could survive as individual agricultural units and settled them on a new tract at Hazelwood, a few miles north of Yellow Medicine Agency. That fall the American Board purchased a small circular sawmill for the new station, and Riggs began to help the farmers build frame houses and fence fields.[26] Murphy and Gorman were pleased with this progress and agreed to pay the farmers for improvements, help break their lands, and purchase oxen for them. Four of the Hazelwood farmers had discarded their blankets by 1854, and three more were considering the change of dress.[27] Accordingly, Riggs viewed Hazelwood as an important symbol of progress. Drawing a parallel to the politics of the times, he dubbed it "Young America against the Old Regime."[28]

Early opposition to this hybrid community came, ironically, from Running Walker, who thought the Hazelwood farmers were receiving more attention than his people and were using too much wood for buildings. Nevertheless, Running Walker continued to support agriculture and even encouraged his people to conceal food from hunting Indians who refused to farm. Such refusals were a serious breach of social mores. His attitude led Williamson to conclude in the fall of 1854 that he had never seen a time "when the prospect for successful labour among the Dakotas was better." Running Walker had fenced his own fields and had begun attending church. More important, his young son and heir Peter Big Fire began building a house at Yellow Medicine in the spring of 1855. Progress seemed assured at the upper agency, at Hazelwood, at Lac qui Parle, where a small residue of native farmers remained after Riggs's departure, and at Patterson Rapids, where Cloud Man, Renville's cross-cousin, had settled with his Sisseton followers.[29]

The farmers still constituted a small minority on the reservations, as missionaries and government officials could easily see. Murphy, Gorman, Manypenny, and the station workers realized that something had to be done for the majority, especially after rumors of rebellion surfaced in the mid-1850s.[30] Yet Indian Bureau officers generally felt that the blame for past failures lay outside their own offices. Throughout the spring of 1855 Murphy pleaded for the government to release money for the construction of mills and buildings. He made some headway with Gorman, who presented his case to Manypenny.[31] "The commissioner will not fail to observe," Gorman wrote to the commissioner, "that these Indians have been told again and again the amount their great father was to give them for farms, schools, mills &c., annually. They know it all, they can recapitulate almost every appropriation in the treaty." Manypenny responded that funds could not be "advantageously applied" until the Indians had settled on the reservations. "If the interests of the Indians have not been as fully promoted as practicable, I am unable to perceive that any blame attaches to this office," Manypenny defensively replied.[32]

The farming program finally produced an excellent crop of corn and potatoes by August 1855. Prescott reported that the Indians who had planted near Redwood Agency "raised nearly enough for their winter supply." Over seven hundred acres had been opened at the lower agency, or about eighty acres on average per band. Riggs still discounted the use of "common" fields, but it seemed they would prevent starvation during the coming fall and winter. He also rejoiced that Joseph Napeśniduta, a mission-trained full-blood, and six or seven companions—some women—had started separate farms that spring at Redwood.[33] Although government administrators gave them little notice, Napeśniduta's people formed the basis for the spread of "individualized" farming from the upper to the lower agency.

By fall, Murphy and Gorman had also managed a smooth distribution of annuities. Over $80,000 in cash reached eager Dakota hands, as did the prescribed amounts of goods and provisions. Troubles with the Yanktons that had broken out that summer on the Missouri River prompted military officials to request that munitions not be distributed, but the Indians seemed so placid by October that even these items had been handed out. In October Gorman submitted his usual optimistic report, with a ring of truth. "A very large quantity of ploughing and planting" had been accomplished over the year, he wrote, and "the crops have yielded abundantly." Mills were taking shape, and the superintendent had expectations of building schools.[34]

Nonetheless, Gorman's optimistic report ignored certain realities. Although the Indians received large sums of money, traders waited at the pay table like vultures to collect past debts, thereby securing large amounts of the cash annuities, occasionally over the vehement denials of the Indians. The Sioux had been called in a full month early to collect their money, and as they waited many were forced to purchase flour and pork on credit at scandalous prices. Agent Murphy had again apparently herded cattle onto the reservation from his farm and sold beef at fifteen cents a pound. The Sissetons and Wahpetons bought heavily from Murphy and others, since they had been without buffalo for some time. Unidentified observers noted that the agent held back the annuities until most of the salable provisions and beef were gone.[35]

Despite the relative success of the 1855 distribution, Sioux leaders still felt they had substantial grievances. In January of the new year many chiefs signed a petition asking for permission to go to Washington and see their Great Father. Leaders noted that the government still owed them money and provisions. Although officials in the Bureau of Indian Affairs disregarded their request, Manypenny did instigate an audit. He soon found that beyond the money he had generally refused to send west, the government still owed the Mdewakantons over $30,000 from the 1837 treaty and owed the other three tribes $12,000. He petitioned Congress for the funds and soon received them.[36] It was hoped that this discovery would alleviate the dissatisfaction in the Sioux bands.

The Indian Bureau also made an administrative change on 15 April, designed to promote Sioux reservation development. It transferred

the Dakota agencies to the supervision of the Northern Superintendency. The new superintendent, Francis Huebschmann, immediately went to Minnesota to survey reservation affairs and straighten
out the tangled financial situation. Huebschmann quickly showed
that he intended to make changes.

The new superintendent's first orders prohibited intertribal fighting. Feuds had begun afresh in the spring when several Dakota parties struck the Chippewas and the victims retaliated by viciously
killing a Dakota girl who had been living with a white family. After
Mdewakanton chiefs refused to hand over the warriors involved and
further infuriated the superintendent by stealing goods from government warehouses, Huebschmann directed that an army guard
be placed around the annuity goods being readied for distribution,
and he took the Sioux money to the fort. On 17 June he counciled
with the four hundred Indians who appeared "in war costume." Little
Crow addressed Huebschmann, telling him emphatically that the
warriors would not be surrendered. The chief quickly moved to other
issues, dwelling on "the very long pocket" of the agent, "into which
their [the Sioux's] funds were slipt." Although Huebschmann sympathized with the Indians, he refused to withdraw his demands.[37]

As he prepared to leave, the superintendent heard that many older
Mdewakanton leaders, including Little Crow, wished to hand over
the warriors. But the young men remained defiant. Left to their own
devices, the moderates soon prevailed. On 16 July fourteen warriors
gave themselves up, and a few days later the list increased to nineteen. At this point Huebschmann handed out the funds in his possession, withholding food until later in the fall. The prisoners
remained in the post stockade until mid-September when the
commandant, tired of feeding them, set them free.[38] Like Taliaferro
and Clark, Huebschmann soon discovered that civil authorities refused to spend money trying Indians, and this made further action
impossible.

Once calm had settled over the agency, Huebschmann investi-
gated Murphy's handling of reservation development. The agent's
absenteeism had left its mark. Gristmills had been poorly con-

structed, and some lands would have to be replowed. The government farmers and their white assistants, now numbering more than fifty and drawing salaries over $13,000 annually, took provisions earmarked for the Indians. Even with this gratuity, employees seldom did a full day's work. One whom the superintendent stumbled onto was lying drunk in the barracks.[39] In the final report for the year, Prescott blamed the problems on the commissioner, who had not trusted Murphy and had held back funds. The funds still due the Dakotas did amount to $163,500, according to Prescott's count.[40] Manypenny, on the other hand, congratulated himself for rescuing "a considerable amount of funds for the object of education, improvement, and other useful ends" from the hands of agency employees. Moreover, he rejoiced in Murphy's replacement on 22 August by the Minnesota lawyer Charles Flandrau. After the new agent made symbolic cuts in the number of whites employed at each agency, Manypenny concluded that this vast reserve of money might now be used with "favorable auspices."[41]

As government officials fought over the expenditure of funds, missionaries continued to set examples that they hoped would lead to the acculturation of the eastern Sioux. In July 1856 Riggs organized the farmers near his mission into the "Hazelwood Republic," a quasi-independent political structure that successfully petitioned agent Murphy for recognition as a Dakota band. Paul Mazekutemani acted as the "governor" of the republic, while Henok Mahpiyahdinape, Antoine Freniere, Simon Anawangmani, and Gabriel Renville assumed positions as cabinet officials. Riggs had no illusions about the republic, since several of the members were not Christians, but he sought to establish a clearer distinction between the small numbers who had rejected tribalism and the majority of the annuity Sioux who had not. By 1857 the farmers at Hazelwood made known their intention to restrict membership in the republic to those Indians who discarded their "medicine sacks," refused to participate in medicine dances or "other foolish feasts," adopted white dress, and constructed houses.[42] Officers of the republic took charge of their own school system and eventually sought integration into white society by applying for Minnesota citizenship. Riggs was behind the latter idea, asking Martin McLeod, who had been a territorial delegate, if it would not be appropriate to confer citizenship upon Indians who dressed like whites and could read and write in their own language. Unfortunately, the framers of the state constitution decided against this course in 1857, and the state court determined that citizens must use the English language.[43]

Indian farmers, like those at Hazelwood, harvested large amounts of corn and potatoes in the fall of 1856, and many sold excess provisions to Flandrau. Receipts the agent kept suggest that while the Hazelwood community, tied together by kinship and at least a nominal interest in Christianity, may have held the most successful farmers, by mid-decade the villages near Yellow Medicine contained larger numbers of men interested in agriculture. They too had surplus crops. Flandrau paid Indian farmers $5 for each barrel of corn and $3 for each of potatoes. In all, the agent bought 225 barrels of provisions in the spring of 1857.[44]

The proliferation of native agriculturalists greatly encouraged government officials. Huebschmann openly discussed the possibility of removing all white farmers and filling their positions with Indians. Flandrau too felt that a new attitude pervaded the reservations, concluding in January 1857 that there existed a "general disposition among all the bands to engage in agriculture" during the coming year.[45] Accordingly, both men were startled when in mid-March news filtered into the snowbound Redwood Agency of a terrible massacre that a small band of Wahpekutes had recently unleashed upon the Iowa frontier.[46] All talk of acculturation programs came suddenly to a halt.

In the decade preceding the 1851 treaties, more and more land in northern Iowa was opened to settlement. Once the territory of the Wahpekutes, this area suffered a slow ecological disintegration as Sac and Fox hunters and white pioneers depleted its resources. Blood feuds had also broken out among the Wahpekutes themselves, resulting in the murders of Tasaugye in 1839 and Wanmdisapa in 1842. One group, led by the descendants of Tasaugye, stayed in the Blue

Earth and Cannon river valleys and eventually moved to the reservation. The second, under the leadership of Sintomniduta, had wandered west, camping occasionally with the Yanktons on the Vermilion River and returning to hunt and trade at the headwaters of the Des Moines River.[47]

During their eastern excursions the western Wahpekutes, seldom numbering even one hundred, fell in with the white squatters who had settled in advance of the general frontier. Several of these whites were horse thieves and whiskey dealers who felt safe in the rather isolated reaches of the upper Des Moines watershed where military patrols seldom ventured. In 1854 Henry Lott and his son axed to death Sintomniduta and nine women and children. Other incidents followed, the reports of which are not always reliable. Nevertheless, the troubles convinced settlers living on Lake Okoboji to surround and disarm the followers of Sintomniduta during the dead of winter 1856–57.[48] Now under the leadership of Inkpaduta, these people depended on their firearms to hunt. Obtaining replacements, they retaliated on 8 March, killing thirty settlers near Lake Okoboji and about a dozen more across the Minnesota border near present-day Jackson. These settlements were so isolated from white civilization that survivors near Jackson headed overland to Fort Ridgely for help, arriving with their stories of horror on 18 March.[49]

The news of the "Spirit Lake Massacre," so called because this lake was the most identifiable landmark in the area, reverberated like a thunderclap on the Minnesota frontier. Militia were quickly raised in the developing towns of Mankato, St. Peter, and Traverse des Sioux. As these units took the field, hundreds of excited settlers fled eastward carrying their most prized possessions. In the confusion, the militia units ambushed innocent Indians. One command under Martin McLeod's brother George attacked Sleepy Eyes's Sisseton village west of Mankato. Another fired on Red Iron's people in the northeastern sections of Watonwan County. These Indians had as usual drifted back onto ceded lands after the distribution of annuities. While the confrontations had the potential for becoming serious, only a few casualties were reported. Agent Flandrau quickly reached other bands then off the reservation, informing them of the trouble and ordering them to return to Redwood at once.[50]

Meanwhile the army sent Captain Bernard E. Bee and a company of troops to Jackson. They battled violent snow and cold for several days, only to arrive on the scene too late to catch Inkpaduta. "The nest was there, but not warm," Bee reported to his superiors. Actually, the Wahpekutes had seen the troops coming and doused their fires. They were only a few miles off, holding four white women prisoner.[51] Upon Bee's return an outcry swept the territory for the punishment of the marauders. Orders from the War Department called for immediate pursuit, yet at the same time troubles in Kansas and Utah had prompted the withdrawal of large numbers of men and supplies from the Minnesota frontier. Colonel E. B. Alexander, in command at Fort Ridgely, informed Washington that he would need more men to pursue the Wahpekute raiders and that he could not start until 1 June. As an afterthought the colonel suggested that the War Department engage fifty "Indians and half breeds" as scouts for a search-and-destroy mission.[52]

On the specified date, as conditions on the reservation deteriorated, the army failed to launch an expedition. Colonel Alexander had marched his troops to Fort Leavenworth, en route to Utah, leaving Captain Bee with a skeleton command at Fort Ridgely. To make matters worse, another upheaval occurred in the administration of the reservations. Huebschmann was replaced by the inexperienced William J. Cullen in May, and Flandrau took a position as a federal judge, abandoning his post in July.[53] The punishment of Inkpaduta and his people had not been given high priority by the federal government, and their success had created great excitement on the reservations.

Cullen assumed the task of defusing the tense situation at Redwood and Yellow Medicine. He had been ordered not to distribute June annuities until Inkpaduta had been punished. Nonetheless, after several Dakota leaders voiced their willingness to join an expedition against the western Wahpekutes Cullen requested that troops come to the agencies to supervise the upcoming payment. He wanted troops stationed especially at the upper agency, where several thousand Yanktons and Yanktonais had arrived to share in the annuities. The Yankton and Yanktonai tribes felt that some of the land ceded in 1851 belonged to them.[54] As troops took up positions on 1 July at Yellow Medicine, word arrived that one of Inkpaduta's sons, Mahpiyahoto-mani, who had married a Sisseton, had foolishly returned to visit his in-laws. As one of his last acts as agent, Flandrau took a dozen men to the Sisseton camp, where they killed Mahpiyahotomani as he attempted to escape and took his wife prisoner. On their return march mobs harassed the party, forcing the troops to hand over the woman.[55]

The confrontation quickly escalated, with hostile camps coming together and traders, friendly Indians, and agency workers barricading themselves at the agency. The beleaguered whites received relief from Major T. W. Sherman's battery and twenty-five men, and Cullen was able to hold council with the discontented Indians on 9 and 10 July, but when a young Sisseton warrior stabbed a soldier shortly thereafter everyone prepared for all-out war.[56] Cullen and Sherman demanded the surrender of the man, who came forward and taunted the troops. Sherman then planned an assault on the Indian camp as soon as promised reinforcements arrived from Fort Randall on the Missouri River. "My opinion is that we are on the eve of a general war with all these Indians," the outnumbered and surrounded Sherman concluded. During the night the Sioux moved off a mile or two; they seemed to be organizing their own campaign.[57] Fortunately, Little Crow arrived on the sixteenth and went into council with the hostile elements. He had married several daughters of Running Walker, giving him strong kinship credentials in Sisseton-Wahpeton circles. In a miraculous display of diplomacy, Little Crow convinced the Sisseton assailant to give himself up and produced a small body of men willing to go in pursuit of Inkpaduta. The party, which ultimately reached between 150 and 200 farmers, mixed-bloods, and "blanket" Indians from both agencies, left on 23 July. Even though no troops accompanied the expedition, Major Sherman had little doubt of the sincerity of the warriors, reporting that they had "a fixed determination to bring in the murderers."[58]

Delighted with this turn of events, Cullen handed out some food, to reciprocate the good intentions of the Sissetons as well as to support the families of the men on the raid. But he referred the larger question of distributing all the annuities to the new Indian commissioner, J. W. Denver. The commissioner quickly instructed Cullen that "there must be no yielding."[59] The Indian Bureau felt compelled to refuse annuities until the old chief Inkpaduta had been eliminated by the reservation Sioux. That the western Wahpekutes were not annuity Indians made no difference to Washington officials.

Meanwhile, Little Crow's men nearly destroyed the Wahpekute marauders during the last week in July, when they came upon a splinter group of Inkpaduta's band. They killed at least five persons and captured several women and children. This prompted reservation leaders to demand the release of their long-overdue annuities, even though Inkpaduta himself had not been taken. Cullen sympathized with them, but he waited for orders from Washington. Commissioner Denver finally agreed to release the goods for distribution on 25 August.[60]

Despite the tension in July, a sense of normality had returned to both agencies by September. Those Indians who had planted—far fewer than the year before—managed to harvest a surplus. The Yanktons and Yanktonais had moved out onto the plains to hunt buffalo, taking many of the discontented Sissetons and Wahpetons with them. At councils with the leaders who had remained, Cullen heard numerous complaints regarding the government's failure to send certain funds, but agents and superintendents had grown accustomed to such criticism. Cullen was able to satisfy many reservation Indians when he distributed an extra $42,000 in annuity money in November, funds that Manypenny had discovered were due the Sioux from the 1837 treaty.[61] Although most of this money went immediately into the pockets of traders, it did help soothe the animosity that many Sioux were nurturing against the government and against the treaties they had signed.

On the other hand, most whites and many Indians on the upper Minnesota realized that Indian-white relations would never be the same after the Inkpaduta massacre. The events of July demonstrated that the government would use annuities as a means to control the Sioux, forcing them to punish people of their own blood for misdeeds, an action that polarized the Dakota bands even more. More important, the troubles at Spirit Lake brought a dramatic increase in tensions between white homesteaders and the Sioux. Native parties would continue to hunt in the Big Woods thereafter, but the government now made every effort to stop such invasions of territorial domain. Red Iron and the leaders of several other small bands moved their villages permanently onto the reservation in 1857. "Concentration" was finally becoming a reality.[62]

Scholars who have examined the Spirit Lake massacre generally believe that the government's failure to punish Inkpaduta proved a decided factor in instigating the Sioux to rebel five years later. Missionaries first offered this explanation in the fall of 1862. At least one contemporary newspaper also decried the military failure, calling the response to the killings "humiliating." [63] The army eventually sent out a large patrol in September 1857 that scoured the Coteau des Prairies west of Fort Ridgely for several weeks before returning empty-handed. Little Crow acted as a guide for the troops. The officers at the fort, however, felt certain that they had demonstrated the mobility of their troops and that the army could "penetrate any part of their [Sioux] country, whenever circumstances may render it necessary." Commissioner Denver agreed that no damage had occurred to the credibility of American forces despite the need to call on Little Crow for men in July.[64] In fact, the government had adopted a policy of using Indians to punish the misdeeds of their fellow warriors several decades before. The response of Washington officials to Spirit Lake conformed to patterns already well established in federal Indian policy.

It seems doubtful, then, that the Inkpaduta affair stimulated a series of discussions in Dakota camps regarding the effectiveness of the American military. More likely it brought a reassessment of Dakota relations with the federal government and the growing number of whites who were slowly overrunning Sioux hunting preserves in

Minnesota. When the Big Woods fell under the white man's plow, as it inevitably would, those Dakota men who preferred to remain hunters would be deprived of a livelihood. Many had already become anachronisms of sorts by the mid-1850s, or so thought a young surveyor named Frederick P. Leavenworth who worked on the reservation. He marveled at the "deference" with which native traditionalists continued to view change. A party he met under Sibley's kin Bad Hail provided a good example of the stoic, unflinching Indian hunter: "the women carried the packs, the men, tall handsome fellows, with a streak of red paint across their faces, stalked along innocent of any other freight than a gun and blanket."[65] Most Dakota men still looked and thought like Bad Hail in 1857.

Convincing warriors like these to adopt farming had been the goal of government programs in 1852. Instead, the treaties that were to reform the Sioux had accomplished little more than the program that Taliaferro had begun fourteen years before. The incompetent handling of early reservation development had no doubt contributed to the failure, yet even if Murphy had constructed a smoothly operating model farm, the example would have had little effect on the Dakota hunters. They had not agreed to treaties in 1851 so they might be made into farmers. In substance, the missionaries had been correct; government officials would have to challenge the tribal fabric of Indian life if agriculture was to make substantial progress. If migratory hunting continued, the possibility of another Spirit Lake was very real.

While tribalism continued to be an important social force on the reservations, a few astute observers did notice that political erosion, under way for several decades, had reached a new stage. Annuities were largely responsible. With most of the government payment coming as cash rather than goods as in the 1840s, it became a simple matter to pay individual heads of households in each Sioux village. Provisions distributed in barrels and boxes might still be given to a band chief, but often these supplies were too meager for a leader to use in gaining prestige. One official sent west to examine reservation affairs in 1857 noted that "the per capita system" of payment directly affected the chiefs' ability to control their young men.[66] Obviously consensus government had not worked effectively for some time. But some Dakota men seemed to be devising alternatives. Soldiers' lodges emerged during the 1851 treaties with the intent of overruling chiefs. This pattern continued in the 1850s. Lodges were select organizations that excluded fictive kin, such as white agents, and they appealed primarily to hunters rather than nonblanket Indians. It was clear that they were the only institutional organizations with any power that could and would protect traditionalism.

The kinship relations that various factions formed with whites also seemed to be in transition. Whereas Dakota "descent groups" remained intact, their members witnessed the infusion of a new array of whites, mostly settlers or government workers who understood very little about the intricacies of Indian social relations. Often they acted like the whites near Spirit Lake. But changes occurred even in top reservation personnel in the 1850s, destroying the continuity that had been the hallmark of Dakota relations with the United States in past decades. Joseph R. Brown, now a newspaper editor, commented in 1857 that neither Cullen nor Huebschmann "could set [sit] down and give a succinct, logical, and intelligent description of the differences between the habits, manners, customs, and peculiarities of a Sioux Indian and a snapping turtle."[67] How different they were from earlier agents, who had in many cases been students of Indian life.

The continuity that had characterized early intercultural relations had also declined in regard to the traders. As Williamson pointed out, "the old traders in whom the [the Sioux] had confidence, had all left them."[68] There were still many whites and mixed-bloods around, such as Prescott and Robertson, who had strong family ties and understood how reciprocity functioned, but the Renvilles, Mooerses, and Fairbaults had long since died or retired. Even Sibley had left the Dakota trade after receiving substantial funds from the 1851 treaties. The men who replaced them, along with the horde of reservation employees who worked on mills and plowed fields, were a new generation. Some quickly made friends among the Indians, while others were completely unsympathetic toward them.

During the first few years of the reservation experience, then, more change occurred in the basic relations between whites and Indians in Minnesota than ever before. Although numerous kinship networks still remained and even seemed to be strengthened among farmer Indians, missionaries, and the white reservation employees who helped them to break land and build houses, evidence suggests that more and more hunting Indians felt that whites had defaulted on their obligations to them. Stealing from warehouses, defying agents, superintendents, and army officers, and threatening violence all illustrated this growing discontent. They were the type of incident that had generally happened in the past when a kinsman had ignored his responsibilities to his relatives and his village. Yet these displays were still very much the exception rather than the rule. For every report of trouble, there were undoubtedly many peaceful exchanges where individuals from different ethnic groups and factions smoked, ate, discussed events, and parted friends. The Dakotas were still not at a point where any segment of them saw whites in general as responsible for their many problems.

Economic relations still contained some threads of continuity as well. Despite the hit-and-miss record of annuity distribution in the first few years of reservation life, many Sioux men did not opt to change their life-style. And up until the Spirit Lake affair they continued to roam freely throughout the countryside, relatively unintimidated either by agency personnel or by the American army. Access to annuities, now an essential supplement to this nomadic existence, had increasingly become a privilege rather than a right, and the belief that treaties would solve the material misfortunes of the Sioux hunter was quickly breaking down, but the overall economic environment remained relatively unchanged. Reports of good hunting in the eastern woods of Minnesota did occasionally surface, and each year the Sissetons and Wahpetons went in search of buffalo on the western prairies. Though some Indians now wore pants rather than breechcloths, hoarded food, and lived on farms, hunting Indians still returned to villages with the game they had taken, and children celebrated their success with cries of adoration. The old Dakota world was not unrecognizable; the Sioux warrior-hunter still had the opportunity to imitate the existence that had been the meaning of life itself to his ancestors, even though it no longer provided sustenance for survival.

11

The Dissolution of Kinship and Reciprocity Bonds

The Inkpaduta massacre unveiled an obvious flaw in the government's reservation policy—concentration had failed, and many Dakota villagers continued to roam at large across Minnesota's frontier. Inkpaduta had likewise illustrated that many western counties in the new state would be unsafe as long as the Sioux were permitted off the reservation. American pioneers had reason to be concerned. Even though a corridor of prairie still separated the reservation from lands being developed west of St. Paul, a large number of annuity Indians had sympathized with Inkpaduta. As Superintendent Cullen argued in his 1857 annual report, the Spirit Lake marauders were "connected by marriage and blood to both the upper and lower bands," and the conduct of several "prominent" annuity bands suggested a strong willingness to assist the "murderers."[1] Inkpaduta had demonstrated the potential for conflict in western Minnesota, despite the history of friendship and reciprocity that had existed among ethnic groups.

Concerned officials in Washington called for an immediate study of the Minnesota situation. After several months of assessing the eastern Sioux, special agent Kintzing Pritchette filed a discouraging report. "The hope of making them a permanent agricultural people," Pritchette concluded, "is a vain dream of impractical philanthropy." His solution emphasized isolation, enforced by a military presence. On the other hand, Cullen expressed some optimism. He first implored government officials to fulfill treaty promises. In regard to

Dakota migratory habits, he suggested that when a "comfortable" atmosphere existed on the reservations, Sioux warriors would stay home. Finally, in September 1857 Cullen openly advocated the development of individual farms as a way to improve the social and economic environment on the reservations and to ease tensions on the frontier.[2] One month later, Joseph R. Brown was appointed Sioux agent and joined him in implementing this program.

Brown's appointment came as no surprise. He had been an active Democrat for many years, and he understood Sioux culture as well as any white man. Furthermore, Brown had launched a newspaper campaign in 1856 designed to foster Indian policy reforms. He argued that the Sioux had shown considerable patience with government failures, and he cautioned the public of "serious troubles" if better management of the reservations was not forthcoming. Brown then clamored for a division of the reservations "in severalty" and a discontinuation of the "community of interest" system used in the distribution of annuity goods. The new agent also proposed that common fields be broken up and the Indians be given every encouragement to stop their custom of sharing sustenance with kinsmen and friends.[3]

Considering his energy, knowledge of the Indians, and compassion for their cause, the Indian Bureau made a wise choice in Brown. Yet he had one overriding fault: Brown was sexually immoral. Riggs was aghast at his selection, being well aware of his penchant for young Sioux girls and also of his questionable business background. Rumor also had it that Brown intended to put two of his brothers, both as licentious as himself, in positions of trust. Although Williamson had more tolerance for the federal patronage system, even he fretted over Brown's appointment. Both missionaries wondered how a man who had spent much of his life debauching Indian women and trading liquor to their men could ever be an effective instrument of acculturation.[4]

The concern of these critics seemed warranted when Brown cast his support behind a new treaty negotiation. Brown and traders William H. Forbes, Louis Roberts, and Andrew J. Myrick had originally introduced the idea in January 1856, convincing eastern Sioux leaders that if they petitioned to visit Washington they might see the Great Father and find out what had happened to their annuity funds. The final petition, however, contained clauses acknowledging Dakota debts to traders for $90,000, admissions that a handful of Dakota leaders quickly repudiated.[5] Murphy and Gorman both opposed the document, and the effort never obtained serious consideration until Flandrau, who had been speculating in land before his appointment as agent, called for a land cession in 1857. He advised bureau officials to bring some Dakota chiefs to Washington, thus negating the influence of radical "young men," and to negotiate with them for their land northeast of the Minnesota River.[6] The eastern Sioux would supposedly gain permanent ownership of the southwest bank from the sale—the five-year guarantee given them by the president was about to expire—and their agent would be empowered to sanction individual ownership of allotted farm plots.

The men behind the scheme employed the patterns used so successfully in 1851. Most were living with Dakota women, establishing kinship ties, yet they had traded with the Sioux for less than a decade, and it is doubtful that they had accumulated credits of major proportions. Besides kinship alliances, the traders had friends in government, especially Brown and Flandrau. Brown had several thousand dollars in trader claims, and both he and Flandrau had designs on the land north of the Minnesota River. Brown intended to use the "half-breed scrip" that originated from the final sale of the mixed-blood Lake Pepin reserve in 1857 to lay claim to a large tract of acreage. Each mixed-blood Sioux was allowed land in the west as partial compensation. Williamson assessed the situation succinctly in March 1858 when he concluded that so many land speculators and traders were involved in the scheme to convince the Sioux to sell part of their lands that it would be difficult for the Indians to refuse.[7]

The Dakota delegation headed to Washington when the rivers cleared of ice in March. Sixteen leaders came from Redwood and ten from Yellow Medicine. Fully half the latter group were farmers, and the Lake Traverse Sissetons were poorly represented. The lower bands fell under the leadership of men heavily involved in the negotiations of 1851. Most chiefs felt the trip offered them a chance to lay their grievances before the president, and it seems unlikely that they were aware of the designs on the remainder of their reservation lands. Stories had been printed in the local newspapers, however, intimating that if the Dakota leaders refused to negotiate the president would allot natives lands southwest of the Minnesota River and open the region northeast of the river to white settlement. When the Indians arrived in Washington they were faced with a fait accompli and could only hope to get the best possible bargain.[8]

The delegates met with Acting Commissioner Charles Mix on four occasions in late March and early April. Little Crow ably presented the Indians' case, arguing that several funds connected to both the 1837 and 1851 treaties had not been paid. In addition, he complained about agent Murphy, who had on occasion "lost" provisions and blankets and then opened a store to sell these very items. "If I were to give you an account of all the money [due us] that was spilled" into the Minnesota River, the chief said at one point, "it would take all night." Mix listened patiently, since he knew that Manypenny had withheld funds. He labored to convince the Indians that the time was near when their Great Father intended to forward this money; it now rested safely "in a strong box of the treasury" and would be sent when it could be used to advantage. In an awkward attempt to disarm his disgruntled charges, Mix admitted that Superintendent Cullen had "pushed" him on the money matter and that it had perhaps been responsible for his premature baldness. The traders and interpreters laughed, but Little Crow remained in bad humor. Finally, growing impatient, Mix shifted the discussion to the land issue.[9]

Here Mix made no joke in responding to Little Crow: "I do not wish to frighten or unnecessarily alarm him," he said through an interpreter, "but he and his people are now living on the land they occupy by the courtesy of their Great Father." Mix asserted that he wanted the Sioux to have permanent tenure to the acres southwest of the river, but that the Great Father now needed the rest for his white children. Mix then told the delegates he wanted to develop a severalty program and organize an agency police force. On 25 May these proposals were presented in writing for the Indians to consider.[10]

At this point Little Crow displayed unusual anger: "You [Mix] talk well and use fine language and that's all." For Little Crow, it seems, the promise of occupancy granted by the president had been forever, rather than for five years. This impression had arisen from an 1854 meeting between Little Crow and Mix in Washington. "You then promised that we should have this same land forever," Little Crow told the acting commissioner, "and yet . . . you now want to take half of it away." Perhaps the chief, who apparently went east alone, had been led to believe the Sioux would not have to move. Congress had passed a resolution authorizing the president to grant the Sioux permanent tenure, but it was never acted upon. At any rate, Little Crow was caught off guard by the treaty proposal. He finally promised to see if he could "find anything good in it."[11]

On 4 June the Mdewakanton and Wahpekute delegates reassembled to discuss the proposed session. Although most leaders were in a testy mood, Little Crow and Wabasha ultimately submitted a counterproposal that called for the distribution of a sum of money "to settle their affairs." Mix demanded to know how they intended to use the money. Little Crow seemed unwilling to tell him, complaining that "although he [the Great Father] has got the land . . . the money he holds fast." Finally, the chief admitted that the funds were primarily for the traders, "who have lost money by us." "They wanted to be paid, and I am willing to set apart $50,000 for that purpose." Little Crow then listed the debts: to Myrick $11,000, to A. J. Campbell $11,000, to Madison Sweetser $8,000, to Brown $5,000, to Forbes $3,000, and to Roberts $2,500. Since the figures did not add up to the total, $45,000 was reserved for debts and $25,000 for the Dakota people. With this understanding the Indians reluctantly signed the treaty on 19 June after many more hours of useless debate. At one point Mix told the delegates to sign or else deal with the new, unsympathetic state of Minnesota, which would soon have jurisdiction over the entire Minnesota River valley. The final document never included a price for the lands surrendered, leaving that up to the Senate.[12]

Mix used similar tactics with the upper Sioux, who signed a treaty on the same day. The farmer Mazamani listed the traders to whom the tribes owed money—seventeen in all—and indicated his willingness to compensate them with $17,000. The Sissetons and Wahpetons expressed less discontent with the government, but they acknowledged that most of the chiefs who did have complaints were back at Lake Traverse. Even so, some delegates castigated the government for failing to fulfill obligations under the 1851 accord, and those Indian farmers present pointed out that the northeast side of the Minnesota River, which they would lose, contained most of the prime timber for building. Yet many of these men agreed in principle with the idea of severalty.[13] Indeed, some already lived on separate farms.

The Senate finally ratified the treaties on 9 March 1859, but it waited over a year before assigning a price for the cession. Ultimately a figure of thirty cents an acre was agreed upon, though it represented perhaps one-twentieth of what the land was worth. More important, by 1860, when the government decided to distribute the money—$96,000 to the lower Sioux and $170,880 to the upper bands— the traders had increased their claims, leaving the lower Sioux with virtually nothing. Had the delegates known that Congress and the traders were about to treat them so shabbily, it is doubtful they would have signed the documents. As it was, they departed for home in 1858 "in apparent bad humor." The chief's coats, medals, and other miscellaneous gifts did not make up for their ill treatment at the hands of government officials.[14]

While the delegates were absent, however, radical improvements occurred at the agencies. Money recently released by the Indian commissioner was now available for massive construction projects. Brown had invested some of the funds in three steam sawmills and had purchased 150 yokes of oxen, making the spring plowing much easier. When the delegates disembarked from the steamboat that had brought them up the Minnesota River they landed in the midst of a boom. By fall, some forty-five houses had been constructed for the Indians at the lower agency and bountiful crops had been harvested and stored for the winter.[15] Cullen had convinced Mix of the need to spend all the funds that had accumulated for the eastern Sioux over the years.

The new agent also proposed new guidelines for the expenditure of annuity money. In his September 1858 report Brown attested that "the idea that the agricultural and educational funds are the common property of all [Sioux Indians] should be discarded." He believed they should be spent only on those natives "who evince an anxiety to profit by their expenditure." Flandrau and others had been saying for some time that large numbers of Indians would adopt "civilization" if they had the right incentives and support. Brown agreed, arguing in essence that the bulk of reservation resources should be used in a reciprocal fashion to effect change. He obviously intended to assist with plowing and house building only those natives who were willing to adopt white customs.[16] He said as much in an 1858 newspaper article, indicating that his charges "seem to appreciate their position, and to see the necessity of allying themselves, by as close bonds as possible, to the white man."[17]

Brown indicated to the commissioner that he already had "many applicants" for houses and farming equipment. One band of sixteen Mdewakantons had adopted "articles of association" and had cut their hair and donned white clothes. Joseph Napeśniduta, a missionary convert, headed this movement, along with White Dog. Cullen organized them into a "pantaloon band" in November 1858.[18] Many more Indians expressed an interest in conversion over the next winter, knowing it could mean the difference between eating and starving. Indeed, after the annuities had been handed out in June 1859, more than two hundred Sioux men flocked to the agencies for haircuts and store-bought clothes. "I can only partially convey to you the highly encouraging conditions of the Sioux," Cullen wrote to Commissioner A. B. Greenwood in jubilation over the change. "This desire to become civilized is of such a character [that] not any who have taken that step have returned to their Indian dress." Throughout 1859–60 the farmers did their own field work, raising surplus crops. The "improvement Sioux," as they were called, had swollen to about one-sixth of the Mdewakanton and Wahpekute tribes—four hundred people. At Yellow Medicine they numbered nearly as many.[19]

The transformation came so unexpectedly that neither Brown nor Cullen was prepared for it. Even the agent seemed surprised that so many Indians had been willing to change their appearance in exchange for annuity help. Brick houses soon replaced wooden ones, which had been poorly built and were susceptible to prairie fires. Large amounts of stock also had to be imported. Initially each farmer received a yoke of oxen, but the supplies soon ran out. Although the Dakotas took good care of the animals they received, delays in getting them discouraged some would-be farmers. Brown also distributed two dozen cows, a few chickens, and some pigs. By the time Brown left office in 1861 he had been instrumental in constructing at least 125 individual farms with a substantial output: eastern Sioux farmers were growing at least sixty thousand bushels of corn and twenty thousand bushels of potatoes a year.[20]

Cullen believed that allotting lands and locating the Indians on farms would end their roaming. Although this proved untrue, a new settlement pattern did emerge on the reservations. Clusters of farms were now strung out like the spokes of a wheel along the roads leading to each agency. Most were relatively close to the Minnesota River, where wood could be found. Brown opened schools near the largest concentrations, financing seven in all by 1860. Those Indians living under the tutelage of Wabasha, Wakute, Mankato (Penichon's old band), Little Crow, and Passing Hail, who succeeded the Mdewakanton Cloud Man, seemed most interested in farming. The first three chiefs had cut their hair and donned white clothing. Near Yellow Medicine the improvement Indians came primarily from the Wahpeton and Sisseton bands of Running Walker, Red Iron, Extended Tail Feathers, and Cloud Man.[21] In each of these bands, however, young men still could be found who preferred the chase.

Other villages, more isolated from the agencies, fell under the control of nonimprovement Indians. The men of Red Legs's Wahpe-

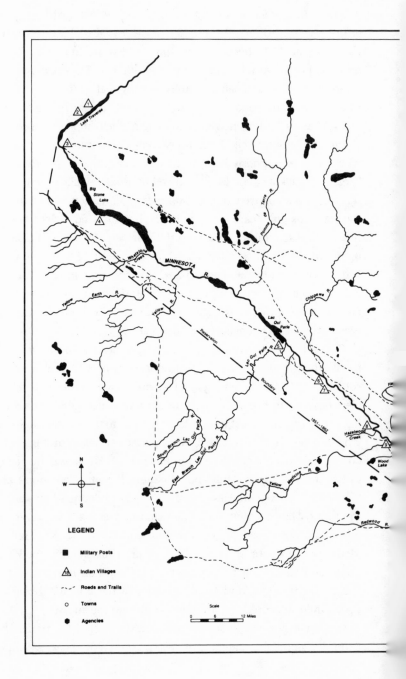

LEGEND

■ Military Posts

△ Indian Villages

- - - Roads and Trails

○ Towns

● Agencies

Scale

0   6   12 Miles

1. Wanata
2. Sweet Corn
3. Standing Buffalo
4. Scarlet Plume
5. Extended Tail Feathers
6. Sleepy Eyes
7. Red Iron
8. Cloud Man

9. Running Walker
10. Red Middle Voice
11. Shakopee
12. Big Eagle
13. Little Crow
14. Mankato
15. Wakute
16. Wabasha
17. Red Legs

kute camp and Shakopee's Mdewakanton band resisted the farming movement. Red Legs's people had settled in an isolated area on the southernmost edge of the reserve, and Shakopee's partisans had two villages, both north of the Redwood River. Shakopee's band had divided after the old chief died in 1857, and the seceding group, under his brother Red Middle Voice, had moved to Rice Creek with the more militant portion of the village. The Sisseton villages at Lake Traverse and on Coteau des Prairies also resisted severalty. The people under Wanata, Sweet Corn, and Standing Buffalo, although party to the 1851 accords, hunted bison on the plains most of the year. Other factions under Scarlet Plume, Sleepy Eyes, Lean Bear, and Limping Devil joined them.[22] In most cases these people were so mobile that the government never tried very seriously to settle them on individual farms.

Nonetheless, the strongest resistance came from within the bands most affected by improvements. Sioux leaders saw that the acculturation program was a threat to their authority. It weakened tribal unity, limiting the power of civil chiefs; it encouraged the rejection of traditional religion, challenging the role of the shamans; and it demanded that men no longer take the warpath, weakening the influence of war leaders. In addition, when a Dakota man became a farmer he left the village, seeming to turn his back on kinship obligations. Indeed, the farmhouses built by the government had separate cellars that encouraged families to hoard food. This was acceptable practice in white society but not among the Sioux. Little Crow fretted over these changes, telling Cullen once that he would never abandon the old ways and that he wished to go to the place where his father was when he died. Cullen tried to convince him that Dakota men could continue in their old religious beliefs and still be husbandmen. Little Crow disagreed, as did many traditional Indians, believing that religion and livelihood worked conjointly. He even talked his brother-in-law Peter Big Fire out of teaching in the mission school at Yellow Medicine, arguing that education was a component of white religion and farming.[23]

Even though the Mdewakanton chief and many other civil and

religious leaders struggled to hold the line against cultural change, increasing numbers of Indians gave up the ways of their fathers. Some called for schools and missionaries, convinced that they should embrace Christianity and learn to read when they put on white man's clothes; others reluctantly disavowed the warpath. The symbolic severing of the scalp lock with scissors, a practice that government personnel assisted in, affirmed their commitment to the new life. Brown felt sure that a Dakota warrior would *"never go to war without a scalp lock."*[24] While Brown may have overstated the impact of the haircuts, certainly traditionalists like Little Crow viewed them as illustrating a degeneration in Dakota society. The Sioux had been able to adjust to the economic decline that attended the destruction of animal herds, but this new acculturation challenge struck at the heart and soul of Dakota being.

Understandably, many Dakota leaders believed it was their duty to resist the acculturation movement. The first signs of violent opposition to conversion surfaced in the summer of 1859 when warriors began assaulting Sioux farmers. By November, Williamson learned that a dozen or so men in the agricultural community who were leaning toward Christianity had been poisoned and that several others had been shot. Two of the men "supposed to be poisoned acted as speakers for those who applied to the agent for a missionary," Williamson reported to his superiors.[25] The assaults continued into the winter, causing some desertions from the farmers' ranks at Yellow Medicine. The men who left continued to farm but wanted protection before they would wear "white man's dress." Even the Hazelwood people were not immune to the onslaught. After the murder of a close relative, Henok Maḣpiyahdinape retaliated by attacking the assailant's cousin. The blood feud threatened to break up the entire experiment, and several members fled north to escape the troubles.[26]

Dakota shamans were behind much of the opposition to the farm program. Both those who worked as conjurers curing the sick and those who were military leaders felt that cutting one's hair and donning white man's clothes were clear signs that one had abandoned significant aspects of the Sioux world view. Not all Dakota men believed this, and a few worked as farmers one day only to change into leggings and breechcloths the next to participate in feasts and dances. But the *wicaśta wakan*, or supernatural people, could not accept cultural compromise and did everything possible to break up the farmer movement. Whenever they caused the death of an Indian farmer they boasted of their success and threatened others with the same fate.[27]

Pressures also came from tribal organizations. Secret societies and dances, institutions that had gotten little attention in the 1850s, suddenly gained popularity in Dakota villages. The Bear Dance Society, the Buffalo Dance Society, the Elk Lodge, the Raw Fish Eater's Lodge, the Dog Liver Eater's Lodge, and the Wakanwacipi, or Sacred Dance, all with their attendant trappings, competed for members. The Wakanwacipi was by far the most important. It carefully recruited members, demanding that they never divulge the secret powers that came from its mystical ceremonies. This social and religious revival acted as a catalyst for resistance, and farmers found it difficult to deny themselves the fellowship these organizations afforded. This revitalization even caused the usually optimistic Brown to admit in October 1860 that to withdraw the Dakotas from their "sacred feasts and superstitious worship, is at best an uphill business."[28]

The militant atmosphere that lingered at the Yellow Medicine Agency after the Inkpaduta affair also posed problems for developmentalists. Yet the old Wakpekute chief was not responsible. The Yanktonais and their influence on the Sissetons now caused the most concern for reservation officials. The Yanktonais were angry over the construction of Fort Abercrombie above Lake Traverse in 1857; they wanted a share of the annuities and occasionally threatened to raid agency warehouses. Cullen attempted to give them a peace offering of $5,000 worth of presents in the fall of 1858, but they refused to see him.[29] The next June, as he departed Yellow Medicine with the gifts, one hundred Sisseton warriors forcibly turned him back. The Sissetons wanted their annuities before anything was given to the Yanktonais.[30]

Enraged, Cullen asked Colonel John Abercrombie for troops and headed west to find the Yanktonais and punish the Sissetons. The former again refused to see him, since Yanktonai leaders obviously mistrusted American soldiers. However, once near the Sisseton camps at Lake Traverse, Cullen went into council with Burning Earth, Standing Buffalo, and several other leaders and demanded the surrender of the men who had stopped him. "If you are not prepared to deliver up those who insulted me," Cullen said, "you had better send your women away to gather turnips. It will be men's and not boy's play you may expect." Burning Earth slyly asked if "the President authorized you to say this," and if so, "how could he relay the message in a mere 20 days?" Cullen smugly replied; "We talk by lightning." Of course Cullen told the chiefs that no annuities would be paid until the men were turned over, and a handful were eventually surrendered.[31]

The incident near Lake Traverse drove a further wedge between government-supported improvement bands and the traditionalists at the upper agency. By February 1860 Brown believed the farmers were in great danger of being exterminated by the Lake Traverse faction. "They [the farmers] are told that no Indian who persists in wearing pantaloons next summer shall see the leaves fall," he reported to Cullen. The militants claimed that the Yanktonais would join them in an all-out war on the agency, a claim that Brown believed was true. To counter the onslaught, he begged Cullen to have troops permanently stationed nearby.[32] The War Department responded by billeting K Company of the Fourth Artillery at the upper agency in April. The troops quickly seized prominent men who had been shooting farmers and their oxen. This precipitated a major migration of Sissetons and Wahpetons from the reservation out onto Coteau des Prairies. Cullen immediately asked the army for more troops, and the young captain in command at Yellow Medicine seconded the request.[33]

Despite the excitement, Brown paid the annuities at both agencies in July 1860, but he made several important changes. Using troops to take a census of adult males, Brown excluded all Indians who had fled out onto Coteau des Prairies as well as more than two hundred warriors who had participated in intertribal war. This increased the per capita distribution, but it excluded many traditionalist or blanket Indians. According to agency reports, those not receiving annuities were "disaffected individuals" who had "exhibited their hostility to the 'agriculturists,' and their opposition to the peaceful pursuits of civilization by leaving the reservation on war and hunting excursions." At least $2,700 due this group went to farmer Indians as "premiums" for good behavior. When telling these warriors they would receive nothing, Brown warned them that thereafter any hunting trips into the white settlements or assaults on the Chippewas would be severely punished.[34]

Brown's efforts to keep the Sioux at home were all the more important after whites settled along the northeast bank of the Minnesota River and threatened to cut off Dakota hunters from their established hunting grounds. Most settlers were Germans who had arrived under the sponsorship of an emigrant society from Chicago and had begun the land rush along the upper Minnesota in 1854 by staking claims along the Big Cottonwood River in the fall and creating the town site of New Ulm. After cold weather set in, the boomers moved into the abandoned summer lodges of some remnants of Red Iron's and Sleepy Eyes's Sisseton bands. When spring arrived and the Indians returned, the first serious confrontation took place. The Dakota women "became enraged and struck the ground with their fists to indicate that that land belonged to them." The Germans refused to be intimidated even after the young Dakota warriors threw down the survey flags and began killing cattle. Only the arrival of the army prevented violence. The Indians were informed that New Ulm was on land ceded to the government, and the Sioux reluctantly moved off in the face of overwhelming force.[35]

More and more Germans settled on the southern border of the reservation in the late 1850s, and they seldom got along with their Indian neighbors. Complicating matters, the government failed to survey the reservation border until 1858, so neither side knew exactly where its land terminated. The geographic points used to determine the reservation in 1851 also were obscure, causing many Indians to believe they had been cheated after surveyors completed the lines. Land office officials ultimately supported Sioux claims by stating that the boundary actually crossed the Minnesota River "four to six miles" east of where it had been located. Nevertheless, nothing was done to correct the error.[36]

With the issue unresolved in the south, it is no wonder many Sioux became incensed when the lands on the northeast bank of the Minnesota River were opened to settlement in the summer of 1858. The Washington treaty had not been ratified and the Dakotas had received no money from the sale, yet the Henderson land office registered the patents of a dozen or so German settlers who had taken up farms on Beaver Creek, just across the Minnesota River from Shakopee's village. When the Indians tried to drive them out, the Germans suspected that agent Brown, who wanted the land himself, had put them up to it.[37] By the spring of 1859 constant complaints from agents, Indians, and settlers were pouring into Colonel Abercrombie at Fort Ridgely. "I feel much embarrassed as to what course in relation to the matter it would be proper for me to pursue," the beleaguered colonel wrote in asking for instructions.[38]

Initially, the secretary of interior decided to remove the Germans and a handful of Scandinavians who had joined them, since the land was still under the control of the president. But Colonel Abercrombie demurred, waiting for orders from the War Department. Meanwhile the Germans solicited support from Senator Henry M. Rice, who stopped the contemplated eviction. As news of the decision leaked out, hundreds of whites flocked into the area. The commandant at Fort Ridgely estimated that five hundred families had settled on the northeast bank of the Minnesota River by March 1860. Most were hardworking, pietistic Protestants; others sold whiskey to the Indians, thereby inciting trouble. Brown became so exasperated with the situation that he tried to convince the army to patrol the river and slap into irons anyone, white or Indian, who was caught with contraband.[39]

The close proximity of the white settlers increasingly taxed the patience of most Sioux warriors. The Sauk and Crow river valleys in the "Big Woods" were quickly filling with pioneers, with fields and cabins lining the trails leading to these old hunting preserves. Most of these settlers were foreigners who knew nothing about the Indians and did not understand the importance of reciprocity in Sioux society. If they aided a passing hunting party, it was usually out of fear rather than from a willingness to share. Consequently many Dakota men came to hate their German and Scandinavian neighbors. They derogatorily called them "eyasica," or more correctly *iaśica*, which meant "bad speakers." The whites had taken the land, run off the game, and often seemed unwilling to share what resources they possessed. Their failure to adopt reciprocal patterns made it impossible for them ever to become a part of the Sioux kinship system. The Indians came to see them as intruders.[40]

This sense of cultural dissimilarity is illustrated in the many individual encounters between the two groups just before the Sioux war of 1862. Only one German woman, Mrs. Helen M. Tarble, is recorded to have learned the Dakota language and come to appreciate native culture after moving into the Beaver Creek settlement in 1858. She frequently visited the Dakota villages across the river and even established rapport with a shaman. This hospitality was reciprocated when Sioux hunters came calling, since Mrs. Tarble "supplied them with meals." But she was an exception, as she quickly pointed out. Settlers were more apt to be like her neighbors the Hendersons, who "ridiculed" shamans and steadfastly refused to share provisions. In the Dakota world such conduct was antisocial and unbecoming to human beings.[41]

The dislike for the "Dutchmen," or Germans, may have stemmed from other problems. New Ulm quickly became a center for the liquor trade, and Indians often got spirits from German farmers. Once sober again, however, they felt the German settlers had taken advantage of them. Some chiefs complained of this to the military. Once they even asked the commanding officer at Fort Ridgely to rescue a Dakota man whom the Germans had imprisoned in the New Ulm jail for disturbing the peace. Traders had used liquor to acquire furs for nearly two centuries, but the Germans were more inclined to trade it for necessities such as blankets or knives, leaving the Indians destitute. The practice only added to the distrust that these foreigners naturally engendered because of their strange customs and language.[42]

A second rationale for the dislike of the Germans resulted from their occupations. Little Crow mentioned the aggressiveness of the German populations in the 1858 treaty negotiation, pointing out that they were farming lands close to the reservation and scaring off game. By 1860, *iaśica* came to be synonymous with "farmer" in the Dakota language. Eastern Sioux hunters were using it in a derogatory sense to refer to Indian farmers and mixed-bloods as well as German settlers. In other words, the Germans became noticeable symbols of the harm that farming in general was doing to the Sioux. "The Indians were particularly vindictive against the Germans, Eyasica [*iaśica*], or 'bad language,'" a close observer noted after the 1862 war, "because most of the new settlers, who had driven out the game by their coming, were foreigners."[43]

The rejection of reciprocity by most settlers characterized the changes that had occurred in intercultural relations since the 1830s. Whites and mixed-blood people no longer needed to maintain close relations with the Indians; the Sioux had degenerated militarily and economically to the point where kinship bonds were no longer useful or understood by white settlers and were even neglected at times by Indian farmers. This was just as true on the reservations, where a new breed of bureaucrats and traders had taken over, as in the settlements.[44]

Traders had by this time given up all thoughts of courting native leaders. The trade had become a business where political connections in Washington and access to information on the annuity distributions, not the reinforcement of kinship ties, led to profits. One trader, Louis Roberts, even had a system of double-ledger accounting. In one book he listed the number of dependents a particular Indian could collect money on, and in the other he logged daily sales of merchandise to annuity recipients. In the accounts from his

Yellow Medicine post for 1861, almost all the debtors ended up owing five, ten, fifteen, or twenty dollars, corresponding with the amounts they received at the distribution.[45]

Robert's accounts might have been beyond suspicion had the claims shown some deviation in values and had Sarah Wakefield, the wife of the agency physician at Yellow Medicine, not been present at the July 1861 distribution. Wakefield wrote two years later that four trading establishments existed at the agency, "cheating the creatures [Indians] very much." Dakota men did not keep track of what they purchased, she noted, "so the traders have their own way at the time of payment." As the money was handed out, traders brought their books forward and claimed it. Many Indians protested, and one even swallowed his money before anyone could take it from him, exclaiming to those present, "I do not owe him [the trader nearby]."[46]

Traders employed other methods at the distributions. When a small operator, identified as D. Carothers, had a few blankets stolen from his store at Big Stone Lake by two Sissetons in 1860, he filed a damage claim for $5,500 and lobbied strongly for it in Washington. Commissioner Mix issued a warrant for the funds to be deducted from the upper Sioux annuity in 1861, causing a flurry of anger when the Indians realized what had happened. They quickly petitioned the commissioner for redress, but he in turn refused to admit his error, especially after other Minnesota politicians came to the defense of the claimant.[47] In substance, by 1860 those Indians who remained hunters and who relied heavily on annuities had few people, in or out of government, who would help them receive fair treatment during the annuity distributions. Even missionaries said little, since they wanted Sioux men to be independent of such handouts and had no sympathy for those who were not.

The new economic dependency that pervaded the reservations by the late 1850s also led to the abuse of marriage customs. White men in contact with the Sioux now commonly bought women, then left them. The practice had occurred on a small scale in the past; Sibley and Taliaferro had both left half-Sioux children behind them, and Joseph R. Brown had a reputation for womanizing. But Brown,

Sibley, and Taliaferro seemed to be exceptions, at least in the 1830s and 1840s. Hazen Mooers, Joseph Renville, Jean Baptiste Faribault, Oliver Faribault, and Louis Provençalle were more typical of early-nineteenth-century traders; they did little philandering and maintained close family ties, even though this put Renville in debt and cost Mooers his job. The new breed of whites who came to build the reservation and trade with the Sioux in the 1850s acted more like Brown. At one point Riggs described the entire lot as "licentious," especially Brown and his brothers. But traders and employees alike kept women, whom they abandoned when they returned east. James W. Lynd, a trader who was being considered as a replacement for Brown in 1861, was thought to be the worst of all; Riggs noted that he already had several mixed-blood children and had yet to marry. The presence of troops at the agencies only added to the demoralization, since officers and enlisted men commonly purchased women for a day, using food or clothing as enticements.[48]

Dakota leaders had never opposed interracial marriage. The union of one of their women with a white man brought wealth to the descent group. But when traditional institutions of bride purchase were ignored and women prostituted themselves for food and clothing, chiefs began to complain. Little Crow spoke out against the immoral practices of James Magner, a superintendent of farming, at the 1858 treaty negotiation. He managed the warehouse and used his power over the distribution of goods to gain favors from native women. The Mdewakanton chief Big Eagle made the same complaint in a later memoir, noting that on the reservation "the white men abused the native women ... and disgraced them."[49] Traders also used their powerful positions to extract sexual favors, a practice that had occurred in the past but that seemed to be more obvious in the later 1850s. One chief reportedly told a merchant: "If I was your kept squaw I could get all the credit I wanted; but as I am a man, I can not."[50]

Traders and government employees were joined in this debauchery by the mixed-bloods. Although some no doubt were legitimate farmers, many observers argued that as a class they excelled in carrying liquor from the settlements to the reservations and had generally become a debilitating social influence. "Nearly all of them are addicted to the use of whiskey," one critic recorded in 1861, "and act as Agents and pimps of the Devil in human form." Even full-blood leaders had grown tired of them, and several chiefs petitioned as early as 1857 to have them removed from the annuity rolls.[51] Government agents did their best to stop this nefarious trade, since it harmed the farming program. Even Brown argued that mixed-bloods ought to be removed from the reservation. But failing in this, he petitioned the army to have any of them caught with alcohol confined in the fort *"subject to police duty in irons."* Both the promiscuity, which spread venereal disease, and the increased use of alcohol did severe damage to Sioux institutions and buttressed the arguments of traditionalists, who increasingly blamed their troubles on whites.[52]

As social discord seemed to reach a peak in the spring of 1861, yet another political upheaval occurred in the nation. The election of Abraham Lincoln the year before brought to power a new superintendent of Indian affairs, Clark W. Thompson, and a new agent, Thomas J. Galbraith. Neither had any experience with Indians, and they intended to replace most reservation workers with new appointees. Both expressed surprise at the material progress on the reservations when they arrived in the spring, but they soon realized that Brown had also left a legacy of problems. The former agent had spent $292,000 on reservation development, but he left a debt of $52,000. Worse, Brown had abandoned the agency in early 1861 to complete a luxurious, three-story mansion east of the Yellow Medicine Agency, where he and his mixed-blood children had filed land claims originating from the sale of the Lake Pepin reserve. As a result, crops went unplanted. Galbraith did his utmost to plant two thousand acres late in the spring, but it rained only sporadically thereafter, and cutworms attacked the immature cornstalks. The resulting light yield forced Galbraith to seek funds in Washington to feed destitute Indians as reports circulated that the Sissetons on the plains were suffering terribly from want of food.[53]

While Sioux hunters fought off starvation, Galbraith made extensive plans for a spring campaign to enlist more native men in the farming program. "Funds can only be given as rewards for industry and economy," he concluded in describing his philosophy to superiors. Despite the suffering and the great need for food, the agent ordered seventy-nine yokes of oxen, forty-seven cows, and eighty-eight sheep along with several hundred plows, wagons, and hoes. After he distributed much of the equipment in spring 1862, nearly three thousand acres of land fell under cultivation, and by July the crop looked excellent. The promise of implements had convinced another 175 men to cut their hair and join the farming bands.[54] Riggs wondered if this policy would really produce a permanent "foundation" for change. Yet he remained optimistic, especially after two new mission stations, one under Thomas Williamson's son John and the other under Samuel D. Hinman, an Episcopalian, sprang up at the lower agency. Galbraith, much the same as Brown, seemed intent on pushing acculturation at a fast pace.[55]

The attention given the farming program inflamed the already ill-humored Dakota hunters. The poisoning of improvement Indians increased, and the leaders of the blanket bands near Yellow Medicine voiced strong disapproval of Galbraith's favoritism. The agent "did everything for the 'dutchmen' [farmer Indians]," even allowing them free access to the agency storehouses.[56] The hunters could not understand how it was that they received supplies only once a year and the farmers took them at will. Many blanket chiefs demanded that Galbraith treat farmers as "white men," or "Germans" and refuse to give them annuities. Nearly every council that Galbraith conducted with blanket Indians during the fall of 1861 and the spring of 1862 showed them to be "restive, turbulent, saucy, insolent, impudent and insulting."[57]

With such conditions, the army would have been well advised to keep troops at both agencies. Instead, regular army detachments were being ordered east to fight in the Civil War. Minnesota Volunteers slowly replaced them, and two companies visited Yellow Medicine in July, but at a crucial stage in the "civilization program" agency workers and farmer Indians were left to defend themselves. The lack of protection inaugurated a reign of terror at the upper agency. Disgruntled Sissetons formed a soldiers' lodge in the summer of 1861 to extract a more equitable annuity distribution and to harass farmers. Galbraith noted that "peaceably disposed Indians" feared to speak against them "lest their cattle be killed, or their lives taken." Even chiefs accepted the dictates of the soldiers.[58] If this were not enough, six Yanktonai chiefs suddenly appeared demanding the goods that Cullen had been unable to deliver to them. Although somewhat unnerved, Galbraith listened patiently and promised to send the president their petition. Simultaneously, he sent an urgent request for troops to Fort Ridgely. Luckily the Indians left peaceably, because the soldiers never came.[59]

The lack of cooperation that Galbraith received from the militia seemed to characterize his administration over the next twelve crucial months. Many incompetent office seekers who had no experience with Indians were thrust upon him, and he believed that men in the Indian Bureau were plotting his recall. Perhaps A. T. C. Pierson, the new school superintendent, best personified the rabble now working at the agencies. Pierson wrote Thompson candidly that he wished the superintendent to "secure" for him control of the entire education fund. Of course he expected to share with Thompson whatever could be skimmed from it. To make it appear that the previous administration had failed in its educational duties toward the Indian and thus justify large expenditures in this area, Pierson promptly fired all the teachers Brown had hired.[60]

Even this contemplated fraud failed to match the scheme hatched in Washington in May 1862. Galbraith heard that Commissioner Mix intended to substitute depreciated greenbacks for the $80,000 in gold due the Indians that summer. Unwilling to depend upon Thompson, since Galbraith thought he was scheming with Pierson, the agent wrote Henry Benjamin Whipple, the new Episcopalian bishop in Minnesota, who was deeply interested in the welfare of the Indians. "The Blackest '*trick*' of Indian Swindles has just been revealed to me," Galbraith wrote; "God only knows what will be the result."[61] Galbraith had been depending upon the annuity money to relieve hunger at both agencies until the crops could be harvested. His warehouses had been so depleted during the winter that he wondered whether he would have enough supplies to sustain the Indians for any length of time.

Meanwhile, rumors that the government was unable to meet its annuity obligations surfaced in June, after large numbers of Sissetons had arrived at Yellow Medicine. Galbraith assured their leaders that this was not so. He told them to send their people home until the cash arrived. On 7 July he traveled to the lower agency and told the Mdewakantons and Wahpekutes that adverse rumors about the annuities were untrue. They demanded rations, and Galbraith issued a good supply of pork, flour, and tobacco, later learning that they were "well satisfied" with the supplies. The lower Sioux had suffered less than the Sissetons over the winter. Even so, a few had traded their guns and horses to settlers for food.[62]

At this point most of the discontent existed among the Sissetons and Wahpetons, who were expected to cause trouble during the annuity distribution. Galbraith had asked Major John S. Marsh at Fort Ridgely to send troops to the upper agency for this event, and Lieutenant Timothy J. Sheehan of the Fifth Minnesota Volunteers reached the agency with 101 men on 2 July. Six days later, warriors from the soldiers' lodge came to council and spoke frankly. They demanded rations and expressed their determination not to let the traders "come to the paytable." "They take all of our money out of our hands," the spokesman explained. Sheehan professed to have nothing to do with the annuities, but he did assure the warriors that he would talk with Galbraith about the traders.[63]

When Galbraith returned to Yellow Medicine on 10 July he found, surprisingly, that none of the upper Sioux had left. Sheehan counted 659 lodges, or roughly seven thousand people. Besides the Sissetons and Wahpetons, the large mass included Yanktonais, Cutheads (Yanktonai-Sissetons), and a few Mdewakantons and Wahpekutes. Their leaders immediately asked for the payment and demanded to be fed. The agent could fulfill neither request.[64] On 19 July he sent off a desperate letter to Thompson. "I need to urge you [to] appreciate the situation," he wrote, "'Hurry up,' come right up here and make this payment at once." In closing, he cursed "Damned Old Mix, the consummate old scamp," for putting him in such a bind. Galbraith believed Mix was withholding the money to embarrass him.[65]

The tense situation finally broke on 4 August when four hundred warriors chopped down the door to the Yellow Medicine warehouse and began to carry off sacks of flour. Lieutenant Sheehan quickly unlimbered his artillery piece and threatened to "blow them to hell in less than a minute" if they refused to leave the building. As his men took up positions near the scene, a few warriors physically assaulted one or two, and other soldiers were insulted "in all manner possible." As confusion reigned, Galbraith cowered in his house. The job of defusing the situation fell to Sheehan, who counciled with the warriors and promised to issue some rations if they would return to their camps. This quieted them, but when Sheehan tried to recover the flour that had been removed from the warehouse he was rebuffed.[66]

The next day Galbraith tried to reassert his control by ordering the young lieutenant to capture the men responsible for the break-in. Sheehan seized two and put them in the agency jail. As he did so, Galbraith stealthily left the agency, only to be intercepted and turned back by the disgruntled Sioux warriors. Sheehan then heard that the members of the soldiers' lodge were planning an assault on his troops. He sent an urgent request to Captain Marsh for reinforcements and released the Dakota prisoners. While waiting for Marsh, who arrived on 6 August, Galbraith held two days of discussions with the Indians, but these councils solved nothing. When Marsh arrived he ordered the agent to surrender to the Sioux whatever supplies still remained in the warehouse. Galbraith reluctantly did so on 8 August, and the angry Indians left. Four days later most of the militant Sissetons reached Big Stone Lake.[67]

Most white observers felt that Sioux discontent had peaked at Yellow Medicine during the first week of August. War seemed imminent on several occasions, especially after Dakota leaders, prompted by Little Crow, asked the traders for credits and supposedly were told by Andrew Myrick: "So far as I am concerned, if they are hungry, let them eat grass."[68] Although historians, following the lead of William Watts Folwell, have generally described this exchange as taking place at the lower agency on 14 or 15 August and have seen it as the trigger for the war that began on the seventeenth, the sequence of events and the people involved make that impossible.[69] Winifred W. Barton first reported the incident in a biography of her father, John P. Williamson. She notes that after the regular interpreter refused to translate the comment, Galbraith asked Williamson to repeat it in Dakota for the Sioux. Williamson complied, whereupon Dakota representatives "broke into weird and savage war-whoops." Williamson's personal letters, however, clearly show that he left for Ohio on 11 August—Barton suggests that he departed just after a major council broke up—reached St. Peter, Minnesota, on the twelfth, and could not have participated in a council held on either the fourteenth or the fifteenth. Thus Barton's description of the Myrick insult must refer to a council that took place at Yellow Medicine rather than at the lower agency, undoubtedly sometime between 5 and 8 August. Galbraith supports this by stating in his report that he had no councils with the Sioux after 8 August.[70]

This revised chronology of Myrick's statement puts a different light on events immediately preceding the Minnesota-Sioux War of 1862. It does much to discredit the argument that it was a spontaneous outburst, triggered by a series of events put in motion by Myrick's bad manners. On the other hand, it is clear that several traders repeated Myrick's insult, or modifications of it, after the council took place, and Indian warriors often answered them by threatening to cut off access to essential wood and food. Myrick and his cohorts' unmistakable warning to the Sioux was that as long as the soldiers' lodge continued to prevent trader access to the pay tables, the Dakotas would be forced to live by their own means. The insult, then, more than anything else, symbolized white rejection of reciprocity. After the war began, Little Crow dictated a letter to government authorities in which he outlined its causes. The Mdewakanton chief cited Myrick's comments as an example of the mistreatment afforded Indians.

Yet it must not be forgotten that Myrick's famous paraphrase of a French queen's remark took place nearly two weeks rather than two days before the war broke out, and much happened in the meantime.[71] Indeed, Galbraith felt the crisis had passed by 10 August, since the specter of starvation, strongly evident a week before, had disappeared. Green corn from Indian fields was now ready for roasting. The atmosphere at Yellow Medicine had changed so drastically that Galbraith busied himself on 12 August with aiding in the recruitment of thirty mixed-bloods under a volunteer militia company called the Renville Raiders. He agreed to accompany these men to St. Paul and, anticipating no trouble, took leave of his family on the thirteenth and marched to the lower agency, where he added nearly two dozen more recruits. Sheehan also slackened his vigilance, letting his men fish and rest before the trip back to Fort Ridgely. His two companies later received orders to occupy Fort Ripley, along the upper Mississippi River, and the troops left for their new assignment on 18 August. Galbraith had passed through Fort Ridgely a day before with the Renville Raiders, leaving only two companies of volunteers on the western Minnesota frontier.[72]

Much has been made of the fact that the departure of these men left Minnesota defenseless and thereby encouraged the Indians to go to war. Yet Fort Ridgely had been understaffed in the past, and Galbraith saw the removal of the mixed-blood raiders as a blessing. Besides, both reservations had been quiet for over a week. Even Little Crow, an antagonist in the past, seemed well disposed. He had made his first serious commitment to farming in the spring, digging with his own hands a cellar for a new brick house. When Galbraith spoke with him informally on 15 August at the lower agency, he seemed "well pleased and satisfied."[73] With the Indians peacefully harvesting crops, whites at the agencies harbored no suspicions of the frightful war that was to follow.

Notwithstanding this outward calm, much was happening in the Indian camps, especially among the Mdewakanton people. In July a soldiers' lodge formed at Shakopee's village and the Rice Creek village, encampments that were still decidedly in the hands of nonfarmers. The soldiers apparently held nightly discussions regarding the increasing number of white settlers, the actions of the traders, and the delay in the cash payment.[74] Older pioneers living across the river noted that many of these hunters had become "disagreeable and ill-natured." One had flown into a rage when a settler refused to share some fish he had caught in the Minnesota River.[75] Many Mdewakanton soldiers had no doubt witnessed the test of wills at Yellow Medicine in early August. Like their upper Sioux relatives, who hunted buffalo, they too had found it nearly impossible to get credit from traders and depended greatly on the money due them. The Mdewakanton chief Big Eagle later confessed that the possibility of war had been discussed in the soldiers' lodge well before the outbreak of fighting, though he had not been present at the meetings. Some soldiers apparently felt that fighting the whites would cause the Dakotas, as Big Eagle put it, to "forget the troubles among themselves" and unify their society once again.[76]

Disappointed over the delayed cash payment, a few members of the lodge had decided to hunt to the east in the Big Woods. They had customarily traded for whiskey on these forays, and on 17 August four members left the main party to call on Robinson Jones of Acton, who had supplied them in the past. Even though they were Wahpetons by birth, they hailed from the Rice Creek village, a splinter faction of Shakopee's band, the most militant on the lower reservation. Near Jones's house, they discovered several chicken eggs and debated whether to take them. The horseplay evolved into a dare as one man taunted another over his unwillingness to kill white settlers. Aroused, they met Jones and quarreled with him, then shot him, his wife, and three others.[77]

Before word filtered out to local authorities, the miscreants had arrived at Rice Creek to tell their story to the soldiers' lodge. Although lodge members had been debating the annuity delay over the weekend, new discussions ensued once it was known that white blood had been spilled. Everyone in the lodge realized that the cash annuity would be withheld until the murderers were surrendered. Sometime in the early morning the excited soldiers traveled the few miles to Little Crow's house, recounting every step of the way the ills the whites had inflicted upon them. Reaching their destination, Red Middle Voice, the Rice Creek leader, his nephew young Shakopee, or "Little Six," and more than a hundred soldiers pressured Little Crow to join them in a war against the whites.[78]

According to oral accounts, Little Crow at first demurred, telling the assemblage to see Passing Hail, who had just been elected speaker of the Mdewakanton people. Little Crow had generally sided with traditional Dakota factions, but he had many relatives who were farmers and was well aware of the futility of the proposed war. Indeed, Passing Hail was a farmer and a friend of the whites, and Little Crow may have been hoping to defuse the hostility of the soldiers by bringing calmer heads into the discussion. Unfortunately, the soldiers saw Passing Hail's election as another victory for the farmer groups, and they refused Little Crow's advice, demanding again that he join them. The chief begged off a second time, telling the soldiers that the whites had many soldiers of their own in spite of the war they were fighting in the east. The warriors countered by pointing to Galbraith's recruitment of the mixed-bloods. Was not the "Great Father" weak if he had to call on these men to fight for him? When this did not move Little Crow, the Mdewakanton soldiers resorted to calling him a coward. Rising to his feet Little Crow reluctantly said, "Taoyateduta [Little Crow's Dakota name] is not a coward; he will die with you." He joined the hundred or so Dakota warriors from the soldiers' lodges, and they attacked the lower agency at dawn, killing whites both at the government buildings and at the traders' stores.[79]

The ironies surrounding the Sioux Outbreak are many. A reluctant chief who had recently turned to farming and who had attended church the morning before the fighting began has been perceived as the leader of the Indian campaigns. The Sioux had suffered through many unpleasant winters for lack of food, but 1862–63 would not have been one of them. Despite the difficulty of procuring food that spring, all thoughts of scarce rations had passed, and the bountiful harvest precluded suffering over the coming winter. Galbraith later estimated that the crops would have yielded 75,000 bushels of corn and potatoes.[80] Finally, the Mdewakanton-Wahpekute people had been the recipients of most of the government resources that had reached the agencies. The Sissetons and Wahpetons had more reason to fault the government, were in a much worse humor, yet consistently had stopped short of war. What, then, brought the Mdewakantons to rebellion?

Early scholars have identified several causes, including discontent over the terms of the treaties of 1851 and 1858, the army's failure to make an example of Inkpaduta, the illicit practices of the traders, the agents' inability to keep promises regarding annuities, and the murders at Acton. Most recent historians have added to these the acculturation pressures of the "civilization" program. These arguments are compelling because they reflect the judgments of on-the-scene observers. In other words, they chronicle what whites perceived as the causes for discontent on the reservations in 1862.[81] Nevertheless, these explanations fail to incorporate any understanding of the rationalization the Mdewakantons used for starting the war, thus telling only half the story and leaving the impression that the rebellion was an irrational response to an unbearable material situation. Finally, the traditional causes cited for the war say little about the complexities of interethnic relations and how it was that after so many years of peaceful coexistence the bond that prevented hostilities broke down. Indeed, whites who survived the initial attack later could not explain how it was that such a peaceful atmosphere could exist on Sunday, 17 August, and such a nightmare follow the very next day.

Perhaps the motivation for the rebellion can best be examined by understanding the men who actually prompted the assault on the lower agency. By 1862 they were clearly a minority of warriors from the Mdewakanton soldiers' lodges: a tribal or band council never even met to consider the prospect of war. In the two or three years before, these young men came to realize that their relationship with whites and mixed-bloods was at the root of their social, economic, and political problems and that it had resulted in a degenerative polarization on both reservations, making farmers and warriors into two distinct Indian groups. Many of these Dakota soldiers had been boys when the 1851 treaties were signed, and none had visited Washington seven years later to negotiate the 1858 accords. Certainly they knew of the particulars surrounding past negotiations, but they had had little contact with government officials and were not active in a political or diplomatic sense. More important, their lives were dominated by hunting as an occupation, warfare as a sacred endeavor to demonstrate bravery and obtain revenge, kinship as a form of social cohesiveness, and reciprocity as a means to solidify friendly relations with outsiders.[82]

Clearly, warriors and hunters were slow to perceive that government policies sought to end their nomadic life and were responsible for the polarization on the reserves. They had consistently viewed the treaty process as a means to subsidize hunting and gathering. Many years after the war, Chief Big Eagle delineated what he thought were its most important causes. High on the list was the desire of traditional Dakota men to continue to earn glory in intertribal war and "to live as they did before the Treaty of Traverse des Sioux [1851] ... hunt game wherever they could find it [and] sell their furs to the traders."[83] The influx of whites on old hunting grounds had effectively limited this way of life. The realization that the 1851 and 1858 accords fostered a policy of "confinement" and would work against hunters and warriors came as a shock to many Indians, especially in the Rice Creek village and Shakopee's village.

Although government policies purposely attempted to end age-old hunting and gathering cycles, acculturation programs also struck at the foundations of village life. In essence, to receive federal assistance of any substance Indians had to leave the village and at least show an inclination to adopt farming. Every Mdewakanton camp was affected in some fashion by this policy in 1862, and many native family bonds were severely strained. Cullen noted the polarizing social impact when he left office. "One class of them [Dakota people] rejects with scorn and contempt the overtures made to induce them to abandon their present life," he wrote. "On the other hand, those who have become converts . . . have zealously devoted themselves to their new life."[84] The social polarization became a major factor in prompting the soldiers to begin the outbreak. "They [soldiers] were envious of them [farmers]," Big Eagle later said, "and disliked them because they had gone back on the customs of the tribe and because they were favored."[85] Becoming farmers, living away from villages and accordingly not participating in communal-consensus decision making, adopting white dress, and seemingly abandoning religious ceremonials all were tangible changes that the warrior societies found unacceptable.

The agents' use of annuities as bribes to recruit farmers only enhanced the bitter civil discord that was evident on the reservations by 1859. Dakota traditionalists could not understand how it was that the agents let farmers come and go at the warehouses, receiving goods periodically, and excluded them from such haphazard distributions. The Dakotas had always based giving on need, and the warriors and hunters rightfully argued that they needed the annuities more than farmers did. Many members of the soldiers' lodges saw the war as a way to end this unjust system and restore past bonds of reciprocal sharing and support. Once they decided to fight, the cry went up at Little Crow's village: "Kill the whites and kill all those cuthairs [Dakota farmers] who will not join us."[86]

Besides these fundamental concerns, an obvious change had occurred in Indian–mixed-blood–white social relations by 1862. What is unique about early Dakota contact with whites is the long years of friendship, initiated by early fur traders. Friendly relations were based upon a system of reciprocity and kinship that traders and government agents like Taliaferro continued well into the nineteenth century. The treaties of 1830, 1837, and even 1851 expanded these well-established reciprocal patterns, and the eastern Sioux came to believe that the government would take care of all their needs. But once the Indians were on the reservations, the promises of assistance initially fell short of expectations and eventually proved limited to those who nominally became whites. Thus the treaties became instruments of cultural change rather than reinforcers of reciprocal friendship. Yet some Dakota leaders continued to believe in the humanitarian ideal of the Great Father as late as 1858. The delegates who went east that year agreed to pay their own expenses in order to put their grievances before the president, whom they still believed was good. The trip did much to expose the fiction of a benevolent father, illustrated the reality of dependence upon the government, and weakened lingering beliefs in a reciprocal and evenhanded relationship between whites and Indians. Agents Brown and Galbraith only reinforced this realization in the four-year period after the negotiation by closing warehouses to hunters and even refusing them their rightful annuities.

While tribal relations with the government slowly disintegrated, a similar degeneration occurred among individuals on the reservations. Indians like Big Eagle detected a sense of racial superiority among the white reservation population by the late 1850s. They seemed to say, "I am much better than you," the old chief noted.[87] The actions of traders like Myrick and Lynd only added to the growing perceptions of cultural dissimilarity. Lynd's loose ways with Sioux women offended Dakota leaders, and Myrick's insulting refusal to extend credit struck at the core of reciprocity. In addition, mixedbloods were increasingly seen in the same light: as traders, whiskey peddlers, or farmers who took advantage of their Indian relatives rather than honestly attempting to help them in their quest for survival. When Little Crow was in Washington in 1858, he willingly agreed to compensate the traders for past assistance. But he expected the traders to continue supplying his people. As Big Eagle so aptly put it, "the Indians seemed to think [by 1862] that the traders ought not to be too hard on them ... but do as the Indians did among one another, and put off payment until they were better able to make it."[88] The Dakota sense of individual obligation did not correlate with the growing adoption of a capitalist ethic on the reservations.

While kinship and reciprocal relations deteriorated between traders and Indians, they seldom if ever matured between Indians and white settlers. Big Eagle noted that just before the outbreak white neighbors commonly abused Dakota Indians. "Perhaps they had an excuse," he said, "but the Indians did not think so."[89] The Dakota people had traditionally justified warfare by convincing themselves that their opponents were less than human and were undeserving of life. By calling Germans and even Indian farmers *iaśica*, Sioux warriors showed the contempt in which they held them.[90] Unwilling and often culturally unable to share for the common good of the village, mixed-bloods, Indian farmers, and white settlers were increasingly becoming social outsiders, not unlike the Chippewas with whom the Sioux had fought, on and off, for over a hundred years.

Finally, war resulted from the utter failure of political institutions to prevent it. By so obviously manipulating the process of consensus that had governed Indian-white negotiations in the past, white officials discredited council government. Many traditional Indians simply did not trust the consensus process by the 1850s. The Mdewakanton soldiers' lodges, traditionally hunting and quasi-military organizations, evolved into institutions that represented traditional views. These lodges excluded Indian farmers and mixed-bloods by the later 1850s, thereby keeping their deliberations secret. Such a political trend had been in the making since before the treaties of 1851. Nonetheless, even as late as 1862 leaders of the rebellion still realized that they represented a minority of the Dakota people. Their success in recruiting Little Crow to the movement on the evening of 17 August lent the prestige necessary to make the rebellion into a general war.

In sum, the causes of the Sioux Outbreak are complex and best understood by tracing the economic, political, and social motivations that constituted the basis for Indian-white relations in the upper Mississippi watershed. During the early years of contact the Dakota world view dominated and fur traders assimilated much of what their customers saw as essential to the creation of friendly bonds. But as the relationship matured, it was the Indian who soon became a cultural foreigner in his own land. Political forums became corrupted, social kinship networks were neglected, and economic subsistence patterns were co-opted. It was not, then, so much that traders and even politicians lined their pockets with gold, for the Sioux had never been materialists, or that Congress asked them to share the land—they had always shared what they had with whites. Nor was it that the examples set at Spirit Lake or Acton proved how easily whites could be killed. In the final analysis, a substantial number of Sioux men concluded that the white man had abandoned, seemingly forever, the obligations and promises of assistance that formed the basis for the Dakota communal existence and all relations with people. Revenge through war, even though a futile gesture, was the only response to such a betrayal.

12

Epilogue: The Upheaval, August–December, 1862

The history of the Sioux Outbreak is a story of two engagements—
one between Indians and whites, the second the futile struggle of
militant Dakota leaders to reestablish cultural cohesiveness. Many
detailed accounts of the first have been written, several of which
carefully document the terrible carnage inflicted upon Minnesota's
white settlement by the Sioux. In all, nearly five hundred whites lost
their lives in the fray, four-fifths of them noncombatants.[1] Since so
many narratives of the destruction exist, there is little need to do
more than briefly outline the fighting. Events within the Dakota
community, on the other hand, offer a final illustration of how dramatic social, political, and economic change had been in the later
1850s, the degree of polarization that had occurred as a result of
these changes, and the means the soldiers' lodge would employ to
reverse this cultural deterioration.

Tragically for the hostiles, they would soon discover that the social, political, and economic bonds that tied their people to Euroamericans were not as easy to dispose of as they had initially supposed. While some Sioux warriors blamed whites for their troubles,
other Dakota men and women disagreed with them or thought war
was an extreme, immoral response. Individual kinship bonds among
whites, mixed-bloods, and Indians, though strained in the later 1850s,
still remained. In addition, the Dakota people were simply not accustomed to fighting the kind of sustained campaign that would be
necessary to gain advantages in western Minnesota, especially when

many of their soldiers had once viewed individual whites as human beings and allies. The truth was that the eastern Sioux had moved too far along the road: revitalization, or a reversal of the culture change that had become commonplace by the later 1850s, was an unattainable goal.

The elusiveness of this primary goal seemed unimportant during the first few days of fighting. Such necessary items as guns, ammunition, and food were readily obtained from plundered white farms and traders' stores. The question of what would be done once these supplies ran out never came up. Thus from the start the eastern Sioux warrior and his family lived on bread and beef and fought with shotguns and rifles. It was impossible to return to a traditional hunter-gatherer life or to fight whites with bows and arrows.

Still, Dakota soldiers did believe that some social revitalization could occur. Most agreed that farmer Indians had failed to reinforce kinship ties; almost immediately after starting the war, members of the soldiers' lodges forced farmers to demonstrate allegiance to the cause, threatening most with death. Second, while soldiers recognized that for years the tribal council had failed to act as a political forum, they turned the soldiers' lodges into a political body that served as a medium to discuss the future of the war. Although historians have suggested that Little Crow acted as the leader of the outbreak, nothing could be further from the truth. The lodge made decisions by consensus. Ironically, farmers who opposed the war slowly gained access to the new "tribal" council and used it as a forum for their own views. However, farmer opposition formed rather late in the fighting; initial successes made resistance unpopular.

News regarding the Dakota assault at the lower agency reached Fort Ridgely by midmorning 18 August. Captain John S. Marsh, a seasoned commander, immediately assembled a platoon and started toward the agency. Dakota warriors ambushed the command, killing interpreter Peter Quinn and about two dozen men. Marsh, who underestimated the seriousness of the trouble, later drowned while attempting to withdraw his troops from the engagement. With the exception of the handful of soldiers who quickly returned to the fort under Lieutenant Timothy J. Sheehan, no military units existed in the west to stop the vengeful Sioux from sweeping down the Minnesota valley.[2]

The hostile elements in the Dakota camps, buttressed by the victory over Marsh, quickly launched a campaign against Minnesota's white settlements. Marauding parties first attacked the German farmers living just north of New Ulm and east of the lower agency, then carried their assault into the Big Woods. When the rampages were over, no fewer than twenty-three western Minnesota counties had been evacuated.[3] Large-scale battles followed at New Ulm on 19 and 23 August and at Fort Ridgely on the afternoons of August 20 and 22. The struggle at New Ulm on the twenty-third was carried into the streets of the town. Houses were burned so the Sioux could not use them for cover. The fighting was every bit as vicious as the clashes then occurring in the eastern United States. Despite suffering considerable losses at New Ulm, white settlers and the army held out at both the town and the fort, though at times it appeared that both would fall. During the week of intense fighting, the state organized its own offensive, placing militia under the command of Colonel Henry Hastings Sibley, the former Minnesota fur trader. This force of several hundred men relieved Fort Ridgely on 27 August, ending any possibility of a major Indian victory.[4]

The easternmost Sioux, especially the Mdewakantons and Wahpekutes, had little chance of winning a prolonged war with the United States. They were less prepared for fighting than their western relatives, and they lacked mobility. Even more ominous was the indecisiveness of native leaders, who could not agree on how to proceed. Some wanted to limit the fighting to military objectives, engaging and defeating American armies. Indeed, had the soldiers' lodge followed up the victory over Marsh with an immediate attack on the fort, Sheehan's small garrison no doubt would have fallen.[5] Unfortunately for the hostiles, many warriors wasted time plundering and killing in the settlements, while whites fled to the fort for protection. Once the orgy of killing in the settlements had ended—by the afternoon of 19 August—the Mdewakanton soldiers' lodge faced yet another difficulty: members had to sustain support for an increasingly unpopular war effort in the face of growing opposition from Indian farmers. Almost from the beginning it became clear that the extensive ties that had linked the native farming communities to whites made a unified Dakota front impossible.

Intratribal strife over past interethnic ties surfaced within minutes of the first attack at the lower agency. As the fighting commenced, many Dakota people did their best to save friends and kinsmen, many of whom were white. Most often, farmer Indians who did not support the war were involved in this, but even many of the Dakota soldiers who were actively fighting made exceptions, saving whites from death at the hands of their fellow tribesmen. For example, on the first day Little Crow and his head soldier, Wakinyantawa, saved the lives of trader George Spencer and Charles Blair, Joseph R. Brown's white son-in-law. According to one account, Wakinyantawa had a unique relationship with Spencer, based upon "a species of freemasonry." Spencer's kinship ties obviously averted his death, since all the other traders, including Myrick, Lynd, and several less important clerks, were killed at their stores.[6]

In most cases, those saved from the tomahawk had demonstrated friendship with certain Sioux people and attained some degree of fictive kinship ties. The experience of Helen M. Tarble illustrates the role of these interlinking ties. A settler's wife, Tarble had moved into the German community across from the lower agency at Beaver Creek four years before the outbreak. She spent many hours thereafter with an old shaman, believed to be Parent Hawk, who showed her many of the medical secrets of his trade. She, in turn, fed the man and his friends. When Dakota warriors overtook the Tarbles and several of their fleeing neighbors on 18 August, Mrs. Tarble talked to them in Dakota, pleading for the lives of the party.[7] Although the Sioux men saved her and her children, they purposefully killed eleven others, among whom were the wife and children of a settler named Henderson. As Tarble noted, the Indians "seemed especially enraged against her [Mrs. Henderson]. I have since believed that they were instigated in their feeling by the old medicine man . . . who took revenge for the insults and abuse which Mr. Henderson had heaped upon him." One Henderson girl, only two and a half, was beaten to death and another was hacked to pieces. Their helpless mother was burned to death while lying ill on an old mattress. The Dakota warriors responsible for the killings were quick to assure Mrs. Tarble that she need not fear for her life, and even in captivity she was allowed to do as she pleased.[8]

Other whites benefited in similar ways because of fictive kinship ties. The wife of the physician at the upper agency, Sarah F. Wakefield, found that the generous assistance her husband had given to various Indian patients proved invaluable after her capture. Taken to Little Crow's camp on the afternoon of 18 August Wakefield found Indian women and children competing among themselves to "spread down carpets for me to sit on . . . they prepared my supper, and tried in every way possible to make me comfortable."[9]

Some reservation employees received warning to flee on 18 August. Among them were Joseph Reynolds and his wife, owners of a boardinghouse and government schoolteachers; John Narin, a government carpenter; Samuel Hinman, missionary at the lower agency; and old Philander Prescott. With the exception of Prescott, all were saved while other whites around them were being slaughtered. Prescott probably would have survived had he stayed indoors as he was told. Reynolds and his wife were convinced to leave by no other than young Shakopee, later thought to be one of the most active Dakota participants in the killing of white civilians.[10] The saving of whites provoked discord within the Dakota camp; their fate as captives prompted even more intense squabbling.

While a few whites benefited from past generosity, the kinship ties fostered by mixed-bloods made them practically immune to the assaults of Dakota soldiers. Killing mixed-bloods would have invited retribution from full-blood kinsmen. In an exhaustive study of the war, Marion Satterlee found only one mixed-blood who had been killed by hostile parties.[11] Yet many mixed-bloods clearly functioned in a white world and in some respects were hated by traditional Dakota people as much as were the Germans. This was surely the case with Louis Brisbois and his wife, who, according to one account, had mistreated Dakota men and women when they came to their house seeking aid. Just as the couple were to be killed for their social indiscretion, some whites distracted the warriors, and Brisbois and his wife escaped.[12]

Despite threats and assaults, many mixed-bloods attempted to help white friends. Joseph La Framboise and Narcisse Freniere, for example, warned traders and government workers at the upper agency. Most escaped without harm.[13] Missionaries likewise were protected by their flocks, many of whom were mixed-bloods. Both the Riggs and the Williamson families stayed near the upper agency for some time after news of the war had reached them. When it became clear they could not safely remain, they received food and horses from friendly Indians and mixed-bloods and escaped onto the prairies east of Yellow Medicine.[14]

Perhaps the most illustrative use of kinship connection by mixed-bloods came during the capture of Mrs. Joseph R. Brown, a Sisseton woman who was the wife of the former agent, her eleven children, and nearly a dozen white settlers. The Brown party had fled from a farm near Yellow Medicine the day after the killing started at the lower agency. Unfortunately, while moving south they came upon a party led by Cut Nose, Dowanniye, and young Shakopee. Fearful of a frightful slaughter, Mrs. Brown "stood up in the wagon, waved her shawl and cried in a loud voice, in the Dakota language, that she was a Sisseton and relative of Wannatan, Scarlet Plume, Sweet Corn, Ah-kee-pah [Joseph Akipa Renville], and the friend of Standing Buffalo." She demanded protection for her family and the whites with them.[15]

The tactic worked, and the Dakota warriors, spattered with blood from earlier killings, escorted the Brown party to Little Crow's camp. Even so, along the way they taunted the whites who had been saved by Mrs. Brown's actions. Shakopee was particularly troublesome, shaking his tomahawk at a German settler and at one of Mrs. Brown's white sons-in-law, all the while shouting, "The Dutch [Germans] have made me so angry, I will butcher them alive." Once at Little Crow's village, all members of the party received good treatment, and several whites were freed. Shortly thereafter, full-blood relatives came and took charge of the Browns, removing them to Yellow Medicine.[16]

Unfortunately, most whites on the upper Minnesota had made no attempt to develop kinship bonds with the nearby Sioux. This was true of some government employees, but more particularly so of the Germans, who generally received no quarter in the war. Men, women, and children were indiscriminately slaughtered or, in some cases, taken captive. Most often the chance to live as a captive depended upon the mood of the war party. In the case of Dr. John Humphrey and his wife and two children the Sioux manifested no compassion. Humphrey, physician at the lower agency, was an unbending man with a strong penchant for preaching "Christian doctrine." Dakota warriors trapped him and his family in a cabin not far from Fort Ridgely and massacred them.[17] The same fate befell fifty or so German settlers living just north of New Ulm. Virtually all of them— men, women, and children—were slaughtered, because most had been responsible for forcing the eviction of the lower Sioux from this region back in 1855. Mass killings likewise occurred in the Beaver Creek settlements, regions that the Sioux felt had been wrongly occupied in 1858.[18] So few people survived in these areas that there are no reliable accounts of the carnage.

Although numerous stories about these killings quickly surfaced in the Minnesota newspapers, there is some question about their trustworthiness. Clearly some Sioux warriors used knives and hatchets to mutilate their victims. Traditionally, Dakota men had scalped, decapitated, and disfigured the bodies of enemies. Women occasionally were stripped of clothes, a practice meant to offend their menfolk rather than to gratify sexual deviance.[19] The extent to which mutilation occurred in 1862 is still somewhat clouded, however. Dr. Jared W. Daniels, who accompanied the burial party to the lower agency, denied that bodies had been disfigured; yet reliable sources too numerous to list contradict him.[20] Several eyewitnesses attest that Sioux warriors frequently disrobed female corpses. One badly wounded woman, thought to be dead, was stripped at night while still conscious.[21] Clearly Dakota warriors had come to view whites as enemies in the traditional sense, unworthy to be treated as human beings. On the other hand, such actions lent credence to charges by whites that the Dakotas deserved no better fate than extermination.

Undoubtedly the most serious charge levied by newspapers was rape, or the "fate worse than death." Some white women were saved from the tomahawk with the intent of incorporating them into the tribes as wives, a practice occasionally applied in intertribal war. But there were strong taboos against rape by a war party; the Sioux believed it would displease native spirits. Accordingly, far fewer women were assaulted than the Minnesota press implied.[22] The evidence shows that members of Sleepy Eyes's village did sexually abuse two women sometime after taking them captive near Lake Shetek. Testimony also indicates that two other women were raped while prisoners in the Mdewakanton camp, both giving sworn statements to the fact.[23]

Once captured women reached the Indian camp, however, they fell under the protection of tribal institutions, such as the family, designed to prevent abuse. Mary Schwandt, a German teenager, was adopted by Snana, and once she was part of the kinship group no harm came to her. Ćaska, a friendly Indian, protected Sarah Wakefield, even claiming to have taken her as a wife in order to stop other men from bothering her. Rumors of this relationship spread among other white captives, and the army later executed Ćaska despite Mrs. Wakefield's courageous defense of his actions. She undoubtedly realized that her futile attempt to save Ćaska's life would result in her condemnation by every white person in Minnesota. Another female captive reported that native matrons slept on each side of her to prevent abuse.[24] Clearly Sioux men felt that once in camp taboos against the assault of white women ended. Indeed, it was not uncommon for men to waylay women of their own tribe while out gathering wood or fetching water. For this reason farmer Indians did their best to gain control of female captives and keep them out of sight.

On the evening of 18 August the white captives reached Little Crow's village, which quickly became the nucleus of the hostile movement. There they discovered a celebration in progress. "We saw papooses of all sizes robed in rich laces and bedecked in many fantastic styles," Mrs. N. D. White later reported.[25] For the first time in months there was an abundance of fresh meat from slaughtered oxen, flour, dried fruit, tea, and coffee. Ransacked trunks were strewn over the ground, and sunbonnets and jewelry graced Sioux women. A few Indians smashed clocks to get the gears, which they used for earrings. Captives, mixed-bloods, and farmer Indians alike were told to discard their white clothes and don Indian dress. Mixed-bloods ran frantically about the camp searching for breechcloths, leggings, native dresses, and skins and cloth for tepees.[26] Those living in houses were forced to abandon them, and the soldiers burned many homes. Warriors were doing their best to force a rebirth of Sioux life-style amid the confusion of continuous dancing, singing, beating of drums, and departure and return of war parties.

The celebrations lasted only a short while, however, and as soon as it became obvious that Fort Ridgely and New Ulm would not be overrun the Indian soldiers decided to withdraw north. The Indian train that left the lower agency on 26 August extended over five miles of Minnesota prairie. Soldiers struggled to maintain order, but as one reporter noted, the caravan soon resembled "the confusion of Babel." Stopping for a day at Rice Creek, the assemblage finally reached Yellow Medicine River, or the upper agency, on the twenty-eighth.[27]

While near the upper agency, the soldiers organized two war parties, one heading east toward the Big Woods and the second south, supposedly to attack New Ulm. This latter camp soon discovered a reinforced burial detail of two companies of troops surveying the ruins of the lower agency. Under the joint command of Joseph R. Brown and Captain Joseph Anderson, the military patrol camped for the evening near Beaver Creek on Birch Coulee. Little care was taken to select a defensive camp, since Colonel Sibley had sent scouts nearly to Yellow Medicine River the previous day and they had failed to see any hostile Indians. But at dawn on 2 September the Indians, following various leaders, quietly surrounded the troops and attacked. The battle of Birch Coulee lasted through most of the day, with the white soldiers suffering heavy losses. In all, the Sioux killed twenty troopers and wounded upward of sixty. Every horse in the command save one—eighty-seven in all—fell to Sioux bullets. Fortunately Colonel Sibley arrived on 3 September with a relief column to save the exhausted and nearly defeated militia.[28]

In the aftermath of the Birch Coulee debacle, Sibley adopted a cautious course in dealing with the eastern Sioux, aware that a like disaster could befall his poorly equipped army of twelve hundred men. He seemed especially concerned about the determination with which the Sioux fought; most whites had generally believed Dakota warriors would never fight a pitched battle, and traditional Indian warfare almost precluded it. Obviously the hostile Indians had adopted many of the military techniques of their white opponents, assaulting positions in force.[29] Hopeful of averting such a struggle, Sibley left a note at the Birch Coulee battlefield calling on the supposed leader of the hostiles, Little Crow, to explain why he had opted for war. Sibley hoped to negotiate a release of the prisoners in the main Sioux camp and possibly to convince the hostiles to surrender without further bloodshed. To obtain better information on Indian movements, he also enlisted at least one full-blood Dakota scout, John Otherday, who offered to serve Sibley's army on 4 September.[30] Sibley increasingly sought assistance from friendly Indians throughout the campaign that followed, a recruiting pattern that formed the basis for a permanent organization of Sioux scouts.[31]

Meanwhile, strong factional divisions surfaced at the main Mdewakanton-Wakpekute camp on Yellow Medicine River. The trouble began on 28 August, before the Birch Coulee battle, when Mdewakantons attempted to convince Sissetons and Wahpetons, who had stayed near the upper agency, to join them. Instead a large number of Sissetons and Wahpetons under the leadership of Gabriel Renville, Joseph Akipa Renville, Solomon Two Stars, Henok Mahpiyadenape, the Sisseton Cloud Man, Iron Walker, and Paul Mazakutemani spoke against the war, demanding to know why the Mdewakantons and Wahpekutes had brought such a disaster upon themselves. Fearful of reprisals, the men above then formed a soldiers' lodge of their own. Its organization came none too soon, since on 29 August about three hundred Mdewakanton-Wahpekute warriors surrounded the Sisseton-Wahpeton camp and threatened to kill those men who refused to join them. But upon seeing the main lodge of the soldier group in the center of the Sisseton-Wahpeton village the hostile warriors withdrew, knowing it meant the upper Sioux intended to resist them militarily. A long dialogue followed in which farmers, mixed-bloods, and nonhostile elements tried their best to negotiate an end to the rebellion, presenting their arguments both individually and in what one observer described as a "big council."[32]

One important council discussion got under way sometime between 29 and 31 August. Paul Mazakutemani spoke for those Indians professing friendship toward whites, and various soldiers represented the hostile Mdewakanton camp. As in most council debates during this period, Little Crow played only a minor role. More than a thousand Indians were present as Mazakutemani asked the soldiers why they had started the war. He complained that it was begun "without a council being called." Furthermore, he could not understand how warriors could make war on women and children, and he told the Mdewakanton soldiers to give up their captives and fight Sibley's soldiers. But the vast majority of soldiers present refused to accept his logic, prompting him to make several more attempts to convince the Mdewakantons of their folly. Finally, on 6 September he gathered large quantities of food and invited the Mdewakantons to a feast in the Sisseton-Wahpeton village, a ploy traditionally used to create a sense of obligation. This time the Mdewakanton soldiers strongly warned him against bringing up the subject of the captives again, one soldier declaring: "The Mdewakantons are *men*, and as long as one of them lives they will not stop pointing their guns at the Americans."[33]

Despite initial diplomatic failures, a new series of discussions commenced after Little Crow received Sibley's message on 4 September. Even though the previous councils had demonstrated that the soldiers' lodge was running the war rather than Little Crow, the chief was able to convince lodge members that the query should be answered. Little Crow selected two mixed-bloods, Tom Robinson and Thomas A. Robertson, to deliver his message to Colonel Sibley on 8 September. In the reply Little Crow attempted to justify the war, citing the government's failure to distribute annuities and the traders' stinginess as primary causes for discontent. Little Crow also reminded Sibley that the hostiles had many prisoners and asked the colonel to pass along his explanation to Alexander Ramsey, now governor of the state of Minnesota.[34]

Sibley found little encouraging in the note, but the information he received from the mixed-blood messengers proved fruitful. He learned from them that the white captives were being reasonably well treated, that considerable numbers of Mdewakantons—mostly farmers—had been forced to participate in the battles, and that many Sissetons and Wahpetons remained steadfastly opposed to the war. Sibley remained hopeful that the captives could be saved, and he instructed Robinson and Robertson to tell Little Crow that he wanted the Indians to surrender them.[35]

After the two messengers arrived back at Yellow Medicine River, the soldiers' lodge ordered a further retreat north to Lac qui Parle. It seems likely that Robinson and Robertson not only had given the Mdewakanton soldiers Sibley's message but had also reported on the large number of troops now near Fort Ridgely. The march north began early on 9 September, the Sissetons and Wahpetons joining in with the Mdewakantons and Wahpekutes, making a train five miles long. Toward evening the lead elements were within fourteen miles of Lac qui Parle when the Wahpeton Red Iron met them at the head of 150 Sisseton and Wahpeton warriors. Red Iron was still a farmer and still friendly to whites despite his confinement by Ramsey in 1852. He now told the Mdewakantons to proceed no further: "You commenced the Outbreak, and must do the fighting in your country. We do not want you here to excite our young men." Standing Buffalo, a major chief from Lake Traverse, joined Red Iron a few days later in condemning the war.[36] Although elements of the Lake Traverse Sissetons had joined the Mdewakanton and Wahpekute camp and some of their young men had even harassed the garrison at Fort Abercrombie north of Lake Traverse, the defection of the main leaders to the peace party seriously hampered the hostile cause.[37]

Even before the upper Sissetons made known their disapproval of the war, however, factions within the main Mdewakanton-Wahpekute camp began suing for peace. Little Crow even joined the effort, writing Sibley on 12 September that the hostiles had failed to obtain the support of the Sissetons and Wahpetons and closing with an interesting plea: "I want to know from you as a friend what way that I can make peace for my people."[38] Little Crow was trying to use his past fictive ties with Sibley to help extricate his people from the war. Robinson and Robertson again delivered the message, giving Sibley more information about the situation near Lac qui Parle. They told him of the extreme divisions among the Dakotas, even within the Mdewakanton camp. Little Crow's life had been threatened, presumably for raising the issue of peace. Robinson and Robertson also carried a private note from Wabasha, Taopi, the principal farmer at the lower agency, and a dozen others—mostly farmers—who said that they had favored peace all along and had not participated in the murder of the whites. They noted that the Mdewakanton soldiers had carefully guarded them and even used threats to keep them in line. While again demanding the captives from Little Crow, Sibley told Robinson and Robertson to have the friendly Sioux separate themselves from the main hostile group. On 14 September many of those who opposed the war left the Mdewakanton-Wahpekute camp.[39] Robinson and Robertson had given these people the distinct impression that Sioux warriors who had not killed civilians would be well treated by Sibley.

Over the next week, tensions reached extreme levels in the two Indian camps, which were separated by only a mile. Squabbles especially erupted over the captives, who were slowly being removed, a few at a time, to the friendly camp. "Raids" of a sort also occurred, with hostile Indians descending upon the friendly camp and destroying tepees and goods. This sort of destruction was characteristic of warriors, who felt their kinsmen had failed to demonstrate loyalty. Fighting was miraculously averted. The struggles reached a climax on 22 September when news arrived that Sibley's force had reached Wood Lake, just south of the upper agency. The colonel had been prodded by authorities in the east to do something to punish the Sioux and save the captives. He had finally decided to force the issue.[40]

In the Mdewakanton camp, the soldiers' lodge ordered every able-bodied man to prepare for war, forcing Indians friendly to whites to join them. Rewards were offered to those who could procure the scalps of Sibley, Brown, or any of the better-known whites. In all, 738 warriors left the camps below Lac qui Parle on the afternoon of the twenty-second, but only about 300 engaged Sibley the next morning at Wood Lake. Large numbers of Indians who went to the battle-ground could not be prodded into fighting. Losses during the engagement that followed were minimal on both sides, Sibley losing only four men and the Sioux sixteen. The unwillingness of many Indians to participate doomed the assault from the start. Tired and discouraged, the main body of Dakota men returned to their old camp below Lac qui Parle on the evening of 23 September, now aware that they must either surrender or flee out onto the western prairies.[41]

Back in camp, the hostiles learned that the friendly Indians had removed most of the remaining white captives to Red Iron's village and were prepared to defend them with their lives. They had dug rifle pits in the floors of the tents and organized a perimeter guard. Sibley learned of the removal of the captives to the friendly camp on the twenty-third from A. J. Campbell, a mixed-blood, who carried the message to Wood Lake. Many members of the Mdewakanton soldiers' lodge wanted to overrun the friendly camp, yet the lodge had steadily been losing power, and Little Crow strongly advised against hurting the captives, arguing that it would only enrage the white soldiers. Little Crow now urged those who had taken part in the war to divide up and flee.[42]

Before leaving, Little Crow called on A. J. Campbell, a relative who had played a major role in organizing the friendly camp, to come and feast with him. Campbell went, not knowing what to expect.

The meeting that followed illustrates the tragedy of the entire Sioux Outbreak. When Campbell arrived in Little Crow's lodge, the chief greeted him as "cousin," then asked if there was anything he could do for him before leaving for the west. Campbell asked him to surrender to Sibley, whereupon Little Crow laughed and said, "Sibley would like to put the rope around my neck, but he won't get the chance." Little Crow then agreed to do what he could to have any captives still held by hostile warriors—there were perhaps a dozen—turned over to Campbell, and the two men parted, still friends and relatives despite the different roles they had taken in the war.[43]

Several hundred hostiles did follow Little Crow onto the plains west of Lac qui Parle, leaving the friendly Indians in charge of ninety-four white captives. The mixed-bloods who were held against their will totaled 162. For unexplained reasons, Sibley waited until 26 September to march on the friendly village, now called Camp Release, and claim the unfortunate captives. It was a joyous day for most, though the two dozen or so white women fretted over their appearance. All were dressed in "squaw suits," and Sibley had nothing better for them to wear.[44] The only mission remaining for the army was to capture and punish those responsible for the war—no small order, since Sibley's soldiers lacked horses and the supplies necessary to operate on the plains.

The hostile Indians seemed reluctant to escape out onto the plains. Most were Mdewakantons or, to a lesser degree, Wahpekutes, who had always lived in the woodlands. They viewed the plains as a forbidding place where food would be difficult to find. A few moved in with relatives at Camp Release, hoping that Robinson and Robertson had spoken the truth about Sibley's intentions and no doubt convinced that their kinship ties with nonhostile Indians could afford them protection from punishment. Indeed, this camp grew from 150 lodges on the twenty-third to nearly 250 by the twenty-sixth, and more Dakotas kept moving in after the army arrived, usually at night.[45]

Sibley soon realized that he might persuade many hostiles to surrender if it appeared that he had forgiven the farmer groups and did not intend to punish them. His early promise to Robinson and Robertson to punish only those directly involved in killing civilians was clearly understood by the Sioux. In addition, on 24 September he wrote both to members of the friendly camp and to the upper Sissetons, assuring them that they had nothing to fear if they had not been involved in the murder of civilians. Nonetheless, as the friendly camp grew in number, Sibley ordered the formation of a military tribunal to gather evidence against all those present. He made no move to take large numbers of prisoners, however, securing only sixteen men. Other Dakota men were even allowed to keep their weapons, a move that encouraged still more to surrender.[46]

During the two weeks that followed, Camp Release slowly increased to more than a thousand people. Some men who returned to it had been deeply implicated in the fighting; others were tied to the killing of civilians. Finally, on 11 October, when Sibley was convinced that he had "three-fourths of those primarily concerned in the Outbreak," he surrounded Camp Release and arrested more than 100 men. He apprehended others over the next few days, including a large number of warriors who had been sent back to Yellow Medicine to dig potatoes. By 17 October Sibley had close to 400 prisoners, only 68 of whom were deemed to have been "friendly" throughout the entire war. Their dependents totaled another 1,400 people. Perhaps 200 hostile Mdewakanton warriors were still at large on the plains.[47]

For those in custody, trials moved at a fast pace. By 21 October, 120 had been judged guilty, 40 cases being determined on one day alone. At this point Sibley moved the prisoners and their dependents south, building log jails along the way to accommodate the guilty men. The last case was determined at Fort Ridgely on 4 November. In all, the military commission condemned 303 Dakota men. While the government debated their eventual fate, they were moved to a stockade near Mankato. En route a mob attacked the chained men in New Ulm, killing two prisoners. A second assault by civilians was narrowly averted on 9 December.[48]

The dependents of the prisoners, 1,658 people, were marched to St. Paul on 9 November. The government built a walled enclosure for them below Fort Snelling to keep angry whites from abusing them. Protection was necessary, since the caravan of old men, women, and children had been attacked by enraged whites while passing through Henderson, Minnesota, and further abuse occurred when the party reached St. Paul. Washington officials, aware that these people could no longer stay in Minnesota, selected Crow Creek on the Missouri as a new home for them, and they were moved west in the spring. More or less uninhabited, Crow Creek was a dreadfully barren place where many eastern Sioux Indians later perished.[49]

All along, Sibley had wanted to execute en masse the men judged guilty. Even the missionary Riggs, who acted as military chaplain for Sibley and as occasional interpreter during the trials, reluctantly concurred, noting that "the great majority of those who are condemned should be executed."[50] Yet President Abraham Lincoln, warned by Bishop Henry Benjamin Whipple and others of the haste with which the trials had been conducted, demanded to see the proceedings of the military commission. What he saw undoubtedly disturbed him. Only two cases showed credible evidence of rape, though congressmen from Minnesota had informed Lincoln that nearly all of the condemned had sexually abused white women. Most trials contained only a paragraph or two of testimony, frequently only a man's admission that he had been present at one of the major battles and had fired a gun. The military court had agreed to condemn any Indian who admitted to firing either at the fort or at New Ulm. Time and again men who had not sided with the hostiles testified that although they had charged their guns with powder and fired them, they had not used balls, thus harming no one. Evidence also frequently demonstrated that members of the soldiers' lodge had to threaten reluctant Sioux men—mostly farmers—to make them participate in the fighting.[51]

Lincoln finally agreed to execute 39 men, partly to satisfy the thirst for revenge in Minnesota and partly because circumstantial evidence indicated that these men had been party to the killing of civilians. On 26 December, 38 were hanged in Mankato, one man in the group receiving a reprieve. The springing of the trap by a white man who had lost most of his family symbolically ended the Sioux Outbreak in Minnesota.[52]

Federal officials removed the remaining 250 male prisoners to Davenport, Iowa, where they served sentences of one to three years. Those who survived the internment—nearly one-half died of disease—eventually joined their families at Crow Creek. In 1866 the government allowed the Crow Creek remnants of the once-powerful eastern Sioux to settle at Santee, Nebraska, where their descendants have a reservation today.[53]

Despite their freedom, the 500 or so people who followed Little Crow and the 2,800 Sissetons and Wahpetons who continued to roam north of Lake Traverse suffered nearly as much as the main body of Indians who surrendered. Forced out onto the prairies late in the fall, many perished during the winter. Buffalo had all but disappeared from the lands east of the Missouri River. Both Little Crow's group and the Sissetons and Wahpetons sought aid in Canada, partly out of desperation and partly because of lingering memories of kinship bonds that had once existed between the Sioux and English agents representing the crown. Others joined western Sioux bands and fought alongside Red Cloud, Sitting Bull, and Crazy Horse. Little Crow resorted to raiding the Minnesota frontier, where he was killed by a farmer while picking berries. Upon learning the identity of the corpse, white boys desecrated the body. It was an inglorious end for the once important chief who had tried hard to maintain the ways of the past as well as live peaceably alongside whites. A handful of his followers stayed behind in Canada, where they eventually received a small reservation. By the late 1860s many Sissetons and Wahpetons were being resettled on reservations in northeastern South Dakota and central North Dakota.[54]

Overall, the uprising of 1862 was a terrible tragedy. Hundreds of whites and Indians lost their lives, most of whom had neither started nor condoned the conflict. Although the Dakota men who started the war had hoped it would lead to a rejuvenated society, the fighting accentuated the split in eastern Sioux camps so that it threatened the very fabric of Dakota existence. The reliance on kinship systems to provide identity in one's descent group and tribe, loyalty to native culture, and assistance in time of trouble seemed on the point of dissolution. Yet Sioux warriors did not openly fight among themselves in 1862, and when differences over the war could not be resolved the hostiles fled to the plains, leaving the friendly camp unmolested. Indeed, some protagonists such as Little Crow and A. J. Campbell could even part friends.

Even so, it is important to remember that the antagonisms the outbreak unveiled were historical exceptions in the chronicle of early Dakota-white contact. The ethnic relations that evolved on the upper Mississippi River after 1650 by and large were characterized by peaceful trade, the creation of strong kinship bonds, and fruitful negotiation. Although these relations underwent change as traders came and went and after the federal government built Fort Snelling, the age was one in which individuals like Le Sueur, Dickson, Taliaferro, and even Sibley met, smoked, and worked out their differences with their Dakota kinsmen Sacred Born, Wabasha, Running Walker, and Little Crow. Differing world views seemed compatible, even complementary, for nearly two centuries. Relations with Euroamericans had brought the Dakotas time-saving items that made life easier as well as new and powerful allies. If ever the eastern Sioux had a golden age, it was this period.

But, as they always do, the golden age came to an end, and the era passed when the game no longer could support villages, white pioneers began to invade Sioux lands, and acculturation programs sought to destroy native culture. Even with such pressures, Dakota people continued to trust their white kinsmen and believed the "Great Father" would always assist them. This lingering faith no doubt explains why so many Mdewakantons who had participated in the war decided to stay near Camp Release and be captured by Sibley. One can only marvel at the patience of the eastern Sioux and their commitment to whites.

Thus, when we remember the Minnesota Sioux we should not recall simply the horrors of those days in late August. The outbreak was begun by a minority of Sioux warriors who were unable to unify their people behind a policy of violence even after initial successes at the lower agency and Birch Coulee gave the leaders of the movement reason to be optimistic. Furthermore, we should not assume that those Indians who counseled peace were unpatriotic or were weaklings who became cultural traitors in exchange for annuities. As is often true in history, the opposing groups both had worthy convictions that must be considered in the context of the time.

Finally, we should also remember that, though early whites willingly assimilated aspects of the Dakota world view, the tendency to do so decreased as the potential for economic exploitation and the need to manipulate Sioux institutions declined. Herein lies the tragedy of this interethnic relationship: successful and peaceful patterns, so well established in the past, were abandoned as whites succumbed to the immensely strong urge to impose the cultural conformity that dominated the American frontier experience. This illiberal attitude brought violence to the land and to people who generally had been committed to living in peace with their white neighbors.

Notes

Abbreviations in Notes

ABCFM	American Board of Commissioners for Foreign Missions
AFC-MHS	American Fur Company Papers, New York Public Library (photostats and microfilm in Minnesota Historical Society)
AFCP	American Fur Company Papers
AGO	Adjutant General's Office
DPL	Detroit Public Library
DRNRUT	Documents Relating to the Negotiation of Ratified and Unratified Treaties
HD	House Document
HED	House Executive Document
LR	Letter Received
LS	Letter Sent
NARG	National Archives Record Group
OIA	Office of Indian Affairs
PRO	Public Record Office, London
SED	Senate Executive Document

Notes

PREFACE

1 Ella C. Deloria, *Speaking of Indians* (New York: Friendship Press, 1944), 24–26.
2 Raymond J. DeMallie has argued that kinship systems remain very much intact on Sioux reservations today. See his "Change in American Indian Kinship Systems: The Dakota," in Robert E. Hinshaw, ed., *Currents in Anthropology: Essays in Honor of Sol Tax, Studies in Anthropology*, vol. 3 (The Hague and New York: Mouton, 1979), 221–41.
3 *Minnesota Pioneer* (St. Paul), 9 August 1849.

CHAPTER 1

1 Arthur T. Adams, ed., *The Explorations of Pierre Esprit Radisson* (Minneapolis: Ross and Haines, 1961), 136–43.
2 Reuben Gold Thwaites, ed., *The Jesuit Relations and Allied Documents, Travels and Explorations of the Jesuit Missionaries in New France, 1610–1793*, 73 vols. (New York: Pageant Book Company, 1959), 54:191–93, 56:115–17 (hereafter cited as *Jesuit Relations*).
3 "Relation of sieur de Lamothe Cadillac, Captain on Full Pay Commanding a Company of the Marine Troops in Canada; formerly Commandant of Missilimackinac and other Posts in Distant Countries," 1718, *Wisconsin Historical Society Collections*, 31 vols. (Madison: Wisconsin Historical Society, 1855–1931), 16 (1902):362–63 (hereafter cited as *Wisconsin Collections*).
4 Le Sueur spent the winter of 1700–1701 with the Sioux on the Blue Earth River in present-day south-central Minnesota. Although his original journal has not been discovered, an abridged copy in the hand of Claude Delisle, dated 1702, is in the Archives Nationales, Paris, under the title "Mémoires de Mr le Sueur." Mildred

Mott Wedel graciously allowed me to consult her copy of this journal, which I hereafter cite as Delisle, "Mémoires de Mr le Sueur." Le Sueur gives the Cree description on page 57 and the quotation relative to Sioux warfare on page 43. Bénard de la Harpe, a contemporary of Le Sueur's, used a small portion of the explorer's journal for his "Historical Journal of the Establishment of the French of Louisiana," translated and edited by B. F. French in the *Historical Collections of Louisiana*, 5 parts (New York: D. Appleton, 1851), 3:1–118. In turn, small extracts of La Harpe are found in the *Wisconsin Collections*, 16(1902):177–93, and in Pierre Margry, ed., *Découvertes et établissements des Français dans l'Ouest et dans le Sud l'Amérique Septrionale (1614–1754): Mémoires et Documents Originaux*, 6 vols. (Paris: Maisonneuve Preres et Ch. LeClerc, editeurs, 1876–88), 6(1888):69–87 (hereafter *Découvertes et établissements*).

5 Extraites des Lettres d'Antoine Raudot sur l'Amérique Septrionale, in *Découvertes et établissements*, 6(1888):15.

6 See Stephen Return Riggs, *Dakota Grammar Texts, and Ethnography*, in *Contributions to North American Ethnology*, ed. James Owen Dorsey (Washington, D.C.: Government Printing Office, 1893), 9:156–60 (hereafter Riggs, *Dakota Grammar*); Adams, ed., *Radisson's Explorations*, 136–43; Delisle, "Mémoires de Mr le Sueur," 52.

7 The term "Sioux," a derivative of the Algonquin "Naudoweissious," meaning enemy, is consistently used by authors even though the easternmost Sioux called themselves the "Dakota," a word that translates as "league" or "ally." Another term, "Santee," a corruption of "Issati," promotes even more confusion, since authors have used it to denote the four eastern Sioux tribes when it referred only to a Mdewakanton band in the seventeenth century. In this study, "eastern Sioux" and "Dakota" are used interchangeably. The spelling of Dakota words is from Stephen Return Riggs, *A Dakota-English Dictionary*, ed. James Owen Dorsey (Minneapolis: Ross and Haines, 1968). For a discussion of "Santee," see Riggs, *Dakota Grammar*, 159–60.

8 "Relation de Pénicaut [Pénigauît]," *Découvertes et établissements*, 5 (1887): 417; Delisle, "Mémoires de Mr le Sueur," 43–44; Mildred Mott Wedel, "Le Sueur and the Dakota Sioux," in *Aspects of Upper Great Lakes Anthropology: Papers in Honor of Lloyd A. Wilford*, ed. Elden Johnson, 157–71 (St. Paul: Minnesota Historical Society, 1974).

9 Pierre de Charlevoix, *Journal of a Voyage to North-America*, 2 vols. (London: R. Dodsley in Pall-Mall, 1761), 1:280.

10 See Harold Hickerson, *Sioux Indians*, vol. 1. *Mdewakanton Band of Sioux Indians* (New York and London: Garland Publishing, 1974), 20–28; Louise Phelps Kellogg, ed., "Father Alouez's Journey to Lake Superior, 1665–1667," in *Early Narratives of the Northwest, 1634–1699* (New York: Barnes and Noble, 1967), 132.

11 The use of corn by the Sioux is mentioned very early by Pierre Radisson and the

Jesuits, and there were substantial cornfields on the Minnesota River in 1774. Yet Father Louis Hennepin in 1680 and Le Sueur in 1700 indicated that the Dakotas were nonagricultural. Adams, ed., *Radisson's Explorations*, 134, 143; "The Journey of Raymbault and Jogues to the Sault, 1641," in *Early Narratives*, 24; Louis Hennepin, *A Description of Louisiana*, ed. John G. Shea (New York: John G. Shea, 1880), 228–29, 254–55; Delisle, "Mémoires de Mr le Sueur," 43–44; Charles M. Gates, ed., "The Narrative of Peter Pond," in *Five Fur Traders of the Northwest* (St. Paul: Minnesota Historical Society, 1965), 56; John Parker, ed., *The Journals of Jonathan Carver and Related Documents, 1766–1770* (St Paul: Minnesota Historical Society, 1976), 95.

12 Samuel W. Pond, "The Dakota or Sioux in Minnesota as They Were in 1834," *Minnesota Historical Society Collections*, 17 vols. (St Paul: Minnesota Historical Society, 1860–1920), 12(1905–8):340–75 (hereafter cited as *Minnesota Collections*); Ruth Landes, *The Mystic Lake Sioux: Sociology of the Mdewakantonwan Santee* (Madison: University of Wisconsin Press, 1968), 161–214.

13 Pond, "The Dakota . . . in 1834," *Minnesota Collections*, 12 (1905–8):360–66; Harold Hickerson, *The Chippewa and Their Neighbors: A Study in Ethnohistory* (New York: Holt, Rinehart and Winston, 1970), 106–19; Thomas G. Anderson, "Narrative of Captain Thomas G. Anderson," *Wisconsin Collections*, 9 (1909):183–85.

14 Delisle, "Mémoires de Mr le Sueur," 44; Hennepin, *Description of Louisiana*, 216–17; Parker, ed., *Carver's Journal*, 105–7.

15 Hennepin, *Description of Louisiana*, 224–25, 228–29, 232–33.

16 Ibid., 238–39, 244–45, 250–54, 322–23. Hennepin indicated that the women *boucanned*, or smoked meat after cutting it into strips (p. 323).

17 Nicholas Perrot, "Memoir on the Manners, Customs, and Religion of the Savages of North America," in *The Indian Tribes of the Upper Mississippi Valley and the Region of the Great Lakes*, ed. Emma H. Blair, 2 vols. (Cleveland: Arthur H. Clark, 1911), 1:119.

18 Delisle, "Mémoires de Mr Sueur," 56; "Relation of Pénicaut [Pénigault]," *Découvertes et établissements*, 5(1887):413; Frank Gilbert Roe, *The North American Buffalo: A Critical Study of the Species in Its Wild State* (Toronto: University of Toronto Press, 1970), 367–413, 489–520; Tom McHugh, *The Time of the Buffalo* (New York: Alfred A. Knopf, 1972), 16–17; David A. Dary, *The Buffalo Book: The Full Saga of the American Animal* (Chicago: Swallow Press, 1974), 28–29; Adams, ed., *Radisson's Explorations*, 134–43.

19 Delisle, "Mémoires de Mr le Sueur," 47–48.

20 "Memoir of Duluth on the Sioux Country, 1678–1682," in *Early Narratives*, 331; Charles R. Watrall, "Virginia Deer and the Buffer Zone in the Late Prehistoric–Early Protohistoric Periods in Minnesota," *Plains Anthropologist* 13 (May 1968):81–86.

21 Recent anthropological arguments suggest that an efficient hunter-gatherer so-

286

ciety in balance with its ecosystem could easily produce sufficient food each year. Marshall Sahlins, *Stone Age Economy* (Chicago and New York: Aldine, Atherton, 1972), 1–39; Frederick L. Dunn, "Epidemiological Factors: Health and Disease in Hunter-Gatherers," in *Man the Hunter*, ed. Richard B. Lee and Irven De Vore (Chicago: Aldine, 1968), 223; Landes, *Mystic Lake Sioux*, 38–39, 204–14; Hennepin, *Description of Louisiana*, 217–18.

22 Landes, *Mystic Lake Sioux*, 122–28; Hennepin, *Description of Louisiana*, 217–18. Pond wrote that the Dakota hunter "wished to be as generous as his neighbors and was ashamed to eat of their food while they never tasted of his. He wanted to make as good a show of ability as others, and, prompted by generosity or vanity, incurred greater expense than his means would justify." Pond, "The Dakota ... in 1834," *Minnesota Collections* 12 (1905–8):412.

23 The quotation is from Parker, ed., *Carver's Journals*, 103.

24 Philander Prescott, "The Dakota or Sioux of the Upper Mississippi," in *Information Respecting the History, Condition, and Prospects of the Indian Tribes of the United States*, ed. Henry R. Schoolcraft, 6 vols. (Philadelphia: J. B. Lippincott, 1865), 3:227–30; Parker, ed., *Carver's Journals*, 103–5; Pond, "The Dakota ... in 1834," *Minnesota Collections*, 12 (1905–8), 405–17; James H. Lockwood, "Early Times and Events in Wisconsin," *Wisconsin Collections*, 2 (1856):182–83; Landes, *Mystic Lake Sioux*, 48–66, 181–84.

25 Prescott, "Contributions to the History, Customs, and Opinions of the Dacota Tribes," in *Information Respecting the History, Condition, and Prospects of the Indian Tribes*, ed. Schoolcraft, 2:189; Gideon Pond, "Power and Influence of Dakota Medicine Men," ibid., 4:641–51.

26 Calvin Martin, *Keepers of the Game: Indian-Animal Relationships and the Fur Trade* (Berkeley: University of California Press, 1978), 17–18, 38; Christopher Vecsey, "American Indian Environmental Religions," in *American Indian Environments: Ecological Issues in Native American History*, ed., Christopher Vecsey and Robert W. Venables (Syracuse, N.Y.: Syracuse University Press, 1980), 1–37.

27 Parker, ed., *Carver's Journals*, 103–5; Hennepin, *Description of Louisiana*, 211, 231–33; Extrait du Mémoire de M. Le Chevalier de Beaurain sur la Louisiane, *Découvertes et établissements*, 6 (1888):86; Delisle, "Mémoires de Mr le Sueur," 54; Prescott, "The Dakota or Sioux of the Upper Mississippi," in *Information Respecting the History, Condition, and Prospects of the Indian Tribes*, ed. Schoolcraft, 3:227.

28 Hennepin, *Description of Louisiana*, 217–18; Delisle, "Mémoires de Mr le Sueur," 56.

29 Quotation from Royal B. Hassrick, *The Sioux: Life and Customs of a Warrior Society* (Norman: University of Oklahoma Press, 1964), 174; Perrot, "Memoir on the Manners, Etc.," in *Indian Tribes*, ed. Blair, 1:105, 107.

30 Landes, *Mystic Lake Sioux*, 31.

31 Hennepin, *Description of Louisiana*, 232.

32 Pond, "The Dakota ... in 1834," *Minnesota Collections*, 12 (1905–8):359–69; Landes, *Mystic Lake Sioux*, 95–160; Raymond J. De Mallie, "Teton Dakota Kinship and Social Organization" (Ph.D. diss., University of Chicago, 1971), 41–42, 98; Alan Michael Klein, "Adaptive Strategies and Process on the Plains: The 19th Century Cultural Sink" (Ph.D. diss.: State University of New York, Buffalo, 1977), 90; Marcel Mauss, *The Gift: Forms and Functions of Exchange in Archaic Societies* (New York: W. W. Norton, 1967), 3–35; Robin Fox, *Kinship and Marriage: An Anthropological Perspective* (Harmondsworth, England: Penguin Books, 1976), 20–43; Hennepin, *Description of Louisiana*, 207, 215, 220.

33 Pond, "The Dakota ... in 1834," *Minnesota Collections*, 12 (1905–8):382–83; De Mallie, "Teton Dakota Kinship and Social Organization," 93; Landes, *Mystic Lake Sioux*, 78–94; Prescott, "Contributions to the History, Customs, and Opinions of the Dacota Tribe," in *Information Respecting the History, Condition, and Prospects of the Indian Tribes*, ed. Schoolcraft, 2:182.

34 Landes, *Mystic Lake Sioux*, 44–78; "Account of George Quinn," *Minnesota History* 38 (September 1962):147.

35 Hennepin, *Description of Louisiana*, 205–7.

36 O'Fallon to William Clark, 20 May 1818, in *The Territorial Papers of the United States*, ed. Clarence E. Carter and John P. Blum, 28 vols. (Washington, D.C.: Government Printing Office, 1934–), 15:407–8.

37 Pond, "The Dakota ... in 1834," *Minnesota Collections*, 12 (1905–8):390; Landes, *Mystic Lake Sioux*, 38–40, 135–39.

CHAPTER 2

1 Sahlins, *Stone Age Economy*, 2–9; Annuity Rolls for the Mdewakanton, Sisseton, and Wahpeton Sioux Tribes, 1853, National Archives Record Group 75 (hereafter NARG), Records of the Bureau of Indian Affairs.

2 Henry F. Dobyns, "Estimating Aboriginal American Population: An Appraisal of Techniques with a New Hemispheric Estimate," *Current Anthropology* 7 (October 1966):395–416; Francis Jennings, *The Invasion of America: Indians, Colonialism, and the Cant of Conquest* (New York: W. W. Norton, 1976), 29; Wilbur R. Jacobs, "The Tip of an Iceberg: Pre-Columbian Indian Demography and Some Implications for Revisionism," *William and Mary Quarterly* 31 (January 1974):123–32; John Duffy, "Smallpox and the Indians in the American Colonies," *Bulletin of the History of Medicine* 25 (1951): 324–41; Bruce G. Trigger, *Children of Aataentsic: A History of the Huron People to 1660*, 2 vols. (Montreal and London: McGill–Queens University Press, 1976), 2:449, 588–89.

3 Richard White, "The Winning of the West: The Expansion of the Western Sioux in

the Eighteenth and Nineteenth Centuries," *Journal of American History* 65 (September 1978):319–43.

4 Roy Meyer, *History of the Santee Sioux: United States Indian Policy on Trial* (Lincoln: University of Nebraska Press, 1967), 12. Meyer uses a 1736 unidentified estimate that gave the number of Dakota warriors as 300 and those of the prairie Sioux as *"over"* two thousand men" (italics added). From these figures, he places the total number of men at 2,300 and arrives at a Sioux population of 10,000. Comparatively, the new British commandant at Mackinac concluded in 1763 that the Sioux were "variously computed, but by the best accounts they exceed 10,000 men [50,000 people]." Of the many estimates available for Sioux populations in the seventeenth and eighteenth centuries, Meyer elected to believe the most conservative. See Census of Western Nations, November 1763, in *The Papers of Sir William Johnson*, ed. James Sullivan, 14 vols. (Albany: University of the State of New York, 1921–65), 4 (1925):245.

5 Delisle, "Mémoires de Mr le Sueur," 44, 56.

6 James R. Mooney, *The Aboriginal Populations of America North of Mexico*, ed. John R. Swanton, *Smithsonian Institution Miscellaneous Collections*, 80, no. 7 (Washington, D.C., 1928):12–13.

7 John Upton Terrell, *Sioux Trails* (New York: McGraw-Hill, 1974), 195; Robert H. Lowie, *Indians of the Plains* (Garden City, N.Y.: Natural Press, 1954), 12–13; Donald Jackson, ed., *The Journals of Zebulon Montgomery Pike*, 2 vols. (Norman: University of Oklahoma Press, 1966), 1:222.

8 "The Journey of Raymbault and Jogues to the Sault, 1641," in *Early Narratives*, 24; *Jesuit Relations*, 44:245–251, 54:167; Delisle, "Mémoires de Mr le Sueur," 57.

9 "Memoir of Duluth on the Sioux Country, 1678–1682," in *Early Narratives*, 332; Adams, ed., *Radisson's Explorations*, 142; Wedel, "Le Sueur and the Dakota Sioux," in *Aspects of Upper Great Lakes Anthropology*, 165–70.

10 See Arthur J. Ray, *Indians in the Fur Trade: Their Role as Trappers, Hunters, and Middlemen in the Lands Southwest of Hudson Bay, 1660–1870* (Toronto: University of Toronto Press, 1974), 4–12.

11 *Jesuit Relations*, 45:161–63, 235–39; Perrot, "Memoir on the Manners, Etc.," in *Indian Tribes*, ed. Blair, 1:170–71.

12 Adams, ed., *Radisson's Explorations*, 142–43, lx–lxi; Hennepin, *Description of Louisiana*, 203.

13 *Jesuit Relations*, 45:235–39; "Relation des aventures de Mr. de Boucherville à son Retour des Sioux en 1728 et 1729, Suivie d'Obervations [d'Observations] (par l'auteur) sur les moeurs, coutumes, & en de ces Sauvages, Accompagnée de Notes et Suivie d'un Appendice, par J. Viger," Archives du Séminaire de Québec, ASQ, Fonds Verreau 0107, Saherdache rouge, 1:74. Polygamy was less evident among the eastern Sioux in the nineteenth century, as were losses from warfare. See Pond, "The

Dakotas . . . in 1834," *Minnesota Collections*, 12 (1905–8):455.

14 "Memoir on the Savages of Canada as Far as the Mississippi River, Describing Their Customs and Trade," 1718, *Wisconsin Collections*, 16 (1902): 371.

15 Jackson, ed., *Pike Journals*, 1:222; Adams, ed., *Radisson's Explorations*, 92. Indian agent Lawrence Taliaferro compiled incomplete data for the Mdewakanton Sioux near Fort Snelling that indicated sex ratios of 72:100 for 1822 and 63:100 for 1826, and an annuity roll for 1831 had a ratio of 81:100. A second surviving annuity roll for 1844, again of the Mdewakanton tribe, demonstrates clearly that warfare affected sex ratios. Those villages well outside the reach of the troops at Fort Snelling, who discouraged intertribal war, had a ratio of 76:100, while the three villages within a few miles of the fort had an average ratio of 103:100, or more men than women. Consult the Taliaferro journal, entries following 7 April 1822 and 4 June 1826, and the 1831 annuity roll in Taliaferro's papers, both in the Minnesota Historical Society, St. Paul; annuity roll for 1844, Henry Hastings Sibley Papers, Minnesota Historical Society, St. Paul.

16 Dunn, "Epidemiological Factors," 222–23; Santiago Genovés, "Estimation of Age and Mortality," in *Science and Archaeology*, ed. D. R. Brothwell and Eric Higgs (New York: Basic Books, 1963), 354; Robert L. Blakeley, "Comparison of the Mortality Profiles of Archaic, Middle Woodland, and Middle Mississippian Skeletal Populations," *American Journal of Physical Anthropology* 34, no. 1 (1971):46–51; Homer Aschmann, "The Central Desert of Baja California: Demography and Ecology," *Ibero-Americana* 42 (1959):133; Douglas H. Ubelaker, *Reconstruction of Demographic Profiles from Ossuary Skeletal Samples: A Case Study from the Tidewater Potomac* (Washington, D.C.: Smithsonian Institution Press, 1974), 59–70; Pond, "The Dakotas . . . in 1834," *Minnesota Collections*, 12 (1905–8):472.

17 Jackson, ed., *Pike Journals*, 1: 222; vaccination census for the Yankton Sioux, 1832, NARG 75, Letter Received (hereafter LR), St. Louis Superintendency; Lawrence Taliaferro to Lewis Cass, 22 June 1832, NARG 75, LR, St. Peter's Agency. Disease had profoundly altered Dakota society by 1844, but the Mdewakanton annuity roll of that year still lists 42 percent of the tribe as children. Annuity roll, 1844, Sibley Papers.

18 Jennings, *Invasion of America*, 29; Dobyns, "Estimating Aboriginal American Population, 395–416.

19 William Whipple Warren, "History of the Ojibway Nation," *Minnesota Collections*, 5 (1885):157–233; Doane Robinson, *A History of the Dakota or Sioux Indians* (Minneapolis: Ross and Haines, 1958), 20, 48–67; Meyer, *History of the Santee Sioux*, 12–13; Gary Clayton Anderson, "Early Dakota Migration and Intertribal Warfare: A Revision," *Western Historical Quarterly* 11 (January 1980):17–36.

20 French "Census" for 1736, *Wisconsin Collections*, 17 (1906):247; Delisle, "Mémoires de Mr le Sueur," 43.

21 Trigger, *Children of Aataentsic*, 2:624–25; Louise Phelps Kellogg, *The French Regime in Wisconsin and the Northwest* (Madison: State Historical Society of Wisconsin, 1925), 84–100.

22 Perrot, "Memoir on the Manners, Etc.," in *Indian Tribes*, ed. Blair, 1:161–65; Adams, ed., *Radisson's Explorations*, 96–97, 133.

23 Perrot, "Memoir on the Manners, Etc.," 1:187–90, 210–25.

24 The quotation is from *Jesuit Relations*, 54:229. See also ibid., 51:241, 54:167, 191–93, 223.

25 Perrot, "Memoir on the Manners, Etc.," in *Indian Tribes*, ed. Blair, 1: 269, note 188; La Potherie, "History of the Savage Peoples Who Are Allies of New France," ibid., 1:358, 2:34–35, 97–105, 113–17; Kellogg, *French Regime*, 270–78; Delisle, "Mémoires de Mr le Sueur," 82; Extrait du Mémoire de M. Le Chevalier de Beaurain sur la Louisiane, *Découvertes et établissements*, 6 (1888):85–86; Cadillac's Report, 31 August 1703, *Michigan Pioneer and Historical Society Collections*, 40 vols. (Lansing, Mich.: The Society, 1877–1929), 33 (1904):162–76 (hereafter *Michigan Collections*); Speeches of Miscouaky, Chief of the Outaouas, ibid., 288–89; Philippe de Rigaud, Marquis de Vaudreuil au Ministre, 19 Octobre 1705, *Rapport de L'Archiviste de la Province de Québec pour 1938–1939* (LS.-A. Proulx, Imprimeur de Sa Majesté le Roi, 1939), 91–92.

26 La Potherie, "History of the Savage Peoples Who Are Allies of New France," in *Indian Tribes*, ed. Blair, 1:293, 340–41.

27 "Memoir of Duluth on the Sioux Country, 1678–1682," *Early Narratives*, 331; Kellogg, *French Regime*, 122–23, 205.

28 For quotation see Richard Glover, ed., *David Thompson's Narrative, 1784–1812* (Toronto: Champlain Society, 1962), 236. Consult also Charles de la Boische de Beauharnois to the French Minister, 1 and 30 May 1733, *Wisconsin Collections*, 17 (1906):172–73, 181; Lawrence J. Burpee, ed., *Journals and Letters of Pierre Gaultier de Varennes de la Vérendrye and His Sons, with Correspondence between the Governors of Canada and the French Court, Touching the Search for the Western Sea* (Toronto: Champlain Society, 1927), 256–58, 282–83.

29 Parker, ed., *Carver's Journals*, 86, 117; *Jesuit Relations* 43:181–85, 237–39, 50:169, 53:241–59, 66:125, 69:189. According to William McNeill, Indians had no genetic resistance to malaria, which was probably of African origin. See McNeill, *Plagues and Peoples* (Garden City, N.Y.: Doubleday Books, 1976), 211–13. The standard study on malaria in the Mississippi valley is Erwin H. Ackerknecht, *Malaria in the Upper Mississippi Valley, 1760–1900* (Baltimore: Johns Hopkins Press, 1945).

30 Hennepin, *Description of Louisiana*, 203; Delisle, "Mémoires de Mr le Sueur," 52; "Journal de Monsieur Marin Fils Commandant pour le Roy à LaBaye des puans et dépendances chargé de faire et de faire faire les Découvertes dans le haut de mississipi [Mississippi], des mines, minière, et minéraux qui pourroient si trouver et dy Lier [se lier?] aussi Commerce avec les nations qui pourroient habitter

ces contrés [contrées]," 11 Novembre 1753, Henry E. Huntington Library and Art Gallery, San Marino, California. A useful translation, though with numerous editorial errors, is Kenneth P. Bailey, ed. and trans., *Journal of Joseph Marin, French Colonial Explorer and Military Commander in the Wisconsin Country August 7, 1753–June 20, 1754* (Published by the author, 1975). See also Riggs, *Dakota Grammar*, 177–78, 184.

31 Hennepin, *Description of Louisiana*, 203; Perrot's proclamation, 8 May 1689, *Découvertes et établissements*, 5 (1887):33–34; Delisle, "Mémoires de Mr le Sueur," 52; "Journal de Monsieur Marin Fils," 2 Decembre 1753. Duluth estimated the distance separating the Issati and "Songaskitons" village as twenty-six leagues, or about sixty-five miles. See "Memoir of Duluth on the Sioux Country, 1678–1682," in *Early Narratives*, 330.

32 Perrot's proclamation, 8 May 1689, *Découvertes et établissements*, 5 (1887):33–34.

33 Perrot does not identify these Sioux as Mantantons, but the chief of the tribe, Sacred Born, later described their defeat to Le Sueur. Extrait du Mémoire de M. Le Chevalier de Beaurain sur la Louisiane, *Découvertes et établissements*, 6 (1888):85–87; La Potherie, "History of the Savage Peoples Who Are Allies of New France," in Indian Tribes, ed. Blair, 2:97–99.

34 Wedel, "Le Sueur and the Dakota Sioux," 165–70.

35 Ibid., 166–67; Riggs, *Dakota Grammar*, 177–78, 184.

36 Delisle, "Mémoires de Mr le Sueur," 52; Wedel, "Le Sueur and the Dakota Sioux," 165–70.

37 Ibid.

38 Ibid. Perrot's proclamation, 8 May 1689, *Découvertes et établissements*, 5 (1887):33–34.

39 Delisle, "Mémoires de Mr le Sueur," 52; Extrait du Mémoire de M. Le Chevalier de Beaurain sur la Louisiane, *Découvertes et établissements*, 6 (1888):69–89; "Journal de Monsieur Marin Fils," 11 Novembre 1753. E. D. Neill offers a fascinating piece of oral history regarding the origins of the Mdewakantons that he obtained from tribal members in the 1850s. It made no sense to Neill at the time, and he simply added it to a footnote without explanation. Neill learned that the Mdewakantons traditionally had consisted of two bands, the Mantantons and the "Wakpaatonwedans," or Watpatons. This suggests that Hennepin's Issati people eventually dissolved, perhaps after they abandoned Mille Lacs Lake. This left the two bands that Neill recorded to form the modern Mdewakanton tribe sometime in the eighteenth century. See E. D. Neill, *The History of Minnesota: From the Earliest French Explorations to the Present Time* (Minneapolis: T. T. Bacheller, 1873), 144.

40 Delisle, "Mémoires de Mr le Sueur," 52; Wedel, "Le Sueur and the Dakota Sioux," 165–71.

41 "Relation des aventures de Mr. de Boucherville à son Retour des Sioux en 1728,"

292

43–45, 73; extrait d'une lettre de Michel Guignas à Beauharnois, 29 Mai 1728, *Découvertes et établissements*, 6 (1888):552–58; Beauharnois and Giles Hocquart to the French Minister, 25 October 1729, *Wisconsin Collections*, 17 (1906):77–80. Hennepin, *Description of Louisiana*, 241–53.

42 "Relation des aventures de Mr. de Boucherville à son Retour des Sioux en 1728," 73–75; extrait d'une lettre de Guignas à Beauharnois, 29 Mai 1728, *Découvertes et établissements*, 6 (1888):552–58.

43 White, "The Winning of the West," 319–43.

44 See Meyer, *History of the Santee Sioux*, 23.

45 Marin found the Sissetons west of the Mississippi in 1753. In the winter, however, they returned to hunt in the Crow Wing River valley. See the various entries regarding the Sissetons in "Journal de Monsieur Marin Fils."

46 Extrait d'une lettre de Guignas à Beauharnois, 29 Mai 1728, *Découvertes et établissements*, 6 (1888):556–57.

47 "Memoir of the Sioux—A Manuscript in the French Archives, Now First Printed, with Introduction and Notes," in *Macalester College Contributions: Department of History, Literature and Political Science, Number Ten*, ed. E. D. Neill (St. Paul: Pioneer Press, 1890), 236.

CHAPTER 3

1 Hennepin, *Description of Louisiana*, 211–12.

2 Arthur J. Ray and Donald B. Freeman, *"Give Us Good Measure": An Economic Analysis of Relations between the Indians and the Hudson's Bay Company before 1763* (Toronto: University of Toronto Press, 1978), 55, 231–33; W. Raymond Wood, "Plains Trade in Prehistoric and Protohistoric Intertribal Relations," in *Anthropology on the Great Plains*, ed. W. Raymond Wood and Margot Liberty (Lincoln: University of Nebraska Press, 1980), 98–107; Edward M. Bruner, "Mandan," in *Perspectives in American Indian Culture Change*, ed. Edward H. Spicer (Chicago: University of Chicago Press, 1961), 187–277.

3 Joseph Epes Brown, ed., *The Sacred Pipe: Black Elk's Account of the Seven Rites of the Oglala Sioux* (Norman: University of Oklahoma Press, 1953), 101–15; Bruner, "Mandan," 201; E. Leigh Syms, "Cultural Ecology and Ecological Dynamics of the Ceramic Period in Southwestern Manitoba," *Plains Anthropologist* 22, memoir 12 (May 1977): part 2, 57–59; Donald J. Blakeslee, "The Calumet Ceremony and the Origin of Fur Trade Rituals," *Western Canadian Journal of Anthropology* 7, no. 2 (1977): 78–85; Landes, *Mystic Lake Sioux*, 95–96.

4 For a general discussion of family relations consult Fox, *Kinship and Marriage*, 16–177; De Mallie, "Teton Dakota Kinship and Social Organization," 42–43; John S. Wozniak, *Contact, Negotiation, and Conflict: An Ethnohistory of the Eastern*

Dakota, 1819–1839 (Washington, D.C.: University Press of America, 1978); Jacqueline Peterson, "The People in Between: Indian-White Marriage and the Genesis of a Métis Society and Culture in the Great Lakes Region" (Ph.D. diss., University of Illinois, Chicago Circle, 1980); Sylvia Van Kirk, "The Role of Women in the Fur Trade Society of the Canadian West, 1700–1850" (Ph.D. diss., University of London, Queen Mary College, 1975); Ray and Freeman, *"Give Us Good Measure,"* 55–58, 219–23.

5 *Jesuit Relations,* 57:255–63.

6 Ibid., 255–63; Lettre du Sieur Duluth au M. le Comte de Fontenac, 5 Avril 1679, *Découvertes et établissements,* 6 (1888): 26–36.

7 "Memoir of Duluth on the Sioux Country, 1678–1682," in *Early Narratives,* 329–31. Perrot noted that the Dakotas "were not very solicitous for the friendship of anyone whomsoever; but because they could obtain French merchandise only through the agency of the Saulteurs, they made a treaty of peace with the latter by which they were mutually bound to give their daughters in marriage." Perrot, "Memoir on the Manners, Etc.," in *Indian Tribes,* ed. Blair, 1:227.

8 "Memoir of Duluth on the Sioux Country, 1678–1682," *Early Narratives,* 330, 333.

9 Kellogg, *French Regime,* 225; Jean Enjalran au Antoine Lefebre de la Barre, 26 Août 1683, *Découvertes et établissements,* 5 (1887):3–7.

10 Kellogg, *French Regime,* 231–33; Perrot, "Memoir on the Manners, Etc.," in *Indian Tribes,* ed. Blair, 1:242–45.

11 Perrot, "Memoir on the Manners, Etc.," 1:245–49; La Potherie, "History of the Savage Peoples Who Are Allies of New France," in *Indian Tribes,* ed. Blair, 1:358, 365, 2:34–35.

12 La Potherie, "History of the Savage Peoples Who Are Allies of New France," 2:30–35.

13 Ibid., 44–65, 70–71.

14 Ibid., 97–99.

15 Ibid., 102–5, 111–17.

16 Delisle, "Mémoires de Mr le Sueur," 42; Kellogg, *French Regime,* 252; Neill, *History of Minnesota,* 148–51. Le Sueur later said in his journal that he was ordered to the western Great Lakes in 1693 "pour ménager la paix entre les Sioux & les Sauteurs [Chippewas]." His choice of words suggests that he was referring to the arrangement Duluth had helped establish more than a decade before. See Extrait du Mémoire de M. Le Chevalier de Beaurain sur la Louisiane, *Découvertes et établissements,* 6 (1888):69–70.

17 Neill, *History of Minnesota,* 148–51. The literal translation of Tioscate, or Tiyoskate, is "plays in the lodge."

18 Ibid.; Extrait du Mémoire de M. La Chevalier de Beaurain sur la Louisiane, *Découvertes et établissements,* 6 (1888):86–88.

19 Kellogg, *French Regime,* 257–59.

20 Wedel, "Le Sueur and the Dakota Sioux," 59–71.

21 Delisle, "Mémoires de Mr le Sueur," 46–51; Extrait du Mémoire de M. Le Chevalier de Beaurain sur la Louisiane, *Découvertes et établissements*, 6 (1888): 70, 73–76.

22 Delisle, "Mémoires de Mr le Sueur," 42–57. Le Sueur's journal indicates that after he departed from his Mississippi River post in 1696 other traders stayed behind and traded with the Sioux from wintering posts north of St. Anthony Falls (see folio 42 of the "Mémoires"). Consult also "Relation de Pénicaut [Pénigault]," *Découvertes et établissements*, 5 (1887):413. Le Sueur met Frenchmen who had been robbed below Lake Pepin. It seems the Sioux protected voyageurs who traded exclusively with them and dealt harshly with others. Delisle, "Mémoires de Mr le Sueur," 47; extract of a letter of Governor Louis Hector de Callieres-Bonnevue to Louis Phélypeaux, Comte de Pontchartrain, 16 October 1700, *Wisconsin Collections*, 16 (1902):200–203.

23 Extrait du Mémoire de M. Le Chevalier de Beaurain sur la Louisiane, *Découvertes et établissements*, 6 (1888): 81. Consult also Delisle, "Mémoires de Mr le Sueur," 52–53.

24 Extrait du Mémoire de M. Le Chevalier de Beaurain sur la Louisiane, *Découvertes et établissements*, 6 (1888): 84; Raymond J. De Mallie, "Touching the Pen: Plains Indian Treaty Councils in Ethnohistorical Perspective," in *Ethnicity on the Great Plains*, ed. Frederick C. Luebke (Lincoln: University of Nebraska Press, 1980), 50. Wakantapi is likely a corruption for Wakantonpi, meaning Sacred Born.

25 Delisle, "Mémoires de Mr le Sueur," 52–54.

26 Ibid., 56.

27 "Relation de Pénicaut [Pénigault]," *Découvertes et établissements*, 5 (1887):417; Cadillac to Jérôme Pontchartrain, 31 August 1703, ibid., 322–24; summary of an inspection of the posts of Detroit and Michilimackinac by François Clairambault d'Aigrement, 14 November 1708, *Wisconsin Collections*, 16 (1902):258; Kellogg, *French Regime*, 268–70, 273.

28 Kellogg, *French Regime*, 270–73; Speeches of Ottawa, Huron, and Miami chiefs at Montreal, 27 September 1703; Philippe de Rigaud, Marquis de Vaudreuil, and Claude Michel Bégon to the French Minister, 15 November 1713 and 20 September 1714, and extracts from the letters of Claude de Ramesay and Bégon to the French Minister, 13 and 16 September 1715, *Wisconsin Collections*, 16 (1902): 222–27, 300, 303–6, 311–22; report from Detroit, Cadillac Papers, 31 August 1703, and speeches of Miscouaky, 26 September 1706, *Michigan Collections*, 33 (1904):173–76, 288–89.

29 Vaudreuil and Bégon to the French Minister, 15 November 1713, and 20 September 1714, Ramesay and Bégon to the French Minister, 7 November 1715, and proceedings in the French Council of Marine, 28 March 1716, *Wisconsin Collections*, 16 (1902):300, 303–6, 331, 338–40; Yves F. Zoltvany, *Philippe de Rigaud de*

Vaudreuil: Governor of New France, 1703–1725 (Toronto: McClelland and Stewart, 1974), 136, 144.

30 See Louis de la Porte de Louvigny's reports, 14 and 30 October 1716, *Wisconsin Collections*, 5 (1868): 78–81; R. David Edmunds, *The Potawatomis: Keepers of the Fire* (Norman: University of Oklahoma Press, 1978), 24–38; Kellogg, *French Regime*, 285–89.

31 Vaudreuil letters to the Council of Marine, 28 October 1719 and 22 October 1720, *Wisconsin Collections*, 16 (1902):380, 392; extrait d'une lettre de Vaudreuil, 4 Novembre 1720, *Découvertes et établissements*, 6 (1888):508.

32 The Mantanton chief Sacred Born had pledged to abandon the Fox cause, but apparently he, or other woodland Dakota warriors, had decided to ignore French advice. Vaudreuil to the Council of Marine, 22 October 1720, *Wisconsin Collections*, 16 (1902):393–94.

33 Extrait d'une lettre de Vaudreuil, 4 Novembre 1720, *Découvertes et établissements*, 6 (1888):508–11; "résumé" of French policy, 1726, *Wisconsin Collections*, 16 (1902):463–68; "résumé" of French relations with the Fox, 27 April 1727, ibid., 17 (1906):1–7.

34 Vaudreuil to the French Minister, 2 October 1723, and extract from Vaudreuil to Pierre Dugue de Boisbriant, *Wisconsin Collections*, 16 (1902):428–31, 441–42; Lettre de Bougmont au MM. les Commissaires et Membres du Counseil de la Louisiane, 11 Janier 1724, *Découvertes et établissements*, 6 (1888): 396–97.

35 Father Louis d'Avaugour's letter, 15 April 1723, and extract from a Vaudreuil letter to Boisbriant, 20 May 1724, *Wisconsin Collections*, 16 (1902):427–28, 441–42; extract from a De Longueil letter to the French Minister, 25 July 1726, ibid., 3 (1857):157–58; Extrait d'une lettre des sieurs de Vaudreuil et Bégon, 4 Octobre 1723, and extrait d'une lettre de M. de Longueil et M. Bégon au Ministre de la Marine, 31 Octobre 1725, *Découvertes et établissements*, 6 (1888):541–42, 542–43.

36 "Relation des aventures de Mr de Boucherville à son Retour des Sioux en 1728"; trade agreement between Governor Beauharnois and Montreal merchants, 6 June 1727, Marchand de Lignery to Beauharnois 30 August 1728, Beauharnois to the French Minister, 24 March 1729, Beauharnois and Hocquart to the French Minister, 25 October 1729, and Nicholas Coulon, Sieur de Villiers, to Beauharnois, 23 September 1730, *Wisconsin Collections*, 17 (1906):10–15, 31–35, 58–59, 78–79, 113–18.

37 Villiers to Beauharnois, 23 September 1730, Louis Henri Deschamps, Sieur de Boishebert, to Beauharnois, 28 February 1732, and Beauharnois to the French Minister, 15 October 1732, *Wisconsin Collections*, 17 (1906): 113–18, 148–52, 167–69.

38 Beauharnois to the French Minister, 1 October 1731, ibid., 139–41; Burpee, ed., *La Vérendrye's Journals*, 8–9.

39 Trade agreement for the Sioux country, 6 June 1731, *Wisconsin Collections*, 17 (1906):135–39; reply of Beauharnois and Hocquart to the king's memorandum, 1 October 1731, *Michigan Collections*, 34 (1904):97–98.

40 The quotation is from Father Nau to Father Bonin, 2 October 1735, *Jesuit Relations*, 68:283–85. The number of Winnebagos must have steadily increased, since approximately thirty or forty lodges were reported to be near the fort in 1729 and 1734 whereas this latter number had doubled by 1736. Beauharnois to the French Minister, 1 September 1729, Beauharnois and Hocquart report, 7 October 1734, and census of western tribes, 1736, *Wisconsin Collections*, 17 (1906):67–68, 206–8, 248.

41 Hocquart to the French minister, 26 October 1735, *Wisconsin Collections*, 17 (1906):230.

42 Burpee, ed., *La Vérendrye's Journals*, 9; "Relation de Pénicaut [Pénigault]," *Découvertes et établissements*, 5 (1887):417.

43 Beauharnois and Hocquart to the French Minister, 25 October 1729, *Wisconsin Collections*, 17 (1906):78–79; Beauharnois and Hocquart to the French Minister, 10 October 1731, in Burpee, ed., *La Vérendrye's Journals*, 84–85.

44 La Vérendrye to Beauharnois, 2 and 25 May 1733, and *La Vérendrye's Journals*, 27 May 1733 to 12 July 1734, in Burpee, ed., *La Vérendrye's Journals*, 96, 100–101, 135–38, 145, 174–86.

45 *La Vérendrye's Journals*, 27 May 1733 to 12 July 1734, ibid., 174–86; Beauharnois to the French Minister, 14 October 1737, *Wisconsin Collections*, 17 (1906):267–68; W. J. Eccles, *The Canadian Frontier, 1534–1760* (New York: Holt, Rinehart and Winston, 1969), 149.

46 Beauharnois to Jean-Frédéric Phélypeaux Maurepas, 14 October 1736, *Wisconsin Collections*, 17 (1906):208–13. Bourassa told La Vérendrye that the Sioux party "had a grievance against the French for distributing arms to their enemies wherewith to kill them." See *La Vérendrye's Journals*, 2 June 1736 to 3 August 1737, in Burpee, ed., *La Vérendrye's Journals*, 218.

47 Relation du sieur de Jacques le Gardeur de St. Pierre, commandant au poste des Sioux, jointe à la lettre de M. le Marquis de Beauharnois, 14 Octobre 1737, *Découvertes et établissements*, 6 (1888):575–76.

48 Ibid., 576–77.

49 Ibid.

50 Ibid., 577–80.

51 Ibid., 576–80.

52 Trade agreements between Governor Beauharnois and Montreal merchants, 6 June 1727 and 1731, *Wisconsin Collections*, 17 (1906): 10–15, 135–39.

53 La Potherie, "History of the Savage Peoples Who Are Allies of New France," in *Indian Tribes*, ed. Blair, 2:113; Wedel, "Le Sueur and the Dakota Sioux," 164.

54 Meyer, *History of the Santee Sioux*, 13.

55 Support for the Warren thesis has been unanimous. Consult Warren, "History of the Ojibway Nation," *Minnesota Collections*, 5 (1885):157–233; Robinson, *History of the Dakota or Sioux Indians*, 48–67; Newton H. Winchell, *The Aborigines of Minnesota: A Report on the Collections of Jacob V. Brower and on the Field Surveys and Notes of J. Hill and Theodore H. Lewis* (St. Paul, Minn.: Pioneer Company, 1911), 506–7; William Watts Folwell, *A History of Minnesota*, 4 vols. (St. Paul: Minnesota Historical Society, 1921–30), 1:80–84.

56 Warren, "History of the Ojibway Nation," *Minnesota Collections*, 5 (1885):157–62.

57 See, for example, Governor Beauharnois to the French Minister, 24 September 1742 and 9 October 1744, *Wisconsin Collections*, 17 (1906):424–30, 442–43.

58 Theodore C. Blegen and Sarah A. Davidson, eds., *Iron Face: The Adventures of Jack Frazer, Frontier Warrior, Scout, and Hunter* (Chicago: Caxton Club, 1950), 130.

59 "Census" of western tribes, *Wisconsin Collections*, 17 (1906):247.

60 Louis Denys, Sieur de la Ronde to the French Minister, 28 June and 22 July 1738, ibid., 277–79; Kellogg, *French Regime*, 356–57.

61 Beauharnois to the French Minister, 12 October 1739, *Wisconsin Collections*, 17 (1906):315–16.

62 Beauharnois to the French Minister, 26 September 1741, *Wisconsin Collections*, 17 (1906):360–61.

63 Quote in Beauharnois to Maurepas, 24 September 1742, *La Vérendrye's Journals*, 380–81; Eccles, *Canadian Frontier*, 149–50.

64 Beauharnois and Hocquart to the French Minister, 24 September 1742, *Wisconsin Collections*, 17 (1906):416–22.

65 Quotations found in speeches of the Sioux at Montreal, 18 July 1742, *Wisconsin Collections*, 17 (1906):396–97; Beauharnois and Hocquart to the French Minister, 24 September 1742, ibid., 416–22. The Dakota name Wazikute, Leaf Shooter, is used in the document. The name is passed on and is used by a chief in the nineteenth century.

66 Beauharnois to the French Minister, 18 September 1743, 9 October 1744, and 28 October 1745, *Wisconsin Collections*, 17 (1906):435–38, 440–43, 447–49; Kellogg, *French Regime*, 376–79; Eccles, *Canadian Frontier*, 150–54.

67 Abstract of the different movements at Montreal, December 1745 to August 1756, in E. B. O'Callaghan, ed., *Documents Relative to the Colonial History of the State of New York*, 15 vols. (Albany: Weed, Parsons), 10 (1858):34, 37; Green Bay lease agreement, 10 April 1747, diary of events for 1747, and Michel Rolland, Comte de Galissonière, and Bigot to the French Minister, 20 September 1748, in *Wisconsin Collections*, 17 (1906):451–55, 462–63, 477–78, 498–99.

68 Extrait d'une lettre de Jonquière et Bigot au Ministre, 9 Octobre 1749, *Découvertes et établissements*, 6 (1888):637–38; Kellogg, *French Regime*, 379–81.

69 Eccles, *Canadian Frontier*, 146–50; Kellogg, *French Regime*, 381–82.

70 "Journal de Monsieur Marin Fils," 17 Août 1753 to 20 Juin 1754, Huntington Library. The Marin journal consists of fifty-two folios, six letters, and one petition. It is by far the most valuable source on upper Mississippi trade activities at midcentury.

71 Ibid.

72 Ibid., 2 Decembre 1753.

73 Ibid., 14 Octobre 1753; De Mallie, "Touching the Pen," 50–51.

74 "Journal de Monsieur Marin Fils," 14 Octobre, 10 Novembre, 27 Decembre, et 28 Fevrier 1754; Wozniak, Contact, Negotiation, and Conflict, 43–47.

75 "Journal de Monsieur Marin Fils," 10–11 Novembre, 2, 27–28, 31 Decembre 1753, and 18–26 Avril 1754. See also unsigned letters entitled "A Monsieur le General, Lettre du 1ᵉʳ Juin" (1754?) and "A Monsieur Deschambeau," 1ᵉʳ Juin 1754, ibid.; Hickerson, Chippewa and Their Neighbors, 64–79.

76 "Journal de Monsieur Marin Fils," 21 et 27 Avril 1754; "A Monsieur Deschambeau," 1ᵉʳ Juin 1754, ibid.

77 Ibid., 11 Novembre 1753.

78 Paul Marin had carried several chief's medals west with him in 1750. In the spring of 1754, as his son organized a Sioux delegation to go east, he made further recommendations on who should be granted medals in Montreal. "Ouapate" is likely a corruption for "Ouapasha," or Wabasha. "Ouapate" was described as a "good man." He was bringing his uncle Sacred Born's medal back to the French, suggesting that the old chief had recently died. Iroquois also received Marin's recommendation along with several less important war chiefs. See "A Monsieur le General, Lettre du 1ᵉʳ Juin," ibid., as well as entries for 14–15 Octobre, 27–31 Decembre 1753, and 20 Avril 1754; La Jonquière to the French minister, 18 August 1750, Wisconsin Collections, 18 (1908):63–67.

79 "Journal de Monsieur Marin Fils," 14 Octobre, 11 Novembre, 2, 14, 20–21 Decembre 1753.

80 Ibid., 16 Septembre, 20–21 Decembre 1753; La Jonquière to the French minister, 18 August 1750 and 16 September 1751, Wisconsin Collections, 18 (1908):63–66, 78; "Mémoire ou journal sommaire du voyage de Jacques le Gardeur de Saint-Pierre, chevalier de l'ordre royal et militaire de Saint-Louis, captaine d'une compagnie des troupes d'etachées [détachées] de la Marine en Canada, chargé de la découverte de la mer de l'Ouest," 1750–52, Découvertes et établissements, 6 (1888):648–49.

81 "Journal de Monsieur Marin Fils," 10–11 Novembre, 14, 20–21, 27–28 Decembre 1753, 28 Fevrier 1754; "A Monsieur le General, Lettre du 1ᵉʳ Juin," ibid.

82 "Journal de Monsieur Marin Fils," 14 Octobre 1753 et 21 Avril 1754. Leech Lake was commonly spelled "Sensue," or Sangsue, by the French.

83 "A Monsieur le General, Lettre du 1ᵉʳ Juin," in "Journal de Monsieur Marin Fils."

CHAPTER 4

1 Wayne E. Stevens, "The Fur Trade in Minnesota during the British Regime," *Minnesota History* 5 (February 1923):4–6; Marjorie Gordon Jackson, "The Beginning of British Trade at Michilimackinac," *Minnesota History* 11 (September 1930):231–35, 253–60.

2 Alexander Henry, *Travels and Adventures in Canada and the Indian Territories between the Years 1760 and 1777* (New York: I. Riley, 1809), 47; "Lieut. James Gorrell's Journal," *Wisconsin Collections*, 1 (1903):25–26, 36–37, 40–41.

3 Henry, *Travels and Adventures*, 195–98, 203–4.

4 J. Carver, Esq., *Travels through the Interior Parts of North America, in the Years 1766, 1767, 1768* (London: J. Walter and S. Crowder, 1778); Parker, ed., *Carver's Journals*, 1–21.

5 Parker, ed., *Carver's Journals*, 101, 113.

6 Ibid., 95–101, 107, 129–30. See also James Stanley Goddard, "Journal of a Voyage, 1766–1767," ibid., 189.

7 Ibid., 92, 98–99, 115. When Carver first met the Mantantons below the mouth of the St. Croix River, he mentioned that the "chief" of the band, likely Sacred Born or his son, had recently died, leaving Wabasha as head chief. Parker suspects that the war chief Carver stayed with over the winter was Wabasha. He would have been in the prime of life (forty-five years of age?) and, according to Carver, was well known for his "wisdom and abilities in the art of war" (p. 115).

8 Parker, ed., *Carver's Journals*, 92–93, 100, 116; Carver, *Travels*, 59–60, 79–80.

9 Parker, ed., *Carver's Journals*, 116–20, 122.

10 Plan of Robert Rogers, 1767, in Sullivan, ed., *Johnson Papers*, 13:447–48; Jackson, "Beginning of British Trade at Michilimackinac," 255–60; memorial of the merchants and traders of Montreal, 20 February 1765, C.O. 42/2, Board of Trade Papers, Public Record Office (hereafter PRO), London (all PRO material cited is on microfilm); petition of Montreal traders to Guy Carleton, governor of Quebec, 28 March 1767, C.O. 42/2, and Carleton to Lords Commissioners of Trade and Plantations, 28 March 1767, C.O. 42/6, ibid.; Thomas Gage to the Earl of Shelburne, 22 February 1767, in Clarence E. Carter, ed., *The Correspondence of General Thomas Gage with the Secretaries of State, 1762–1775*, 2 vols. (New Haven: Yale University Press, 1931–33), 1:121–24.

11 Review of trade and Indian affairs, 1767, Johnson to the Earl of Hillsborough, 17 August 1768, *Documents Relative to the Colonial History of New York*, 7:966, 989, 8:94.

12 Jackson, "Beginning of British Trade at Michilimackinac," 259–64.

13 Gage to the Earl of Hillsborough, 3 February 1769, 22 July 1769, and 10 November 1770, in Carter, ed., *Gage Correspondence*, 1:215–16, 231, 279–80. Gage claimed

that Montreal traders had captured a "portion" of the upper Mississippi trade by 1773. See Gage to the Earl of Dartmouth, 5 May 1773, ibid., 1:349–51.

14 Gates, ed., "The Narrative of Peter Pond," in *Five Fur Traders*, 30–31, 33, 42–44.

15 Ibid., 44–46.

16 Ibid., 46–47.

17 Ibid., 48–50.

18 Ibid., 51–58.

19 "Gautier's Journal of a Visit to the Mississippi, 1777–1778," *Wisconsin Collections*, 11 (1888):102–5.

20 Ibid.; Hickerson, *Chippewa and Their Neighbors*, 80–84.

21 Lieutenant Governor Patrick Sinclair to Captain Diedrick Brehm, 15 February 1780, *Wisconsin Collections*, 11 (1888):144–46; see also Major Arent Schuyler de Peyster to Sir Frederick Haldimand, 1 June 1779, ibid., 131–33.

22 David A. Armour and Keith R. Widder, *At the Crossroads: Michilimackinac during the Revolution* (Mackinac Island, Mich.: Mackinac Island State Park Commission, 1978), 20–170; Francisco Cruzot to Governor Bernardo Galvez, 19 December, 1780, *Wisconsin Collections* 18 (1908):413–14.

23 Lieutenant Charles Frederick Phillips to Lieutenant George Clowes, 27 April 1780, *Wisconsin Collections*, 12 (1892):49. See also Sinclair to Haldimand, 29 May and 8 July 1780, and Sinclair to Lieutenant Colonel Mason Bolton, 4 June 1780, *Wisconsin Collections*, 11 (1888):151–52, 155–57, and 154–55.

24 Jean Baptiste Perrault, "Narrative of the Travels and Adventures of a Merchant Voyageur in the Savage Territories of Northern America Leaving Montreal the 29th of May 1783 (to 1820)," ed. John Sharpless Fox, *Michigan Collections*, 37 (1909–10):537; Stevens, *Northwest Fur Trade*, 135–37; Joseph Howard to the Committee of Merchants at Montreal, 11 January 1787, C.O. 42/11, Board of Trade Papers, PRO.

25 Perrault, "Narrative of the Travels and Adventures," *Michigan Collections*, 37 (1909–10):539, 546–47; Howard to the Committee of Merchants at Montreal, 11 January 1787, C.O. 42/11, Board of Trade Papers, PRO; Kellogg, *British Regime*, 197–98, 239–40.

26 Perrault, "Narrative of the Travels and Adventures," *Michigan Collections*, 37 (1909–10):537–38; Joseph Tassé, *Les Canadiens de L'Ouest*, vol. 1 (Montreal: Berthiaume et Sabourin, 1882), 138, 145, 310, 316; Willoughby M. Babcock, "Louis Provençalle, Fur Trader," *Minnesota History* 20 (September 1939):259–68; Gertrude W. Ackermann, "Joseph Renville of Lac qui Parle," *Minnesota History* 12 (September 1931):231–32; Louis A. Tohill, "Robert Dickson, British Fur Trader on the Upper Mississippi," *North Dakota Historical Quarterly* 3 (October 1928):9–28: Court of Inquiry, 24 June to 8 July 1787, *Michigan Collections*, 11 (1887):555, 565.

27 Ackermann, "Joseph Renville of Lac qui Parle," 231–33; Tassé, *Canadiens de l'Ouest*, 293; Wozniak, *Contact, Negotiation and Conflict*, 46–47.

28 Neill, *History of Minnesota*, 453; Wozniak, *Contact, Negotiation, and Conflict*, 113.

29 Tohill, "Robert Dickson, British Fur Trader on the Upper Mississippi," 14–15, 19; *Hastings Gazette*, 1 July 1921.

30 Wozniak, *Contact, Negotiation, and Conflict*, 118.

31 De Mallie, "Teton Dakota Kinship and Social Organization," 98; Klein, "Adaptive Strategies and Process on the Plains," 90, 298–301.

32 Tohill, "Robert Dickson, British Fur Trader on the Upper Mississippi," 14–15; "Court of Inquiry," Prosecution of Joseph Rolette, 1814, *Michigan Collections*, 16 (1890):13–17; Court of Inquiry, 24 June to 8 July 1787, *Michigan Collections*, 11 (1887):520–22.

33 Perrault, "Narrative of the Travels and Adventures," *Michigan Collections*, 37 (1909–10):537–48, 556–76.

34 Tassé, *Canadiens de L'Ouest*, 315–17.

35 Court of Inquiry, 24 June to 8 July 1787, *Michigan Collections*, 11 (1887):539, 550, 552, 555.

36 Memorandum of Montreal Merchants, 13 April 1786, *Michigan Collections*, 11 (1887):483–88.

37 Ainsé's report, 16 August 1787, *Michigan Collections*, 11 (1887):501–4.

38 Ibid., 503.

39 Perrault, "Narrative of the Travels and Adventures," *Michigan Collections*, 37 (1909–10):542–43.

40 A copy of the original treaty, dated 12 July 1787, is in the Wayne Edson Stevens Papers, "Miscellaneous Papers Relating to the Fur Trade, 1777–1778," Minnesota Historical Society.

41 Perrault, "Narrative of the Travels and Adventures," *Michigan Collections*, 37 (1909–10):545.

42 Consult the treaty dated 12 July 1787 in the Stevens Papers.

43 Dickson to Robert Hamilton, 14 July 1793, C.O. 42/318, Secretary of State Papers, PRO.

44 Perrault, "Narrative of the Travels and Adventures," *Michigan Collections*, 37 (1909–10):556–57.

45 Thomas Duggan to Joseph Chew, 9 July 1797, *Wisconsin Collections*, 18 (1908):456–57; Warren, "History of the Ojibway Nation," *Minnesota Collections*, 5 (1885):344–48.

46 Glover, ed., *David Thompson's Narrative, 1784–1812*, 196–97, 208–9; Elliott Coues, ed., *The Manuscript Journals of Alexander Henry, Fur Trader of the Northwest Company, and of David Thompson, Official Geographer and Explorer of the Same Company, 1799–1814*, 2 vols. (Minneapolis: Ross and Haines, 1965), 1:56.

47 Ainsé's report, 16 August 1787, *Michigan Collections*, 11 (1887):506.

48 Williams H. Keating, *Narrative of an Expedition to the Source of St. Peter's River, Lake Winnepeek, Lake of the Woods, &c. Performed in the Year 1823 by the Order*

of the Hon. J. C. Calhoun, Secretary of War, under the Command of Stephen H. Long, U.S.T.E., 2 vols. (Minneapolis: Ross and Haines, 1959), 1:401–2.

49 Ainsé's report, 16 August 1787, *Michigan Collections*, 11 (1887):506.

50 Glover, ed., *David Thompson's Narrative*, 236.

CHAPTER 5

1 Lieutenant Governor Simcoe to the Secretary of State, 21 June 1794, and Simcoe to the Committee of the Privy Council for Trade and Foreign Plantations, 1 September 1794, C.O. 42/318, Secretary of State Papers, PRO; Peter Russell to General Prescott, 24 August 1794, C.O. 42/320, ibid.; Prideaux Selby to Russell, 23 January 1799, C.O. 42/324, ibid.

2 Louise Phelps Kellogg, *The British Regime in Wisconsin and the Northwest* (Madison: State Historical Society of Wisconsin, 1935), 233–37.

3 Pierre Chouteau to William Henry Harrison, 22 May 1805, and B. Parks to Harrison, undated [May 1805], NARG 107, LR, Secretary of War Papers, Main Series; Chouteau to Harrison, 10 May 1805, Chouteau Papers, Minnesota Historical Society.

4 Parks to Harrison, undated [May 1805], NARG 107, LR, Secretary of War Papers, Main Series.

5 General Wilkinson to the Secretary of War, 24 August and 8 September 1805, ibid.; General Wilkinson's proclamation, 24 August 1805, NARG 107, LR, Secretary of War Papers, Unregistered File.

6 Wilkinson to the Secretary of War, 10 August and 22 September 1805, NARG 107, LR, Secretary of War Papers, Main Series; Wilkinson to Pike, 30 July 1805, in *Territorial Papers*, ed. Carter and Blum, 13:185–86; Jackson, ed., *Pike Journals*, 1:26–27.

7 Jackson, ed., *Pike Journals*, 1:25–26, 34–37, 211–12, 220. Pike actually lists only four "divisions," represented by Wabasha, Red Wing, Little Crow, and "Chatamucah," who had been recently replaced in council by Penichon. But he met Shakopee at the mouth of the Minnesota River and recognized him as a chief. Thus Shakopee and Penichon undoubtedly headed separate villages. See also Riggs, *Dakota Grammar*, 157; Benjamin O'Fallon to William Clark, 10 May 1817, *Territorial Papers*, 15:262–65.

8 Jackson, ed., *Pike Journals*, 1:37–38, 212.

9 Ibid., 38; Riggs, *Dakota Grammar*, 157.

10 Jackson, ed., *Pike Journals*, 1:221–22; "Lewis and Clarke's [sic] Expedition, Communicated to Congress, 19 February 1806," *American State Papers: Indian Affairs*, 2 vols. (Washington, D.C.: Gales and Seaton, 1834), 1:712, 714.

11 "Lewis and Clarke's Expedition," 19 February 1806, *American State Papers: Indian Affairs*, 1:712, 714; Jackson, ed., *Pike Journals*, 1:220–21.

12 "Lewis and Clarke's Expedition," 19 February 1806, *American State Papers: Indian Affairs*, 1:714; Annie Heloise Abel, ed., *Tabeau's Narrative of Loisel's Expedition to the Upper Missouri* (Norman: University of Oklahoma Press, 1939), 121–23; Jackson, ed., *Pike Journals*, 1:63.

13 "Lewis and Clarke's Expedition," 19 February 1806, *American State Papers: Indian Affairs*, 1:712–14; Jackson, ed., *Pike Journals*, 1:213–14, 221; Anderson, "Early Dakota Migration and Intertribal War: A Revision," 34.

14 Jackson, ed., *Pike Journals*, 1:37–38, 245–47; Meyer, *History of the Santee Sioux*, 26.

15 Pike to Wilkinson, 23 September 1805, in Jackson, ed., *Pike Journals*, 1:238; Wilkinson to the Secretary of War, 26 November 1805, NARG 94, LR, Adjutant General's Office (hereafter AGO).

16 Pike to Wilkinson, 23 September 1805, in Jackson, ed., *Pike Journals*, 1:237–41.

17 Council with the Sioux, 23 September 1805, ibid., 243.

18 Ibid., 41, 118–21, 243.

19 Ibid., 104–5, 110–11, 118–19; "Observations on the Country and the Indians," ibid., 216–17.

20 Pike's journal entry for 11 April 1806 and "Observations on the Country and the Indians," ibid., 118–21, 216–17.

21 Wilkinson to Dearborn, 27 May 1806, ibid., 277–79.

22 The Secretary of War to Nicholas Boilvin, 10 April 1806, and Governor Meriwether Lewis to the Secretary of War, 1 July 1808, *Territorial Papers*, 13:488–89, 14:201; Clark to the Secretary of War, 18 May 1807, NARG 107, LR, Secretary of War Papers, Main Series.

23 "Narrative of Capt. Thomas G. Anderson," *Wisconsin Collections*, 9 (1909):158–59.

24 Dunham to Clark, 20 August 1807, *Territorial Papers*, 10:127–29; Clark to Dearborn, 18 May, 12 September, and 30 October 1807, and Dunham to the Secretary of War, 24 November 1807, all NARG 107, LR, Secretary of War Papers, Main Series; Kellogg, *British Regime*, 260.

25 Reginald Horsman, "Wisconsin and the War of 1812," *Wisconsin Magazine of History* 46 (Autumn 1962):5; Frederick Bates to the Secretary of War, 22 October 1807, NARG 107, LR, Secretary of War Papers, Main Series; Tohill, "Robert Dickson, British Fur Trader on the Upper Mississippi," 3:35–37.

26 Johnston to General John Mason, 4 February 1808, NARG 75, LR, Superintendent of Indian Trade.

27 Varnum to Mason, 10 November 1809, ibid.; Dearborn to Campbell, 9 December 1807, *Territorial Papers*, 14:155; Dunham to the Secretary of War, 7 December 1806, Campbell to Clark, 16 August 1807, and Clark to Dearborn, 30 October 1807, NARG 107, LR, Secretary of War Papers, Main Series.

28 Boilvin to Clark, 21 April 1809, *Territorial Papers*, 14:272–73. Jefferson submitted the Pike Treaty to the Senate in March 1808. After approval, Jefferson indicated that he "had no immediate view" of establishing the trade house the treaty guaranteed. Jefferson to Congress, 29 March 1808, and Senate Committee Report, 13 April 1808, in *American State Papers: Indian Affairs*, 1:753–55.

29 Boilvin to the Secretary of War, 2 August and 17 October 1809, *Territorial Papers*, 14:286–89, 330–32.

30 Boilvin to the Secretary of War, 17 October 1809, ibid., 14:330–32; Tohill, "Robert Dickson, British Fur Trader on the Upper Mississippi," 3:36–39; Frederick Bates to the Secretary of War, 30 October 1807, NARG 107, LR, Secretary of War Papers, Main Series; Kellogg, *British Regime*, 175, 266. Reginald Horsman has attributed the swift change in loyalties in the northwest to a more aggressive British policy. See "British Indian Policy in the Northwest, 1807–1812," *Mississippi Valley Historical Review* 45 (June 1958):51–66.

31 Johnston to Mason, 20 November 1808, and Varnum to Mason, 7 February and 30 September 1810, NARG 75, LR, Superintendent of Indian Trade; "Narrative of Capt. Thomas G. Anderson," *Wisconsin Collections*, 9 (1909):178–85; Governor William Hull to the Secretary of War, 12 July 1810, and Boilvin to the Secretary of War, 30 August 1810, *Territorial Papers*, 10:314–16, 14:410–11; M. Elliott to William Claus, 9 July 1810, C.O. 42/351, Secretary of State Papers, PRO.

32 Boilvin to the Secretary of War, 30 August 1810, and Clark to the Secretary of War, 12 September 1810, *Territorial Papers*, 14:410–11, 412–15.

33 Boilvin to the Secretary of War, 11 February 1811, NARG 107, LR, Secretary of War, Unregistered File.

34 Clark to the Secretary of War, 23 November 1811, *American State Papers: Indian Affairs*, 1:518–20.

35 Dickson to an unidentified officer at Fort George, 10 June 1812, Dickson Papers, Minnesota Historical Society.

36 Dickson to Major General Sir Isaac Brock, 13 July 1812, ibid.

37 Reginald Horsman, *The Frontier in the Formative Years, 1783–1812* (New York: Holt, Rinehart and Winston, 1970), 173.

38 Dickson letter to an officer at Fort George, 10 June 1812, Dickson Papers.

39 Matthew Irwin to Mason, 16 October 1812, and Maurice Blondeau to Governor Howard, 23 January 1813, *Territorial Papers*, 10:411–14, 14:644–45.

40 Joseph Charless to the Secretary of War, 7 February 1813 and the Governor of Illinois Territory to Governor Howard, 5 February 1813, *Territorial Papers*, 14:629–31, 643–44; letter of Le Feuille (Wabasha), 5 February 1813, and traders' report, 10 February 1813, *Michigan Collections*, 15:244–45, 245–46; Dickson to Noah Freer, 23 June 1813, Dickson Papers.

41 Neill, *History of Minnesota*, 281–82; Robinson, *History of the Dakota or Sioux Indians*, 86–87; Captain Richard Bullock to Major General Henry Proctor, 25 Sep-

tember 1813, *Michigan Collections*, 15 (1890):391–93; Louis Grignon to Dickson, 5 October 1813, in "Dickson and Grignon Papers, 1812–1815," ed. Thwaites, *Wisconsin Collections*, 11 (1888):275–76.

42 Declaration of Mellesello, 3 July 1812, Clark to the Secretary of War, 5 December 1812, and Governor Howard to Pierre Chouteau, April 1813, *Territorial Papers*, 14:578–80, 609–11, 674–75; Boilvin to Clark, 25 July 1813, and John Johnson to Clark, 25 July 1813, Clark Papers, Kansas State Historical Society, Topeka, Kansas; "Anderson's Journal at Fort McKay, 1814," 27 September 1814, *Wisconsin Collections*, 9 (1909):238.

43 "Proceedings & Report of a Confidential Board of Inquiry on Expenses Incurred by Robert Dickson," 8 January 1813, Dickson Papers.

44 Blondeau to Governor Howard, 3 April 1813, *Territorial Papers*, 14:685–91.

45 Clark to the Secretary of War, 5 December 1812, 20 August 1814, and 11 December 1815, *Territorial Papers*, 14:609–11, 786–87, 15:95–96; Clark to President James Monroe, November 1814, Monroe Papers, ser. 2, Library of Congress.

46 Louis Grignon to Dickson, 5 October 1813, and Dickson to John Lawe, 13 January 1814, in "Dickson and Grignon Papers, 1812–1815," *Wisconsin Collections*, 11 (1888):275–76, 285–87.

47 Dickson to Lawe, 4 February 1814, *Wisconsin Collections* 11 (1888):289–92; Robinson, *History of the Dakota or Sioux Indians*, 124–26.

48 Testimony in the prosecution of Joseph Renville, 1814, *Michigan Collections*, 16 (1890):7–9, 13, 16–17.

49 Ibid.; Dickson to Lawe, 4 February 1814, in "Dickson and Grignon Papers, 1812–1815," *Wisconsin Collections*, 11 (1888):289–92; Clark to the Secretary of War, 28 March and 5 June 1814, *Territorial Papers*, 14:746–47, 768–69; Lieutenant Colonel Robert McDouall to Lieutenant General Gordon Drummond, 16 and 27 July 1814, Dickson Papers.

50 "Anderson's Journal at Fort McKay, 1814," 27 September 1814, *Wisconsin Collections*, 9 (1909):235, 238, 249, 251.

51 Captain Bulger to McDouall, 23, 30, and 31 December 1814, 7 January and 10 March 1815, all in "The Bulger Papers," ed. Thwaites, *Wisconsin Collections*, 13 (1895):23, 32, 36–37, 51–52, 113; Dickson to Captain Freer, 17 January 1815, Dickson Papers.

52 Duncan Graham to John Lawe, 14 March 1815, in "Lawe and Grignon Papers, 1794–1821," *Wisconsin Collections*, 10 (1909):127–32.

53 Clark to the Secretary of War, 17 April 1815, *Territorial Papers*, 15:25–26; Bulger's instructions to Sioux interpreter Joseph Renville, 8 April 1815, "The Bulger Papers," *Wisconsin Collections*, 13 (1895):129–30.

54 McDouall to Bulger, 25 April and 5 May 1815, *Wisconsin Collections*, 13 (1895):133–34, 137; McDouall to Lieutenant General George Murray, 24 June 1815, Dickson Papers.

55 Alexander J. Dallas to Major General Andrew Jackson, 22 May 1815, NARG 107, LR, Secretary of War Papers, Main Series.

56 Sioux treaties, 19 July 1815, *American State Papers: Indian Affairs*, 2:2–5.

57 Clark, Ninian Edwards, and Auguste Chouteau to the Secretary of War, 18 September and 18 October 1815, *American State Papers: Indian Affairs*, 2:9; McDouall to Major General F. Robinson, 22 September 1815, Dickson Papers.

58 Clark, Edwards, and Chouteau to the Secretary of War, 18 October 1815, *American State Papers: Indian Affairs*, 2:9; Clark to the Secretary of War, 11 December 1815, and extracts from the Executive Journal of the Missouri Territory, 1 October 1815 to 30 September 1816, *Territorial Papers*, 15:95–96, 190–91.

59 "Indian Council," June 1816, *Michigan Collections*, 16 (1890):480–82; William Henry Puthuff to Governor Cass, 20 June 1816, *Wisconsin Collections*, 19 (1910):417–24. See also Francis Paul Prucha, *Broadax and Bayonet: The Role of the Army in the Development of the Northwest, 1815–1860* (Lincoln: University of Nebraska Press, 1967), 18–20.

60 McDouall to the Military Secretary, 19 June 1816, Dickson Papers.

61 Charles J. Kappler, comp. and ed., *Indian Affairs, Laws, and Treaties*, 2 vols. (Washington, D.C.: Government Printing Office, 1904), 2:128–29; Benjamin O'Fallon to Clark, 20 May 1918, *Territorial Papers*, 15:407–13.

62 Unsigned [Brevet Brigadier General Thomas A. Smith] to Clark, 23 September 1816, letters received by Indian agents, Clark Papers; Francis Paul Prucha, *The Sword of the Republic: The United States Army on the Frontier, 1783–1846* (London: Macmillan, 1969), 126–28.

63 Unsigned [Smith] to Clark, 23 September 1816, LR, Clark Papers.

64 Thomas Forsyth to Clark, 3 June 1817, letterbook vol. 4, Forsyth Papers, Draper Collection, Wisconsin Historical Society, Madison; O'Fallon to Clark, 29 November 1817, Western Americana Collection, Beinecke Rare Book and Manuscript Library, Yale University, New Haven, Connecticut; Clark to the Secretary of War, 28 September 1816, *Territorial Papers*, 15:175–76; Clark census, 4 November 1816, NARG 107, LR, Secretary of War Papers Relating to Indian Affairs.

65 Secretary of War William Crawford to Puthuff, 10 May 1816, NARG 107, LR, Secretary of War Papers Relating to Indian Affairs; Clark to the Secretary of War, 28 September 1816, and O'Fallon to Clark, 10 May 1817, *Territorial Papers*, 15:175–76, 262–65.

66 Lucile M. Kane, June D. Holmquist, and Carolyn Gilman, eds., "The Journal of Stephen H. Long," in *The Northern Expeditions of Stephen H. Long: The Journals of 1817 and 1823 and Related Documents* (St. Paul: Minnesota Historical Society, 1978), 49–77.

67 O'Fallon to Clark, 29 November 1817, Western Americana Collection, Beinecke Library; O'Fallon council notes, 26 September 1817, St. Louis Superintendency

Files, Clark Papers; O'Fallon to Edwards, 19 February 1818, *Niles' Register* 14 (1 August 1818):388.

68 O'Fallon to Clark, 20 May 1818, *Territorial Papers*, 15:407–13.

69 Ibid.

70 Ibid.

71 Ibid.; Secretary of War to Governor Cass, 25 March 1818, ibid., 10:738–39. Dickson had apparently tried to bribe the commanding officer at Prairie du Chien to allow him into the upper Mississippi country. When this failed he defied the law and went anyway, necessitating his arrest. See General Smith to the Secretary of War, 16 May 1818, ibid., 15:394–96.

72 O'Fallon to Clark, 20 May 1818, ibid., 15:407–13. Dickson posted bond and soon was again among the Mississippi Indians. See *Niles' Register* 14 (1 August 1818):388.

73 O'Fallon to Clark, 20 May 1818, *Territorial Papers*, 15:407–13.

74 Secretary of War to O'Fallon, 8 March 1819, *Territorial Papers*, 15:520–21.

75 Secretary of War Calhoun to Clark, 13 March 1819, NARG 107, LS, Secretary of War Papers Relating to Indian Affairs.

76 Forsyth, "Journal of a Voyage from St. Louis to the Falls of St. Anthony, in 1819," *Wisconsin Collections*, 6 (1908):188–219; Clark to Forsyth, 1819, Forsyth Papers, LR, and Forsyth to Clark, 23 September 1819, Forsyth Papers, letterbook vol. 4, both documents in Draper Collection.

77 Forsyth, "Journal of a Voyage," *Wisconsin Collections*, 6 (1908):202–3.

78 Forsyth to Clark, 23 September 1819, Forsyth Papers, letterbook vol. 4, Draper Collection.

79 Prucha, *Sword of the Republic*, 147–48; Marcus L. Hansen, *Old Fort Snelling, 1819–1858* (Minneapolis: Ross and Haines, 1958), 22–28.

80 Taliaferro to Commissioner T. Hartley Crawford, 15 July 1839, NARG 75, LR, St. Peter's Agency.

CHAPTER 6

1 David Lavender, *The Fist in the Wilderness* (Albuquerque: University of New Mexico Press, 1964), 227–85; Robert Stuart to J. J. Astor, 5 and 22 July 1818, L5:1816–19, American Fur Company Papers (hereafter AFCP), Burton Collection, Detroit Public Library (hereafter DPL).

2 E. E. Rich, *The History of the Hudson's Bay Company*, 2 vols. (London: Hudson's Bay Record Society, 1959), 2:389, 416–18, 425; John Perry Pritchett, "Some Red River Fur-Trade Activities," *Minnesota History* 5 (May 1924):408–10; William H. Goetzmann, "The Mountain Man as Jacksonian Man," *American Quarterly* 15 (Fall 1963):402–15.

3 Lavender, *Fist in the Wilderness*, 266–68; Ramsay Crooks to James H. Lockwood, 30 January 1821, L5:1820–22, AFCP, Burton Collection.

4 Lavender argues that the company's political clout and its subsequent ability to protect itself prompted other traders to either join Astor's men or sell out to him. See *Fist in the Wilderness*, 291.

5 Crooks to Rolette, 4 September 1821, and Crooks to Stuart, 4 January and 8 April 1822, L5:1820–22, AFCP, Burton Collection; Thomas Hughes, *Indian Chiefs of Southern Minnesota* (Minneapolis: Ross and Haines, 1969), 103–4; Babcock, "Louis Provençalle, Fur Trader," 262–66.

6 Stuart to Mooers, 4 August 1826, L5:1823–30, AFCP, Burton Collection; Crooks to Rolette, 27 June 1827, L5:1824–43, ibid.

7 Taliaferro journal, July (n.d.), 29 August 1821, and 4 and 29 August 1827.

8 Keating, *Narrative of an Expedition*, 1:302–3. Two other journals have survived from the expedition. See Kane, Holmquist, and Gilman, eds., "The Journal of Stephen H. Long, 1823," and "The Journal of James E. Colhoun, 1823," in *Northern Expeditions*, 113–90, 271–327. Consult also idem, "Up the Mississippi in a Six-Oared Skiff," in *Northern Expeditions*, 60–61, 65.

9 Keating, *Narrative of an Expedition*, 1:350.

10 Kane, Holmquist, and Gilman, eds., "The Journal of James E. Colhoun, 1823," in *Northern Expeditions*, 290, 307–23.

11 Ibid., 317–23; idem, "The Journal of Stephen H. Long, 1823," in *Northern Expeditions*, 178.

12 Cass to Calhoun, 21 October 1820, NARG 107, LR, Secretary of War Papers Relating to Indian Affairs; Thomas Forsyth to Calhoun, 3 July 1821, and Forsyth to Clark, 29 May 1826, letterbook vol. 4, Forsyth Papers, Draper Collection, Wisconsin Historical Society; Taliaferro journal, 25 September 1821.

13 Gates, ed., "The Narrative of Peter Pond," in *Five Fur Traders*, 56; James H. Lockwood, "Early Times and Events in Wisconsin," *Wisconsin Collections*, 2 (1856):112; Jackson, ed., *Pike Journals*, 1:213.

14 Journal of Charles Christopher Trowbridge, 2 August 1820, Trowbridge Papers, D5:1820, Burton Collection.

15 Kane, Holmquist, and Gilman, eds., "The Journal of Stephen H. Long, 1823," and "The Journal of James E. Colhoun," in *Northern Expeditions*, 158, 279; Keating, *Narrative of an Expedition*, 1:342–43; Pond, "The Dakotas . . . in 1834," *Minnesota Collections*, 12 (1905–08):343; Prescott, "The Dakota or Sioux of the Upper Mississippi," in *Information Respecting the History, Condition, and Prospects of the Indian Tribes*, ed. Schoolcraft, 3:227.

16 *National Intelligencer*, 11 January 1805; Invoice book, Lockwood's outfit, 28 and 29 April and 9 May 1920, I7:1818–20, AFCP, Burton Collection; invoice book, Bailly's and Mooers's outfits, 23 June and 11 July 1827, I6:1827, ibid.

17 Ibid.

18 Invoice book, Bailly's and Mooers's outfits, 23 June and 11 July 1827, I6:1827, AFCP, Burton Collection.

19 Taliaferro journal, 21 September 1821, 21 June 1823, 10 June 12 July and 11 August 1827, and 3 March 1828; Keating, *Narrative of an Expedition*, 1:359; Pond, "The Dakotas . . . in 1834," *Minnesota Collections*, 12 (1905–8):369–70.

20 Edwin James diary and journal, May 1824, Columbia University Library, Columbia University, New York; Boilvin to Clark, 15 December 1824, NARG 75, LR, St. Louis Superintendency; Taliaferro journal, 11 August 1827.

21 Fort Snelling had become a rendezvous for trade not only with the garrison but also between the Sioux and the Chippewas. Consult Colonel Snelling to General Henry Atkinson, 31 May 1827, NARG 75, LR, St. Louis Superintendency; Hansen, *Old Fort Snelling*, 108–10; George Johnston to Henry Schoolcraft, 20 March 1829, Johnston Papers, L5:1828–29, Burton Collection.

22 Compare the information on hunting techniques in Blegen and Davidson, eds., *Iron Face: The Adventures of Jack Frazer*, with that in Pond, "The Dakotas . . . in 1834," *Minnesota Collections*, 12 (1905–8):360–66.

23 Although an 1824 law required that trading posts have permanent locations, the tendency after the War of 1812 had been to build more substantial stores. Regarding the law; see Taliaferro to Clark, 10 December 1824, NARG 75, LR, St. Louis Superintendency.

24 Several lists of creditors for the 1820s have survived in the Bailly Papers, the Sibley Papers, and the Louis Provençalle Papers, all in the Minnesota Historical Society. Consult also Parker, ed., *Recollections of Philander Prescott*, 28.

25 Taliaferro journal, 10 June 1827, 15 April 1829, 13 August 1833, 25 August 1835, and 30 June 1836.

26 Taliaferro journal, 12 June 1831.

27 Thomas L. McKenney to Clark, 10 January 1828, NARG 75, LS, Office of Indian Affairs.

28 Stuart to the Indian agent at Green Bay, 11 August 1822, L5:1822–25, AFCP, Burton Collection; Lieutenant Colonel William Morgan to General Edmund P. Gaines, 17 November and 4 December 1822, NARG 107, LR, Secretary of War Papers Relating to Indian Affairs; Colonel Ninian Pinkney to Major General W. Scott, 24 August 1822, NARG 107, LR, Secretary of War Papers, Unregistered File.

29 Joseph Street to Taliaferro, 14 June 1830, Taliaferro Papers.

30 Snelling remained unaware of the inspection law until the Secretary of War sent him a copy of the act in February 1825. Secretary of War James Barbour to Snelling, 17 February 1825, and Thomas L. McKenney to Clark, 19 September 1828, NARG 75, LS, Office of Indian Affairs; Snelling voucher, 14 July 1826, and Taliaferro to Snelling, 14 July 1826, Bailly Papers; Rolette to Elias T. Langham, 11 October 1826, John Marsh to Langham, 6 September 1826, and Snelling statement, 9 May 1927, Taliaferro Papers; Stuart to John Jacob Astor, 29 November

1826, L5:1825–30, AFCP, Burton Collection; Langham to Clark, 23 March 1827, NARG 75, St. Louis Superintendency; Taliaferro to Stuart, 2 April 1826, NARG 75, LR, St. Peter's Agency.

31 Stuart to Mooers, 4 August 1826, and Stuart to John Jacob Astor, 29 November 1826, L5:1823–30, AFCP, Burton Collection; Crooks to Rolette, 27 June 1827, Crooks Papers (photostats of originals in New York Public Library), Burton Collection.

32 Taliaferro to Clark, 24 December 1825, Taliaferro Papers; Taliaferro journal, 27 April 1826; Stuart to George Boyd, July (n.d.), 1822, L5:1822–25, AFCP, Burton Collection.

33 Taliaferro journal, 18 June 1827, 3 May 1829, and 30 April 1830. See also Stuart to Rolette, 10 October 1824, L5:1823–30, AFCP, Burton Collection.

34 Crooks to Rolette, 22 March 1822, L5:1820–22, AFCP, Burton Collection; Crooks to Stuart, 8 April 1822, and Crooks to Rolette, 22 January 1823, L5:1822–25, ibid.; Crooks to Rolette, 5 September 1823, Stuart to Crooks, November (n.d.) 1823, and Stuart to Rolette, 10 October 1824, L5:1823–30, ibid.; Taliaferro journal, 12 February and 22 March 1822; Taliaferro to Secretary of War Calhoun, 1 March 1822, Taliaferro Papers.

35 Stuart to Rolette, 16 May 1822, L5:1822–25, AFCP, Burton Collection; Stuart to John Jacob Astor, 26 November 1826, L5:1823–30, ibid.; Rolette to Clark 27 June 1826, NARG 75, LR, St. Peter's Agency; Taliaferro to Clark, May (n.d.) 1827, NARG 75, LR, St. Louis Superintendency.

36 Taliaferro journal, 27 March 1826.

37 Parker, ed., *Recollections of Philander Prescott*, 56–57, 92–93, 120.

38 Taliaferro to Clark, 10 December 1824, NARG 75, LR, St. Louis Superintendency; Clark to Forsyth, 16 May 1825, Forsyth Papers, Draper Collection; Stuart to William B. Astor, 4 June 1825, and Stuart to Rolette, 10 September 1825, L5:1823–30, AFCP, Burton Collection; McKenney to William B. Astor, 22 July 1825, *Territorial Papers*, 11:690–91; Alexander Faribault and Joseph La Framboise to Office of Indian Affairs, 26 June 1826, NARG 75, LR, St. Peter's Agency.

39 McKenney to Clark, 22 July 1825, NARG 75, LS, Office of Indian Affairs.

40 Clark to Barbour, 8 December 1825, and Taliaferro to Clark, May (n.d.) 1827, NARG 75, LR, St. Louis Superintendency; Taliaferro to Stuart, 2 April 1826, NARG 75, LR, St. Peter's Agency; Parker, ed., *Recollections of Philander Prescott*, 80–81; Taliaferro journal, 11 February 1828.

41 Taliaferro journal, 22 September 1821 and 28 May 1828; expense voucher for St. Louis Superintendency, 1 September 1822 to 1 September 1823, NARG 107, LR, Secretary of War Papers Relating to Indian Affairs; Stipe, "Eastern Dakota Acculturation," 215–35; Wozniak, *Contact, Negotiation, and Conflict*, 23.

42 Consult, for example, Taliaferro journal, 6 September and 11 October 1821, 2 and 24 February 1822, and 27 April 1826; Colonel Snelling to Taliaferro, 7 November 1821, Taliaferro Papers; Wozniak, *Contact, Negotiation, and Conflict*, 40–41, 67.

43 *Taliaferro journal, 23 September 1838; Charles Eastman to H. M. Hitchcock, 8 September 1927, Ayer Collection, Newberry Library, Chicago.*

44 Wozniak makes the case for the "network system" in *Contact, Negotiation, and Conflict*, 69–91.

45 Taliaferro, "Auto-biography of Maj. Lawrence Taliaferro," *Minnesota Collections*, 6 (1894):219; Taliaferro journal, 22 September 1821, 19 October 1827, and 28 May 1828; Wozniak, *Contact, Negotiation, and Conflict*, 69–71; expense voucher for St. Louis Superintendency, 1 September 1822 to 1 September 1823, NARG 107, LR, Secretary of War Papers Relating to Indian Affairs; Calhoun to Taliaferro, 27 December 1819, NARG 107, LS, Secretary of War Papers Relating to Indian Affairs.

46 Quotation in Kane, Holmquist, and Gilman, eds., "The Journal of James E. Colhoun, 1823," in *Northern Expeditions*, 274; ibid., 309; Keating, *Narrative of an Expedition*, 389, 403, 423, 448; Klein, "Adaptive Strategies and Process," 298–301; Stipe, "Eastern Dakota Acculturation," 221.

47 Atkinson to Taliaferro, 20 August 1820, and Snelling to Taliaferro, 10 November 1820, Taliaferro Papers; Snelling to Atkinson, 2 October 1820, NARG 107, Secretary of War Papers Relating to Indian Affairs.

48 Quotation is in Snelling to Taliaferro, 13 November 1820, Taliaferro Papers. See also *Niles' Register*, 30 December 1820.

49 Snelling to Taliaferro, 13 November 1820, Taliaferro Papers; Calhoun to Snelling, 5 January 1821, *Territorial Papers*, 15:688–89.

50 Taliaferro journal, 4 and 12 June, 5, 9, and 23 September 1821.

51 Rich, *History of the Hudson's Bay Company*, 2:416–18, 425; Taliaferro journal, 9 September 1821.

52 Snelling to Taliaferro, 7 November 1822, Taliaferro Papers; Gaines to Snelling, 25 October 1822, Atkinson to the Secretary of War, 10 June 1823, Thomas Biddle to Atkinson, 22 July 1824, Snelling to Atkinson, 24 July 1824, and William Laidlaw to Colonel W. Morgan, 25 August 1825, NARG 94, LR, AGO; John Marsh to his father, 22 February 1825, Marsh Papers, Minnesota Historical Society.

53 Atkinson to Snelling, 3 August 1824, and Snelling to Atkinson, 20 August 1824, NARG 94, LR, AGO.

54 See Francis Paul Prucha, *American Indian Policy in the Formative Years: The Indian Trade and Intercourse Acts, 1790–1834* (Cambridge, Mass.: Harvard University Press, 1962), 213–49; Calhoun to Boilvin, 11 November 1820, Calhoun to Taliaferro, 14 August and 13 October 1821 and 26 April 1822, NARG 107, LS, Secretary of War Papers Relating to Indian Affairs.

55 Trowbridge journal, 31 July 1820, D5:1820, Trowbridge Papers. See also Henry R. Schoolcraft, ed., *Narrative Journal of Travels, through the Northwestern Region of the United States, Extending from Detroit through the Great Chain of American Lakes, to the Sources of the Mississippi River, Performed as a Member of the*

Expedition under Governor Cass in the Year 1820 (Albany: E. and E. Hosford, 1820), 282; Taliaferro to Colonel Leavenworth, 30 July 1820, Taliaferro Papers.

56 Taliaferro journal, July (n.d.) 1821 and 17 July 1823; Taliaferro to Clark, 25 May 1829, NARG 75, LR, St. Peter's Agency.

57 Taliaferro journal, 17 June 1823.

58 Ibid., July (n.d.) 1821.

59 Clark to Calhoun, 8 January 1822, NARG 107, LR, Secretary of War Papers Relating to Indian Affairs; Taliaferro to Forsyth, 22 July 1820, and Taliaferro to O'Fallon, 29 August 1822, Taliaferro Papers; Calhoun to Clark, 30 August 1822, NARG 107, LS, Secretary of War Papers Relating to Indian Affairs; Taliaferro journal, 5 September 1821. Also consult the numerous letters of Forsyth to Calhoun dated between 1820 and 1823 in the Forsyth Papers.

60 Forsyth mistakenly identified the murdered Sioux chief as Little Crow. See Calhoun to Clark, 30 August 1822 and 9 December 1823, NARG 107, LS, Secretary of War Papers Relating to Indian Affairs; Forsyth to Clark, 9 September 1824, NARG 75, LR, Prairie du Chien Agency; Clark to Calhoun, 24 December 1824, NARG 75, LR, St. Louis Superintendency; Taliaferro, "Auto-biography of Maj. Lawrence Taliaferro," *Minnesota Collections*, 6 (1894):203–5.

61 Council Notes from Prairie du Chien, 2 August 1825, Clark Papers; Journal of Proceedings, August 1825, NARG 75, Documents Relating to the Negotiation of Ratified and Unratified Treaties (hereafter DRNRUT); *Niles' Register*, 2 July 1825.

62 Council Notes from Prairie du Chien, 8–10 August 1825, Clark Papers.

63 Ibid., 12 and 16 August 1825.

64 Ibid.; Taliaferro to Commissioner Elbert Herring, 5 July 1833, Clark to Herring, 21 July 1833, and Jon L. Bean to Clark, 11 January 1834, NARG 75, LR, St. Peter's Agency; Taliaferro journal, 22 June 1833.

65 Taliaferro to Clark, 31 May 1826, Taliaferro Papers; Taliaferro journal, 22–30 August 1825; Lockwood, "Early Times and Events in Wisconsin," *Wisconsin Collections*, 2 (1856):153; Edwin James diary and journal, July–August 1825, Columbia University Library.

66 Council at Traverse des Sioux, 30–31 August 1826, Taliaferro Papers.

67 Taliaferro journal, 31 May 1827; Snelling to Atkinson, 31 May 1827, NARG 94, LR, AGO; Parker, ed., *Recollections of Philander Prescott*, 83–85. Several other accounts of this incident have survived, but they do contain errors. See Charlotte Ouisconsin Van Cleve, *"Three Score Years and Ten": Life-long Memories of Fort Snelling, Minnesota and Other Parts of the West* (Minneapolis: Harrison and Smith, 1888), 74–78; William J. Snelling, "Running the Gauntlet," *Minnesota Collections*, 1 (1872); 444–55.

68 Translation of Strong Earth's speech, 30 May 1827, Josiah Snelling diary, Minnesota Historical Society.

69 Snelling to Atkinson, 31 May 1827, NARG 94, LR, AGO. See Strong Earth's speech, signed by Taliaferro and Snelling, 30 May 1827, ibid.

70 Ibid.; Taliaferro letter, 6 October 1827, *Niles' Register*; Parker, ed., *Recollections of Philander Prescott*, 83–85.

71 Taliaferro to Clark, 31 May 1827, and Clark to Barbour, 14 June 1827, NARG 75, LR, St. Louis Superintendency; Atkinson to Gaines, 15 June 1827, NARG 94, LR, AGO.

72 Taliaferro journal, 9, 10, 14 July and 1 August 1827; John Marsh to Clark, 30 June 1827, and Forsyth to Clark, 5 July 1827, NARG 75, LR, St. Louis Superintendency; Forsyth to Clark, 9 and 28 July 1827, Forsyth Papers; Snelling to Atkinson, 17 July 1827, NARG 94, LR, AGO; regimental order, 6 August 1827, Snelling diary.

73 Taliaferro to Clark, 8 August 1827, NARG 75, LR, St. Peter's Agency; Forsyth to Clark, 9 and 20 July 1827, letterbook vol. 4, and 28 and 15 July 1827, letterbook vol. 6, Forsyth Papers; Joseph Street to the Secretary of War, 15 November 1827, NARG 75, LR, Prairie du Chien Agency; Lockwood, "Early Times and Events in Wisconsin," *Wisconsin Collections*, 2:(1856), 162; Roger L. Nichols, *General Henry Atkinson: A Western Military Career* (Norman: University of Oklahoma Press, 1965), 122; Tatapiśa, Wahkahuhindeota, and Ahakakos to David Lowry, 26 February 1840, NARG 75, LR, Prairie du Chien Agency.

74 Taliaferro journal, 11 July 1827. See also entries for 28 May to 2 June, 13, 19, 23 June, 11, 14, 17, 23 July, and 3 September 1827.

75 Taliaferro journal, 4 August 1827.

76 Ibid., 29 August 1827.

77 Taliaferro to Clark, 7 October 1827, Taliaferro Papers.

78 Clark to Barbour, 1 March 1826, NARG 75, LR, St. Louis Superintendency.

CHAPTER 7

1 See Bernard W. Sheehan, *Seeds of Extinction: Jeffersonian Philanthropy and the American Indian* (New York: W. W. Norton, 1974); Prucha, *American Indian Policy in the Formative Years*.

2 Thomas L. McKenney to Clark, 22 December 1827, 26 August 1829, and 9 June 1830, NARG 75, LS, Office of Indian Affairs, (hereafter OIA); Joseph Street to Commissioner of Indian Affairs, 22 February 1830, NARG 75, LR, Prairie du Chien; Clark to Taliaferro, 2 May 1830, Taliaferro Papers; Clark to Secretary of War, 26 May 1830, LS, St. Louis Superintendency, Clark Papers.

3 Lavender, *Fist in the Wilderness*, 376–81; Ramsay Crooks to J. J. Astor, 24 May 1827, Crooks Papers; Taliaferro to Clark, 1 October 1827, NARG 75, LR, St. Peter's Agency; Taliaferro journal, 10 November 1827.

4 Contract, dated 21 August 1829, Bailly Papers; Taliaferro journal, 10 November 1827.

5 Taliaferro journal, 31 January and 4 February 1828; credit list, 1828, Sibley Papers.

6 Credit list, 1828, Sibley Papers.

7 Taliaferro journal, 10 November 1827, 31 January and 23 April 1828, and 23 and 24 March 1829.

8 Ibid., 23 April and 28 December 1828 and 30 July 1829; E. T. Langham to Clark, 7 August 1828, and Clark to Taliaferro, 2 May 1830, Taliaferro Papers.

9 Taliaferro journal, 28 December 1828, 12 January, 1 April, and 6 May 1829.

10 Ibid., 15 June 1829.

11 Street to Commissioner of Indian Affairs, 22 February 1830, and John McNeill, Pierre Menard, and Caleb Atwater to John Eaton, 11 September 1829, NARG 75, LR, Prairie du Chien Agency.

12 McKenney to Clark, 5 April 1830, NARG 75, LS, OIA; Clark to Taliaferro, 22 April and 2 May 1830, and Colonel Zachary Taylor to Taliaferro, 14 May 1830, Taliaferro Papers.

13 Clark to McKenney, October (n.d.) 1829, LS, St. Louis Superintendency, Clark Papers; Clark to Taliaferro, 22 April 1830, Taliaferro Papers.

14 Thomas Forsyth to Clark, 6 May, 1 and 7 June 1830, letterbook vol. 6, Forsyth Papers; Clark to Secretary of War, 10 May and 19 June 1830, LS, St. Louis Superintendency, Clark Papers; Street to Taliaferro, 14 May 1830, Taliaferro Papers; Taylor to Major General Edmund P. Gaines, 14 May 1830, NARG 94, LR, AGO.

15 Colonel Willoughby Morgan to Brigadier General Henry Atkinson, 30 July 1830, and Atkinson to Gaines, 28 June 1830, NARG 94, LR, AGO; Taliaferro to Captain J. H. Gale, 18 June 1830, Taliaferro Papers; Clark to McKenney, 6 July 1830, and Clark to Secretary of War, 11 July 1830, LS, St. Louis Superintendency, Clark Papers; Morgan address to delegates, 7 July 1830, NARG 75, LR, Prairie du Chien Agency; minutes of the councils held at Prairie du Chien, 15 July 1830, NARG 75, DRNRUT.

16 The agreement to hand over violators of the peace was not written into the treaty. Rather, Colonel Morgan presented it orally, apparently suggesting that the tribes had accepted such a condition in article 14 of the Prairie du Chien Treaty of 1825. That section reserved to the government the right to "take such measures as they deem proper" in ending the wars. See Morgan to Atkinson, 30 July 1830, and Atkinson to Gaines, 1 August 1830, NARG 94, LR, AGO; Morgan to Secretary of War, 18 July 1830, NARG 75, LR, Prairie du Chien Agency; "Treaty with the Sioux, Etc.," 1830, in Charles J. Kappler, ed., *Indian Treaties*, 2:251–55.

17 "Treaty with the Sack [Sacs] and Foxes, Etc.," 1830, in Kappler, ed., *Indian Treaties*, 2:305–10.

18 Morgan to Atkinson, 5 and 6 August 1830, NARG 94, LR, AGO; Morgan to Eaton, 5 and 8 August 1830, NARG 75, LR, Prairie du Chien Agency; Street to Clark, 8 August 1830, LR, St. Louis Superintendency, Clark Papers.

19 Street to Clark, 8 August 1830, 2 February, 2 March, and 28 May 1831, Morgan to Clark, 9 September 1830, Taliaferro to Clark, 8 and 12 August 1831, LR, St. Louis Superintendency, Clark Papers; Clark to Secretary of War, 1 November 1830, LS, ibid.; Morgan to Taliaferro, 9 September and 10 October 1830, Taliaferro Papers; Taliaferro journal, 31 August 1830 and 7 August 1831; Morgan to Atkinson, 7 September and 8 December 1830, Atkinson to Gaines, 10 August 1831, and Atkinson to Jones, 18 October 1831, NARG 94, LR, AGO; Morgan to Atkinson, 12 October 1831, NARG 393, LR, Jefferson Barracks, 1831–53.

20 Captain W. R. Jouett to Atkinson, 2 November 1831 and Second Lieutenant E. R. Williams to Jouett, 28 November 1831, NARG 393, LR, Jefferson Barracks, 1831–53.

21 William A. Aitkin to Williams, 5 February 1833, Benjamin Baker to Indian Department, 8 February 1833, and Lieutenant Jefferson Vail to Clark, 4 March 1833, NARG 75, LR, St. Peter's Agency; Bliss to Atkinson, 3 May 1834, NARG 94, LR, AGO.

22 Quotation in Taylor to Atkinson, 27 June 1833, NARG 94, LR, AGO. See also Atkinson to Taylor, 13 June and 9 July 1833, Taylor to Atkinson, 23 June 1833, Atkinson to Jones, 11 September 1833, and Vail to Bliss, 9 December 1833, ibid.; Elbert Herring to Clark, 4 May 1833, NARG 75, LS, OIA; Taliaferro to Herring, 6 June and 2 August 1833, and Clark to D. Kurts, 9 September 1833, NARG 75, LR, St. Peter's Agency.

23 Clark to Herring, 21 July 1833 and 24 January 1834, Jon L. Bean to Clark, 11 January 1834, Taliaferro to Clark, 2 September 1835, and Taliaferro to Herring, 20 September 1835, NARG 75, LR, St. Peter's Agency; George Johnston to Herring, 13 June 1835, NARG 75, LR, Prairie du Chien Agency; Taliaferro journal, 12 August 1832, 7 June, 10 August, and 30 August 1835; Prucha, *Sword of the Republic*, 68.

24 Taliaferro journal, 17 and 18 July 1835; Taliaferro to Clark, 17 and 19 July 1835, 31 January and 14 June 1836, and Taliaferro to Major John Bliss, 17 July 1835, NARG 75, St. Peter's Agency.

25 Taliaferro to Clark, 17 August 1830, Clark to the Secretary of War, 22 September 1830, NARG 75, LR, St. Peter's Agency; P. G. Randolph to Clark, 21 October 1830, NARG 75, LS, OIA.

26 Jouett to Atkinson, 2 November 1831 and 3 August 1832, NARG 94, LR, AGO; Herring to Clark, 4 December 1832, NARG 75, LS, OIA; Prucha, *Sword of the Republic*, 202–3.

27 Taliaferro to Clark, 15 August 1833, NARG, LR, St. Peter's Agency; Taliaferro journal, 16 July 1834 and 11 June 1835; Rolette to Bailly, 1 May 1833, Bailly Papers.

28 For quotation see Taliaferro journal, 2 June 1832. Consult also journal entries for 9 and 14 August 1831, 24, 28, 31 May and 11 June 1832.

29 Taliaferro to Clark, 10 July 1833, and Taliaferro proclamation, 12 July 1833, NARG 75, LR, St. Peter's Agency; Alexis Bailly to Bliss, 1 January 1834, NARG 94, LR, AGO; Taliaferro journal, 8 and 9 July 1834.

30 Bailly to Bliss, 1 January 1834, Taliaferro Papers; Taliaferro journal, 9 July 1834.

316

For an example of retaliation, see Blegen and Davidson, eds., *Iron Face*, 115–16; Edmund C. Bray and Martha C. Bray, eds., *Joseph N. Nicolett on the Plains and Prairie: The Expeditions of 1838–39 with Journals, Letters and Notes on the Dakota Indians* (St. Paul: Minnesota Historical Society Press, 1976), 108.

31 Prescott, "Contributions to the History, Customs, and Opinions of the Dacota Tribe," in *Information Respecting the History, Condition, and Prospects of the Indian Tribes*, 2:195.

32 Thomas S. Williamson to David Greene, 5 August 1836, American Board of Commissioners for Foreign Missions Papers (hereafter ABCFM Papers), Houghton Library, Harvard University (transcripts in the Minnesota Historical Society). Rolette to Crooks 8 September 1834, American Fur Company Papers, New York Public Library, photostats and microfilm in Minnesota Historical Society (hereafter AFC-MHS); Joseph R. Brown to Sibley, 20 September 1835, Sibley Papers.

33 Williamson to Greene, 5 August 1835, ABCFM Papers; Taliaferro journal, 15–19 July 1834.

34 Taliaferro journal, 9 October 1835.

35 Smoky Day to Sibley (written by Louis Provençalle), 1 December 1836, Sibley Papers; Taliaferro journal, 7 August 1836.

36 Brown to Sibley, 20 September 1835 and 6 May 1836, Sibley Papers.

37 Taliaferro journal, 17 June 1836; Brown to Sibley, 26 January and 30 November 1836, and Sibley to Crooks, 24 December 1836, Sibley Papers. Mooers did attempt to oppose Brown the next year on the upper Mississippi as an independent trader. See George W. Featherstonhaugh, *A Canoe Voyage up the Minnay Sotor; with an Account of the Lead and Copper Deposits in Wisconsin; of the Gold Region in the Cherokee Country; and Sketches of Popular Manners*, 2 vols. (St. Paul: Minnesota Historical Society, 1970), 2:256.

38 Featherstonhaugh, *Canoe Voyage*, 253–54, 312–14, 384–86; Peterson, "People in Between," 210, 256–58.

39 Fur returns for 1834, Bailly Papers; Taliaferro journal, 24 August and 1 November 1835, and 26 July 1836; fur returns, September 1831, LR, St. Louis Superintendency, Clark Papers; credit lists, 1831, 1833–36, and 1836, and Crooks to Sibley, 17 April 1840, Sibley Papers.

40 Unsigned [Brown] to Sibley, 25 January 1836, and Brown to Sibley, 6 May and 30 November 1836, Sibley Papers; William Johnston to Jane Johnston Schoolcraft, 14 November 1833, *Michigan Collections*, 37 (1909–10):200.

41 Taliaferro journal, 23 January and 7 September 1836; Louis Le Blanc (Provençalle) to Sibley, 18 September 1836, Sibley Papers; Sibley to Crooks, 24 December 1836, AFC-MHS.

42 Taliaferro journal, 10 April and 28 May 1828.

43 Ibid., 15 April, 2 and 20 May, and 12 September 1839; Taliaferro to the Secretary of War, 23 February 1830, NARG 75, LR, St. Peter's Agency.

44 Taliaferro journal, 4 September 1830, 30 April 1831, 14 August 1833, 7 July 1834, and 8 August and 7 September 1835; Williamson to Greene, 12 June 1834, ABCFM Papers; Parker, ed., *Recollections of Philander Prescott*, 126–28.

45 Taliaferro journal, 23 September 1838; Parker, ed., *Recollections of Philander Prescott*, 36; Stephen Return Riggs, *Mary and I: Forty Years with the Sioux* (Boston: Congregational Sunday-School and Publishing Society, 1880) 24; Peterson, "People in Between," 214–16. For a vaccination report see Taliaferro to Cass, 25 June 1832, NARG 75, St. Peter's Agency.

46 Taliaferro journal, 7 July 1834 and 21 July 1835; Taliaferro to Herring, 25 July 1834, and Taliaferro to Clark, 2 August and 2 December 1835, NARG 75, LR, St. Peter's Agency.

47 Taliaferro to Cass, 7 March 1832, and Taliaferro to Clark, 2 October 1832, NARG 75, LR, St. Peter's Agency; Taliaferro journal, 7 June 1832 and 21 July 1835.

48 Taliaferro to Clark, 6 July 1831, NARG 75, LR, St. Peter's Agency; Taliaferro journal, 16 June 1831, 14 June, 26 August, 2 and 9 October 1835, and 6, 18, and 24 February 1836.

49 Taliaferro to Clark, 2 June 1832 and 22 July 1835, Taliaferro to Governor Henry Dodge, 22 September 1836, and Taliaferro to the Commissioner of Indian Affairs, 30 September 1836, NARG 75, LR, St. Peter's Agency; Taliaferro journal, 22 September 1830, 28 May 1832, 22–24 June 1836, and 17 July and 9 August 1836; "claims filed under the treaty of September 29, 1837 with the Sioux of the Mississippi," NARG 75, Special Files of the OIA.

50 Taliaferro to Commissioner of Indian Affairs, 30 September 1836, NARG 75, LR, St. Peter's Agency.

51 Taliaferro to Clark, 15 May 1836, NARG 75, LR, St. Peter's Agency; Taliaferro journal, 1 May 1836.

52 Taliaferro to Clark, 15 May 1836, NARG 75, LR, St. Peter's Agency.

53 Ibid.

54 Clark to Herring, 9 June 1836, NARG 75, LR, St. Peter's Agency.

55 Herring to Clark, 25 June 1836, NARG 75, LS, OIA; Dodge to the Acting Secretary of War, 12 August 1836, and Dodge to Carey Harris, 23 November 1836, *Territorial Papers*, 27:638–39, 673–74; Taylor to Dodge, 28 August 1836, NARG 75, LR, Prairie du Chien Agency.

56 Taliaferro to Dodge, 2 September 1836, NARG 75, DRNRUT; Sibley to Crooks, 24 December 1836, AFC-MHS.

57 Taliaferro journal, 10 August 1836.

58 Ibid., 12 June 1836.

59 Featherstonhaugh, *Canoe Voyage*, 2:256.

CHAPTER 8

1 Harris to Acting Secretary of War Benjamin Butler, 9 January 1837, and Harris to Dodge, 14 January 1837, NARG 75, LS, OIA.

2 Kappler, ed., *Indian Treaties*, 2:307.

3 See Bruce David Forbes, "Evangelization and Acculturation among the Santee Dakota Indians, 1834–1864" (Ph.D. diss., Princeton Theological Seminary, 1977).

4 Dodge to Butler, 12 August 1836, and Dodge to Harris, 23 November 1836, *Territorial Papers*, 27:638–39, 673–74.

5 Quotation in Warren to Sibley, 13 March 1837, Sibley Papers; see also the timber contract, 13 March 1837, Sibley Papers; Dodge to Harris, 23 November 1836, *Territorial Papers*, 27:673–74; Dousman to Taylor, 9 August 1836, and Taylor to Harris, 16 August 1836, NARG 75, LR, Prairie du Chien Agency.

6 Lieutenant Colonel William Davenport to Adjutant General Roger Jones, 27 May 1837, *Territorial Papers*, 27:792–95.

7 Dodge to Harris, 28 December 1836, and Harris to the Secretary of War, 16 March 1837, *Territorial Papers*, 27:697–98, 745–47; Harris to Dodge, 20 March 1837, NARG 75, LS, OIA; House Document 82 (hereafter HD), 9 January 1837, 24th Congress, 2d session, serial 303.

8 Harris to Dodge and Smith, 13 May 1837, NARG 75, LS, OIA. Edmund Jefferson Danziger uses a statement made by trader Lyman Warren to argue that the price paid for Chippewa lands was ridiculously low. In contrast, Taliaferro saw Warren's role in the treaty negotiation as self-serving. See Danziger, *The Chippewa of Lake Superior* (Norman: University of Oklahoma Press, 1978), 87; "Auto-biography of Maj. Lawrence Taliaferro," *Minnesota Collections*, 6 (1896):215–17.

9 Quotation in Sibley to Crooks, 24 December 1836, AFC-MHS; Taliaferro to Dodge, 2 August 1837, NARG 75, LR, St. Peter's Agency; Crooks to Sibley, 28 February 1837, Sibley Papers.

10 Harris to Dodge, 20 March 1837, NARG 75, LS, OIA.

11 Taliaferro to Dodge, 24 July 1837, NARG 75, LR, St. Peter's Agency.

12 Dousman to Crooks, 10 August 1837, AFC-MHS. Roy Meyer suspects that Mdewakanton leaders were unaware of the government's desire to purchase land when they reached Washington, but fur trade correspondence and Taliaferro's activities show otherwise. See Meyer, *History of the Santee Sioux*, 56.

13 Dousman to Sibley, 4 August 1837, Sibley Papers.

14 Taliaferro to Dodge, 6 and 21 August 1837, Taliaferro to Captain M. Scott, 16 August 1837, and Taliaferro's notes and vouchers for board of delegation, September–October 1837, NARG 75, LR, St. Peter's Agency.

15 The proceedings of the council are found in the Chauncey Bush journal, 21–27 September 1837, Michigan Historical Collections, Bentley Library, Ann Arbor, Michigan. A copy is in NARG 75, DRNRUT.

16 Bush journal, 23 September 1837. Grey Iron's Dakota name is Mazahota.

17 Ibid.; Boston *Atlas*, 22 and 30 September 1837.

18 Actual agreement was voiced by several delegates on 23 September, and others accepted the terms on Monday, 25 September. Bush journal, 23 and 25 September 1837.

19 Taliaferro treaty draft, 20 September 1837, NARG 75, LR, St. Peter's Agency; "Auto-biography," *Minnesota Collections*, 6 (1896):218.

20 Bush journal, 25 and 27 September 1837; Kappler, ed., *Indian Treaties*, 2:493–94.

21 Bush journal, 29 September 1837. Iron Cloud, whose Dakota name is Mahpiya-maza, had recently become band chief at Red Wing's village. Iron Walker, or Mazamani, was the only Wahpeton in the Sioux delegation. For information on both men see Taliaferro's journal.

22 Sibley to Crooks, 29 September 1837, AFC-MHS; "Auto-biography," *Minnesota Collections*, 6 (1896):219.

23 Sibley to Crooks, 29 September 1837, AFC-MHS.

24 Bush journal, 6 October 1837.

25 *Niles' Register*, 7 October 1837; Sibley to Crooks, 5 October 1837, AFC-MHS.

26 Scott Campbell to Taliaferro, 7 December 1837, NARG 75, LR, St. Peter's Agency.

27 Dousman to Sibley, 22 December 1837, Sibley Papers.

28 Campbell to Taliaferro, 22 July 1835 and 13 January 1838, NARG 75, LR, St. Peter's Agency; Taliaferro to delegate George Wallace Jones, 21 February 1838, *Territorial Papers*, 27:931–32.

29 Poinsett to Senator Lewis F. Linn, Committee on Indian Affairs, 19 March 1838, NARG 75, LS, OIA.

30 Taliaferro journal, 9 June 1838. See also 7 June and 8 July 1838.

31 Three companies of reinforcements did arrive on 28 June, showing the seriousness of the situation. Ibid., 4 and 28 June 1838; Plympton to Adjutant General, 1 June 1838, and Atkinson to Gaines, 20 June 1838, NARG 94, LR, AGO; Thomas Boyd to Dodge, 15 June 1838, NARG 75, LR, Prairie du Chien Agency.

32 Taliaferro journal, 8 and 9 July 1838.

33 Taliaferro to Harris, 28 June 1838, NARG 75, LR, St. Peter's Agency.

34 Taliaferro to Dodge, 31 July and 10 September 1838; Dodge to Harris, 16 October 1838, and council with the Sioux, 17 October 1838, NARG 75, LR, St. Peter's Agency; Taliaferro journal, 9 July through 13 October 1838.

35 Quotation in Taliaferro journal, 13 October 1838; also consult entries for 3–17 October 1838.

36 Ibid., 21 October 1838.

37 Ibid., 19 and 30 May, 1836, 1 June to 18 August 1839; Taliaferro to Poinsett, 16 July and 27 August 1839, and Taliaferro to T. Hartley Crawford, 15 July and 27 August 1839, NARG 75, LR, St. Peter's Agency; Crawford to Governor Robert Lucas, 7 November 1839, NARG 75, LS, OIA.

38 Annuity distribution list, 1 June 1840, Lucas to Crawford, 24 August 1840, James Doty to President John Tyler, 13 August 1841, Bruce to D. D. Mitchell, 17 November 1841, Bruce to Crawford, 17 November 1841, Bruce to Governor John Chambers, 15 September 1842, and 12 September 1843, NARG 75, LR, St. Peter's Agency.

39 Bruce to Crawford, 1 September 1841, Chambers to Crawford, 22 November 1842, and Bruce's annual report, 1 September 1843, ibid.; Dousman to Sibley, 16 September and 4 November 1842, Sibley Papers.

40 Taliaferro to the Indian Bureau, 30 September 1836, Bruce's annual report, 1 September 1843, and statistical report of Sioux bands, 1 September 1846, NARG 75, LR, St. Peter's Agency; annuity roll, 1849, NARG 75, OIA.

41 Annuity roll, 1844, Sibley Papers; annuity roll, 1849, NARG 75, OIA; Thomas S. Williamson to Bruce, 5 August 1840, NARG 75, LR, St. Peter's Agency; Williamson to David Greene, 28 May 1840 and 5 May 1843, ABCFM Papers; Parker, ed., *Recollections* of Philander Prescott, 215.

42 Taliaferro to Dodge, 21 August 1837, NARG 75, LR, St. Peter's Agency.

43 Harris to S. J. Pease and W. L. D. Ewing, 26 July 1838, NARG 75, LS, OIA; Ewing to the Secretary of War, 7 October 1838, and petition of Sioux mixed-bloods (n.d.) 1839, NARG 75, LR, St. Peter's Agency; Taliaferro journal, 17 August, 17, 19, 21, 23, and 26 September 1838.

44 Sibley to Harris, 22 September 1837, Samuel C. Stambaugh to Harris, 23 September 1837, and petition of Sioux mixed-bloods (initiated by Taliaferro, n.d.), NARG 75, LR, St. Peter's Agency; Crawford to Stambaugh, 20 March 1839, NARG 75, LS, OIA; Crawford to Poinsett, 9 January 1839, and Stambaugh to Poinsett, 1 March 1839, Bailly Papers.

45 Henry Sibley to Solomon Sibley, 9 December 1838, Sibley Papers; Dousman to Crooks, 6 November 1838, AFC-MHS; Taliaferro journal, 1 September 1838; "Claims Filed under the Treaty of September 29, 1837, with the Sioux of the Mississippi," 5 November 1838, NARG 75, Special Files of the OIA.

46 Taliaferro journal, 8 October 1838; Williamson to Bruce, 5 August 1840, ABCFM Papers.

47 Quotation in Taliaferro journal, 21 June 1837; Rolette to Crooks, 19 May 1838, AFC-MHS.

48 The depression convinced Dousman of the soundness of Sibley's new policy. "For besides punishing the *dogs* [Sioux]," he wrote Sibley, "no *new post* can pay the expense at the present rate of furs." Dousman to Sibley, 6 May 1838, Sibley Papers. See also Sibley to Dodge, 23 April 1838, *Territorial Papers*, 27:990–91; John C. Frémont to Poinsett, 8 June 1838, in *The Expeditions of John C. Frémont*, 2 vols., ed. Donald Jackson and Mary Lee Spence (Urbana, Chicago, and London: University of Illinois Press, 1970), 1:12–13; Sibley to Crooks, 2 July 1838, AFC-MHS.

49 Williamson to Sibley, 11 July 1837, Frémont to Sibley, 16 July 1838, and Louis

Provençalle to Sibley, 9 January 1839, Sibley Papers; Taliaferro journal, 6 September 1839; Bray and Bray, eds., *Joseph Nicollet on the Plains and Prairies*, 65, 78; Williamson to Greene, 3 May 1838, ABCFM Papers.

50 Taliaferro to Crawford, 30 September 1839, NARG 75, LR, St. Peter's Agency.

51 Crawford to Governor Chambers, 10 May 1841, NARG 75, LS, OIA; Doty to Secretary of War John Bell, 7 June 1841, *Territorial Papers*, 28:303–5; Dousman to Sibley, 18 June and 6 July 1841, Sibley Papers; Folwell, *History of Minnesota*, 1:457–59.

52 Doty to Bell, 4 and 9 August 1841, Mdewakanton Treaty, 11 August 1841, Doty to Crawford, 31 August 1841, and voucher for presents, 1 September 1841, NARG 75, LR, St. Peter's Agency; Bell to Crawford and Chambers to Doty, 3 September 1841, NARG 75, LS, OIA; Riggs to Samuel Pond, 29 July 1841, Pond Papers, Minnesota Historical Society; HD no. 101, 28 January 1843, 27th Congress, 3d session, serial 420.

53 Treaty with upper Sioux, 4 August 1841, and Mdewakanton treaty, 11 August 1841, NARG 75, LR, St. Peter's Agency.

54 See Taliaferro to Bell, 10 September 1841, ibid.

55 Doty to Bell, 9 August 1841; treaty with Sioux "half-breeds," 31 July 1841, and Doty to Secretary of War John C. Spencer, 9 November 1841, ibid.

56 Doty to Bell, 4 August 1841, NARG 75, LR, St. Peter's Agency.

57 Senator Benton to the President, 14 September 1841, *Territorial Papers*, 28:334–35; Riggs to Greene, 24 August 1841, and Robert Stuart to Greene, 11 February 1842, ABCFM Papers.

58 Stuart to Spencer, 21 February 1842, NARG 75, LR, St. Peter's Agency; Crooks to Sibley, 15 February 1842, and 1 July 1842, Sibley Papers; Henry Sibley to Solomon Sibley, 19 March 1842, Solomon Sibley Papers, Burton Collection, Detroit Public Library; Folwell, *History of Minnesota*, 1:457–59.

59 Taliaferro to Bell, 10 September 1841, NARG 75, LR, St. Peter's Agency.

60 Quotation in Taliaferro journal, 16 June 1839; Dodge to Harris, 16 October 1838, and personnel list, 30 September 1839, NARG 75, LR, St. Peter's Agency.

61 Taliaferro journal, 25 May, 4 June, 17 July, and 24 October 1839; Pope to Sibley, 22 May 1839, Sibley Papers; Bruce to Chambers, 15 June 1841, NARG 75, LR, Iowa Superintendency; James Reed contract, 1 October 1842, NARG 75, LR, St. Peter's Agency.

62 Taliaferro journal, 16 June, 15 July and 3 August 1839; Bruce to Chambers, 15 June and 2 August 1841, NARG 75, LR, Iowa Superintendency; Bruce to Robert Lucas, 11 November 1840, and Bruce to Crawford, 15 September 1842, NARG 75, LR, St. Peter's Agency; Nathaniel Fish Moore, "Journey by Way of Buffalo and the Lakes to the Falls of St. Anthony & return ... by Way of St. Louis and the Ohio River in the autumn of 1845," 19 August 1845, Edward E. Ayer Manuscript Collec-

tion, Newberry Library; Philander Prescott to Superintendent Alexander Ramsey, 25 September 1849, NARG 75, LR, Minnesota Superintendency.

63 Gideon Pond to Greene, 28 August 1840, ABCFM Papers.

64 Riggs, *Mary and I*, 5–12; Riggs, "The Dakota Mission," *Minnesota Collections*, 3 (1880):114–28; Forbes, "Evangelization and Acculturation among the Santee Dakota Indians, 1834–1864," 28–104.

65 Williamson to Greene, 14 August 1837 and 28 May 1840, and Riggs to Greene, October (n.d.) 1838, ABCFM Papers; Prescott, "The Dakota or Sioux," in *Information Respecting the History, Condition, and Prospects of the Indian Tribes*, ed. Schoolcraft, 3:227–30; Stephen Return Riggs, *Tah-koo Wah-kan; or, The Gospel among the Dakotas* (Boston: Congregational Publishing Society, 1869); Pond, "The Dakotas . . . in 1834," *Minnesota Collections*, 12 (1908):401–15; Landes, *Mystic Lake Sioux*, 48–66.

66 Riggs to Greene, 10 September 1839, ABCFM Papers.

67 Quotation in Samuel Pond to Greene, 8 January 1838, ibid.; see also Williamson to Greene, 24 August 1837, Riggs to Samuel Pond, 21 June 1839, Samuel Pond to Samuel Leavitt, 29 November 1838, and J. D. Stevens to Greene, 14 January 1839, ABCFM Papers.

68 See Ackermann, "Joseph Renville of Lac qui Parle," 231–46; Stephen Return Riggs, "Dakota Portraits," *Minnesota History Bulletin* 2 (November 1918):527–28, 532–37, 547–57, 561–68; Williamson to Greene, 4 May 1836, ABCFM Papers; Bray and Bray, ed., *Joseph Nicollet on the Plains and Prairies*, 279–80. Tacanhpitaninya's son, Joseph Napeśniduta, was described by Williamson as the "first male Dakota convert," but other records suggest that this distinction fell to Simon Anawangmani; see Williamson, "Napehshneedoota: The First Male Dakota Convert to Christianity," *Minnesota Collections*, 3 (1880):188–91.

69 Quote in Riggs, "Dakota Portraits," 548. See also Williamson to Greene, 1 October 1836 and 10 May 1837, and Riggs to Greene, 28 March 1838, ABCFM Papers.

70 Bray and Bray, eds., *Nicollet on the Plains and Prairies*, 277–78.

71 Riggs, *Mary and I*, 54–55; Riggs to Greene, 13 July and 1 August 1839, ABCFM Papers; Riggs, "Dakota Portraits," 561–68. See also Raymond J. DeMallie and Robert H. Lavenda, "Wakan: Plains Siouan Concepts of Power," in *The Anthropology of Power: Ethnographic Studies from Asia, Oceania, and the New World*, ed. Raymond D. Fogelson and Richard N. Adams (New York: Academic, 1977), 154–59.

72 Williamson to Greene, 28 May 1840, and Riggs to Greene, 24 February and 17 July 1841, ABCFM Papers; Riggs, *Mary and I*, 71; Riggs, *Tah-koo Wah-kan*, 176–77.

73 Riggs, *Tah-koo Wah-kan*, 146–47; Williamson to Greene, 28 May 1840, 10 May and 29 July 1842, 13 December 1843, 3 April 1844, 3 January 1845, 2 January and 10 April 1846, and Samuel Pond to Greene, 10 May 1842, ABCFM Papers.

74 Forbes, "Evangelization and Acculturation among the Santee Dakota Indians, 1834–1864," 127–66; Williamson to Greene, 15 August 1839, Samuel Pond to Greene, 10

May 1842, Riggs to Greene, 29 April 1846, ABCFM Papers; Gideon Pond to Sibley, 25 November 1848, Sibley Papers.

75 See the Lac qui Parle school reports in the ABCFM Papers.

76 Taliaferro journal, 12 February 1836 and 17 June 1838; Riggs, *Mary and I*, 40; Riggs, "The Dakota Mission," *Minnesota Collections*, 3 (1880):116–20; Bruce to Lucas, 30 September 1840, NARG 75, LR, St. Peter's Agency.

77 Riggs, *Mary and I*, 55; Riggs, *Tah-koo Wah-kan*, 198–99; Riggs to Greene, 28 January 1840 (part of journal dated 27 September 1839) and 1 May 1844, and Williamson to Greene, 2 January 1846, ABCFM Papers.

78 Bruce to Lucas, 6 November 1840, and Bruce to Crawford, 30 October 1841, NARG 75, LR, St. Peter's Agency; Crawford to Chambers, 13 July 1841, William Medill to Thomas H. Harvey, 7 January 15 May, and 28 August 1847, and Medill to Williamson 29 June 1848, NARG 75, LS, OIA; Williamson to Seliah B. Treat, 1 August 1848, and Samuel Pond to Treat, 28 December 1848, ABCFM Papers; Riggs, Williamson, and Samuel Pond to Sibley, 12 September 1845, Sibley Papers.

79 Riggs to Sibley, 26 February 1844, and Gideon Pond to Sibley, 25 November 1848, Sibley Papers; Riggs to Treat, 18 October 1848, ABCFM Papers.

80 Gideon Pond to Greene, 30 May 1839, and Samuel Pond to Greene, 22 September 1841, ABCFM Papers; Taliaferro to Lucas, 24 May 1839, and Bruce to Lucas, 30 September 1840, NARG 75, LR, St. Peter's Agency; Andrew Drips to Harvey, October (n.d.) 1844, NARG 75, LR, Upper Missouri Agency; Drips to Harvey, 25 October 1844 and 6 December 1845, Drips Papers, Bancroft Library, Berkeley, California; McLeod to Sibley, 12 April 1845, 29 January 1846 and 25 February 1848, Sibley Papers.

81 Officers' petition, 19 February 1840, NARG 75, LR, St. Peter's Agency; Captain G. Dearborn to Jones, 6 May 1842, NARG 94, LR, AGO; Second Lieutenant Cyrus Hall to Captain Backus, 10 April 1845, NARG 393, LR, Jefferson Barracks, 1831–53; Bruce to Sibley, 30 August 1842, Sibley Papers; Riggs to Greene, 30 May 1844, and Samuel Pond to Greene, 18 March 1845, ABCFM Papers.

82 Taliaferro journal, 2, 5, 14, 18 July and 6 August 1839; Samuel Pond to Greene, 8 May 1840, ABCFM Papers; Samuel Pond, "Indian Warfare in Minnesota," *Minnesota Collections*, 3 (1880):131–33; "Indian Warfare: Memorial of Stephen R. Riggs, Et Al.," 5 February 1849, HD no. 60, 26th Congress, 1st session, serial 365.

83 Bruce to Chambers, 20 June 1842, 4 August 1843, and 18 February 1844, NARG 75, LR, St. Peter's Agency; Backus to Major L. Cooper, 27 July 1843, NARG 94, LR, AGO; Lieutenant Colonel Henry Wilson to Jones, 13 February 1844, *Territorial Papers*, 28:642–43.

84 Wilson to Cooper, 1 April 1844, NARG 94, LR, AGO; Bruce to Chambers, 1 April and 13 June 1844, NARG 75, LR, St. Peter's Agency.

85 Wilson to Lieutenant H. S. Turner, 24 October 1844, NARG 94, LR, AGO; Wilson to Turner, 19 December 1844, NARG 393, LR, Western Division and Department; Bruce

to Chambers, 2 October and 2 November 1844, and Bruce to Harvey, 21 August 1847, NARG 75, LR, St. Peter's Agency; Norman Kittson to Sibley, 22 August 1844, Sibley Papers; Captain Seth Eastman to Colonel Sanford, 27 May 1847, NARG 393, LR, Jefferson Barracks, 1831–53; Medill to Harvey, 20 August and 4 September 1847, NARG 75, LS, OIA.

86 See Sibley account books for the 1840s, Sibley Papers.

CHAPTER 9

1 William G. Le Duc, *Minnesota Year Book for 1851* (St. Paul: William G. Le Duc, 1851), 34; *Minnesota Pioneer*, 6 May 1849; Folwell, *History of Minnesota*, 1:246–53.

2 See, for example, Riggs to Seliah B. Treat, 5 June 1849, ABCFM Papers; Williamson to Ramsey, 9 June 1849, NARG 75, LR, Minnesota Superintendency; Riggs to Sibley, 3 January 1850, Sibley to G. Pond, 13 May 1850, Fred Sibley to Henry Sibley, 27 June 1850, Fred Sibley to Chouteau, 14 September 1850, and Sibley to Ramsey, 5 September 1849, Sibley Papers (Fred Sibley will be distinguished from his older, more important brother, by the use of his first name in cited correspondence).

3 Riggs to David Greene, 29 April 1846, ABCFM Papers.

4 Quote in Riggs to Sibley, 28 July 1849, Sibley Papers. Consult also "Outline of a Plan for Civilizing the Dakotas, Adopted at a Meeting of the Dakota Mission Held at Kaposia," 6 June 1850, NARG 75, LR, Minnesota Superintendency; Williamson to Ramsey, 7 June 1849, ibid.; Riggs to ABCFM, 28 June 1850, ABCFM Papers.

5 Thomas H. Harvey to William Medill, 17 July 1848, NARG 75, LR, St. Peter's Agency; Brown to Ramsey, 26 July 1849, Brown to Secretary of Interior Thomas Ewing, 5 June 1849, and Murphy to Ramsey, 13 July 1849, NARG 75, LR, Minnesota Superintendency; Murphy to Harvey, 9 October 1849, House Executive Document (hereafter HED), no. 1, 30th Congress, 2d session, serial 537, 474–75; Lea report, 27 November 1850, Ramsey to Lea, 21 October 1850, and McLean to Ramsey, 25 September 1850, HED no. 1, 31st Congress, 2d session, serial 595, 35–36, 75, 103–4, and 110.

6 McLean to Ramsey, 25 September 1850, HED no. 1, 31st Congress, 2d session, serial 595, 103–4.

7 Ewing to Brown, 16 July 1849, and Ewing to Chambers, 25 August 1849, NARG 48, LS, Indian Division of the Interior Department; Brown to Ramsey, 14 July 1849, NARG 75, Minnesota Superintendency; Brown to Ramsey and Chambers, 25 August 1849, HED no. 5, 31st Congress, 1st session, serial 570, 979–80.

8 Sibley to Ramsey, 5 September 1849, Alexander Ramsey Papers, Minnesota Historical Society; Chambers to Ramsey, 30 August 1849, Ramsey to Sibley, 21 September 1849, petition of upper Sioux leaders, 2 November 1849, and Riggs to

Ramsey, 13 October 1849 and 5 November 1849, NARG 75, LR, Minnesota Superintendency.

9 "Journal of Proceedings," 29 September 1849, NARG 75, DRNRUT.

10 Sibley to Ramsey, 15 September 1849 and 9 February 1851, Ramsey Papers; Sibley
and Ramsey to Brown, 10 December 1849, NARG 75, LR, St. Peter's Agency; Ramsey to Brown, 10 December 1849, NARG 75, LR, Minnesota Superintendency.

11 Bailly to Sibley, 6 September 1849, Fred Sibley to Henry Sibley, 26 September 1850,
Sibley to Martin McLeod, 24 October 1850, Sibley Papers; Gideon Pond to Murphy, 27 August 1849, NARG 75, LR, Minnesota Superintendency.

12 Fred Sibley to Henry Sibley, 27 June 1850, and Bailly to Sibley, 6 December 1849,
Sibley Papers. Faribault's "circle of native relatives" was reputed to be "very large"
in Shakopee's camp. See S. W. Pond, Jr., *Two Volunteer Missionaries among the
Dakota; or, The Story of the Labors of Samuel W. and Gideon H. Pond* (Boston:
Congregational Sunday-School and Publishing Society, 1893), 187.

13 Prescott to Ramsey, 23 September 1850, NARG 75, LR, Minnesota Superintendency.

14 Quotation in Sibley to Chouteau, 20 October 1850, Sibley Papers. Consult also
Sibley credit book, March 1851 to April 1852, ibid.; James Clarke to Medill, 2
October 1846, HD no. 1, 29th Congress, 1st session, serial 497, 244; Murphy to
Medill, 9 July 1849, Ramsey to Brown, 4 August 1849, and Murphy to Ramsey, 10
August 1849, NARG 75, LR, Minnesota Superintendency.

15 Quotation in McLeod to Sibley, 25 March 1846, Sibley Papers. The market for
buffalo robes remained stable throughout the 1840s, each dressed skin being
worth three to four dollars. Muskrat, on the other hand, was worth only seven
cents a pelt. Consult Norman Kittson to Sibley, 30 March 1845, McLeod to Sibley,
24 January 1846, 4 January and 10 April 1847, 3 January 1848, 3 January and 21
February 1850, ibid.

16 Quoted in McLeod to Sibley, 2 April 1849, ibid. See also Fred Sibley to Henry
Sibley, 26 September 1850 and 14 January 1851, and McLeod to Sibley, 4 February
1851, ibid.

17 Fred Sibley to Henry Sibley, 14 January 1851, ibid.

18 Quotation in McLeod to Sibley, 22 August 1850, ibid. Consult also Ramsey to
Brown, 22 February 1850, and McLeod to Ramsey, 25 August 1850, NARG 75, LR,
Minnesota Superintendency; McLeod to Sibley, 24 February 1850, 21 and 28 Jan-
uary, and 10 and 26 April 1851, Sibley Papers; Riggs to McLeod, 12 February 1851,
McLeod Papers, Minnesota Historical Society; *Minnesota Pioneer*, 13 March 1851.

19 Fred Sibley to Henry Sibley, 10 September 1850, Sibley Papers; Sibley to Ramsey,
20 April 1850, Ramsey Papers; Charles W. Borup to Chouteau, 11 September 1850,
Chouteau Papers, photostats in Minnesota Historical Society; *Minnesota Pioneer*, 26 June 1851.

20 Riggs to the American Board, 17 May 1850, Robert Hopkins to Treat, 26 December

1848 and 9 April 1849, ABCFM Papers; Hopkins's translation of a letter written by Mah̓piyawicaśta, 26 April 1851, and Hopkins and A. G. Huggins to Ramsey, 29 July 1849, NARG 75, LR, Minnesota Superintendency.

21 For the role of the missionaries and their discussions with traders, see the Riggs translation of a Sisseton petition, 5 September 1849, Sibley to McLeod, 16 December 1849, Sibley to Gideon Pond, 13 May 1850, Riggs to Sibley, 13 January 1850, Alexander Faribault to Sibley, 21 January 1850, and McLeod to Sibley, 13 February 1850, Sibley Papers. Lorenzo Lawrence concluded that those Indians who could "read & write" had agreed to separate themselves from the bands and farm. See Lawrence to Ramsey, 15 February 1851, NARG 75, Minnesota Superintendency.

22 Fred Sibley to Chouteau, 14 September 1850, Sibley Papers. See also Jack Frazer to Sibley, 15 June 1846, ibid.

23 The Ramsey-Chambers report, 17 October 1849, NARG 75, LR, Minnesota Superintendency; Sibley to Ramsey, 14 April and 30 May 1850, Ramsey Papers.

24 Sibley to Chouteau, 3 November 1850, Sibley Papers.

25 Sibley to Ramsey, 26 July and 28 August 1850 and 20 February 1851, and Thomas Foster to Ramsey, 13 October 1850, Ramsey Papers; Folwell, *History of Minnesota*, 1:276–77; Lucile M. Kane, "The Sioux Treaties and the Traders," *Minnesota History* 32 (June 1851):65–80. For a look at the role played by the Ewings see Robert A. Trennert, Jr., *Indian Traders on the Middle Border: The Houses of Ewing, 1827–1854* (Lincoln: University of Nebraska Press, 1981), 176–93.

26 Ramsey to Sibley, 15 May 1851, Sibley to Chouteau, 11 July 1851, and McLeod to Sibley, 26 April 1851, Sibley Papers; Sibley to Ramsey, 21 March 1851, Ramsey Papers; Ramsey to Brown, 27 March 1850, NARG 75, LR, St. Peter's Agency; *Minnesota Pioneer* 5 June 1851.

27 "Journal of the Joint Commission to Treat with the Sioux," is found in NARG 75, DRNRUT. Previous scholars have used the reports taken from this account and published in the *Minnesota Pioneer* by editor James M. Goodhue between 3 July and 4 August 1851. Goodhue's articles later appeared in William G. Le Duc, *Minnesota Year Book for 1852* (St. Paul: Minnesota Historical Society, 1852). There are minor differences between the three accounts, and the original should be consulted.

28 "Journal of the Joint Commission," 18–19 July 1851, NARG 75, DRNRUT; Riggs, "Dakota Portraits," *Minnesota Collections*, 2:491–92.

29 "Journal of the Joint Commission," 21–23 July, NARG 75, DRNRUT; Kappler, ed., *Indian Treaties*, 2:588–90.

30 Ibid. Riggs to the American Board, 28 June 1850, and Williamson to Treat, 7 August 1851, ABCFM Papers; "Outline of a Plan for Civilizing the Dakotas," 6 June 1850, NARG 75, LR, Minnesota Superintendency. Folwell assumes that large annuities were solely the work of traders. Folwell, *History of Minnesota*, 1:281.

31 Kappler, ed., *Indian Treaties*, 2:588–90; "Congressional Report of the Commis-

sioners Appointed by the President of the United States to Investigate the Official Conduct of Alexander H. Ramsey," Senate Executive Document (hereafter SED) no. 61, 33d Congress, 1st session, serial 699, 42, 109–12 (hereafter Ramsey Investigation); traders' paper, 23 July 1851, Sibley Papers.

32 Riggs to Sibley, 16 January 1852 and Sibley statement to Congress, January 1853, Sibley Papers; McLean to Ramsey, 1 September 1851, SED no. 1, 32d Congress, 2d session, serial 658, 351; affidavit of Alexander Faribault, 5 February 1853, and "Half-breed Paper," 1851, Ramsey Papers; Ramsey Investigation, 212.

33 "Journal of the Joint Commission," 29–31 July 1851, NARG 75, DRNRUT.

34 Ibid., 5 August 1851; Reverend Joseph W. Hancock, "Missionary Work at Red Wing, 1849 to 1852," Minnesota Collections 10, part I (1900–1904):177.

35 Kappler, ed., Indian Treaties, 2:591–93; Wahpekute traders' paper, 15 August 1851, Ramsey Papers; Sibley to Dousman, 6 October 1851, Dousman Papers, Wisconsin Historical Society; Sibley to Chouteau, 1 November 1851, Sibley Papers; Williamson to Treat, 11 December 1851, ABCFM Papers.

36 Kappler, ed., Indian Treaties, 2:591–93; Folwell, History of Minnesota, 1:284–85. The Senate later cut out the clause that allowed the Wahpekutes to benefit from the 1837 treaty.

37 Quotation in New York Independent, 16 October 1851, in Grace Lee Nute Papers, Minnesota Historical Society. See also McLean to Ramsey, 1 September 1851, SED no. 1, 32d Congress, 1st session, serial 613, 434.

38 Ramsey to Lea, 3 November 1851, SED no. 1, 32d Congress, 1st session, serial 613, 414–15.

39 Lieutenant Colonel Lee to Captain Irwin McDowell, 20 August 1851, and McLean to Lea, 19 August 1851, NARG 75, LR, St. Peter's Agency; Samuel Pond to Treat, 20 March 1852, ABCFM Papers; McLean to Ramsey, 15 January 1852, NARG 75, LR, Minnesota Superintendency; Minnesota Pioneer, 4 March and 1 April 1852.

40 Sibley to Ramsey, 15 May 1852, Ramsey Papers.

41 McLeod to Sibley, 21 September 1852, Sibley Papers.

42 Sweetser to Colonel George Ewing, 26 October 1851, William G. and George W. Ewing Papers, Minnesota Historical Society (originals in the Indiana State Library); Sibley to Dousman, 31 October 1851, Dousman Papers; Sibley to Joseph La Framboise, 23 November 1851, Sibley Papers; Fred Sibley to McLeod, 24 November 1851, McLeod Papers.

43 The mixed-blood employed was either Joseph Campbell or Henry Auger. Quotation in Sweetser to George Ewing, 26 October 1851, Ewing Papers. See also Sibley to Joseph La Framboise, 23 November 1851, Sibley Papers; petition against the traders' paper, 6 December 1851, NARG 75, LR, St. Peter's Agency.

44 McLean to Lea, 13 December 1851, NARG 75, LR, Minnesota Superintendency.

45 McLeod to Fred Sibley, 20 and 24 December 1851, Sibley Papers; Sibley to Dous-

man, 29 December 1851, Dousman Papers; Sibley to McLeod, 7 January 1852, and D. R. Kennedy to McLeod, 22 February 1852, McLeod Papers.

46 Quotation in Fred Sibley to Chouteau, 6 March 1852, Sibley Papers. See also Sibley to Dousman, 14 February 1851, and Rice to Dousman, 24 February 1851, Dousman Papers; McLeod to Fred Sibley, 1 February 1852 and 22 March 1852, and petition of Sisseton and Wahpeton people, 21 April 1852, Sibley Papers.

47 Alexander Wilkin to Ramsey, 24 April 1852, and Sibley to Ramsey, 26 June 1852, Ramsey Papers; Fred Sibley to Joseph La Framboise, 20 April 1852, and Fred Sibley to Chouteau, 17 June 1852, Sibley Papers; Sibley to McLeod, 30 May 1852, McLeod Papers.

48 Riggs to Treat, 31 July 1852, ABCFM Papers.

49 Quotation in McLeod to Fred Sibley, 3 May 1852, Sibley Papers. Consult also Lee to McDowell, 7 August 1852, NARG 94, LR, AGO.

50 Fred Sibley to Chouteau, 11 July 1852, Sibley Papers.

51 Sibley to Ramsey, 25 July 1852, Ramsey Papers.

52 D. R. Atchison to Lea, 3 August 1852, McLean to Ramsey, 31 August 1852, and Gideon Pond to Ramsey, 31 August 1852, NARG 75, LR, Minnesota Superintendency; Ramsey to Lea, 28 August 1852, ibid., LS; Riggs to Treat, 28 August 1852, ABCFM Papers.

53 Ramsey to Lea, 28 August 1852, NARG 75, LS, Minnesota Superintendency; McLeod to Sibley, 29 July 1852, and Rice to Borup, 2 August 1852, Sibley Papers; Fred Sibley to McLeod, 31 July 1852, McLeod Papers; Parker, ed., *Recollections of Philander Prescott*, 188; Folwell, *History of Minnesota*, 1:294.

54 Quotation in Parker, ed., *Recollections of Philander Prescott*, 187. Ramsey Investigation, 2, 13–14; affidavit of Wallace B. White, 24 May 1853, and affidavit of Prescott, 29 August 1853, Ramsey Papers; Ramsey to Lea, 10 September 1852, NARG 75, LR, Minnesota Superintendency; Alexander H. H. Stuart to Commissioner of Indian Affairs, 2 October 1852, NARG 48, LS, Indian Division of Interior Department.

55 Sibley to Dousman, 16 September 1852, Dousman Papers.

56 Tyler to Sibley, 22 September 1852, Sibley Papers; Wahpekute power of attorney, 8 November 1852, Ramsey Papers.

57 Ramsey Investigation, 76, 81–82, 189, 124–25; Sibley to Dousman, 17 October 1852, Dousman Papers.

58 Ramsey Investigation, 76, 175–76, 189, 277. De Mallie, "Touching the Pen," in *Ethnicity on the Great Plains*, ed. Luebke, 50.

59 Fred Sibley to Chouteau, 16 November 1852, Sibley Papers; Ramsey Investigation, 81–82, 172–74; Pond, *Two Volunteer Missionaries*, 187.

60 See the receipts from Mdewakanton chiefs, 9 and 11 November 1852, Ramsey Papers; Ramsey Investigation, 157, 263–68.

61 Thomas Hughes, *Old Traverse des Sioux* (St. Peter, Minn.: Herald Publishing Company, 1929), 4–5; D. R. Kennedy to Fred Sibley, 22 November 1852, and McLeod to Fred Sibley, 20 September 1852, Sibley Papers; Ramsey Investigation, 275–76, 281–82. A romantic account of Mazasa's (Red Iron's) arrest is related in Hughes, in which the chief is purported to have made an inspiring and condemning speech relative to his treatment. See Folwell, *History of Minnesota*, 301, footnote 80.

62 Ramsey Investigation, 152–53; receipt of Sissetons and Wahpetons, 29 November 1852, Ramsey Papers.

63 Power of attorney to Sweetser, Williamson, and McLean, 2 December 1852, and Sisseton and Wahpeton "national protest," 3 December 1852, Ramsey Papers; Ramsey Investigation, 102–3, 139–40. A third protest, signed on 6 December by a large number of discontented Indians, was sent to the president. Ramsey Investigation, 31–33.

64 Power of attorney to Hugh Tyler, 1 December 1852, Ramsey Papers.

65 Ramsey Investigation, 66, 161, 221–22, 243, 287–88; Folwell, *History of Minnesota*, 303.

66 Ibid., 143–44, 158, 161, 208–10; amount received for account of American Fur Company, December 1852, and Crooks to Sibley, 30 December 1852, Sibley Papers.

67 Fred Sibley to McLeod, 26 January 1853, Sibley memorandum to Congress, January 1853, and Ramsey to Sibley, 23 December 1853, Sibley Papers.

68 Charles E. Mix to Gorman, 28 May and 18 June 1853, NARG 75, LR, Minnesota Superintendency; Franklin Pierce to Young, 18 August 1853, NARG 48, LS, Indian Division of Interior Department.

69 Quotation in Sibley to Ramsey, 23 December 1853, Ramsey Papers. Consult Gorman to George W. Manypenny, 27 August 1853, NARG 75, LR, St. Peter's Agency; Gorman to Manypenny, 14 September 1853, NARG 75, LR, Minnesota Superintendency; Sibley to Ramsey, 7 December 1853, and D. Cooper to Ramsey, 27 January 1854, Ramsey Papers; *Senate Report*, no. 131, 33d Congress, 1st session, serial 706.

70 Sibley to Dousman, 28 May 1854, Dousman Papers.

71 Folwell notes on William Quinn interview, 19 March 1905, Folwell Papers, Minnesota Historical Society. Ramsey's quotation is found in his diary, 8 May 1854, Ramsey Papers.

72 Winchell, *Aborigines of Minnesota*, 554; Meyer, *History of the Santee Sioux*, 87.

73 Ramsey Investigation, 93.

74 Ibid., 117–18.

75 Ibid., 169.

CHAPTER 10

1 McLean to Ramsey, 10 May 1853, J. W. Hancock and William Whreney to Gorman, 17 May 1853, Gorman to George Manypenny, 27 May 1853 and 1 June 1853, NARG 75, LR, Minnesota Superintendency; Prescott to Robert G. Murphy, 1 September 1853, HED no. 1, 33d Congress, 1st session, serial 721, 319.

2 Quoted in Bailly to Gorman, 27 October 1853, NARG 75, LR, Minnesota Superintendency. See also Gorman to Faribault, 18 June 1853, Hancock to Gorman, 1 July 1853, Bailly to Murphy, 9 October 1853, and Gorman to Manypenny, 15 November 1853, ibid.; Gorman to Manypenny, 28 November 1853, NARG 75, LR, St. Peter's Agency; Hancock to Treat, 14 June 1853, ABCFM Papers; Prescott to Alex Faribault, 1 August 1853, Sibley Papers.

3 Fred Sibley to Chouteau, 18 April 1853, Sibley Papers; G. A. McLeod to Martin McLeod, 18 May 1853, McLeod Papers; Gorman to Manypenny, 27 July 1853, NARG 75, LR, St. Peter's Agency; Gorman to Manypenny, 6 September 1853, and Gorman to Mix, 22 September 1853, NARG 75, LR, Minnesota Superintendency; Gorman to Manypenny, 14 September 1853, HED no. 1, 33d Congress, 1st session, serial 721, 296; Ramsey report, 12 September 1853, SED no. 61, 33d Congress, 1st session, serial 699, 34–35.

4 Gorman to Manypenny, 12 August 1853, NARG 75, LR, Minnesota Superintendency; Murphy to Gorman, 3 September 1853, NARG 75, St. Peter's Agency.

5 Gorman to Manypenny, 7 September 1853, NARG 75, LS, Minnesota Superintendency; Mix to Gorman, 27 September 1853, and Manypenny to Gorman, 9 November 1853, NARG 75, LR, ibid.; Manypenny to R. McClelland, 26 November 1853, HED no. 1, 33d Congress, 1st session, serial 721, 245–46.

6 Manypenny to Gorman, 3 February 1854, Gorman to Manypenny, 21 February 1854, and J. P. Wilson to Gorman, 25 February 1853, NARG 75, LR, Minnesota Superintendency. For Ramsey's side of the story see Ramsey to Manypenny, 27 February 1854, and William R. Marshall to Manypenny, 9 March 1854, NARG 75, LR, St. Peter's Agency.

7 Williamson to Treat, 2 December 1853, Riggs to Treat, 5 December 1853 and 30 January 1854, and Treat to Riggs, 11 February 1854, ABCFM Papers. Riggs thought very little of Gorman even before his antics at the agency, reporting that he had been fined in Indiana for "profane swearing," and that he did not know "the a.b.c. of Indian character." Riggs to Treat, 22 June 1853, ibid.

8 Treat to Riggs, 11 February 1854, ibid.; Manypenny to Gorman, 19 April 1854, NARG 75, LR, Minnesota Superintendency.

9 Manypenny to Gorman, 19 April 1854, NARG 75, LR, Minnesota Superintendency. Head farmer Prescott discussed the effects of this order in Prescott to Murphy, 3 September 1856, SD no. 5, 34th Congress, 3d session, serial 875, 606–11.

10 Prescott to Gorman, 16 June 1854, ibid.; Prescott to Murphy, 10 October 1854, SED no. 1, 33d Congress, 2d session, serial 746, 282.

11 Robertson to Gorman, 8 July 1854, NARG 75, LR, Minnesota Superintendency; Riggs to Treat, 3 August 1854, ABCFM Papers.

12 Gorman report, 30 September 1854, NARG 75, LR, Minnesota Superintendency.

13 Murphy to Gorman, 6 January 1854, NARG 75, LR, St. Peter's Agency; *Minnesota Pioneer* 1 June 1854.

14 Lee to Major James Page, 8 July 1854, NARG 393, LR, Department of the West and Western Department, 1853–61. Lee feared above all that the "Indians already in their country [near the reserve] will greatly suffer for want of provisions" owing to Murphy's neglect.

15 Manypenny to Gorman, 21 August 1854, and Brown to Gorman, 28 October 1854, NARG 75, LR, Minnesota Superintendency; Major H. Day to Murphy, 19 October 1854, NARG 393, letterbook, Fort Ridgely, June 1854 to November 1858; Captain J. Hayden to Lieutenant A. F. Bond, 18 November 1854, NARG 393, LR, Fort Ridgely, 1853–68.

16 Day to Assistant Adjutant General, 26 January 1855, NARG 393, letterbook, Fort Ridgely, June 1854–November 1858. Of some of the provisions, Day said: "This same pork is currently said to have been a lot offered by the contractor for this post last year and utterly condemned and rejected on inspection." Day was quite enraged by the entire affair, suggesting that Murphy had been a party to defrauding the Indians.

17 Murphy to Gorman, 10 November 1854, NARG 75, Minnesota Superintendency; Hayden to Bond, 18 November 1854, NARG 393, LR, Fort Ridgely, 1853–68; testimony of James Wells, 6 March 1855, and Moses N. Adams to Manypenny, 3 August 1854, NARG 75, LR, St. Peter's Agency.

18 Day to Assistant Adjutant General, 26 January 1855, NARG 393, letterbook, Fort Ridgely, June 1854 to November 1858; Lee to Page, 8 July 1854, NARG 393, LR, Department of the West and Western Department, 1853–61; Gorman to Manypenny, 9 January 1854, NARG 75, LS, Minnesota Superintendency; Thomas Denter to Gorman, 14 January 1854, and Murphy to Gorman, 4 March and 22 August 1854, ibid.

19 Quotation in Pond to Treat, November (n.d.) 1853, ABCFM Papers. Consult also Pond to Treat, 14 October 1854, ibid.; Adams to Manypenny, 3 August 1854, NARG 75, LR, St. Peter's Agency; Henry Belland to Manypenny, 22 January 1855, NARG 75, LR, Minnesota Superintendency.

20 Prescott to Gorman, 27 June 1854, NARG 75, LR, Minnesota Superintendency; Lee to Page, 30 June, 8 July, and 19 September 1854, and Gorman to Page, 10 August 1854, NARG 393, LR, Department of the West and Western Department, 1853–61.

21 Miscellaneous memorandum, 11 May 1855, NARG 393, LR, Fort Ridgely, 1853–68; Murphy to Gorman, 21 March 1854, Gorman to Manypenny, 9 April 1855, and

Robertson to Murphy, 3 April 1855, and NARG 75, LR, St. Peter's Agency; Williamson to Treat, 13 June 1855, ABCFM Papers.

22 Prescott to Gorman, 2 December 1854, Murphy to Gorman, 12 and 17 May and 5
July 1855, NARG 75, LR, Minnesota Superintendency; Gorman to Murphy, 5 Sep-
tember 1854, NARG 75, LS, ibid.; Gorman to Manypenny, 30 May 1855, NARG 75,
St. Peter's Agency; Day to Murphy, 10 April 1855, NARG 393, letterbook, Fort Ridgely,
June 1854 to November 1858; Riggs to Treat, 29 November 1854, and Williamson
to Treat, 6 March 1855, ABCFM Papers.

23 See the argument Riggs offers in the *Minnesota Pioneer*, 26 May and 9 June 1853.
Consult also Williamson to Treat, 18 July 1853, Riggs to Treat, 19 September 1853,
and Treat to Manypenny, 28 April 1854, ABCFM Papers.

24 Williamson to Treat, 8 June and 30 July 1852, ABCFM Papers.

25 Riggs to Treat, 11 May 1853 and 9 March 1854, ibid.; *Minnesota Pioneer* 9 and 23
March 1854.

26 Riggs to the American Board, 3 March 1854, Indian petition, 3 June 1854, ABCFM
Papers; Riggs, *Mary and I*, 132–33.

27 Riggs to Treat, 23 May 1855, ABCFM Papers; Murphy to Gorman, 1 September
1854, NARG 75, LR, Minnesota Superintendency; Gorman to Manypenny, 13 September 1854, NARG 75, LS, ibid.

28 Riggs to Treat, 26 August 1854, ABCFM Papers.

29 Quotation in Williamson to Treat, 28 March 1854, ibid. Consult also Williamson
to Treat, 14 July and 26 September 1853, 17 February and 28 March 1854, and
Riggs to Treat, 26 August 1854 and 11 and 30 January and 17 February 1855, ibid.;
Riggs to Murphy, 1 September 1854, SED no. 1, 33d Congress, 2d session, serial
746, 274–75.

30 Prescott to Day, 18 March 1855, NARG 393, LR, Fort Ridgely, 1853–68.

31 Murphy to Gorman, 7 April and 17 May 1855, NARG 75, LR, Minnesota Superintendency; Gorman to Manypenny, 21 May 1855, NARG 75, LR, St. Peter's Agency;
Gorman to Murphy, 30 May 1855, NARG 75, LS, Minnesota Superintendency.

32 Quotation in Manypenny to Gorman, 8 May 1855, NARG 75, LS, Minnesota Superintendency; see also Gorman to Manypenny, 22 June 1855, NARG 75, LR, St. Peter's Agency.

33 Prescott to Murphy, 10 September 1855, Robertson to Murphy, 15 September 1855,
and Murphy's annual report, 22 September 1855, HD no. 1, 34th Congress, 1st
session, serial 840, 378–81, 384–85, 386–87; Williamson, "Napehshneedoota: The
First Dakota Convert to Christianity," *Minnesota Collections*, 3 (1880):188–91.

34 Quotation in Gorman to Manypenny, 31 October 1855, HD no. 1, 34th Congress,
1st session, serial 840, 368–70. See also Day to Assistant Adjutant General, 16
April 1855, NARG 393, letterbook, Fort Ridgely, June 1854 to November 1858; Day
to Murphy, 22 September 1855, NARG 393, LR, Fort Ridgely, 1853–68.

35 *Daily Pioneer and Democrat* 6, 19, 27, and 29 November 1855 and 7 January 1856;

"Sioux Papers," petitions dated 1856, NARG 75, LS, Northern Superintendency; J. Rosse Browne to the Secretary of Interior, 3 April 1855, NARG 75, Special Files.

36 Gorman to Manypenny, 16 January 1856, James Shields to Manypenny, 12 February 1856, Manypenny to the Secretary of Interior, 8 April 1856, and W. J. Cullen to J. W. Denver, 23 October 1857, NARG 75, LR, St. Peter's Agency; Gorman to Manypenny, 16 January 1856, NARG 75, LS, Minnesota Superintendency; unsigned report, 1856, NARG 75, LS, Northern Superintendency.

37 Council is reported in Huebschmann to Manypenny, 28 June 1856, NARG 75, LS, Northern Superintendency. Consult also Huebschmann to Murphy, 16 May 1856, and Huebschmann to Manypenny, 20 June 1856, ibid.; Huebschmann to Manypenny, 19 May 1856, NARG 75, LR, St. Peter's Agency; Gideon Pond to Gorman, 12 June 1856, NARG 75, LR, Minnesota Superintendency; Meyer, *History of the Santee Sioux*, 95; *Daily Pioneer and Democrat*, 26 June 1856.

38 Captain Daniel Shaw to Manypenny, NARG 75, LS, Northern Superintendency; Colonel E. B. Alexander to Assistant Adjutant General, 22 July 1856, and Lieutenant Henry E. Magruder to Assistant Adjutant General, 1 September 1856, NARG 393, letterbook, Fort Ridgely, June 1854 to November 1858; Huebschmann to Manypenny, 22 August 1856, NARG 75, LR, St. Peter's Agency; "Order" of J. J. Nash, 16 September 1856, NARG 393, LR, Fort Ridgely, 1853–68.

39 Huebschmann to Manypenny, 19 July 1856, and financial report, 13 January 1856 (1857), NARG 75, LR, St. Peter's Agency.

40 Prescott to Murphy, 3 September 1856, SD no. 5, 34th Congress, 3d session, serial 875, 606–11.

41 Quotation in Manypenny to Huebschmann, 20 November 1856, ibid., 612. See also Mix to Huebschmann, 22 August 1856, NARG 75, LR, Northern Superintendency; Huebschmann to Manypenny, 24 December 1856, NARG 75, St. Peter's Agency; "List of persons employed at Sisseton-Wahpeton Establishment," Flandrau Papers.

42 Riggs to Treat, 31 July 1856 and 22 April 1857, ABCFM Papers; *Daily Pioneer and Democrat* 18 August 1856; *Henderson Democrat* 14 August 1856.

43 Riggs to Treat, 30 November 1857, ABCFM Papers; Riggs to McLeod, 27 February 1857, McLeod Papers; Riggs, *Mary and I*, 133.

44 Williamson to Treat, 17 March 1857, ABCFM Papers; scattered receipts for purchase of food, 17 November 1856 to 31 March 1857, Flandrau Papers; Robertson's report, 20 September 1856, SD no. 5, 34th Congress, 3d session, serial 875, 613–14.

45 Huebschmann to Manypenny, 2 December 1856 and 2 February 1857, NARG 75, LR, St. Peter's Agency; Flandrau to Huebschmann, 13 January 1857, NARG 75, LR, Northern Superintendency.

46 Alexander to Assistant Adjutant General, 23 March and 15 May 1857, NARG 393, letterbook, Fort Ridgely, June 1854 to November 1858; Flandrau to Huebsch-

mann, 10 April 1857, NARG 75, LR, St. Peter's Agency; Riggs to Treat, 13 August 1857, ABCFM Papers.

47 Thomas Hughes, "Causes and Results of the Inkpaduta Massacre," *Minnesota Collections*, 12 (1905–8):264–265, 293–94; Flandrau letter, 11 April 1857, SD no. 11, 35th Congress, 1st session, serial 919, 357–59; Lucius F. Hubbard and Return I. Holcombe, *Minnesota in Three Centuries*, 4 vols. (Mankato: Publishing Society of Minnesota, 1908), 3:220–22; Thomas Teakle, *The Spirit Lake Massacre* (Iowa City, Iowa: State Historical Society, 1918), 64–77.

48 Major Samuel Woods to Gorman, 9 February 1854, and Gorman to the Commissioner of Indian Affairs, NARG 75, LR, Upper Missouri Agency. Iowa historians have argued that Sintomniduta was a brother of Inkpaduta, but they were from different tribes. See the discussion in Hubbard and Holcombe, *Minnesota in Three Centuries*, 3:222–24; Teakle, *Spirit Lake Massacre*, 9–16, 75–83.

49 Hubbard and Holcombe, *Minnesota in Three Centuries*, 3:224–36; Teakle, *Spirit Lake Massacre*, 94–121. The only account of a survivor is L. P. Lee, ed., *History of the Spirit Lake Massacre! And of Miss Abigail Gardner's Three Months Captivity among the Indians According to Her Own Account* (New Britain, Conn.: L. P. Lee, 1857), 1–47.

50 Flandrau to Huebschmann, 16 April 1857, and Huebschmann to Denver, 8 May 1857, NARG 75, LR, St. Peter's Agency; Hubbard and Holcombe, *Minnesota in Three Centuries*, 3:244–45; *Henderson Democrat* 16 April 1857; Captain Theodore Potter, "Captain Potter's Recollections of Minnesota Experiences," *Minnesota History Bulletin* 1, no. 8 (November 1916):431–32.

51 Bee to Lieutenant H. E. Mayandier, 9 April 1857, SD no. 11, 35th Congress, 1st session, serial 919, 351. A volunteer unit from Iowa also reached the scene a day later. For the report it left, see "The Relief Expedition" and "Report of Major Williams," *Palimpsest* 38 (June 1959):253–72.

52 Adjutant General to the commanding officer, Fort Snelling, 5 May 1857, NARG 393, LR, Department of the West and Western Department, 1853–61; Alexander to the Assistant Adjutant General, 13 and 15 May 1857, NARG 393, letterbook, Fort Ridgely, June 1854 to November 1858.

53 Alexander to Assistant Adjutant General, 15 May 1857, and Bee to Adjutant General, 18 June 1857, NARG 393, letterbook, Fort Ridgely, June 1854 to November 1858. Flandrau left during the first week in July, at the height of the troubles at the upper agency. He may have traveled to St. Paul to have better access to telegraphic communications. See Flandrau telegram, 18 July 1857, and report of Kintzing Pritchette, NARG 75, LR, St. Peter's Agency; Cullen to Denver, 28 September 1857, SD no. 11, 35th Congress, 1st session, serial 919, 336–38.

54 Cullen to Major T. W. Sherman, 23 June 1857, NARG 75, LS, Northern Superintendency; J. W. Daniels to Flandrau, 30 June 1857, Flandrau Papers; Cullen to Den-

ver, 20 July 1857, SD no. 11, 35th Congress, 1st session, serial 919, 362–63; Riggs to Treat, 22 July 1857, ABCFM Papers.

55 Bee to Major W. W. Morris, 2 July 1857, NARG 393, LR, Fort Ridgely, 1853–68; Pritchette's report, 15 October 1857, NARG 75, LR, St. Peter's Agency.

56 Riggs quickly informed Flandrau that he could "raise a company" of troops in the vicinity of Hazelwood. Riggs to Flandrau, 1 July 1857, Flandrau Papers; Bee to Lieutenant Colonel John Abercrombie, 12 July 1857, NARG 393, letterbook, Fort Ridgely, June 1854 to November 1858.

57 Sherman to Abercrombie, 16 July 1857, NARG 393, LR, Fort Ridgely, 1853–68.

58 Ibid. Quotation in Sherman to Lieutenant James Hunter, 22 July 1857, ibid. For Little Crow's role, see also *Sketches Historical and Descriptive of the Monuments and Tablets Erected by the Minnesota Valley Historical Society in Renville and Redwood Counties, Minnesota* (Morton: Minnesota Valley Historical Society, 1902), 15; Cullen to Denver, 26 July 1857, NARG 75, LR, St. Peter's Agency; Riggs to Treat, 22 July 1857, ABCFM Papers.

59 Cullen to Denver, 20 July 1857, and Denver to Cullen, 20 July 1857, SD no. 11, 35th Congress, 1st session, serial 919, 362–63; Cullen to Denver, 26 July 1857, NARG 75, LR, St. Peter's Agency.

60 Abercrombie to Assistant Adjutant General, 8 August 1857, NARG 393, letterbook, Fort Ridgely, June 1854 to November 1858; journal of A. J. Campbell (n.d.), council with Sisseton and Wahpeton leaders, 10 August 1857, and Mix to Pritchette, 25 August 1857, SD no. 11, 35th Congress, 1st session, serial 919, 376–77, 383, and 397–99; Hubbard and Holcombe, *Minnesota in Three Centuries*, 3:363–66.

61 Sherman to Abercrombie, 30 July 1857, and Sully to Hunter, 2 August 1857, NARG 393, LR, Fort Ridgely, 1853–68; Denver to Cullen, 10 November 1857, NARG 75, LR, Northern Superintendency; Williamson to Treat, November (n.d.) 1857, ABCFM Papers; council notes, 21 September 1857, and James Magner's farming report, 24 September 1857, SD no. 11, 35th Congress, 1st session, serial 919, 349, 400–403.

62 Red Iron to Flandrau (n.d. [spring 1857]) and A. Robertson to Flandrau, 2 April 1857, Flandrau Papers.

63 *Henderson Democrat* 2 July 1857; Riggs letter of 27 August 1862, and Williamson letter of 29 August 1862, published in *St. Paul Press* 29 August and 3 September 1862.

64 Quotation in Abercrombie to Captain H. C. Pratt, 16 September 1857, NARG 393, letterbook, Fort Ridgely, June 1854 to November 1858. See also Pratt to Abercrombie, 15 September 1857, NARG 393, LR, Fort Ridgely, 1853–68; Denver to J. Thompson, 30 November 1857, SD no. 11, 35th Congress, 1st session, serial 919, 290.

65 Frederick P. Leavenworth to Mary A. Peabody, 21 August 1856, Leavenworth Papers, Minnesota Historical Society.

66 Pritchette to Denver, 16 August 1857, NARG 75, LR, St. Peter's Agency.

67 Brown letter, 7 July 1857, *Henderson Democrat* 16 July 1857.

68 Williamson to Treat, November (n.d.) 1857, ABCFM Papers.

CHAPTER 11

1 Cullen to Denver, 28 September 1857, SD no. 11, 35th Congress, 1st session, serial 919, 336.

2 Ibid.; Pritchette report, 15 October 1857, and Cullen to Mix, 24 December 1857, NARG 75, LR, St. Peter's Agency.

3 *Henderson Democrat* 29 May and 5 June 1856. See also editorials for 14 August 1856 and 17 September 1857.

4 Riggs to Treat, 30 November 1857, and Williamson to Treat, 18 January 1858, ABCFM Papers.

5 Riggs to Treat, 4 March 1856, ibid.; Sioux petition, 11 February 1856, NARG 75, LR, St. Peter's Agency.

6 Flandrau to Cullen, 24 September 1857, SD no. 11, 35th Congress, 1st session, serial 919, 347; Flandrau contract with Gorman and Nathan Hill, 27 May 1854, Flandrau Papers.

7 The Lake Pepin "half-breed" land issue was resolved by a congressional act rather than a treaty. Mixed-bloods were informed through the Minnesota newspaper of their rights to take up land free in March 1857. R. M. McClelland to the Commissioner of Indian Affairs, 2 March 1855, NARG 48, LS, Indian Division of the Interior Department; Gorman to the Commissioner of Indian Affairs, 26 January 1856, NARG 75, LS, Minnesota Superintendency; *Henderson Democrat* 19 March 1857; Williamson to Treat, 18 March 1858; Riggs to Treat, 22 February 1861, ABCFM Papers; Folwell, *History of Minnesota*, appendix 2, 1:482–86.

8 Transcripts of the treaty negotiation dated 15 March through 21 June 1858 are found in NARG 75, DRNRUT; *Henderson Democrat* 3 March and 28 April 1858. For a published account of the treaty see Barbara T. Newcombe, "'A Portion of the American People': The Sioux Sign a Treaty in Washington in 1858," *Minnesota History* 45 (Fall 1976):83–96.

9 Treaty transcripts, 9 April 1858, NARG 75, DRNRUT.

10 Ibid., 25 May 1858.

11 Ibid. For Little Crow's 1854 trip consult the *Minnesota Pioneer*, 5 May 1854.

12 Treaty transcripts, 4 and 19 June 1858, NARG 75, DRNRUT.

13 Ibid., 1 and 19 June 1858.

14 Ibid., 21 June 1858; Folwell, *History of Minnesota*, appendix 9, 2:393–400; Brown to Cullen, 10 September 1859, SED no. 2, 36th Congress, 1st session, serial 1023, 451–52.

15 Brown to Cullen, 4 February 1858 and Cullen to Mix, 3 March and 16 April 1858, NARG 75, LR, St. Peter's Agency; Brown to Cullen, 30 September 1858, SED no. 1, 35th Congress, 2d session, serial 974, 401–4.

16 Brown to Cullen, 30 September 1858, SED no. 1, 35th Congress, 2d session, serial 974, 401–4; Brown to Cullen, 30 November 1859, NARG 75, LR, St. Peter's Agency; *Henderson Democrat* 1 October 1858.

17 *Henderson Democrat* 1 October 1858.

18 Brown to Cullen, 30 September 1858, SED no. 1, 35th Congress, 2d session, serial 974, 401–2; Riggs to Treat, 2 and 27 November 1858, ABCFM Papers.

19 Quotations in Cullen to Greenwood, 13 August 1859, NARG 75, LR, St. Peter's Agency. See also Cullen to Greenwood, 15 August 1859, and Brown to Cullen, 2 August 1859, ibid.; Cullen to Greenwood, 15 September 1859, SED no. 2, 36th Congress, 1st session, serial 1023, 420; Riggs to Treat, 24 August 1859, and Williamson to Treat, 18 November 1859, ABCFM Papers.

20 *Henderson Democrat* 15 June 1859; Cullen to Greenwood, 13 August 1859 and 21 April 1860, NARG 75, LR, St. Peter's Agency; Cullen to Brown, 6 September 1859, SED no. 2, 36th Congress, 1st session, serial 1023, 466–69, 448–49; Cullen to Brown, 22 September 1860, and Brown to Cullen, 25 October 1860, SED no. 1, 36th Congress, 2d session, serial 1078, 291–92, 278–84; Williamson to Treat, 18 November 1850, ABCFM Papers.

21 The best sources for settlement patterns are the Leavenworth diaries and notebooks in the Leavenworth Papers and the J. William Trygg maps, drawn from the original survey work completed in the 1850s. The Trygg maps are available through the Trygg Land Office, Ely, Minnesota. See also Hubbard and Holcombe, *Minnesota in Three Centuries*, 3:271–72; Riggs to Treat, 24 August 1859, ABCFM Papers; Captain Theodore Potter, "Captain Potter's Recollections of Minnesota Experiences," *Minnesota History Bulletin* 1, no. 8 (November 1916):426–27.

22 Captain J. Hayden to Lieutenant A. F. Bond, 18 November 1854, NARG 393, LR, Fort Ridgely, 1853–68; Hubbard and Holcombe, *Minnesota in Three Centuries*, 3:270–71.

23 Williamson to Treat, 18 November 1859 and Riggs to Treat, 21 January 1858, ABCFM Papers; Asa W. Daniels, "Reminiscences of Little Crow," *Minnesota Collections*, 12 (1905–8):524.

24 Quotation in Brown to Cullen, 10 September 1859, SED no. 2, 36th Congress, 1st session, serial 1023, 449. See also Williamson to Treat, 18 November 1859, ABCFM Papers; Brown to Cullen, 3 March and 15 April 1860, NARG 75, LR, St. Peter's Agency.

25 Williamson to Treat, 18 November 1859, ABCFM Papers.

26 Ibid.; Brown to Cullen, 2 August 1859, 3 and 6 February 1860 and 10 and 17 May 1860, and Brown to "Mazakutemoni," 10 May 1860, NARG 75, LR, St. Peter's Agency; Riggs to Treat, 24 August 1859, ABCFM Papers.

27 Williamson to Treat, 19 November 1860, and annual report, 2 January 1862, ABCFM Papers; Prescott, "Contributions to the History, Customs, and Opinions of the Dacota Tribe," in *Information Respecting the History, Condition, and Prospects of the Indian Tribes*, ed. Schoolcraft, 2:189.

28 "Reminiscences of Thomas A. Robertson," a typed manuscript in the Minnesota Historical Society; Brown to Cullen, 25 October 1860, SED no. 1, 36th Congress, 2d session, serial 1078, 278. In the Robertson manuscript there is a reference to a "Monkey Society," which apparently was a temporary organization formed in the 1850s.

29 Brown to Mix, 23 May 1858, Brown to Cullen, 18 December 1858, and Cullen to Mix, 1 July and 23 August 1858, NARG 75, LR, St. Peter's Agency; Abercrombie to Lieutenant George Ruggles, 18 and 24 June 1858, NARG 393, LR, Department of the West and Western Department, 1853–61; Brown to Cullen, 7 September 1858, NARG 75, LR, Northern Superintendency.

30 Cullen to A. B. Greenwood, 24 June 1859, NARG 75, LR, St. Peter's Agency.

31 Cullen to Greenwood, 15 August 1859, ibid.

32 Brown to Cullen, 3 February 1860, ibid.

33 Returns of the Yellow Medicine Command, 19 April 1860, Cullen to Major W. W. Morris, 15 June 1860, Brown to Captain G. A. DeRussy, 10 August 1860, and DeRussy to the Assistant Adjutant General, 2 September 1860, NARG 393, LR, Department of the West and Western Department, 1853–61; unsigned [DeRussy] to Lieutenant J. J. Dana, 5 July 1860, NARG 393, LR, Fort Ridgely, 1853–68; Brown to Cullen, 17 May 1860, NARG 75, LR, St. Peter's Agency.

34 Quotation in Greenwood to the Secretary of War, 30 November 1860, SED no. 1, 36th Congress, 2d session, serial 1078, 237. See also Brown to Cullen, 25 October 1860, ibid.; Brown to Cullen, 7 July 1860, NARG 75, LR, St. Peter's Agency.

35 Alexander Berghold, *The Indians' Revenge; or, Days of Horror. Some Appalling Events in the History of the Sioux* (San Francisco: P. J. Thomas, 1891), 26–36. The army's investigation of the incident showed that several German settlers were so intimidated by the "insolence of the Indians" that they decided to leave. See Captain T. Steele to Major H. Day, 8 August 1855, NARG 393, LR, Fort Ridgely 1853–68.

36 Quotation in Francis Bansen to the Secretary of Interior, 2 February 1859, NARG 75, LR, St. Peter's Agency. The boundary issue is further discussed in Huebschmann to Manypenny, 11 February 1857, C. L. Emerson to Thomas A. Hendricks, 8 February 1859, and L. A. Smith to Greenwood, 15 December 1859, ibid.

37 Brown to Cullen, 5 December 1858, Thomas Martin petitions, 28 December 1858 and 25 February 1859, NARG 75, LR, St. Peter's Agency.

38 Abercrombie to Assistant Adjutant General, 20 February 1859, NARG 393, LR, Department of the West and Western Department, 1853–61.

39 Mix to Jacob Thompson, 23 April 1859, Assistant Adjutant General E. D. Townsend to Colonel E. V. Sumner, 19 July 1859, Morris to Assistant Adjutant General, 7 March 1860, and Brown to Morris, 27 February 1860, NARG 393, LR, Department of the West and Western Department, 1853–61; Cullen to Greenwood, 7 June 1859, Rice to Thompson, 15 June 1859, and Thompson to Greenwood, 5 July 1859, NARG 75, LR, St. Peter's Agency; Williamson to Treat, 30 April 1860, ABCFM Papers.

40 George C. Allanson, "Stirring Adventures of the Joseph R. Brown Family," 19 August 1862 (no page), in *The Garland Library of Narratives of North American Indian Captivities*, ed. Wilcomb E. Washburn (New York: Garland Publishing, 1976), 103 (hereafter *Garland Library*).

41 Helen M. Tarble, "The Story of My Capture and Escape during the Minnesota Indian Massacre of 1862, with Historical Notes, Descriptions of Pioneer Life, and Sketches and Incidents of the Great Outbreak of the Sioux or Dakota Indians as I Saw Them," *Garland Library*, 105 (1976):19–23. See also Wilhelmina B. Carrigan, *Captured by the Indians: Reminiscences of Pioneer Life in Minnesota* (Forest City, S.D.: Forest City Press, 1907), 7; J. E. DeCamp Sweet, "Mrs. J. E. DeCamp Sweet's Narrative of Her Captivity in the Sioux Outbreak of 1862," *Minnesota Collections*, 6 (1894):355; N. D. White, "Captivity among the Sioux, August 18 to September 26, 1862," *Garland Library*, 104 (1976):396. Some captives later claimed they had always treated the Sioux well, but the comments of Mrs. Sweet, who lived on the Sioux reservation, seems closer to the truth: "They [the Dakota people] were daily visitors to our home—not always welcome ones, it is true" (p. 355).

42 Jonas Pettijohn to commanding officer, 30 December 1859, NARG 393, LR, Fort Ridgely, 1853–68; Jonas Pettijohn, *Autobiography, Family History and Various Reminiscences of the Life of Jonas Pettijohn among the Sioux or Dakota Indians. His Escape during the Massacre of August, 1862. Causes That Led to the Massacre* (Clay City, Kans.: *Dispatch* Printing House, 1890), 82–83.

43 Allanson, "Stirring Adventures of the Joseph R. Brown Family," *Garland Library*, 103, no page. See also treaty transcripts, 21 June 1858, NARG 75, DRNRUT.

44 Changes in personnel and traders on the reservations were closely tied to the political changes in the state and nation. When a new administration came to power, as it did in 1860, it often tried to assist traders who had been supportive during the recent campaign. For evidence of the infighting, consult Clark W. Thompson's Papers, Minnesota Historical Society.

45 See the Louis Roberts Papers, Minnesota Historical Society.

46 Sarah F. Wakefield, *Six Weeks in Little Crow's Camp: A Narrative of Indian Captivity* (Shakopee, Minn.: Argus Book and Job Printing Office, 1864), 7.

47 Cullen to Greenwood, 1 February 1860, memorial of upper Sioux, 31 July 1861, and J. W. Ray statement, August (n.d.) 1861, NARG 75, LR, St. Peter's Agency.

48 Riggs to Treat, 28 July 1860 and 22 February 1861, ABCFM Papers; Timothy J. Sheehan diary, 13 and 22 July 1862, Sheehan Papers, Minnesota Historical Society.

49 Return I. Holcombe, "Chief Big Eagle's Story of the Sioux Outbreak of 1862," *Minnesota Collections*, 6 (1894):385; treaty transcripts, 28 June 1858, NARG 75, DRNRUT.

50 Quotation in Isaac V. D. Heard, *History of the Sioux War and Massacres of 1862 and 1863* (New York: Harper, 1865), 48. See also Brown to Cullen, 10 September 1859, SED no. 2, 36th Congress, 1st session, serial 1023, 453–54; Brown to Cullen, 3 March 1860, and Galbraith to Thompson, 3 July 1861, NARG 75, LR, St. Peter's Agency. Berghold also mentions the anger of Indian men over the need for their women to prostitute themselves to acquire credit. "The Indians, compelled to ask for credit on account of their extreme need, would answer the traders: 'If we could, like our women, give ourselves up to you, we could get all the credit we ask for; but, since we are men, we cannot'"; Berghold, *Indians' Revenge*, 77.

51 Quotation in Galbraith to Thompson, 3 July 1861, NARG 75, LR, St. Peter's Agency. See also council with the Sissetons, 27 September 1857, SD no. 11, 35th Congress, 1st session, serial 919, 402–3.

52 Brown to Major W. W. Morris, 27 February 1860, and Morris to Assistant Adjutant General, 7 March 1860, NARG 393, LR, Department of the West and Western Department, 1853–61; Henry Belland to William H. Forbes, 28 July 1860, Corey-Forbes Papers, Minnesota Historical Society.

53 Brown to Mix, 23 September 1861, Galbraith to Thompson, 23 October 1861, NARG 75, LR, St. Peter's Agency; Thompson to William P. Dole, 30 October 1861, SED no. 1, 36th Congress, 1st session, serial 1117, 680. Galbraith to Thompson, 27 January 1863, HED no. 1, 38th Congress, 1st session, serial 1182, 383; G. A. Goodell to Thompson, 31 January 1862, and Galbraith to Thompson, 31 January 1862, Thompson Papers; *Henderson Democrat* 16 March 1862.

54 Quotation in Galbraith to Thompson, October 1861, SED no. 1, 37th Congress, 1st session, serial 1117, 704; Galbraith to Thompson, 27 January 1863, HED no. 1, 38th Congress, 1st session, serial 1182, 388, 398.

55 John P. Williamson to Treat, 16 March 1861, and Riggs to Treat, 14 August 1861, ABCFM Papers; S. D. Hinman to Henry Benjamin Whipple, 31 October 1861, Whipple Papers, Minnesota Historical Society; Henry Benjamin Whipple, *Lights and Shadows of a Long Episcopate, Being Reminiscences and Recollections of the Right Reverend Henry Benjamin Whipple, D.D., L.L.D., Bishop of Minnesota* (New York and London: Macmillan, 1912), 61–62.

56 Quotation in Galbraith to Thompson, 27 January 1863, HED no. 1, 38th Congress, 1st session, serial 1182, 398. See also Wakefield, *Six Weeks in Little Crow's Camp*, 6–7.

57 Cyrus Aldrich to W. P. Dole, 16 July 1861, NARG 75, LR, St. Peter's Agency.

58 Quotations in Galbraith to Thompson, 27 August 1861, ibid. Galbraith believed that the soldiers' lodge had formed a "league" with other discontented groups, including some of Inkpaduta's people. See also Galbraith to Thompson, 24 and 30 July 1861, ibid.; Dakota mission annual report, 2 January 1862, ABCFM Papers; Berghold, *Indians' Revenge*, 77; Assistant Adjutant General to Brigadier General W. S. Harney, 5 April 1861, NARG 393, LR, Department of the West and Western Department; A. Jeremiah Chester memoir, 21 November 1905, Minnesota Historical Society.

59 Galbraith to Thompson, 5 September 1861, NARG 75, LR, St. Peter's Agency; Galbraith to Lieutenant Colonel James George, 5 September 1861, and Galbraith to Captain A. K. Skarr, 14 September 1861, NARG 393, LR, Fort Ridgely, 1853–68.

60 Pierson to Thompson, 30 January, 1 and 7 February, and 24 April 1862, and Galbraith to Thompson, 28 February 1862, Thompson Papers; Jonas Pettijohn to Riggs, 6, 12, and 17 March 1862, Amos Huggins to Riggs, 10 and 13 March 1862, and Galbraith to Riggs, 30 April 1862, Riggs Papers.

61 Galbraith to Whipple, 31 May 1862, Aldrich to Whipple, 12 June 1862, and Hinman to Whipple, 19 June 1862, Whipple Papers.

62 Galbraith to Thompson, 27 January 1863, HED no. 1, 38th Congress, 1st session, serial 1182, 388–89; Mrs. N. D. White, "Captivity among the Sioux, August 18 to September 26, 1862," *Minnesota Collections*, 9 (1898–1900):396; Galbraith to Thompson, 19 July 1862, Thompson Papers; Benjamin Armstrong, *Early Life among the Indians. Reminiscences from the Life of Benj. G. Armstrong. Treaties of 1835, 1837, 1842, and 1854. Habits and Customs of the Red Men of the Forest. Indians, Biographical Sketches, Battles, Etc. Dictated to and Written by Thos. P. Wentworth* (Ashland, Wisc.: Press of A. W. Brown, 1892), 75–76.

63 Sheehan diary, 2–9 July 1862, Sheehan Papers. See also Sheehan deposition, 11 September 1901, "Evidence for Defendant," 270–83, *The Sisseton and Wahpeton Bands of Sioux Indians vs. the United States*, Court of Claims, docket no. 22,524.

64 Sheehan diary, 14 July 1862; Galbraith to Thompson, 27 January 1863, HED no. 1, 38th Congress, 1st session, serial 1182, 389.

65 Galbraith to Thompson, 19 July 1862, Thompson Papers.

66 Sheehan diary, 4 August 1862, Sheehan Papers; Galbraith to Thompson, 27 January 1863, HED no. 1, 38th Congress, 1st session, serial 1182, 389.

67 Galbraith later claimed that he immediately consented to hand out food and goods, but Sheehan's diary suggests that he was trying to withhold what annuities he had until the money arrived. Hungry Indians were more likely to agree to pay their debts to traders. See Galbraith to Thompson, 27 January 1863, HED no. 1, 38th Congress, 1st session, serial 1182, 389; Sheehan diary, 4–9 August 1862, Sheehan Papers.

68 Winifred W. Barton, *John P. Williamson: A Brother to the Sioux* (New York and

Chicago: Fleming H. Revell, 1919), 49. Barton supposedly heard the details of the council from her father, John P. Williamson. Unfortunately, she failed to identify the agency where the council took place or the date when it occurred.

69 Consult Gary Clayton Anderson, "Myrick's Insult: A Fresh Look at Myth or Reality," *Minnesota History* 48, no. 5 (Spring 1983):198–206. Folwell showed decided misgivings regarding the Barton account in his private papers. But he gives the exchange complete coverage in his study of the outbreak, hedging only on the date assigned for the council. Other scholars have failed to notice the uncertainty of the date assigned by Folwell and have exaggerated the impact of the council. See Folwell's memorandum, 28 March 1919, Folwell to A. W. Daniels, 20 February 1919, Folwell to Barton, 20 September 1920 and 29 September 1922, Folwell to Thomas Robertson, 4 August 1922, and Folwell to George G. Allanson, 12 December 1922, Folwell Papers; Priscilla Ann Russo, "The Time to Speak Is Over: The Onset of the Sioux Uprising," *Minnesota History* 45 (Fall 1976): 97–106; Theodore C. Blegen, *Minnesota: A History of the State* (Minneapolis: University of Minnesota Press, 1963), 266–67; Ralph K. Andrist, *The Long Death: The Last Days of the Plains Indians* (New York: Collier Books, 1964), 31; Meyer, *History of the Santee Sioux*, 114, 117; Dee Brown, *Bury My Heart at Wounded Knee: An Indian History of the American West* (New York: Bantam Books, 1970), 40.

70 John Williamson to Treat, 25 August 1862, ABCFM Papers; Barton, *John P. Williamson*, 49–50; Galbraith to Thompson, 27 January 1863, HED no. 1, 38th Congress, 1st session, serial 1182, 387–403.

71 Heard, *History of the Sioux War*, 49; Wakefield, *Six Weeks in Little Crow's Camp*, 9–10; Hubbard and Holcombe, *Minnesota in Three Centuries*, 3:285–86; *Executive Documents of the State of Minnesota for the Year 1862* (St. Paul: Wm. R. Marshall, 1863), 444.

72 Galbraith to Thompson, 27 January 1863, HED no. 1, 38th Congress, 1st session, serial 1182, 390–406; Sheehan diary, 9–18 August 1862, Sheehan Papers; Charles S. Bryant and Abel B. Murch, *A History of the Great Massacre by the Sioux Indians in Minnesota, Including the Personal Narratives of Many Who Escaped* (Cincinnati: Rickey and Carroll, 1864), 72.

73 Quotation in Galbraith to Thompson, 27 January 1863, HED no. 1, 38th Congress, 1st session, serial 1182, 387, 402.

74 Heard, *History of the Sioux War*, 48; Berghold, *Indians' Revenge*, 77; Galbraith to Thompson, 27 January 1863, HED no. 1, 38th Congress, 1st session, serial 1182, 403. Wabasha later testified that mixed-bloods were excluded from the lodge, since they were perceived as being in league with whites. See Wabasha's testimony in *Papers Relating to Talks and Councils Held with the Indians in Dakota and Montana Territories in the Years 1866–1869* (Washington, D.C.; Government Printing Office, 1910), 91.

75 Carrigan, *Captured by Indians*, 7.

76 Holcombe, "Chief Big Eagle's Story of the Sioux Outbreak of 1862," *Minnesota Collections*, 6 (1894):387. Apparently those leaders opposed to a war were able to stop a clash on several occasions by arguing that the crops were looking so good that starvation would be averted.

77 Ibid., 389; Folwell, *History of Minnesota*, appendix 2, 2:415–17; Holcombe to Marion P. Satterlee, April (n.d.) 1915, and Satterlee to Thomas A. Robertson, 26 March 1923, Satterlee Papers.

78 Holcombe, "Chief Big Eagle's Story of the Sioux Outbreak of 1862," *Minnesota Collections*, 6 (1894):388–90.

79 "Taoyateduta Is Not a Coward," *Minnesota History* 38 (September 1962):115; Kenneth Carley, ed., "As Red Men Viewed It: Three Indian Accounts of the Uprising," *Minnesota History* 38 (September 1962):147; Hubbard and Holcombe, *Minnesota in Three Centuries*, 3:285.

80 Galbraith to Thompson, 27 January 1863, HED no. 1, 38th Congress, 1st session, serial 1182, 406; *Sketches Historical and Descriptive*, 17.

81 Folwell, *History of Minnesota*, 2:212–41; Marion P. Satterlee, *A Detailed Account of the Massacre by the Dakota Indians of Minnesota in 1862* (Minneapolis: Marion P. Satterlee, 1923), 4; Riggs to Treat, 15 September 1862, ABCFM Papers.

82 See the list of participants in the 1858 negotiation, treaty transcripts, 1858 treaty, NARG 75, DRNRUT.

83 Holcombe, "Chief Big Eagle's Story of the Sioux Outbreak of 1862," *Minnesota Collections*, 6 (1894):384–85.

84 Cullen to Greenwood, 29 September 1860, SED no. 1, 36th Congress, 2d session, serial 1078, 270.

85 Holcombe, "Chief Big Eagle's Story of the Sioux Outbreak of 1862," *Minnesota Collections*, 6 (1894):388.

86 Ibid., 389.

87 Ibid., 385.

88 Ibid.

89 Ibid.

90 Allanson, "Stirring Adventures of the Joseph R. Brown Family," in *Garland Library*, 103, 19 August 1862.

CHAPTER 12

1 For further reading on the Sioux Uprising, consult the following: Marion P. Satterlee, *Detailed Account*; Robert Huhn Jones, *The Civil War in the Northwest: Nebraska, Wisconsin, Iowa, Minnesota, and the Dakotas* (Norman: University of Oklahoma Press, 1960); Isaac V. D. Heard, *History of the Sioux War and Massacre*; Folwell, *History of Minnesota*, 2:109–301; Board of Commissioners, *Minnesota in*

the Civil and Indian Wars, 1861–1865, 2 vols., (St. Paul: Pioneer Press, 1893), vol. 2, *Official Reports and Correspondence*; Charles M. Oehler, *The Great Sioux Uprising* (New York: Oxford University Press, 1959); Kenneth Carley, *The Sioux Uprising of 1862* (St. Paul: Minnesota Historical Society, 1961).

2 See the report of John F. Bishop in *Minnesota in the Civil and Indian Wars*, 2:166– 70; Report of Lieutenant Governor Ignatius Donnelly, HED no. 1, 37th Congress, 3d Session, serial 1157, 205; *Sketches Historical and Descriptive*, 21–22.

3 Satterlee, *Detailed Account*, 23–26, 39–47.

4 "Extract from the Narrative of the Fifth Regiment, by Gen. L. F. Hubbard," in *Minnesota in the Civil and Indian Wars*, 2:182–86; Flandrau to Ramsey, 27 August 1862, ibid., 203–7; Holcombe, "Chief Big Eagle's Story of the Sioux Outbreak of 1862," *Minnesota Collections*, 6 (1894):391–92; Carley, ed., "As Red Men Viewed It," *Minnesota Collections*, 38 (September 1962):144–45; Sibley to his wife, 28 August 1862, Sibley Papers; Flandrau, *History of Minnesota*, 158–59.

5 Jones, *Civil War in the Northwest*, 39. In a speech recorded by A. J. Campbell, just after the carnage at the lower agency, Little Crow strongly urged warriors to refrain from killing civilians and concentrate on military targets. See *Sketches Historical and Descriptive*, 18; Oscar Garrett Wall, *Recollections of the Sioux Massacre: An Authentic History of the Yellow Medicine Incident, of the Fate of Marsh and His Men, of the Siege and Battles of Fort Ridgely, and of Other Important Battles and Experiences, Together with a Historical Sketch of the Sibley Expedition of 1863* (Lake City, Minn.: Home Printery, 1908), 77.

6 Big Eagle, or Wamditanka, states that he joined the men headed toward the lower agency on the morning of 18 August in order to "save the lives of two particular [white] friends, if I could. I think others went for the same reason, for nearly every Indian had a friend that he did not want killed." Holcombe, "Chief Big Eagle's Story of the Sioux Outbreak of 1862," *Minnesota Collections*, 6 (1894):390. See also Daniels, "Reminiscences of Little Crow," *Minnesota Collections*, 12 (1905– 8):526–27; Harriet E. Bishop, *Dakota War Whoop; or, Indian Massacres and War in Minnesota, of 1862–'3* (Minneapolis: Ross and Haines, reprint, 1970), 33–37; Bryant, *History of the Great Massacre*, 94.

7 Helen M. Tarble, "The Story of My Capture and Escape," in *Garland Library*, 105:25– 30; White, "Captivity among the Sioux," in *Garland Library*, 104:399–404; Satterlee, *Detailed Account*, 23–26.

8 Tarble, "The Story of My Capture and Escape," in *Garland Library*, 105:28.

9 Wakefield, *Six Weeks in Little Crow's Camp*, 14.

10 Heard argues that many whites at the lower agency escaped because the Sioux were initially more interested in stealing goods from the traders' houses. Yet after the traders had been killed the goods could have been taken at any time. It seems obvious that Dakota warriors had no intention of killing whites indiscrim-

inately. Heard, *History of the Sioux War*, 65–66; Satterlee, *Detailed Account*, 15–17; *Sketches Historical and Descriptive*, 64–66.

11 See Satterlee's compilation of the victims of the war, both white and Indian, in the Satterlee Papers, Minnesota Historical Society.

12 Nancy Huggins McClure to W. R. Marshall, May (n.d.) 1894, Huggins Papers, Minnesota Historical Society.

13 *Sketches Historical and Descriptive*, 67–68; Satterlee, *Detailed Account*, 48–61.

14 Riggs, *Mary and I*, 154–63; Riggs to Treat, 24 August 1862, ABCFM Papers.

15 Quotation in Allanson, "Stirring Adventures of the Joseph R. Brown Family," in *Garland Library*, 103:n.p.

16 Quotation in Samuel J. Brown, "In Captivity: The Experiences, Privations and Dangers of Sam'l J. Brown, and Others, While Prisoners of the Hostile Sioux, during the Massacre and War of 1862," in *Garland Library*, 76:n.p. The literal translation of the Dakota phrase used to describe the "Dutch" is "speakers with evil hearts," or "guttural speakers."

17 John Ames Humphrey, "Boyhood Reminiscences of Life among the Dakotas and the Massacre in 1862," *Minnesota Collections*, 15 (1909–14):339–45.

18 Satterlee, *Detailed Account*, 39–47.

19 For an example consult Blegen and Davidson, ed., *Iron Face*, 7.

20 Statements regarding Daniels's testimony are found in the Daniels Papers, in the possession of Karen Petersen, St. Paul. For other evidence see Allanson, "Stirring Adventures of the Joseph R. Brown Family," in *Garland Library*, 103:n.p.; Brown, "In Captivity," in *Garland Library*, 76:n.p.; Tarble, "The Story of My Capture and Escape," in *Garland Library*, 105:38; Sweet, "Mrs. J. E. DeCamp Sweet's Narrative," *Minnesota Collections*, 6 (1894):365; Aaron Meyers to Neil Currie, August (n.d.) 1862, Currie Papers, Minnesota Historial Society. The most gruesome account of atrocities is found in George W. Doud's diary, Minnesota Historical Society. Although Doud had no reason to embellish the firsthand accounts he acquired, they undoubtedly are filled with fabrication.

21 "Narrative of Justina Keiger," in Bryant, *History of the Great Massacre*, 315.

22 Sibley to General John Pope, 27 September 1862, NARG 393, LS, Sibley's Indian Campaign; Sibley to his wife, 27 September 1862 and 1 October 1862, Sibley Papers; Riggs to Martha Riggs, 27 September 1862, Riggs Papers.

23 Trial transcripts of the Sibley military commission, 24 September to 3 November 1862, Senate Records, National Archives. See case no. 2, "Te-he-hdo-ne-cha," and case no. 4, "Tazoo"; "Incidents of the Indian Massacre as Told by Mrs. Kock" (n.d.), Currie Papers. Wakefield believed that only two women were "abused." Wakefield, *Six Weeks in Little Crow's Camp*, 55.

24 Mary Schwandt left no fewer than three drafts of her later-published captivity narrative, all found in the Schwandt Papers, Minnesota Historical Society. See

346

also Schwandt, "The Story of Mary Schwandt: Her Captivity during the Sioux Outbreak," in *Garland Library*, 99:461–70; "Narrative of a Friendly Sioux, by Snana, the Rescuer of Mary Schwandt," *Minnesota Collections*, 9 (1898–1900):429–30; Sibley to his wife, 28 September 1862, Sibley Papers; Wakefield, *Six Weeks in Little Crow's Camp*, 13–37, 50–55; Dorothy Kuske Reminiscences (n.d.), Minnesota Historical Society.

25 White, "Captivity among the Sioux," *Minnesota Collections*, 9 (1898–1900):405.

26 Ibid., 406–7; Wakefield, *Six Weeks in Little Crow's Camp*, 32–33; Alex Seifert reminiscences, 12 August 1894, Minnesota Historical Society; Tarble, "The Story of My Capture and Escape," in *Garland Library*, 105:33.

27 Wakefield, *Six Weeks in Little Crow's Camp*, 32–33; Sweet, "Mrs. J. E. DeCamp Sweet's Narrative," *Minnesota Collections*, 6 (1894):365–70.

28 Hubbard and Holcombe, *Minnesota in Three Centuries*, 3:343–51; *Sketches Historical and Descriptive*, 29–40.

29 Sibley wrote to his wife the day after the battle that the Sioux "fight like devils; no one has seen anything like it." Sibley to his wife, 4 September 1862, Sibley Papers. See also Robert Knowles Boyd, "How the Indians Fought: A New Era in Skirmish Fighting, by a Survivor of the Battle of Birch Coulee," *Minnesota History* 11 (September 1930):299–304.

30 Alexander Ramsey to Sibley, 4 September 1862, NARG 393, "Two or More Name File," Department of the Northwest, 1862–65; Sibley to the Adjutant General, 7 September 1862, Sibley Papers.

31 There is no history of the Sioux scouts, but more than one hundred were in the employ of the army by 1863. See the J. R. Brown Papers for information on them.

32 Brown, "In Captivity," in *Garland Library*, 76:n.p.; Gabriel Renville, "A Sioux Narrative of the Outbreak in 1862, and of Sibley's Expedition in 1863," *Minnesota Collections*, 10, part 2 (1905):599–603.

33 "Declaration of Paul Mazakootemani," 3 May 1869, ABCFM Papers. Another account of this council, though of questionable authenticity, is in Heard, *History of the Sioux War*, 151. See also Wakefield, *Six Weeks in Little Crow's Camp*, 28; Mary Butler Renville, *A Thrilling Narrative of Indian Captivity* (Minneapolis: Atlas Company Book and Job Printing Office, 1863), 24.

34 Hubbard and Holcombe, *Minnesota in Three Centuries*, 3:396–97; Renville, "A Sioux Narrative of the Outbreak in 1862," *Minnesota Collections*, 10, part 2 (1905):604; "Reminiscences of Thomas A. Robertson," typed manuscript, Minnesota Historical Society; Sibley to General Oscar Malmros, 8 September 1862, Sibley Papers.

35 Ibid.

36 Quotation in Brown, "In Captivity," in *Garland Library*, 76:n.p.; Heard, *History of the Sioux War*, 154–60.

37 "Fort Abercrombie 1862," from *Richland County Farmer Globe* 22 September 1936, Newberry Library; Lyman Goff, *An 1862 Trip to the West* (Pawtucket, R.I.: Paw-

tucket Boy's Club, 1926), 114–27; Hubbard and Holcombe, *Minnesota in Three Centuries*, 3:385–88.

38 Little Crow (by a mixed-blood) to Sibley, 12 September 1862, NARG 393, LR, Sibley's Indian Expedition.

39 Sibley to Malmros, 13 September 1862, and Sibley to Wabasha, Taopi, and others, 13 September 1862, NARG 393, LS, Sibley's Indian Expedition; Statement of "Good Thunder and Wahacankamaza" (n.d.), Whipple Papers.

40 Renville, "Sioux Narrative of the Outbreak in 1862," *Minnesota Collections*, 10, part 2 (1905):606–7; Brown, "In Captivity," in *Garland Library*, 76:n.p.; Wakefield, *Six Weeks in Little Crow's Camp*, 45; Pope to Sibley, 16, 17, and 19 September 1862, NARG 393, LS, Northwestern Department.

41 Hubbard and Holcombe, *Minnesota in Three Centuries*, 3:401–9; recollections of Brevet Captain Ezra T. Champlin, *Minnesota in the Civil and Indian Wars*, 2:244–47; Brown, "In Captivity," in *Garland Library*, 76:n.p.; "Reminiscences of Thomas A. Robertson," Minnesota Historical Society; Sibley to Ramsey, 3 September 1862, NARG 393, LS, Sibley's Indian Expedition.

42 Sibley to Ramsey, 3 September 1862, NARG 393, LS, Sibley's Indian Expedition; Brown, "In Captivity," in *Garland Library*, 76:n.p.; *Sketches Historical and Descriptive*, 19; "Reminiscences of Thomas A. Robertson," Minnesota Historical Society.

43 Celia M. Campbell, "Reminiscences," Celia Stay Papers, Minnesota Historical Society. Celia Stay was A. J. Campbell's daughter.

44 Brown, "In Captivity," in *Garland Library*, 76:n.p.; Sibley to his wife, 1 October 1862, Sibley Papers; White, "Captivity among the Sioux," in *Garland Library*, 104:422.

45 Brown, "In Captivity," in *Garland Library*; 76:n.p.

46 Holcombe, "Chief Big Eagle's Story of the Sioux Outbreak of 1862," *Minnesota Collections*, 6 (1894):397; Sibley to "Ya-tan-ka-nazin and Yah-tanka-wakinyan," 24 September 1862, NARG 393, LS, Sibley's Indian Expedition; "order no. 54," 24 September 1862, and Sibley to Flandrau, 28 September 1862, Sibley Papers.

47 Quotation in Sibley to Pope, 7 October 1862, NARG 393, LS, Sibley's Indian Expedition. See also Sibley to Pope, 3, 5, 10, 11, 13, 15, and 17 October 1862, ibid.; Riggs to Treat, 11 October 1862, ABCFM Papers; John Kinsley Wood diary, 9–28 October 1862, Minnesota Historical Society.

48 Sibley to his wife, 22, 25, and 30 October and 3 and 12 November 1862, Sibley Papers; trial transcripts, Senate Records; Riggs, *Tah-koo Wah-kan*, 333–34; Williamson to Treat, 1 December 1862, ABCFM Papers; Colonel Stephen Miller to R. C. Olin, 9 December 1862, NARG 393, "Two or More Name File," Department of the Northwest.

49 Brown, "In Captivity," in *Garland Library*, 76:n.p.; John Williamson to Treat, 28 November 1862, ABCFM Papers; Meyer, *History of the Santee Sioux*, 146–47.

50 Riggs to Treat, 24 November 1862, ABCFM Papers; Sibley to Whipple, 7 December 1862, Whipple Papers.

51 Whipple, *Lights and Shadows of a Long Episcopate*, 133–41; Riggs to Lincoln, 17 November 1862, Riggs Papers; Whipple to Sibley, 4 December 1862, and Lincoln to Sibley, 6 December 1862, Sibley Papers; Sibley to Whipple, 7 December 1862, Whipple Papers; J. P. Usher to Sibley, 10 December 1862, NARG 48, LS, Indian Division of Interior Department; M. S. Wilkinson, Cyrus Aldrich, and William Windom to Lincoln, 11 December 1862, SED no. 7, 37th Congress, 3d Session, serial 1149; Lincoln's message, 11 December 1862, ibid.

52 The condemned men did implicate twenty-two of their fellow tribesmen just before their execution, charging generally that they had killed whites. No action was taken against them despite this belated testimony. See Eli Picket to his wife, 26 December 1862, Picket Papers, Minnesota Historical Society; miscellaneous correspondence, 1862, NARG 393, "Two or More Names File."

53 For the events at Davenport, see the Williamson and Riggs papers; Riggs, *Mary and I*, 194.

54 Canadian policy toward the Sioux refugees is treated in Alvin C. Gluek, Jr., "The Sioux Uprising: A Problem in International Relations," *Minnesota History* 34 (Winter 1955):317–24; Roy W. Meyer, "The Canadian Sioux: Refugees from Minnesota, *Minnesota History* 41 (Spring 1968):13–28; Edmund Jefferson Danziger, Jr., "The Crow Creek Experiment: An Aftermath of the Sioux War of 1862," *North Dakota History* 37 (Spring 1970):104–23.

Bibliography

MANUSCRIPTS

Archives du Séminaire de Québec, Quebec, Canada
"Relation des aventures de Mr. de Boucherville à son Retour des Sioux en 1728 et 1729, Suivie d'Obervations [d'Observations] (par l'auteur) sur les moeurs, coutumes, & en de ces Sauvages, Accompagnée de Notes et Suivie d'un Appendice, par J. Viger."
Archives Nationales, Paris, France
"Mémoires de Mr le Sueur" (microfilm)
Bancroft Library, Berkeley, California
Andrew Drips Papers
Beinecke Rare Book and Manuscript Library, Yale University, New Haven, Connecticut
Benjamin O'Fallon Letter of 29 November 1817
Bentley Library, Ann Arbor, Michigan
Chauncey Bush Journal, 1837 (microfilm)
Columbia University Library, New York City, New York
Edwin James Diary and Journal (microfilm)
Detroit Public Library, Burton Collection, Detroit, Michigan
American Fur Company Papers
Ramsay Crooks Papers (microfilm)
Charles Christopher Trowbridge Journal
George Johnston Papers
Solomon Sibley Papers
Henry E. Huntington Library and Art Gallery, San Marino, California
"Journal de Monsieur Marin Fils Commandant pour le Roy à LaBaye des puans et dépendances chargé de faire et de faire faire les Découvertes dans le haut de mississipi [Mississippi], des mines, minière, et minéraux qui pourroient si trou-

ver et dy Lier [se lier?] aussi Commerce avec les nations qui pourroient habitter ces contrés [contrées]" (microfilm)

Kansas State Historical Society, Topeka, Kansas

William Clark Papers (microfilm)

Library of Congress, Washington, D.C.

James Monroe Papers (microfilm)

Minnesota Historical Society, St. Paul, Minnesota

Moses N. Adams Papers

John Felix Aiton Papers

American Board of Commissioners for Foreign Missions Papers (transcripts)

American Fur Company Papers (photostats and microfilm)

Alexis Bailly Papers

George Biscoe Papers

Blackwood Letterbook (photostat)

Joseph R. and Samuel J. Brown Papers

Scott Campbell Papers

A. Jeremiah Chester Memoir

Pierre Chouteau Papers (microfilm)

Miss Phoebe Frances Cory and Mrs. William H. Forbes Papers (Cory-Forbes Papers)

Neil Currie Papers

Robert Dickson Papers (photostats)

George W. Doud Diary

William G. and George W. Ewing Papers (microfilm)

Charles E. Flandrau Papers

William Watts Folwell Papers

Peter Garrioch Diary

Willis Gorman Papers

James Hart Papers

Edwin A. C. Hatch Papers

Alexander G. Huggins Papers

Nancy Huggins (McClure) Papers

Dorothy Duske Reminiscences

Frederick P. Leavenworth Papers

John Marsh Papers

Martin McLeod Papers

Thomas Montgomery Papers

Grace Lee Nute Papers

Eli Pickett Papers

Gideon H. and Samuel W. Pond Papers

Louis Provençalle Papers

Alexander Ramsey Papers (microfilm)

Stephen Return Riggs Papers

Louis Roberts Papers

Thomas A. Robertson Reminiscences

Marion P. Satterlee Papers

Mary Schwandt (Schmidt) Papers

Alex Seifert Reminiscences

Timothy Sheehan Papers

Henry Hastings Sibley Papers (microfilm)

Josiah Snelling Diary

Mrs. Frank Stay Papers

Wayne Edson Stevens Papers

Lawrence Taliaferro Journals and Papers

Clark Thompson Papers

Martin Weld Papers

Henry Benjamin Whipple Papers

Thomas S. Williamson Papers (microfilm)

John Kinsley Wood Diary

National Archives, Washington D.C., Documents on Microfilm

Record Group 48, Letters Sent, Indian Division of the Interior Department

Record Group 75, Documents Relating to the Negotiation of Ratified and Unratified Treaties with Various Tribes of Indians

Record Group 75, Special Files of the Bureau of Indian Affairs

Record Group 75, Letters Sent, Office of Indian Affairs

Record Group 75, Letters Received and Sent, St. Louis Superintendency

Record Group 75, Letters Received and Sent, Wisconsin Superintendency

Record Group 75, Letters Received and Sent, Iowa Superintendency

Record Group 75, Letters Received and Sent, Minnesota Superintendency

Record Group 75, Letters Received and Sent, Northern Superintendency

Record Group 75, Letters Received, Superintendent of Indian Trade

Record Group 75, Letters Received, St. Peter's Agency

Record Group 75, Letters Received, Upper Missouri Agency

Record Group 75, Letters Received, Prairie du Chien Agency

Record Group 94, Letters Received and Sent, Adjutant General's Office

Record Group 107, Letters Received, Secretary of War, Main Series

Record Group 107, Letters Received and Sent by the Secretary of War Relating to Indian Affairs

Record Group 107, Letters Received, Secretary of War, Unregistered

National Archives, Washington, D.C., Original Documents

Senate Records 37A–F2, Original Transcripts of the Records of Trials of Certain Sioux Indians Charged with Barbarities in the State of Minnesota

Record Group 75, Annuity Rolls for the Sioux

Record Group 75, Letters Received and Sent, Northern Superintendency

Record Group 393, Letters Received and Sent, Western Division and Department

Record Group 393, Letters Received and Sent, Jefferson Barracks

Record Group 393, Letters Received by Brigadier General Henry Atkinson

Record Group 393, Letters Received and Sent, Department of the West and Western Department

Record Group 393, Letters Received, Sent, Letterbooks, and Miscellaneous, Fort Ridgely

Record Group 393, Letters Received, Sent, and Letterbooks, Fort Abercrombie

Record Group 393, Letters Sent, Sibley's Indian Campaign

Record Group 393, Letters Received and Sent, Sibley Indian Expedition (Field Records)

Record Group 393, Letters Received and Sent, Department of the Northwest

Record Group 393, Department of the Northwest, "Two or More Names File"

Record Group 393, Letters Received, District of Minnesota

Newberry Library, Edward E. Ayer Manuscript Collection, Chicago, Illinois

   H. L. Dousman Papers

   Nathaniel Fish Moore Journal

   John Howard Payne Reminiscences

Public Records Office, London, England

   Board of Trade Papers (microfilm)

   Secretary of State Papers (microfilm)

Wisconsin Historical Society, Madison, Wisconsin

   H. L. Dousman Papers

   Thomas Forsyth Papers, Draper Collection (microfilm)

PUBLISHED PRIMARY SOURCES

Newspapers

Atlas (Boston), 1837

Daily Pioneer and Democrat (St. Paul), 1855–56

Dakota Tawaxitkakin or *Dakota Friend*, 1851

Henderson Democrat, 1856–61

Mankato Independent, 1857–63

Minnesota Pioneer (St Paul), 1849–55

National Intelligencer (Washington), 1837

Niles' Register (Washington); *Niles' Weekly Register* and *Niles' National Register* are cited as *Niles' Register*

Nor' Wester (Winnipeg)

Richland County Farmer–Globe (Wahpeton, North Dakota), Supplement of 22 September 1936

St. Paul Press, 1862

Government and Congressional Documents

American State Papers, Indian Affairs. 2 vols. Washington, D.C.: Gales and Seaton, 1832–34.

American State Papers, Military Affairs. 7 vols. Washington, D.C.: Gales and Seaton, 1832–61.

Carter, Clarence E., and John P. Bloom. *The Territorial Papers of the United States.* 28 vols. Washington, D.C.: Government Printing Office, 1934–.

Kappler, Charles J., comp. and ed. *Indian Affairs, Laws, and Treaties.* 2 vols. Washington, D.C.: Government Printing Office, 1904.

Minnesota in the Civil and Indian Wars, 1861–1865. 2 vols. Comp. and ed. Board of Commissioners for Minnesota. St. Paul: Pioneer Press, 1893.

Sisseton Claims Case, Bound Testimony, 1901. Minnesota Historical Society Library.

U.S. Congress. House and Senate Documents and Reports. Serial Set.

Books and Articles (Primary Sources)

Abel, Annie Heloise, ed. *Tabeau's Narrative of Loisel's Expedition to the Upper Missouri.* Norman: University of Oklahoma Press, 1939.

Adams, Arthur T., ed. *The Explorations of Pierre Esprit Radisson.* Minneapolis: Ross and Haines, 1961.

Allanson, George C. "Stirring Adventures of the Joseph R. Brown Family." In *The Garland Library of Narratives of North American Indian Captivities,* ed. Wilcomb E. Washburn, vol. 103. New York: Garland Publishing, 1976.

Armstrong, Benjamin G. *Early Life among the Indians. Reminiscences from the Life of Benj. G. Armstrong. Treaties of 1835, 1837, 1842, and 1854. Habits and Customs of the Red Men of the Forest. Indians, Biographical Sketches, Battles, Etc.* Dictated to and Written by Thos. P. Wentworth. Ashland, Wisc.: Press of A. W. Brown, 1892.

Babcock, Willoughby, M., ed. "Up the Minnesota Valley to Fort Ridgely in 1853." *Minnesota History* 11 (June 1930):161–84.

Bailey, Kenneth P., ed. and trans. *Journal of Joseph Marin, French Colonial Explorer and Military Commander in the Wisconsin Country, August 7, 1753–June 20, 1754.* Published by the author, 1975.

Beltrami, J. C. *A Pilgrimage in America.* Chicago: Quadrangle Books, 1962.

Berghold, Alexander. *The Indians' Revenge; or, Days of Horror. Some Appalling Events in the History of the Sioux.* San Francisco: P. J. Thomas, 1891.

Bishop, Harriet E. *Dakota War Whoop; or, Indian Massacres and War in Minnesota of 1862–3.* Minneapolis: Ross and Haines, reprint, 1970.

Blair, Emma Helen, ed. *The Indian Tribes of the Upper Mississippi Valley and the Region of the Great Lakes, as Described by Nicolas Perrot, French Commandant in the Northwest; Bacqueville de la Potherie, French Royal Commissioner to Canada, Morrell Marston, American Army Officer, and Thomas Forsyth, United States Agent at Fort Armstrong.* Cleveland: Arthur H. Clark, 1911.

Blegen, Theodore C., ed. "The Unfinished Autobiography of Henry Hastings Sibley." *Minnesota History* 8, no. 4 (December 1927):329–62.

Blegen, Theodore C., and Sarah A. Davidson, eds. *Iron Face: The Adventures of Jack Frazer, Frontier Warrior, Scout, and Hunter.* Chicago: Caxton Club, 1950.

Boyd, Robert Knowles. "How the Indians Fought: A New Era in Skirmish Fighting, by a Survivor of the Battle of Birch Coulee." *Minnesota History* 11 (September 1930):299–304.

———. *The Battle of Birch Coulee: A Wounded Man's Description of the Battle with the Indians.* Eau Claire, Wisc.: Herges Printing, 1925.

[Bracket, George A.]. *A Winter Evening's Tale.* New York: Printed by the author, 1880.

Bray, Edmund C., and Martha C. Bray, ed. *Joseph N. Nicollett on the Plains and Prairie: The Expeditions of 1838–39 with Journals, Letters and Notes on the Dakota Indians.* St. Paul: Minnesota Historical Society Press, 1976.

Brown Joseph Epes, ed. *The Sacred Pipe: Black Elk's Account of the Seven Rites of the Oglala Sioux.* Norman: University of Oklahoma Press, 1953.

Brown, Samuel J. "In Captivity: The Experiences, Privations and Dangers of Sam'l J. Brown, and Others, While Prisoners of the Hostile Sioux, during the Massacre and War of 1862." In *The Garland Library of Narratives of Indian Captivities*, ed. Wilcomb E. Washburn, vol. 67. New York: Garland Publishing, 1977.

Bryant, Charles S., and Abel B. Murch. *A History of the Great Massacre by the Sioux Indians, in Minnesota, Including the Personal Narratives of Many Who Escaped.* Cincinnati: Rickey and Carroll, 1864.

Buck, Daniel. *Indian Outbreaks.* Minneapolis: Ross and Haines, 1965.

Burpee, Lawrence J., ed. *Journals and Letters of Pierre Gaultier de Varennes de la Vérendrye and His Sons, with Correspondence between the Governors of Canada and the French Court, Touching the Search for the Western Sea.* Toronto: Champlain Society, 1927.

Carley, Kenneth, ed. "As Red Men Viewed It: Three Indian Accounts of the Uprising." *Minnesota History* 38 (September 1962):126–49.

Carrigan, Wilhelmina B. *Captured by the Indians: Reminiscences of Pioneer Life in Minnesota.* Forest City, S.D.: Forest City Press, 1907.

Carter, Clarence E., ed. *The Correspondence of General Thomas Gage with the Secretaries of State, 1762–1775.* 2 vols. New Haven: Yale University Press, 1931–33.

Carver, J., Esq. *Travels through the Interior Parts of North America, in the Years 1766, 1767, 1768.* London: J. Walter and S. Crowder, 1778.

Charlevoix, Pierre. *Journal of a Voyage to North-America.* 2 vols. London: R. Dodsley in Pall-Mall, 1761.

Clements, William L., ed. "Roger's Michillimackinac Journal." *Proceedings of the American Antiquarian Society,* n.s. 28 (10 April–16 October 1918): 224–73.

Coleson, Ann. *Miss Coleson's Narrative of Her Captivity among the Sioux Indians! . . . in Minnesota.* Philadelphia: Barclay, 1864.

Collins, Mary C. *The Story of Elizabeth Winyan, a Dakota Woman.* Chicago: American Missionary Association, n.d.

Connolly, Alonzo P. *A Thrilling Narrative of the Minnesota Massacre and the Sioux War of 1862–63.* Chicago: A. P. Connolly, 1896.

Coues, Elliott, ed. *The Manuscript Journals of Alexander Henry, Fur Trader of the Northwest Company, and of David Thompson, Official Geographer and Explorer of the Same Company, 1799–1814.* 2 vols. Minneapolis: Ross and Haines, 1965.

Dally, Captain Nate. *Tracks and Trails; or, Incidents in the Life of a Minnesota Territorial Pioneer.* Walker, Minn.: Cass County Pioneer, 1931.

Daniels, Arthur M., ed. *A Journal of Sibley's Indian Expedition during the Summer of 1863, and Record of the Troops Employed. By a Soldier in Company "H," 6th Regiment.* Winona, Minn.: Republican Office, 1864.

Emerson, Charles L. *Rise and Progress of Minnesota Territory, Including a Statement of the Business Prosperity of Saint Paul; and Information in Regard to the Different Counties, Cities, Towns, and Villages in the Territory, Etc.* Saint Paul: C. L. Emerson, 1855.

Featherstonhaugh, G. W. *A Canoe Voyage up the Minnay Sotor; with an Account of the Lead and Copper Deposits in Wisconsin; of the Gold Region in the Cherokee Country; and Sketches of the Popular Manners.* St. Paul: Minnesota Historical Society, 1970.

French, Benjamin F. "Historical Journal of the Establishment of the French of Louisiana," *Historical Collections of Louisiana,* vol. 3. New York: Appleton, 1851.

Gates, Charles M., ed. *Five Fur Traders of the Northwest.* St. Paul: Minnesota Historical Society, 1965.

Glover, Richard, ed. *David Thompson's Narrative, 1784–1812.* Toronto: Champlain Society, 1962.

Goff, Lyman. *An 1862 Trip to the West.* Pawtucket, R.I.: Pawtucket Boy's Club, 1926.

Hachi-Wakanda [Lightning Blanket]. *Story of the Battle of Fort Ridgely, Minn., August 20 and 22, 1862.* Morton, Minn.: O. S. Smith, 1908.

Heard, Isaac V. D. *History of the Sioux War and Massacres of 1862 and 1863.* New York: Harper, 1865.

356

Hennepin, Louis. *A Description of Louisiana*, ed. John G. Shea. New York: John Gilmary Shea, 1880.

Henry, Alexander. *Travels and Adventures in Canada and the Indian Territories between the Years 1760 and 1777.* New York: I. Riley, 1809.

Hibschman, H. J. "The Shetek Pioneers and the Indians." In *The Garland Library of Narratives of North American Indian Captivities*, ed. Wilcomb E. Washburn, vol. 104. New York: Garland Publishing, 1976.

Huggins, Nancy. "Mrs. Huggins the Minnesota Captive." In *The Garland Library of Narratives of North American Indian Captivities*, ed. Wilcomb E. Washburn, vol. 86. New York: Garland Publishing, 1978.

Jackson, Donald, ed. *The Journals of Zebulon Montgomery Pike.* 2 vols. Norman: University of Oklahoma Press, 1966.

Jackson, Donald, and Mary Lee Spence, eds. *The Expeditions of John C. Frémont.* 2 vols. Urbana, Chicago, and London: University of Illinois Press, 1970.

James, Edwin, ed. *A Narrative of the Captivity and Adventures of John Tanner (U.S. Interpreter at the Sault Ste. Marie) during Thirty Years Residence among the Indians of the Interior of North America.* New York: G. and C. and H. Carvill, 1830.

Kane, Lucile M., June D. Holmquist, and Carolyn Gilman, eds. *The Northern Expeditions of Stephen H. Long: The Journals of 1817 and 1823 and Related Documents.* St. Paul: Minnesota Historical Society, 1978.

Keating, William H. *Narrative of an Expedition to the Source of St. Peter's River, Lake Winnepeek, Lake of the Woods, &c., Performed in the Year 1823 by the Order of the Hon. J. C. Calhoun, Secretary of War, under the Command of Stephen H. Long, U.S.T.E.* 2 vols. Minneapolis: Ross and Haines, 1959.

Kellogg, Louise Phelps. *Early Narratives of the Northwest, 1634–1699.* New York: Barnes and Noble, 1967.

Kelly, Fanny Wiggins. *Narrative of My Captivity among the Sioux Indians.* Hartford, Conn.: Mutual Publishing, 1872.

Le Duc, William G. *Minnesota Year Book for 1851.* Saint Paul; William G. Le Duc, 1851.

———. *Minnesota Year Book for 1852.* St. Paul: Minnesota Historical Society, 1936.

Lee, L. P., ed. *History of the Spirit Lake Massacre! And of Miss Abigail Gardner's Three Months Captivity among the Indians According to Her Own Account.* New Britain, Conn.: L. P. Lee, 1857.

Margry, Pierre. *Découvertes et établissements des Français dans l'Ouest et dans le Sud l'Amérique Septrionale (1614–1754).* 6 vols. Paris: Maisonneuve Preres et Ch. LeClerc, Editeurs, 1876–88.

Marshall, William R., comp. *Executive Documents for the State of Minnesota: For the Year 1862.* Saint Paul: William R. Marshall, 1863.

Michigan Pioneer and Historical Society Collections. 40 vols. Lansing, Mich.: The Society, 1877–1929.

Minnesota Historical Society Collections. 17 vols. St. Paul, Minn.: The Society, 1860–1920.

Neill, E. D., ed. *The History of Minnesota: From the Earliest French Exploration to the Present Time*. Minneapolis: T. T. Bacheller, 1873.

———. *History of Ramsey County and the City of St. Paul, Including the Explorers and Pioneers of Minnesota and Outlines of the History of Minnesota*. Minneapolis: North Star Publishing, 1881.

———. *Macalester College Contributions: Department of History, Literature and Political Science, Number Ten*. St. Paul: Pioneer Press, 1890.

Neill, E. D., and Charles S. Bryant. *History of Fillmore County, Including Explorers and Pioneers of Minnesota, and Outline History of the State of Minnesota by Rev. Edward D. Neill; also, Sioux Massacre of 1862, and State of Education, by Charles Bryant*. Minneapolis: Minnesota Historical Company, 1882.

O'Callaghan, E. B., ed. *Documents Relative to the Colonial History of the State of New York*. 15 vols. Albany: Weed, Parsons, 1858.

Parker, Donald D., ed. *The Recollections of Philander Prescott*. Lincoln: University of Nebraska Press, 1966.

Parker, John, ed. *The Journals of Jonathan Carver and Related Documents, 1766–1770*. St. Paul: Minnesota Historical Society, 1976.

Perrin du Lac, François-Marie. *Voyage dans les deux Louisianes, et chez les nations sauvages de Missouri, par les Etats-Unis, L'Ohio et les provinces que le bordent en 1801, 1802 et 1803; avec un aperçu des moeurs, des usages, du caractère et des coutumes religieuses et civiles des peuples de ces diverse contrées*. Paris: Capelle et Renand, 1805.

Pettijohn, Jonas. *Autobiography, Family History and Various Reminiscences of the Life of Jonas Pettijohn among the Sioux or Dakota Indians. His Escape during the Massacre of August, 1862. Causes That Led to the Massacre*. Clay Center, Kans.: *Dispatch* Printing House, 1890.

Pond, S. W., Jr. *Two Volunteer Missionaries among the Dakota; or, The Story of the Labors of Samuel W. and Gideon H. Pond*. Boston: Congregational Sunday-School and Publishing Society, 1893.

Ravoux, Msgr. A. *Reminiscences, Memoirs and Lectures*. Saint Paul: Brown, Treacy, 1890.

Renville, Mary Butler. *A Thrilling Narrative of Indian Captivity*. Minneapolis: Atlas Company Book and Job Printing Office, 1863.

Riggs, Stephen Return. *A Dakota-English Dictionary*, ed. James Owen Dorsey. Minneapolis: Ross and Haines, 1968.

———. *Dakota Grammar Texts, and Ethnography*. In *Contributions to North American Ethnology*, ed. James Owen Dorsey. Washington, D.C.: Government Printing Office, 1893.

———. "Dakota Portraits." *Minnesota History Bulletin* 2 (November 1918):481–568.

———. *Grammar and Dictionary of the Dakota Language*. Washington, D.C.: Smithsonian Institution, 1852.

358

———. *Mary and I: Forty Years with the Sioux.* Boston: Congregational Sunday-School and Publishing Society, 1880.

———. *Tah-koo Wah-kan; or, The Gospel among the Dakotas.* Boston: Congregational Publishing Society, 1880.

Scantlebury, Thomas. *Wanderings in Minnesota during the Indian Troubles of 1862.* Chicago, 1867.

Schoolcraft, Henry R., ed. *Information Respecting the History, Condition, and Prospects of the Indian Tribes of the United States.* 6 vols. Philadelphia: J. B. Lippincott, 1865.

———. *Narrative Journal of Travels, through the Northwestern Region of the United States, Extending from Detroit through the Great Chain of American Lakes, to the Sources of the Mississippi River, Performed as a Member of the Expedition under Governor Cass in the Year 1820.* Albany: E.E. Hosford, 1820.

Schwandt, Mary. "The Story of Mary Schwandt: Her Captivity during the Sioux Outbreak." In *The Garland Library of Narratives of North American Captivities,* ed. Wilcomb E. Washburn, vol. 99. New York: Garland Publishing, 1976.

Seymour, E. S. *Sketches of Minnesota, the New England of the West. With Incidents of Travel in That Territory during the Summer of 1849.* New York: Harper, 1850.

Snelling, William J. *Tales of the Northwest, 1804–1848.* Minneapolis: University of Minnesota, 1936.

Sullivan, James, ed. *The Papers of Sir William Johnson.* 14 vols. Albany: University of the State of New York, 1921–65.

"Taoyateduta Is Not a Coward." *Minnesota History* 38 (September 1962):115.

Tarble, Helen M. "The Story of My Capture and Escape during the Minnesota Indian Massacre of 1862, with Historical Notes, Descriptions of Pioneer Life, and Sketches and Incidents of the Great Outbreak of the Sioux or Dakota Indians as I Saw Them." In *The Garland Library of Narratives of North American Indian Captivities,* ed. Wilcomb E. Washburn, vol. 105. New York: Garland Publishing, 1976.

Thwaites, Reuben Gold, ed. *The Jesuit Relations and Allied Documents: Travels and Explorations of the Jesuit Missionaries in New France, 1610–1793.* New York: Pageant Book Company, 1959.

Van Cleve, Charlotte Ouisconsin. *"Three Score Years and Ten": Life-long Memories of Fort Snelling, Minnesota and Other Parts of the West.* Minneapolis: Harrison and Smith, 1888.

Wakefield, Sarah F. *Six Weeks in Little Crow's Camp: A Narrative of Indian Captivity.* Shakopee, Minn.: Argus Book and Job Printing Office, 1864.

Wall, Oscar Garrett. *Recollections of the Sioux Massacre: An Authentic History of the Yellow Medicine Incident, of the Fate of Marsh and His Men, of the Siege and Battles of Fort Ridgely, and of Other Important Battles and Experiences, Together with a Sketch of the Sibley Expedition of 1863.* Lake City, Minn.: Home Printery, 1908.

Whipple, Henry Benjamin. *Lights and Shadows of a Long Episcopate, Being Reminiscences and Recollections of the Right Reverend Henry Benjamin Whipple, D.D., L.L.D., Bishop of Minnesota.* New York and London: Macmillan, 1912.

White N. D. "Captivity among the Sioux, August 18 to September 26, 1862." In *The Garland Library of Narratives of North American Indian Captivities,* ed. Wilcomb E. Washburn, vol. 104. New York: Garland Publishing, 1976.

[Williams, William]. "Report of Major Williams." *Palimpsest* 38 (June 1957):265–72.

Williamson, John P. "Removal of the Sioux Indians from Minnesota." *Minnesota History Bulletin* 2 (1918):420–25.

Wisconsin Historical Society Collections. 31 vols. Madison: Wisconsin Historical Society, 1855–1931.

SECONDARY SOURCES

Ackerknecht, Erwin H. *Malaria in the Upper Mississippi Valley, 1760–1900.* Baltimore: Johns Hopkins Press, 1945.

Ackermann, Gertrude W. "Joseph Renville of Lac qui Parle." *Minnesota History* 12 (September 1931):231–46.

Anderson, Gary Clayton. "Early Dakota Migration and Intertribal Warfare: A Revision." *Western Historical Quarterly* 11 (January 1980):17–36.

Anderson, Raoul R. "Alberta Stoney (Assiniboin) Origins and Adaptations: A Case for Reappraisal." *Ethnohistory* 17 (Winter–Spring 1970):49–61.

Andrist, Ralph K. *The Long Death: The Last Days of the Plains Indians.* New York: Collier Books, 1964.

Armour, David A., and Keith R. Widder. *At the Crossroads: Michilimackinac during the Revolution.* Mackinac Island, Mich.: Mackinac Island State Park Commission, 1978.

Aschmann, Homer. "The Central Desert of Baja California: Demography and Ecology." *Ibero-Americana* 42 (1959):1–315.

Babcock, Willoughby M., Jr. "Louis Provençalle, Fur Trader." *Minnesota History* 20 (September 1939):259–68.

———. "Major Lawrence Taliaferro, Indian Agent." *Mississippi Valley Historical Review* 11 (December 1924):358–75.

———. "Sioux Villages in Minnesota prior to 1837." *Minnesota Archaeologist* 12 (October 1945):126–46.

Barton, Winifred W. *John P. Williamson: A Brother to the Sioux.* New York and Chicago: Fleming H. Revell, 1919.

Beider, Robert S. "Scientific Attitudes toward Indian Mixed-Bloods in Early Nineteenth Century America." *Journal of Ethnic Studies* 8 (Summer 1980):17–30.

Berkhofer, Robert, Jr. "The Political Context of a New Indian History." *Pacific Historical Review* 40 (August 1971):357–82.

Blakely, Robert L. "Comparison of the Mortality Profiles of Archaic, Middle Woodland and Middle Mississippian Skeletal Populations." *American Journal of Physical Anthropology* 34, no. 1 (1971):43–53.

Blegen, Theodore C. *Minnesota: A History of the State.* Minneapolis: University of Minnesota Press, 1963.

Brown, Dee. *Bury My Heart at Wounded Knee: An Indian History of the American West.* New York: Bantam Books, 1970.

Bruner, Edward M. "Mandan." In *Perspectives in American Indian Culture Change,* ed. Edward H. Spicer, 187–277. Chicago: University of Chicago Press, 1961.

———. "Two Processes of Change in Mandan-Hidatsa Kinship Terminology." *American Anthropologist* 57 (1955):840–50.

Carley, Kenneth. *The Sioux Uprising of 1862.* St. Paul: Minnesota Historical Society, 1962.

Clayton, James L. "The Growth and Economic Significance of the American Fur Trade, 1790–1890." *Minnesota History* 40 (Winter 1966):210–20.

Cook, Sherburne F. "The Extent and Significance of Disease among the Indians of Baja California, 1697–1773." *Ibero-Americana* 12 (1937):1–39.

———. "Interracial Warfare and Population Decline among the New England Indians." *Ethnohistory* 20 (Winter 1973):1–24.

———. "The Significance of Disease in the Extinction of the New England Indians." *Human Biology* 45 (September 1973):485–508.

Cross, Marion E., ed. *Father Hennepin's Description of Louisiana.* Minneapolis: University of Minnesota Press, 1938.

Danziger, Edmund Jefferson, Jr. *The Chippewa of Lake Superior.* Norman: University of Oklahoma Press, 1978.

———. "Civil War Problems in the Central and Dakota Superintendencies: A Case Study." *Nebraska History* 51 (Winter 1970):411–24.

———. *Indians and Bureaucrats: Administering the Reservation Policy during the Civil War.* Urbana: University of Illinois Press, 1974.

Dary, David A. *The Buffalo Book: The Full Saga of the American Animal.* Chicago: Swallow Press, 1974.

Delanglez, Jean. *Hennepin's Description of Louisiana: A Critical Essay.* Chicago: Institute of Jesuit History Publications, 1941.

Deloria, Ella C. *Speaking of Indians.* New York: Friendship Press, 1944.

De Mallie, Raymond J. "Joseph N. Nicollet's Account of the Sioux and Assiniboin in 1839." *South Dakota History* 5 (Fall 1975):343–59.

———. "Teton Dakota Kinship and Social Organization." Ph.D. diss., University of Chicago, 1971.

De Mallie, Raymond J., and Robert H. Lavenda. "Wakan: Plains Siouan Concepts of

Power." In *The Anthropology of Power: Ethnographic Studies from Asia, Oceania, and the New World*, ed. Raymond D. Fogelson and Richard N. Adams, 153–65. New York: Academic Press, 1977.

Dobyns, Henry F. "Estimating Aboriginal American Population: An Appraisal of Techniques with a New Hemispheric Estimate." *Current Anthropology* 7 (October 1966):395–416.

Duffy, John. "Smallpox and the Indians in the American Colonies." *Bulletin of the History of Medicine* 25 (1951):324–41.

Dunn, Frederick L. "On the Antiquity of Malaria in the Western Hemisphere." *Human Biology* 37 (1965):385–93.

———. "Epidemiological Factors: Health and Disease in Hunter-Gatherers." In *Man the Hunter*, ed. Richard B. Lee and Irven De Vore, 221–28. Chicago: Aldine, 1968.

Eccles, W. J. *The Canadian Frontier, 1534–1760*. New York: Holt, Rinehart and Winston, 1969.

Edmunds, R. David. *The Potawatomis: Keepers of the Fire*. Norman: University of Oklahoma Press, 1978.

Eggan, Fred. "Lewis H. Morgan in Kinship Perspective." In *Essays in the Science of Culture in Honor of Leslie A. White*, ed. Gertrude E. Dole and Robert L. Carneiro, 179–201. New York: Thomas Y. Crowell, 1960.

Ellis, Richard. "Political Pressures and Army Policies on the Northern Plains, 1862–1865." *Minnesota History* 42 (Summer 1970):43–53.

Eschambault, Antoine d'. "La Vie Aventureuse de Daniel Greysolon, Sieur Dulhut." *Revue d'Histoire de l'Amérique Français* 5 (December 1951):320–39.

Ewers, John C. "Influence of the Fur Trade upon the Indians of the Northern Plains." In *People and Pelts: Selected Papers of the Second North American Fur Trade Conference*, ed. Malvina Bolus, 1–26. Winnipeg: Peguis Publishers, 1972.

———. "Intertribal Warfare as the Precursor of Indian-White Warfare on the Northern Great Plains." *Western Historical Quarterly* 6 (October 1975):397–410.

Feraca, Stephen E., and James H. Howard. "The Identity and Demography of the Dakota or Sioux Tribe." *Plains Anthropologist* 8 (1963):81–84.

Folwell, William Watts. *A History of Minnesota*. 4 vols. St. Paul: Minnesota Historical Society, 1921–30.

Forbes, Bruce David. "Evangelization and Acculturation among the Santee Dakota Indians, 1834–1864." Ph.D. diss., Princeton Theological Seminary, 1977.

Fox, Robin. *Kinship and Marriage: An Anthropological Perspective*. Harmondsworth, England: Penguin Book, 1976.

Fridley, Russell W., Leota M. Kellett, and June D. Holmquist. *Charles E. Flandrau and the Defense of New Ulm*. New Ulm, Minn.: Brown County Historical Society, 1962.

Galbraith, John. "British-American Competition in the Border Fur Trade of the 1820s." *Minnesota History* 36 (September 1959):241–49.

Genovés, Santiago. "Estimation of Age and Mortality." In *Science and Archaeology*, ed. D. R. Brothwell and Eric Higgs, 353–64. New York: Basic Books, 1963.

Gilman, Rhoda R. "Decline of the Upper Mississippi Fur Trade." *Minnesota History* 49 (Winter 1970):123–40.

———. "The Fur Trade in the Upper Mississippi Valley, 1630–1850." *Wisconsin Magazine of History* 58 (Autumn 1974):3–18.

Gluek, Alvin C., Jr. *Minnesota and the Manifest Destiny of the Canadian Northwest: A Study in Canadian-American Relations*. Toronto: University of Toronto Press, 1965.

———. "The Sioux Uprising: A Problem in International Relations." *Minnesota History* 34 (Winter 1955):317–24.

Goetzmann, William H. "The Mountain Man As Jacksonian Man." *American Quarterly* 15 (Fall 1963):402–15.

Gray, John S. "The Santee Sioux and the Lake Shetek Settlers: Capture and Rescue." *Montana: The Magazine of Western History* 25 (January 1975): 42–54.

Hagan, William T. *The Sac and Fox Indians*. Norman: University of Oklahoma Press, 1958.

Hansen, Marcus L. *Old Fort Snelling, 1819–1858*. Minneapolis: Ross and Haines, 1958.

Hardcastle, David Paul. "The Defense of Canada under Louis XIV, 1643–1701." Ph.D. diss., Ohio State University, 1970.

Hassrick, Royal B. *The Sioux: Life and Customs of a Warrior Society*. Norman: University of Oklahoma Press, 1964.

———. "Teton Dakota Kinship System." *American Anthropologist* 46 (1944):338–48.

Heilbron, Bertha L. *With Pen and Pencil on the Frontier in 1851*. St. Paul: Minnesota Historical Society, 1932.

Henig, Gerald S. "A Neglected Cause of the Sioux Uprising." *Minnesota History* 45 (Fall 1976):107–10.

Herriott, F. I. "Dr. Isaac H. Herriott, One of the Victims of the Spirit Lake Massacre Killed on the Evening of Sunday, March 8, 1857." *Annals of Iowa* 18 (April 1932): 243–94.

———. "The Origins of the Indian Massacre between the Okobojis, March 8, 1857." *Annals of Iowa* 18 (July 1932):323–82.

Hickerson, Harold. *The Chippewa and Their Neighbors: A Study in Ethnohistory*. New York: Holt, Rinehart and Winston, 1970.

———. "Fur Trade Colonialism and the North American Indians." *Journal of Ethnic Studies* 1 (1973):15–44.

———. *Sioux Indians*. Vol. 1. *Mdewakanton Band of Sioux Indians*. New York and London: Garland Publishing, 1974.

———. "The Virginia Deer and Intertribal Buffer Zones in the Upper Mississippi Valley." In *Man, Culture and Animals: The Role of Animals in Human Ecological Adjustments*, ed. Andrew P. Vayda, 43–65. Washington, D.C.: American Association for the Advancement of Science, 1965.

Hinshaw, Robert E., ed. *Currents in Anthropology: Essays in Honor of Sol Tax.* Studies in Anthropology, vol. 3. The Hague and New York: Mouton, 1979.

Horsman, Reginald. "American Indian Policy and the Origins of Manifest Destiny." *University of Birmingham Historical Journal* 11 (December 1968):128–40.

———. "British Indian Policy in the Northwest, 1807–1812." *Mississippi Valley Historical Review* 45 (June 1958):51–66.

———. *Expansion and American Indian Policy, 1783–1812.* East Lansing: Michigan State University Press, 1967.

———. *The Frontier in the Formative Years, 1783–1812.* New York: Holt, Rinehart and Winston, 1970.

———. "Wisconsin and the War of 1812." *Wisconsin Magazine of History* 46 (Autumn 1962):3–15.

Howard, James H. "The Cultural Position of the Dakota: A Reassessment." In *Essays in the Science of Culture in Honor of Leslie A. White,* ed. Gertrude E. Dole and Robert L. Carneiro, 249–68. New York: Thomas Y. Crowell, 1960.

———. "The Dakota or Sioux Indians: A Study in Human Ecology." *Dakota Museum Anthropological Papers,* no. 2 (Vermillion, S.D.), 1966.

———. "Yanktonai Ethnohistory and the John K. Bear Winter Court." *Plains Anthropologist, Memoirs* 21 (August 1976):1–64.

Hubbard, Lucius F., and Return I. Holcombe. *Minnesota in Three Centuries.* Vol. 3 of *Minnesota in Three Centuries, 1655–1908,* ed. Lucius F. Hubbard, William P. Murray, James H. Baker, and Warren Upham. Mankato: Publishing Society of Minnesota, 1908.

Hughes, Thomas. *History of Blue Earth County.* Chicago: Middle West Publishing Company, 1901.

———. *Indian Chiefs of Southern Minnesota.* Minneapolis: Ross and Haines, 1969.

———. *Old Traverse des Sioux.* St. Peter, Minn.: Herald Publishing Company, 1929.

Jackson, Marjorie Gordon. "The Beginning of British Trade at Michilimackinac." *Minnesota History* 11 (September 1930):231–70.

Jacobs, Wilbur R. "The Tip of an Iceberg: Pre-Columbian Indian Demography and Some Implications for Revisionism." *William and Mary Quarterly* 31 (January 1974): 123–32.

Jennings, Francis. *The Invasion of America: Indians, Colonialism, and the Cant of Conquest.* New York: W. W. Norton, 1976.

Johnson, Elden. *The Arvilla Complex: Based on the Field Notes of Lloyd A. Wilford.* Minnesota Prehistoric Archaeology Series no. 9. St. Paul: Minnesota Historical Society, 1973.

Johnson, Roy P. "The Siege of Fort Abercrombie." *North Dakota History* 24 (January 1957):4–79.

Jones, Robert Huhn. *The Civil War in the Northwest: Nebraska, Wisconsin, Iowa, Minnesota, and the Dakotas.* Norman: University of Oklahoma Press, 1960.

364

Kane, Lucile M. "The Sioux Treaties and the Traders." *Minnesota History* 32 (June 1951):65–80.

Kellogg, Louise Phelps. *The British Regime in Wisconsin and the Northwest.* Madison: State Historical Society of Wisconsin, 1935.

———. "Fort Beauharnois." *Minnesota History* 8 (September 1927):232–46.

———. *The French Regime in Wisconsin and the Northwest.* Madison: State Historical Society of Wisconsin, 1925.

Klein, Alan Michael. "Adaptive Strategies and Process on the Plains: The 19th Century Cultural Sink." Ph.D. diss., State University of New York, Buffalo, 1977.

Landes, Ruth. *The Mystic Lake Sioux: Sociology of the Mdewakantonwan Santee.* Madison: University of Wisconsin Press, 1968.

Lass, William E. "The Removal from Minnesota of the Sioux and Winnebago Indians." *Minnesota History* 38 (December 1963):353–64.

Lavender, David. *The Fist in the Wilderness.* Albuquerque: University of New Mexico Press, 1964.

———. "Some American Characteristics of the American Fur Company." *Minnesota History* 40 (Winter 1966):178–87.

Lee, Lorenzo Porter. *History of the Spirit Lake Massacre, 8th March 1857.* Iowa City, Iowa: State Historical Society, 1971.

Lowie, Robert H. *Indians of the Plains.* Garden City, N.Y.: Natural Press, 1954.

Luebke, Frederick, ed. *Ethnicity on the Great Plains.* Lincoln: University of Nebraska Press, 1980.

McHugh, Tom. *The Time of the Buffalo.* New York: Alfred A. Knopf, 1972.

McManus, John. "An Economic Analysis of Indian Behavior in the North American Fur Trade." *Journal of Economic History* 32 (March 1972):36–53.

McNeill, William. *Plagues and Peoples.* Garden City, N.Y.: Doubleday Books, 1976.

Martin, Calvin. *Keepers of the Game: Indian-Animal Relationships and the Fur Trade.* Berkeley: University of California Press, 1978.

———. "The War between Indians and Animals." *Natural History* 87 (June–July 1978): 92–96.

Mauss, Marcel. *The Gift: Forms and Functions of Exchange in Archaic Societies.* New York: W. W. Norton, 1967.

Meister, Cary W. "Demographic Consequences of Euro-American Contact on Selected American Indian Populations and Their Relationship to the Demographic Transition." *Ethnohistory* 23 (Spring 1976):161–72.

Meyer, Roy W. "The Canadian Sioux: Refugees from Minnesota." *Minnesota History* 41 (Spring 1968):13–28.

———. *History of the Santee Sioux: United States Indian Policy on Trial.* Lincoln: University of Nebraska Press, 1967.

Mooney, James R. *The Aboriginal Populations of America North of Mexico,* ed. John

R. Swanton. Smithsonian Institution Miscellaneous Collections, vol. 80, no. 7. Washington, D.C.: Government Printing Office, 1928.

Morton, William L. "The Northwest Company: Peddlars Extraordinary." *Minnesota History* 40 (Winter 1966):157–65.

Nasatir, Abraham P. "The Anglo-Spanish Frontier on the Upper Mississippi, 1786–1796." *Iowa Journal of History and Politics* 29 (April 1931):155–64.

Newcombe, Barbara T. "'A Portion of the American People': The Sioux Sign a Treaty in Washington in 1858." *Minnesota History* 45 (Fall 1976):83–96.

Nichols, David. "The Other Civil War: Lincoln and the Indians." *Minnesota History* 44 (Spring 1974):2–15.

Nichols, Roger L. *General Henry Atkinson: A Western Military Career.* Norman: University of Oklahoma Press, 1965.

Oehler, Charles M. *The Great Sioux Uprising.* New York: Oxford University Press, 1959.

Paulson, Howard W. "Federal Indian Policy and the Dakota Indians: 1800–1840." *South Dakota History.* 3 (Summer 1973):285–309.

Peake, Ora B. *A History of the United States Indian Factory System, 1795–1822.* Denver: Sage Books, 1954.

Peterson, Jacqueline. "The People in Between: Indian-White Marriage and the Genesis of a Métis Society and Culture in the Great Lakes Region." Ph.D. diss., University of Illinois, Chicago Circle, 1980.

Pratt, Julius. "The Fur Trade Strategy and the American Left Flank in the War of 1812." *American Historical Review* 40 (January 1935):246–73.

Pritchett, John Perry. "Some Red River Fur-Trade Activities." *Minnesota History* 5 (May 1924):401–23.

Prucha, Francis Paul. "American Indian Policy in the 1840s: Visions of Reform." In *The Frontier Challenge: Response to the Trans-Mississippi West,* ed. John G. Clark, 81–110. Lawrence: University of Kansas Press, 1971.

———. *American Indian Policy in the Formative Years: The Indian Trade and Intercourse Acts, 1790–1834.* Cambridge: Harvard University Press, 1962.

———. "Andrew Jackson's Indian Policy: A Reassessment." *Journal of American History* 56 (December 1969):527–39.

———. "Army Sutlers and the American Fur Company." *Minnesota History* 40 (Spring 1966):22–31.

———. *Broadax and Bayonet: The Role of the United States Army in the Development of the Northwest, 1815–1860.* Madison: State Historical Society of Wisconsin, 1953.

———. *The Sword of the Republic: The United States Army on the Frontier, 1783–1846.* London: Macmillan, 1969.

Rapport de L'Archiviste de la Province de Québec. Quebec: Imprimeur de Sa Majesté le Roi, 1920–.

Ray, Arthur J. *Indians in the Fur Trade: Their Role as Trappers, Hunters, and Middle-*

men in the Lands South of Hudson Bay, 1660–1870. Toronto: University of Toronto Press, 1974.

Ray, Arthur J., and Donald B. Freeman. *"Give Us Good Measure": An Economic Analysis of Relations between the Indians and the Hudson's Bay Company before 1763.* Toronto: University of Toronto Press, 1978.

Rich, E. E. *The History of the Hudson's Bay Company.* 2 vols. London: Hudson's Bay Record Society, 1959.

————. "Trade Habits and Economic Motivation among the Indians of North America." *Canadian Journal of Economics and Political Sciences* 26 (February 1960):35–53.

Robinson, Doane. *A History of the Dakota or Sioux Indians.* Minneapolis: Ross and Haines, 1956.

Roddis, Louis H. *The Indian Wars of Minnesota.* Cedar Rapids, Iowa: Torch Press, 1956.

Roe, Frank Gilbert. *The North American Buffalo: A Critical Study of the Species in Its Wild State.* Toronto: University of Toronto Press, 1970.

Ruckman, J. Ward. "Ramsay Crooks and the Fur Trade of the Northwest." *Minnesota History* 7 (March 1926):18–31.

Russo, Priscilla Ann. "The Time to Speak Is Over: The Onset of the Sioux Uprising." *Minnesota History* 45 (Fall 1976):97–106.

Sahlins, Marshall. *Stone Age Economy.* Chicago and New York: Aldine, Atherton, 1972.

Satterlee, Marion P. *A Detailed Account of the Massacre by the Dakota Indians of Minnesota in 1862.* Minneapolis: Marion P. Satterlee, 1923.

————. *The Story of Captain Richard Strout and Company, Who Fought the Sioux Indians at the Battle of Kelly's Bluff, at Acton, Minnesota, on Wednesday, September 3, 1862.* Minneapolis: Marion P. Satterlee, 1909.

Satz, Ronald. "Indian Policy in the Jacksonian Era: The Old Northwest as a Test Case." *Michigan History* 60 (Spring 1976):71–93.

Schneider, David M. "What Is Kinship All About?" In *Kinship Studies in the Morgan Centennial Year,* ed. Priscilla Reining, 32–63. Washington, D.C.: Anthropological Society of Washington, 1972.

Sheehan, Bernard W. *Seeds of Extinction: Jeffersonian Philanthropy and the American Indian.* New York: W. W. Norton, 1974.

Sketches Historical and Descriptive of the Monuments and Tablets Erected by the Minnesota Valley Historical Society in Renville and Redwood Counties, Minnesota. Morton: Minnesota Valley Historical Society, 1902.

Skinner, Alanson. "Eastern Dakota Ethnology." *American Anthropologist* 21 (April 1919):167–74.

Smith, G. Hubert. *The Explorations of the La Vérendryes in the Northern Plains, 1738–43,* ed. W. Raymond Wood. Lincoln: University of Nebraska Press, 1980.

Stevens, Wayne E. "The Fur Trade in Minnesota during the British Regime." *Minnesota History* 5 (February 1923):3–13.

———. *The Northwest Fur Trade, 1763–1800*. Urbana: University of Illinois Press, 1928.

Stewart, William J. "Settler, Politician, and Speculator in the Sale of the Sioux Reservation." *Minnesota History* 39 (Fall 1964):85–92.

Stipe, Claude E. "Eastern Dakota Acculturation: The Role of Agents of Culture Change." Ph.D. diss., University of Minnesota, 1968.

Symes, Oliver C. *Ecology and Cultural Continuity as Contributing Factors in the Social Organization of the Plains Indians*. University of California Publications in American Archaeology and Ethnology, no. 48. Berkeley: University of California, 1962.

Syms, E. Leigh. "Cultural Ecology and Ecological Dynamics of the Ceramic Period in Southwestern Manitoba." *Plains Anthropologist* 22, memoir 12, no. 76 (May 1977): 1–142.

Tassé, Joseph. *Les Canadiens de L'Ouest*. Vol. 1. Montreal: Berthiaume et Sabourin, 1882.

Taylor, Joseph H. "Inkpaduta and Sons." *North Dakota Historical Quarterly* 4 (April 1930):152–64.

Teakle, Thomas. *The Spirit Lake Massacre*. Iowa City, Iowa: State Historical Society, 1918.

Terrell, John Upton. *Sioux Trails*. New York: McGraw-Hill, 1974.

Thompson, H. Paul. "Estimating Aboriginal American Population: A Technique Using Anthropological and Biological Data." *Current Anthropology* 7, no. 1 (1966):417–24.

Tohill, Louis A. "Robert Dickson, British Fur Trader on the Upper Mississippi." *North Dakota Historical Quarterly* 3, no. 1 (October 1928):5–49; no. 2 (January 1929): 83–128; no. 3 (April 1929):182–203.

Trennert, Robert A., Jr. *Indian Traders on the Middle Border: The House of Ewing, 1827–1854*. Lincoln: University of Nebraska Press, 1981.

Trigger, Bruce G. *Children of Aataentsic: A History of the Huron People to 1660*. 2 vols. Montreal and London: McGill–Queens University Press, 1976.

Ubelaker, Douglas H. *Reconstruction of Demographic Profiles from Ossuary Skeletal Samples: A Case Study from the Tidewater Potomac*. Washington, D.C.: Smithsonian Institution Press, 1974.

Van Kirk, Sylvia. "The Role of Women in the Fur Trade Society of the Canadian West, 1700–1850." Ph.D. diss., University of London, Queen Mary College, 1975.

Vecsey, Christopher. "American Indian Environmental Religions." In *American Indian Environments: Ecological Issues in Native American History*, ed. Christopher Vecsey and Robert W. Venables. Syracuse, N.Y.: Syracuse University Press, 1980.

Watrall, Charles R. "Virginia Deer and the Buffer Zones in the Late Prehistoric–Early Protohistoric Periods in Minnesota." *Plains Anthropologist* 13 (May 1968):81–86.

Wedel, Mildred Mott. "Le Sueur and the Dakota Sioux." In *Aspects of Upper Great Lakes Anthropology: Papers in Honor of Lloyd A. Wilford*, ed. Elden Johnson, 157–71. St. Paul: Minnesota Historical Society, 1974.

Wedel, Waldo R. *Prehistoric Man in the Great Plains*. Norman: University of Oklahoma Press, 1961.

West, Nathaniel. *The Ancestry, Life and Times of the Hon. Henry Hastings Sibley*. St. Paul: Pioneer Press, 1889.

White, Richard. "The Winning of the West: The Expansion of the Western Sioux in the Eighteenth and Nineteenth Centuries." *Journal of American History* 65 (September 1978):319–43.

Willand, John. *Lac qui Parle and the Dakota Mission*. Madison, Minn.: Lac qui Parle Historical Society, 1964.

Winchell, Newton H. *The Aborigines of Minnesota: A Report on the Collections of Jacob V. Brower and on the Field Surveys and Notes of J. Hill and Theodore H. Lewis*. St. Paul, Minn.: Pioneer Company, 1911.

Wood, W. Raymond. "Plains Trade in Prehistoric and Protohistoric Intertribal Relations." In *Anthropology on the Great Plains*, ed. W. Raymond Wood and Margot Liberty, 98–109. Lincoln: University of Nebraska Press, 1980.

Wozniak, John S. *Contact, Negotiation, and Conflict: An Ethnohistory of the Eastern Dakota, 1819–1839*. Washington, D.C.: University Press of America, 1978.

Zoltvany, Yves F. *Philippe de Rigaud de Vaudreuil: Governor of New France, 1703–1725*. Toronto: McClelland and Stewart, 1974.

Index